Thoughts
on my
Thoughts
V

Thoughts
on my
Thoughts
V

The <u>TALES</u> That Wagged This Veterinarian

Walter R. Hoge, DVM

Printed in the United States of America

ISBN 979-8-89114-178-0 (hc)
ISBN 979-8-89114-177-3 (sc)
ISBN 979-8-89114-179-7 (e)

Library of Congress Pre-assigned Control Number: 2025904019

2025.03.26

MainSpring Books
5901 W. Century Blvd
Suite 750
Los Angeles, CA, US, 90045

www.mainspringbooks.com

Table of Contents

About the Cover vii

Chapter 1   Fine-Tuning Our Planet Earth. 1

Chapter 2   First Observe, Then Serve. 13

Chapter 3   Life Long Battles. 20

Chapter 4   Man's Journey. 35

Chapter 5   Guinea Worms. 52

Chapter 6   Anesthetics. 68

Chapter 7   Propofol. 85

Chapter 8   One of Many Sins. 104

Chapter 9   Diuretics. 120

Chapter 10   Calcium Blockers. 128

Chapter 11   The Statins. 137

Chapter 12   Sympathetic Nervous System. 150

Chapter 13   Phlorizin, Glucose and Pee. 164

Chapter 14   Metformin. 180

Chapter 15   Gila Monsters. 188

Chapter 16   Snake Island and The Golden
             Lancehead Snake. 208

Chapter 17   Cruising with The Devil's Breath. 219

Chapter 18   Saving Lives By Breathing Up Their
              Butt... 230
Chapter 19   Mercury – Good and Bad... 246
Chapter 20   Hookworms Anyone.................. 267
Chapter 21   Covid, US and The Animals... ...... .295
Chapter 22   Cats and Toxo... 312
Chapter 23   Living with Rabies... 334
Chapter 24   Donkeys.......................... 352
Chapter 25   Don't Get Spoiled Before Your Time... . 367
Chapter 26   Near Sighted – Myopia............... 378
Chapter 27   Anthrax Anyone.................... 389
Chapter 28   Terrorists... 412
Chapter 29   Cannibalism...................... 424
Chapter 30   Shocking What Man Will Do........ 443
Chapter 31   A Caring Moment.................. 454
Chapter 32   Finally Got It Right... 464

ABOUT THE COVER

It is God who fills the clouds with water and keeps them from bursting with the weight. He hides the full moon behind a cloud. He divided light from darkness by a circle drawn on the face of the sea. When he threatens the pillars that hold up the sky, they shake and tremble with fear.

It is his strength that conquered the sea. It is his breath that made the sky clear. These are only hints of his power, only the whispers that we have heard. Who can know how truly great God is? *Job 26:8-14*

Let us not forget that in Nature, death recycles into a source that gives the gift of new life. How should we think of Nature's gift across the boundaries of species? Man is entirely dependent on Nature and its resources of land, air, water, fauna, and flora. Many living plants and animals have revealed relevant knowledge for the use of man, from virus' to humans. We have all evolved together, or because we are all the creatures of a creating God, or even the sons and daughters, sisters and brothers of the union of Father Sky and Mother Earth, or of one mystic ancestor? *Altered: from Philippe Chanial*

"There isn't anything to worry about between science and religion, because the contradictions are just in your own mind. Of course they are there, but they are not in the Lord's mind because He made the whole thing, so there is a way, if we are smart enough, to understand them so that we will not have any contradictions." *Henry J. Eyring*

CHAPTER 1

FINE-TUNING OUR PLANET EARTH...

Geneticist Michael Denton writes, "although the tiniest bacterial cells are incredibly small, weighing less than (0.0000000000001grams), each is in effect a veritable micro-miniaturized factory containing thousands of exquisitely designed pieces of intricate molecular machinery, made up of (one hundred billion) atoms, far more complicated than any machinery built by man and absolutely without parallel in the non-living world." Just how has it become possible for an Earth like ours to be formed after the "big Bang" created the heavens?

We know if our own Earth were any bigger or smaller, life here would not exist. The first question must be why the size of a planet would have anything to do with whether life could flourish, and the first and simplest answer has to do with our magnetic field. If Earth were any smaller, our magnetic field would be weaker, and what we call the "solar wind" would quickly strip our atmosphere down to almost nothing, so that we would end up like Mars, which is a lifeless world. Solar wind is a stream of charged particles – "ion gas" or plasma – made up of electrons, protons, and some alpha rays blasted toward us every moment from the sun. But because of the size of our planet, or "magnetosphere" is just powerful enough to protect us from radiation. On Earth, the solar winds would have long ago stripped our hydrogen and oxygen, which make water.

If the Earth were any larger, it would have more powerful gravity, so that no water or methane or carbon dioxide could escape the atmosphere, which would be so thick we couldn't breathe. Our air would be more "viscous." If the Earth were slightly smaller there could also be no life here.

If Earth were slightly closer to the sun, most of our water would have evaporated, and life couldn't exist. If it were slightly farther away all water would be frozen.

The presence in our solar system of the so called "gas giants" Jupiter and Saturn, which are very colossally large and very distant away, are critical to the life on this Earth. The tremendous mass and gravity of these two planets protect us from being pelted with perhaps thousands of meteorites and asteroids. In 1908 a tiny 300-foot diameter asteroid exploded above a region in Siberia. When it did, it flattened eighty million trees and caused so much atmospheric disturbance that the effects were noticed in London.

We know that if the moon were slightly smaller or larger, life here couldn't exist. Early Earth was hit by an exceeding rare event in the galaxies, in a perfect way, by a Mars-sized object at just the perfect angle and just the perfect speed in such a way that after the collision it just happened to have everything necessary to support life. If the planet-sized object that collided with the planet that became Earth had been different in size or composition, we also would not be here.

The part of the Mars-sized object that did not become part of the Earth exploded away into outer space, and then congealed to form the moon. Earth's moon is large when compared to other moons in our solar system. But anything at all smaller would not have been sufficient to stabilize the wobble of the Earth's axis. This enables us to have just the right seasonal variation, the seasons mild enough that the temperature does not fluctuate wildly, which would make life impossible. The moon has enough gravity to cause our oceans' tides, which are also crucial to the ecosystems of our coasts, which are themselves vital to the rest of life on Earth. If the Earth were closer to the galaxy's center, the radiation hitting us would be far greater, because there are many more stars in the center and "active galactic nucleus outbursts", as well as more super novae and more gamma ray bursts. That would make life on Earth impossible. If we were any farther from the center, there would be other problems. Stars farther out are orbited by planets significantly smaller than Earth would mean no atmosphere capable of supporting life. Neither would they be able to sustain the Earth's plate tectonics, which is another element absolutely crucial to life as we know it.

The power of water to erode rock is so powerful that it ought to have eroded every mountain down to nothing, and to have destroyed all life on the planet millions of years ago. For some idea of waters' extraordinary power of erosion, we may consider the dramatic example of Niagara Falls, where the rushing water over the ages has eroded the solid rock so much that the falls are now seven miles farther back than they were merely twelve thousand years ago. Over hundreds of millions of years, even the mildest erosion becomes dramatic. The level of erosion in many places is two to ten millimeters per year, so in ten thousand years, that would erode twenty to a hundred thousand meters. Mount Everest is less than ten thousand meters high. If this is the case, how have the mountains of the worlds managed to avoid being ground into the oceans many times over? The answer was found in the 1960s when the sustainability of life on Earth was found to be credited to plate technology. Water erodes rocks, but the moving continental plates work in the opposite direction, continually creating new mountains. We know that the process of plate tectonics gives our planet its variety of climates and altitudes, and most crucially, ensures a constant recycling of all the minerals and metals in our rocks and soils.[1]

Scientists are becoming more aware of the remarkable number of things that had to go right for life on Earth to work out the way it did. A small change in gravity or tweak to another fundamental force could have made the difference between our universe and one that's completely uninhabitable. This idea has led some scientists to examine the universe's metaphorical dials and knobs and wonder why complex systems like galaxies, planets, and life were able to form when that didn't have to be the case, what's called the "fine-tuning" of our universe. A report published by the Foundational Questions Institute explains the major recent milestones in an ongoing debate whether the universe is fine-tuned and what that even means.

The universe has lots of fixed properties, like the strength of gravity or the cosmological constant—which measures how fast the universe is expanding–that dictate how the universe took shape. Physicists have pondered why these values are what they are for at least a century and tried to find scientific answers to this question for decades. Based on theoretical models, some scientists argue that if one of the many fundamental constants of the universe was significantly different, life wouldn't have been able to form. This leads to a dilemma: If it's vanishingly unlikely that the universe happened to have all the right values necessary for life, why did it work out that way?

Theologians and even some scientists have used the fine-tuning argument to suggest that the universe must have been created for life to form. But recent research in the field provides other alternatives and suggests fine-tuning itself might be an illusion, possibly due to a lack of big-picture view in analyses of potentially different universes. And some scientists have argued that this universe, though it produced life, is not optimally friendly to it.

Cosmological constants directly influenced the formation of life through the creation of stars and the elements produced by stars. If you shifted a fundamental value like the strength of electromagnetism, it would change the way stars form and potentially stop them from producing carbon—a necessary ingredient for life on Earth. However, some stellar models indicate stars are more versatile than scientists thought. They might be able to produce the conditions for life under different universal values.

It's also conceivable that life could form without carbon, though the case for life based on another element, silicon, is not solid. Scientists tend to look for ways that Earth-like life could form, but ultimately they don't know what kind of life–possibly unrecognizable–might be able to form in a differently structured universe.

Most research that has looked into what happens when you change a universal constant has focused on only one constant at a time. For example, if the force of gravity was too much weaker or stronger, it would prevent life as we know it from forming. Recent evidence shows that changing multiple constants together might be more likely to make a working universe, giving the changes a chance to even out against other tweaks, the report says.

Other experiments have hinted that the universal constant related to the expansion of the universe might have changed over time—which means it wouldn't really be constant at all. If this and similar findings pan out, they would undermine the whole concept of fine-tuning. Features of the universe, far from being perfectly tuned at the start, would be constantly, if slowly, changing. Attempts to explain fine-tuning are missing the central fact that there will always be another level to explain. If the multiverse, or a simulated reality, or even some godlike entity is responsible, we still end up with the same question: Why this explanation and not something else?[2]

Caught up in the wonder of this expanding view of the cosmos, we can only kneel in awed reverence before Him, the creator and sustainer of it, and express gratitude that this divine, all-powerful Being is our Father. And we stand in stunned astonishment to learn that the purpose of all the work He has done is to bring about our immortality and eternal life (Moses 1:39). Knowing all this, should we not gladly obey His counsel and, with eagerness, receive the ordinances and covenants that will guide us to eternal life with Him?

Our sun was created to give light and life to the earth on which we live. For example, the miracle of photosynthesis enables plants to convert sunlight into the matter we eat and to release into the environment the oxygen we breathe. Our planet is just the right distance from the sun—neither too far away (and thus too cold) nor too close (and thus too hot) to sustain the amazing diversity of animals, plants, and people that populate it.

Light travels at 186,282 miles (299,792 km) per second. As far as we can tell, nothing in the physical universe can go faster. Because light travels so fast, and because its speed is constant, we can use it to measure the incredible distances in the universe. Light from the sun takes only eight minutes to reach earth, which revolves around the sun at an average of 93 million miles (149.7 million km). A number of other planets and objects revolve around the sun. Circling the sun at the edge of this solar system is a cloud of small, icy objects. They are so far away that it takes seven hours for light from the sun to reach them. That is nothing compared with the distance to our nearest stellar neighbor. Light from Proxima Centauri travels more than four years to reach us. Light from the nearest galaxy, Andromeda, travels to us in about two million years. Because of the sheer size of the universe, astronomers commonly measure distances in light-years, so Andromeda is said to be two million light-years away.

Most stars are grouped into communities called galaxies. Our own, the Milky Way, is a medium-sized spiral galaxy more than 100 thousand light-years in diameter. It has between 200 and 400 billion stars. Yet it is only one of billions of galaxies—estimates range from 100 billion to 500 billion. The largest galaxy discovered so far has 100 trillion stars. All those stars come in a dazzling array of colors and sizes, some more than a thousand times larger than our own.

Together, all the galaxies in the visible universe contain an estimated 30 billion trillion stars. Yet that number may be a small fraction of all there are. Evidence suggests that we can see only about 5 percent of all there is (the rest is "dark matter" and "dark energy," so called because it can't be seen or detected directly by the instruments we have). The universe, in fact, may be infinite in size.

In recent years, with advanced telescopes and other instruments, scientists have begun to search not just for stars but also for planets around those stars. The number of planets discovered is growing rapidly. As of March 2013, the number surpassed 900, and some appeared to lie in the same habitable zone as our earth. The number of planets in our galaxy alone could easily be in the hundreds of billions. Considering that there are hundreds of billions of galaxies in the visible universe, the number of planets is so large as to be incomprehensible—truly worlds without number. And scattered among them, as the Prophet Joseph Smith testified, are worlds whose "inhabitants ... are begotten sons and daughters unto God."[3]

Jamie L. Jensen, Ass Professor of Biology gave the following distinctions between scientific and spiritual truths. "1. Knowing through scientific explanation is a process through which we gather evidence from the natural world to find explanations for natural phenomena. 2.

Knowing through religious faith is a process through which we gather spiritual evidence through study and revelation to find explanations for spiritual truths.

As a scientist, I find comfort and friendly familiarity in the walls of a scientific laboratory. I find joy and wonder in the beauty of logic and evidence and all things analytical. I find comfort and safety in the defendable explanations provided by science.

Now let's talk about the nature or seeking of religious truths. It is an entirely different epistemology, but it is not entirely different in the process. The main difference is in the evidence. When I was in graduate school, my major professor often challenged me about my belief in God and how I could possibly reconcile it with the science I was studying. He was clearly not a believer. I argued that the God hypothesis is not testable through scientific means. He argued that it was testable and that the evidence clearly showed that God does not exist. He claimed that religious people accept without evidence and would even ignore the evidence against God if it was presented to them.

I answered back that although I was religious, I was not one who accepts without evidence. When I was seventeen, I decided to find out for myself if God was real. Since then, I have been convinced again and again, by evidence, that God does, in fact, exist. Unfortunately, the type of evidence I have to offer is mine, and mine alone. It is not the type of evidence that I can share with anyone else because it is based on intense, undeniable feelings as well as personal experiences that wouldn't mean the same thing if I explained them to someone else. However, I have performed tests.[4]

So here are some thoughts discussed about who we are, where we came from and where we are headed after our sojourn on this earth:

- Nevertheless, despite the insignificance of our planet and the ultimate meaningless of human life, Krauss argues that we still have cause for optimism, and joy. As he explains, "So in a purposeless universe that may have a miserable future you may wonder, 'well how can I go about each day?' And the answer is we make our own purpose. We make our own joy. We are here by a cosmic accident as I've tried to show, but it's a remarkable accident that's allowed you and I to be here to talk, to think and appreciate the beauty and splendor of the universe." *Lawrence Krauss, physicist & writer.*

- "Just because we don't have a scientific proof, or it's speculative does not mean all the answers are equally plausible," Waller says, some positions will be more or less probable. Barring completely unexpected discoveries that rewrite our understanding of the universe, he says, going forward, "I think the discoveries are going to be conceptual, or philosophical, rather than scientific." *Jason Waller, a philosopher at Kenyon University who wrote a 2020 book on fine-tuning arguments.*

- Seneca the Younger (4 BC – AD 65), was a Stoic philosopher and a statesman of Ancient Rome. Stoics believed that the meaning or purpose of life is the pursuit of wisdom and virtue, first and foremost, rather than seeking pleasure or tranquility. He wrote, "Of all the people only those are at leisure who make time for philosophy, only they truly live. Not satisfied to merely keep good watch over their own days, they annex every age to their own. All the harvest of the past is added to their store. Only an ingrate would fail to see that these great architects of venerable thoughts were born for us and have designed a way of life for us."

– Eternal perspective provides peace "which passeth all understanding." (Philip. 4:7) In speaking at a funeral of a loved one, the Prophet Joseph Smith offered this admonition: "When we lose a near and dear friend, upon whom we have set our hearts, it should be a caution unto us. ... Our affections should be placed upon God and His work, more intensely than upon our fellow beings." (Teachings of the Prophet Joseph Smith, p. 216) Life does not begin with birth, nor does it end with death. Prior to our birth, we dwelled as spirit children with our Father in Heaven. There we eagerly anticipated the possibility of coming to earth and obtaining a physical body. Knowingly we wanted the risks of mortality, which would allow the exercise of agency and accountability. "This life [was to become] a probationary state; a time to prepare to meet God." (Alma 12:24) But we regarded the returning home as the best part of that long-awaited trip, just as we do now. Before embarking on any journey, we like to have some assurance of a round-trip ticket. Returning from earth to life in our heavenly home requires passage through—and not around—the doors of death. We were born to die, and we die to live. (See 2 Cor. 6:9.) As seedlings of God, we barely blossom on earth; we fully flower in heaven. *Doors of Death, Russell M. Nelson of the Quorum of the Twelve Apostles April 1992.*

In his *Philosophiae Naturalis Principia Mathematica,* Sir Isaac Newton proclaimed: "We are to admit no more causes of natural things than such as are both true and sufficient to explain their appearances. To this purpose the philosophers say that Nature does nothing in vain, and more is in vain when less will serve; for Nature is pleased with simplicity and affects not the pomp of superfluous causes."

Matthew 7:7-8: Ask, and it shall be given you; seek, and ye shall find; knock, and it shall be opened unto you: for every one that asketh receiveth; and he that seeketh findeth; and to him that knocketh it shall be opened.

"This is a paradox of man: compared to God, man is nothing; yet we are everything to God. While against the backdrop of infinite creation we may appear to be nothing, we have a spark of eternal fire burning within our breast. We have the incomprehensible promise of exaltation—worlds without end—within our grasp. And it is God's great desire to help us reach it." *President Dieter F. Uchtdorf, Second Counselor in the First Presidency, "You Matter to Him," Ensign, 2011.*

1– *Is Atheism Dead, Eric Metaxas, 2021.*

2– *That life in the universe arose thanks to extremely lucky circumstances may be a misconception, by Leto Sapunar, Popular Science, 2022.*

3– *Worlds without Number, By R. Val Johnson, Church Magazines, 2013.*

4– *Faith and Science: Symbiotic Pathways to Truth, Jamie L. Jensen, Ass Professor of Biology, BYU, 2020.*

CHAPTER 2

FIRST OBSERVE,
THEN SERVE...

Blessings come in numerous ways. Many are recognized immediately, while others seem to unfold slowly over time. Anything that contributes to our true happiness, well-being or prosperity is a blessing, and these blessings come from God. Some of God's blessings feel extraordinary, leaving little doubt that we are the recipient of divine favor. Yet others seem, well, ordinary. But gratitude for the ordinary blessings of life can give us extraordinary power to transform our lives. Gratitude unlocks the fullness of life. It turns what we have into enough, and more   It can turn a meal into a feast, a house into a home, a stranger into a friend. In a way, gratitude can grow our blessings. It's not that the blessing itself changes, but gratitude expressed for the root blessing causes our perspective to grow and expand, leading to an increased appreciation for our blessings.[1]

Ignaz Semmelweis (1818-1865) is known for being the first medical professional to demonstrate over time that hand washing was a blessing that could prevent infections:

He was the first to show that puerperal fever, also known as childbed fever, was contagious and could be prevented by hand washing. He observed that women delivered by physicians and medical students had a 10% mortality rate and only 4% from those delivered by midwives. He hypothesized that doctors were transferring a "morbid poison" from autopsies to the delivery room. Dr. Semmelweis concluded that the only significant difference was that his was a teaching clinic where corpses were examined. He observed that doctors went directly from performing autopsies to delivering babies. He concluded that somehow the corpses had contaminated their hands and caused the deadly fevers. The "morbid poison" is now known as Group A hemolytic streptococcus.

When he began to recommend that doctors scrub their hands with a chlorinated lime solution, he was met with indifference and even scorn. His conclusions contradicted the "truths" of other doctors. Some of his colleagues even believed that it was absurd to think that a doctor's hand could be impure or cause sickness. Semmelweis became known as the "father of infection control." His discovery directly confronted the beliefs of science and medicine in his time. The blessings of hand hygiene alone also reduced healthcare-associated infections by at least half. Handwashing improvements also lead to a 48% reduction of diarrheal diseases in the community.

In 2010, a South Jordon Utah man's obsession to bless others, began a journey attempting to meet a human's very basic needs. John Renouard was in Africa with his family after his son had been doing missionary work there. He was surprised to see how much time Africans spent collecting water – in fact, dirty water that one wouldn't let their dog drink from swamps and other areas.

His driver informed him that the girls were carrying water in buckets, yet the boys didn't have to. And on top of that, they had to bring the water to the school because the school didn't have any water even though they we're living in the middle of the second-largest city in Tanzania. It really bothered Renouard that this was still a problem in today's world. Children miss a lot of school while they're fetching contaminated water, plus they were often getting sick from drinking it.

He just couldn't believe everybody was still carrying water on their heads. It just didn't make any sense to him when he found out that according to the World Health Organization, at least 2 billion people worldwide use a drinking water source contaminated with feces. He questioned himself, "Who was I to try to solve the world's water crisis? I have no engineering background or advanced degrees." He just really wanted to help, so he started thinking about simple solutions that others either hadn't considered or had quickly dismissed. Many told him that his ideas would never work.

Renouard eventually came up with a rough sketch of a possible solution: a human-powered drill that could create water wells. He called it the Village Drill. The sketch made enough sense and a team of engineering students from Brigham Young University – Renouard's alma mater – spent months helping him design it as part of their capstone project.

They traveled to Tanzania to test the drill, and the first version was ready to be deployed in 2011. According to

Renouard, many people think there's no water in Africa. But there is. It's just 120 to 150 feet underground. There's really nothing out there like the Village Drill. It works because it's so simple, and it actually gets easier to drill the deeper that you go.

So far, the Village Drill has created an estimated over 12,000 wells. The drill can fit in the back of a pickup truck (or even a canoe!) and takes less than an hour to assemble, making it much more cost-effective than a typical drilling rig, plus the Village Drill can reach remote areas that aren't accessible by the big drilling trucks.

Renouard's nonprofit, WHOlives, trains entrepreneurs in the developing world to start their own drill teams using the technology. The organization offers zero-interest loans to those businesses to make the drill affordable. Drill teams generally reach water within a couple of days or weeks at a depth of about 150 feet (45 meters). The Village Drill's maximum depth is 270 feet (80 meters).

In addition, the nonprofit's Community-Funded Loan Program has helped many villages afford a well. Villagers make a down payment and then make small monthly payments to cover the cost of the well, which averages between $3,500 and $5,000. A lifetime of clean water costs about $5 per person, and for context, a day laborer in an African village makes an average of $6 per day. "One day's work for a lifetime of clean water is a bargain," Renouard said. "It's very, very affordable. This is a win-win for the drill teams and the communities."

John Renouard is affectionately known in Africa as "Bwana Maji," or Mr. Water. However, John's impact extends beyond water access. He is a formidable force in the fight to end female genital mutilation (FGM) and child marriages, employing common-sense solutions that make a real difference. John has distributed thousands of copies of his book, "The Value of a Daughter," to help men understand the importance of valuing and empowering their daughters. His efforts are not only raising awareness but actively contributing to the eradication of these brutal practices, transforming communities, and creating a safer, more equitable future for countless girls.[2]

To bring water out of a deep well without electricity, the force used is manual labor, typically through a hand pump which requires physical effort to draw the water up from the well using a lever mechanism; essentially, the force of your arms pulling on the pump handle is what brings the water to the surface.

There was a man who got lost in the desert. After wandering around for a long time his throat became very dry, about that time he saw a little shack in the distance. He made his way over to the shack and found a water pump with a small jug of water and a note. The note read: "Pour all the water into the top of the pump to prime it, if you do this you will get all the water you need."

Now the man had a choice to make, if he trusted the note and poured the water in and if it worked, he would have all the water he needed. If it didn't, he would still be thirsty and might die. Or he could choose to drink the water in the jug and get immediate satisfaction, but it might not be enough and he still might die. After thinking about it the man decided to risk it. He poured the entire jug into the pump and began to work the handle, at first nothing happened but he kept going and water started coming out.

So much water came out he drank all he wanted, took a shower, filled all the containers he could find and gratefully filled the small jug and placed the note where it could easily be found. *Author Unknown*

The night before Jennifer would have a double-lung transplant at age 16, she leaned over to her dad and said, "Don't worry! Tomorrow I will wake up with new lungs, or I will wake up in a better place. Either way will be great." After the surgery and upon taking her first breath unaided by a breathing tube and ventilator, Jennifer began to cry.

Seeing the concern on her family's face, Jennifer quickly exclaimed, "It's just so good to breathe."

Witnessing this, Gary himself found new appreciation for the ordinary blessing of breath. He said: "Ever since that day, I have thanked [God] morning and night for my ability to breathe. We are surrounded by innumerable blessings that we can easily take for granted if we are not mindful. Conversely, when nothing is expected and everything is appreciated, life becomes magical." *(see "Hallmarks of Happiness," by Elder Gary B. Sabin, then a General Authority Seventy, Liahona, November 2023.)* He continued, "[I have determined that] we will never be happier than [we] are grateful."

For Jennifer and Gary, the ordinary blessing of breath became extraordinary. May we all develop what some call an attitude of gratitude, not only for the extraordinary but also the seemingly ordinary blessings of our lives.[1]

Recently I noticed a scantly clothed man walking along the road near my home holding a thin cushion from a couch. I was hurriedly driving the other way running errands and picking up some lunch to share with my wife.

Driving home I began to think about this man and maybe I should have turned around, driven home, picked up a couple of bottles of water, driven directly to the restaurant picked up some food and hurried back to share it with him before he had a chance to disappear from the highway.

Then thoughts filled my mind as to what could happen to me if I had taken this approach. Was he on drugs and dangerous to approach, would he over power me and take my wallet and car, would have he…???

I had closely observed but during my hurried daily life chose not to serve. I failed an opportunity by being more concerned for my wellbeing than serving another (maybe for good reason at least short term). Whether or not the man was grateful, I missed another opportunity of feeling true happiness and joy that comes from following the Savior's example: "If any man will come after me, let him deny himself, and take up his cross, and follow me. For whosoever will save his life shall lose it: and whosoever will lose his life for my sake shall find it." *Matthew 16:24–25; see also Matthew 10:39*

1– *Music & the Spoken Word: The ordinary blessings of life, Derrick Porter, 11/23/2024.*

2– *Nonprofit WHOlives empowers 12 million people with clean water, health and opportunity, 06/12/2023.*

CHAPTER 3

LIFE LONG BATTLES...

In the logbooks of the Butler Hospital for the Insane, there appears in May 1886 the feeble signature of a "William Stewart." Like most patients at the Rhode Island hospital, the 33-year-old did not enter of his own volition but at the insistence of loved ones who witnessed his dark unraveling. William Stewart Halsted—his full name, which he was presumably too ashamed to sign—may have been the most promising surgeon in America at that time.

For six years, rotating among six different hospitals in New York City and teaching sought-after classes at night, he had been transforming the field from one of rushed butchery into a meticulous, sterilized art. A refined and intellectual young man, often seen sporting a mustache and top hat, Halsted indulged in a vibrant social life and possessed an infinite and somewhat untamed curiosity.

With that investigative spirit, Halsted had embarked on experiments with cocaine—then touted as a wonder drug—with a group of colleagues in 1884. Submitting themselves as test subjects, they explored the drug's pain-numbing abilities by injecting it into their peripheral nerves. In doing so, they would advance the concept of local anesthetic, a critical leap for medical procedures, including dental work. They also became enslaved to the drug, whose dangerously addictive properties were not yet understood. Two of Halsted's colleagues died within months.

After a string of unexplained absences and erratic behavior at work, Halsted's close friend William Welch—a pathologist he'd met through New York medical circles—stepped in to lead a series of interventions. The first attempt was rehabilitation by sea, a three-month voyage aboard a schooner to the Windward Islands during which Halsted was supposed to wean himself incrementally from cocaine. By all accounts, the trip was a failure, with a restless Halsted breaking into the captain's storage to hunt for drugs.

When Halsted returned to land, his family and Welch demanded that he seek treatment at Butler, a well-regarded mental hospital. Welch also dangled encouraging bait for his friend's recovery: the opportunity to move to Baltimore to help form a new hospital and the nation's first research university.

For Halsted, this was also a chance to escape the life he'd scorched in New York. Arriving in the new city in December 1886, Halsted joined Welch's pathology lab while Johns Hopkins Hospital and its medical campus remained under construction.

Despite Halsted's lifelong battles with addiction, not only cocaine but later morphine, he revolutionized surgery in America by elevating three concepts: anesthesia to control pain, fine instruments to stop bleeding, and antisepsis to prevent infection. One intern observed that the surgeon's technique was so measured and precise that "there was never a moment of anxiety. I could not believe my eyes. It was like stepping into a new world."

"He was one of the first surgeons to employ courtesy in surgery, to show any consideration for the insides of a man he was operating on," journalist H.L. Mencken wrote in the 1930s. "The old method was to slit a man from the chin down, take out his bowels, and spread them on a towel while you sorted them out. Halsted held that if you touched an intestine with your finger, you injured it, and the patient suffered the effects of the injury."

Equally significant was the surgical residency program Halsted pioneered at Johns Hopkins, based on the German system he revered. This model, whereby medical school graduates enter university-sponsored, hospital-based training, progressively increasing their responsibilities—endures today across the United States.

Halsted's innovations in the practice of surgery were remarkable. His approach to breast cancer, the "radical mastectomy," removing not only the breast but also the muscles beneath—was the dominant treatment for decades before modern radiation and chemotherapy. During his New York years, Halsted performed what was possibly the first successful blood transfusion in the U.S., on his own sister, whom he injected with blood from his arm after finding her unconscious from a postpartum hemorrhage. He later performed the nation's first gallstone surgery, on his own mother, saving her life through a 2 a.m. operation on her kitchen table.

In an act of chivalry for his future wife, Halsted introduced surgical gloves to the operating room. Caroline Hampton, then Halsted's chief nurse, found her skin so inflamed by the chemical dip he required before surgery that she threatened to quit. "As she was an unusually efficient woman," Halsted wrote, "I gave the matter my consideration and one day in New York requested the Goodyear Rubber Company to make, as an experiment, two pairs of thin rubber gloves with gauntlets. On trial these proved to be so satisfactory that additional gloves were ordered." As one researcher remarked, that might have been the first time the start of a love story was recorded in a medical journal.

William Halsted and Caroline Hampton were both born into privilege and pedigree, their marriage a union of "the wealthy merchant class of the North with the planter aristocracy of the South," as medical historian Peter Olch wrote. Born in Manhattan on Sept. 23, 1852, Halsted grew up in a grand townhouse on Fifth Avenue, where his family was well established in the dry goods industry and wielded societal influence. He attended the prestigious Phillips Academy in Andover, Massachusetts, then Yale, where he was a middling student but exceptional athlete, captaining the football team. Only as a senior did Halsted's interest in medicine awaken, when he devoured Gray's Anatomy and Dalton's Physiology. He entered the College of Physicians and Surgeons, which would later become Columbia University's medical school, and graduated among the top 10 of his class in 1877.

Nine years Halsted's junior, Caroline Hampton was born on Nov. 10, 1861, into the family of famous Confederate General Wade Hampton III, her uncle, and she grew up in the shadow of his ruined Millwood Plantation in Columbia, South Carolina, which Union soldiers burned during the Civil War. Orphaned as a baby, Caroline was raised by three unmarried aunts, and she and her sister attended Edgehill in Virginia, a girls' school associated with the family of Thomas Jefferson.

In 1885, Hampton made the surprising choice to head to New York City to study nursing. She graduated from New York Hospital three years later before landing the position of chief nurse in the surgical division of the new Johns Hopkins Hospital.

Independent, aristocratic, and practical in nature, Hampton was by some accounts delightful to friends but perhaps a bit curt and intolerant to others. When frictions arose with another nurse in her unit, Halsted stepped in to appoint Hampton chief nurse of his own operating room. They later married.

If Caroline was no-nonsense, William was fussy. Known for his elegant fashion, he ordered suits from London and shoes from Paris, where he also mailed some of his dress shirts to be laundered. In the fireplace he would burn only hickory logs aged at least three years. One friend compared the couple to Charles Dickens characters—"so peculiar, eccentric, so unlike other people, yet so interesting doubtless because of their oddities."

In Baltimore, the married Halsted's remained childless, they kept company with dogs, most memorably a pair of dachshunds named Nip and Tuck. The bond between the couple was intellectual, and though Caroline left nursing after her wedding, she is thought to have had "a powerful effect on Halsted's career," as Mencken said. "Many of the Halsted techniques for surgery were due to her suggestions."

In the spring of 1922, the National Dental Association honored Halsted for his pioneering work with local anesthetic—the positive result of his otherwise disastrous experiments with cocaine. Halsted must have had mixed emotions that evening, at the banquet at Baltimore's Belvedere Hotel. He later told a friend that his happiness was "tinged with regret for the lost opportunities—for the time wasted from loss of health"— seemingly acknowledging the damage cocaine had wrought.

In those early experiments with the white powder, Halsted was truly working at the cutting edge of medicine. Although cocaine was a common and perfectly legal ingredient in tonics and eventually the famous Coca-Cola, its medical potential was unappreciated and undocumented until 1884. That year, famed Austrian psychoanalyst Sigmund Freud published "Über Coca," the first scientific analysis of cocaine, and his colleague, ophthalmologist Carl Koller, followed with a seminal paper heralding the drug's promise as an anesthetic for eye surgery.

With the perspective of time, Halsted's life can be understood in two distinct phases: before cocaine and after. The energetic, affable man he was in New York—socializing and entertaining often, highly engaged with students— was not the Halsted people knew later in Baltimore, a withdrawn, wary, and enigmatic figure. His friend Harvey Cushing described him as "caring little for the gregarious gatherings of men." According to Welch, Halsted could still be charming with close friends, "full of original, whimsical humor," but he often failed to restrain his "caustic irony" at inappropriate times.

In the phase in between, Halsted completed two separate stints rehabilitating at Butler, which together consumed more than a year of his life. Many believe that his treatment there to ease cocaine withdrawal included daily injections of morphine—in effect, trading one highly addictive drug for another.

The morphine addiction haunted Halsted throughout his life. Although it was the subject of whispers around Johns Hopkins, he guarded his secret from all but a few intimates. He had never been able to reduce the amount of morphine to less than three grains daily; on this he could do his work comfortably and maintain his excellent physical vigor. (For context, that dosage is equivalent to 195 milligrams, while modern pain treatment calls for just 10 to 20 milligrams every four hours.)

Caroline certainly knew of her husband's addiction, but it's not clear how she coped with it—and Daniel Nunn, former historian for the Halsted Society, found anecdotal evidence that morphine may have hooked her too. One caretaker recalled her becoming "very upset because a package had not arrived from Parke-Davis"—a pharmaceutical company that sold the drug.

In an otherwise storied career, Halsted was notorious for spotty attendance and prolonged absences that would have ended the employment of a lesser surgeon. Meeting notes from the hospital's board of trustee's express frustration and concern. "We have much troubled over Halsted," says one 1891 note. "He went to South Carolina a month ago for his health and will not be back until the middle of the month. He was looking dreadfully when he left."[1]

Medical gloves can be made of natural or synthetic polymers. Latex gloves are made of natural latex, which comes from rubber trees. Nonlatex gloves are made of a variety of materials, including polyvinyl chloride, neoprene, and nitrile. Glove powder essentially acts as a lubricant. The first powder, used in the late 1880s, was made of spores (from Lycopodium, i.e. club moss) or pollen (from pine trees). These materials caused wound granulomas and adhesions. Talcum powder (i.e. magnesium silicate), used in the 1930s, also caused adhesions and granulomas. The year 1947 saw the first absorbable powder: modified cornstarch powder. Until recently, starch was the most commonly used type of glove powder.

In January 2017, the FDA banned the use of powdered gloves. As a result, physicians, nurses, dentists, kitchen workers, and veterinary professionals cannot buy them or use them. According to the FDA "unused supplies…will need to be disposed of according to established procedures of the local community's solid waste management system." In plain English, the gloves can be disposed of in regular trash.

Bottom line: The ban affects all glove users and are now obligated to use unpowdered surgical and exam gloves. More than a year later, many professionals still are trying to understand the reason for this perplexing ban.[2]

The earliest evidence of the use of natural latex comes from the ancient Mesoamerican Olmec culture in 1500 BCE, the oldest known major civilization in the Mexico region. It was apparently used for making balls for a game that is not entirely dissimilar to racquetball.

The Frenchman Charles Marie de La Condamine is credited with the introduction of rubber samples to Europe in 1736, and in 1770 the Englishman Joseph Priestly observed that it was particularly good at rubbing off pencil marks from paper, hence the name "rubber."

The first rubber processing procedure, vulcanization, was developed by Charles Goodyear in 1839. He treated crude rubber with sulfur and subjected it to heat. This process made the rubber less plastic and increased its strength and durability. Following this, the use of rubber became increasingly popular, and in the 1870s the commercial cultivation of rubber was introduced by British planters in India, at the Calcutta Botanical Gardens. By the latter part of the 19th-century rubber was widely available and was being used for an increasingly diverse number of commercial and industrial uses.

In the late 1890s surgery still had a 50% mortality rate and infection caused the majority of these deaths. Most of these deaths were preventable as surgeons did not wash hands between procedures or carry out even the most basic of hygiene practices. This began to change with the introduction of the use of carbolic acid to sterilize surgical instruments by Joseph Lister. He initially used the carbolic acid to clean compound fracture wounds, and the results were quite remarkable, reducing mortality rates. This spurred him to invent a machine that distributed a fine mist of carbolic acid into the operating theatre around the surgical site. The surgical instruments were also washed in the same solution. The combination of these antiseptic measures resulted in a dramatic fall in the death rate of

Lister's surgical patients from close to 50% to only 15% in 1870.

Following the work by Lister, Halsted decided to use a combination of carbolic acid and mercuric chloride as a disinfectant during his surgical procedures. Caroline Hampton, acting as his scrub nurse would have to handle these chemicals regularly, and as a consequence, she developed severe contact dermatitis on her hands and was being forced to leave her profession. Halsted had personal interests in Caroline, did not want her to leave and reached out to the Goodyear Rubber Company to create a rubber glove that she could wear during surgery to protect her hands. Halsted explains, (as quoted by Sherwin Nuland in 'Doctors: The Biography of Medicine'): "In the winter of 1889 and 1890, I cannot recall the month, the nurse in charge of my operating-room complained that the solutions of mercuric chloride produced a dermatitis of her arms and hands. As she was an unusually efficient woman, I gave the matter my consideration and one day in New York requested the Goodyear Rubber Company to make as an experiment two pair of thin rubber gloves with gauntlets. On trial these proved to be so satisfactory that additional gloves were ordered. In the autumn, on my return to town, an assistant who passed the instruments and threaded the needles was also provided with rubber gloves to wear at the operations. At first the operator wore them only when exploratory incisions into joints were made. After a time, the assistants became so accustomed to working in gloves that they also wore them as operators and would remark that they seemed to be less expert with the bare hands than with the gloved hands."

The two were married in June of 1890, shortly after he presented her with two pairs of rubber gloves made to fit plaster casts of her hands. Before long other theatre staff and surgeons began wearing the gloves too, and in time their use became commonplace. At this time the gloves were only used to protect the hands of the staff, but in 1894 Lister became the first person to sterilize the rubber gloves used in surgery.

By the early 1900s, all surgeons were wearing sterile rubber gloves. The first disposable latex medical gloves were manufactured in 1964 by the Ansell Rubber company. These disposable gloves were sterilized using gamma irradiation and cornstarch powder lubricant applied before packaging. Disposable surgical gloves are now the standard in the operating room and many surgeons 'double glove' when performing procedures to reduce the danger of infection from glove failure or puncture.[3]

The fine cornstarch powder was used to make getting gloves on (donning) and off (doffing) more easily. Glove powder's main benefit is that the powder simplifies the application and removal of gloves. The FDA decided this sole benefit was overshadowed by the downsides.

Glove powder adheres to latex protein, causing it to become aerosolized when gloves are manipulated. In turn, this increases the exposure to latex, which can cause various reactions ranging from sensitivity and airway inflammation to severe allergies. This can affect both patients and health-care workers.

In addition, the body reacts to the powder which acts as a foreign substance. This has been shown to potentiate wound infection, peritoneal adhesions, and granulomatous reactions. Most of the research was done primarily in humans and lab animal models.[2]

After 1980, manufacturers devised innovative techniques without dusting powder. It had been well documented that cornstarch powders on gloves presented a health hazard to patients and health care workers by 5 different mechanisms. First, the glove powder has documented detrimental effects on wound closure techniques. Second, it potentiates wound infection. Third, cornstarch induces peritoneal adhesion formation and granulomatous peritonitis. Finally, these powders serve as carriers of latex allergen and they can precipitate a life-threatening allergic reaction in sensitized patients. These well-documented hazards of glove powder have caused countries to ban cornstarch powder on medical gloves.[4]

In the days leading to his death, in the summer of 1922, Halsted relied on constant use of morphine to treat his escalating pain, as gallstones in his liver caused nausea, fever, vomiting, and jaundice. As his condition worsened, he ended his vacation early to be admitted to Johns Hopkins Hospital.

Strikingly, Halsted's death featured a mix of elements that also defined his life. Halsted died at his own workplace, under the care of two chief residents he had trained himself. "The irony is, Halsted performed the first gallstone operation and the first blood transfusion—then what does he die from? Gallstones. And one of the residents sticks a needle in his own vein to give Halsted his blood."

Despite the efforts of his former students, Halsted succumbed to post-operative infection on Sept. 7, 1922, just shy of his 70th birthday. Caroline survived her husband by a mere three months. Deep in grief, she died of pneumonia on Nov. 27, 1922.

If William Halsted were alive today, he would surely wince in shame that his legacy as the father of modern surgery is so intertwined with addictions he sought to keep private. But if not for his cocaine addiction, Halsted probably wouldn't have accepted Welch's invitation to Baltimore. An unusual set of circumstances led Halsted to Baltimore and Johns Hopkins Hospital, and the result was an amazing productivity that led to the creation of our surgical heritage.

Moreover, Halsted's accomplishments at Johns Hopkins seem all the more remarkable considering he was wrestling with morphine the entire time. He never overcame it. He lived with it. And yet he achieved more than most people, and here we are still talking about him.

Today, the medical principles that Halsted advanced are taken for granted. But 100 years past his death, his mark is still there—every time a dentist numbs a mouth, every time a doctor or nurse gloves up, every time a gallstone is removed or blood transfused. Every time a patient lies on the operating table, succumbing to the fog of anesthesia, fading into the trust of a surgeon.[1]

Working for my MD father, during my high school years, a part of my tasks included sharpening reusable hypodermic needles, cleaning glass syringes and preparing used disposable latex surgery gloves to be autoclaved. Practicing veterinary medicine during the 70s we continued to clean and autoclave single use surgery gloves and plastic syringes that had become available.

Since the ban on using powdered disposable surgery gloves, I have changed my glove size from a 7 ½ to an 8 and need to spend extra time drying my hands before donning them. I have difficulty getting all my fingers properly in place and the gloves fit loosely. They accumulate sweat inside from my hands and when doffing the gloves I need to remove myself from the surgical field and bend over towards the floor. Instead of an easy lubricated removal, there is effort pulling them inside out from my hands and sweat sprays towards the floor. Often before my next surgery I need to change to another sterile gown because of moisture accumulating around the cuff and sleeve.

Using instruments during surgery I often use an instrument called Halsted (Halstead), hemostats, or Mosquito forceps. They are a lightweight instrument designed for clamping blood vessels or other small tissues and to provide a secure grip that minimizes hand fatigue during surgery. They are often called Mosquito forceps because they resemble the slender legs of a mosquito. Since there is always tissue to be clamped and cut blood vessels to ligate - surgery is rarely performed without the use of various sized straight or curved Halsted forceps named for guess who - William Stewart Halsted.

1– *Angels and Demons: The peculiar and haunted genius of Dr. Halsted, John Hopkins Hospital, Katie Pearce, Fall 2022 Issue.*

2– *Life after the FDA's powdered glove ban, Phil Zeltzman, DVM, DACVS, CVJ, Veterinary Practice News,October 2018.*

3– *The History of Surgical Gloves, Past Medical History, Marc Barton, 09/19/2018.*

4– *Dangers of Cornstarch Powder on Medical Gloves, Annals of Plastic Surgery, July 2009.*

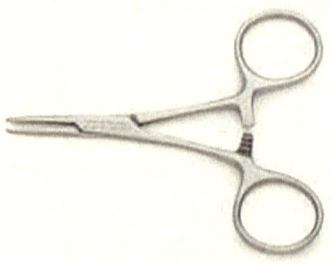

CHAPTER 4

MAN'S JOURNEY...

Soon after I started my medical studies, I was standing before a long metal table with three other medical students one day when I faced my ultimate challenge. On the table was a long black bag with a zipper running down the middle. In the air around us, assaulting our sinuses, was the sharp chemical smell of formaldehyde. Inside the bag was a dead person - a cadaver.

It had been assigned to our group, and we were expected to dissect it, organ by organ, limb by limb, learning by touch, sight, and firsthand experience the contours, textures, colors, and inner realms of the human body. I had known this was coming. We all did, and everyone felt some degree of discomfort about this part of our education. The cadaver stage of medical school has been chronicled profusely. Some students name their cadavers - names like Louise, Jim or Butch. It is a tactic to relieve the discomfort of knowing that before us lies a person who lived life as we do, felt jealousy and fear, and perhaps made art, wrote poetry, raised children and sacrificed for them, decorated

Christmas trees, wrapped birthday presents, had been in love and in lust, had had a broken heart.

But beyond all of this, I had to combat another level of discomfort; Navajos do not touch the dead. Ever. It is one of the strongest rules in our culture. The dead hold ch'iindis, or evil spirits, that are simply not to be tampered with. When a person dies, the "good" part of the person leaves with the spirit, while the "evil" part stays with the physical body. That belief is so strong that before the advent of mortuaries, Navajos sought out Pueblo Indians, missionaries, white traders or other outsiders to bury their dead. When a person dies in a hogan, the hogan is destroyed. Sometimes Navajo people nowadays bring their dying relatives to the hospital simply to prevent them from dying in their home. In many other cases hospitals are avoided. Navajo people know that death lies inside hospital walls, and therefore hospitals are filled with ch'iindis.

Many strong superstitions about the dead are woven throughout our beliefs. Sometimes a dead person can become a skinwalker. A young woman from a sheep camp near Farmington, N.M., above the San Juan River was said to have turned into a skinwalker. A mud clan man from Lukaichukai was made lame after he touched the body of a dead horse, which had also been lame. A healthy man from Tuba City, Ariz., died in his sleep after touching the body of his dead uncle. While there was no shortage of such stories, they were whispered things that I'd caught only in passing conversations between the old people or my aunts or my grandmother and her sister. Mostly these things, thought too terrible, were not discussed. Even speaking the word "death" holds bad karma for a Navajo.

There may have been sound reasons for the Navajo taboo about touching the dead, as there are for the Jewish stricture against eating pork. At the time when the Jewish taboo was set in place, pork often carried the dreaded trichinosis. Dead bodies, too, can be infected with possibly contagious disease. Perhaps long ago an astute Navajo medicine man figured out that touching a corpse might unknowingly spread disease. But whatever the reason, from the earliest age, a Navajo person becomes aware of this aversion. My grandmother and aunts spoke many times of the terrible things that could transpire if someone were to touch or brush against a dead person: things like madness, loss of fertility, death. One who has brushed against a corpse needs to undergo a ceremony (Enemy Way) to purify and release the ch'iindi spirit. It is an elaborate and costly event.

In medical school this taboo confronted me on every level. Never before had I been asked to do anything that directly violated the beliefs of my culture. Had I been more sophisticated, I might have requested some kind of permission from the dean of students to watch instead of touch, on the grounds that it violated my culture. Certain schools today may make allowances or concessions for such a taboo -- much of what is learned from dissecting a cadaver can be gotten from books, from 3-D holograph computer programs whose images simulate the human body or from "virtual" body programs. But at the time I felt that I had no option. If I wanted to become a doctor, I had to dissect. Civilization has discarded many of the taboos of primitive societies, but some have survived into modern times. As late as the 1920s, for example, it was taboo for a doctor to touch the living human heart. By that time surgeons, aided by advances in anesthesiology, had invaded most areas of the body. They had begun to operate routinely on the abdominal organs, limbs, the face, even the brain – but not the heart. In the few instances in the preceding centuries when, in emergencies, surgeons had entered the chest to cut and sew the heart, the patient generally had died.

Well into the twentieth century, to touch the heart was to molest a sacred area of the body, its spiritual center, and most doctors feared to tamper with it. Even if they had not been afraid of incurring God's wrath, there were seemingly unsolvable physical problems. The heart constantly pumped blood; when cut, it bled profusely. How could anyone survive such a hemorrhage?

Furthermore, the heart seemed inaccessible. It lies at most three inches beneath the skin, but it is enclosed by a bony cage of ribs that protects both it and the lungs. Were a surgeon to open the chest cage to operate on the lungs or heart, air could suddenly rush in, collapsing one lung and possibly both.

By World War II, knowledge of the heart's functions and the physiology of the lungs was still rudimentary, much of the intimate physiological relationship between the two yet to be revealed. In 1628, when William Harvey discovered the circulatory system, he taught us that the heart pumps blood over and over again through a closed system of arteries and veins. But three centuries after Harvey's discovery, few doctors could consistently diagnose a heart condition. Physicians could rely on little more than their hands and ears as diagnostic aids.

With the discovery of anesthesia in the mid-nineteenth century, surgeons experimented and devised new operations, but touching the heart remained taboo. In 1880 Dr. Theodor Billroth, the most influential European surgeon of his time said: "A surgeon who tries to suture a heart wound deserves to lose the esteem of his colleagues." The medical profession adopted an attitude about heart surgery so fatalistic that in 1896 Dr. Stephen Paget, a noted English physician, wrote: "Surgery of the heart has probably reached the limits set by Nature to all surgery: no new method, and no new discovery, can overcome the natural difficulties that attend a wound of the heart."

By the turn of the twentieth century, surgeons had opened the chest, but not the heart. Then, in 1903, Cr. Ferdinand Sauerbruch, a famous German surgeon, performed an operation that was to make history – and it came about accidentally. One of Sauerbruch's patients was a woman with heart failure, and Sauerbruch believed it was due to constriction of the pericardium, the membrane that covers the heart. He decided to relieve this constriction. Sauerbruch, a great teacher, operated in an amphitheater before a group of observant doctors. When he cut open the woman's chest, he saw what he thought was a cyst in her pericardium and he began to cut it out. Suddenly blood spurted, Sauerbruch realized immediately that it was not a cyst in the membrane but a ballooning of the heart wall itself, known as an aneurysm, and the pericardium had become attached to it. This brutally bold, fearless surgeon quickly repaired the aneurysm and sewed the heart. The patient recovered.[2]

In 1955, Nelson M. Nelson (09/09/1924 -) returned to where he had been born, Salt Lake City, and accepted a faculty position at the University of Utah School of Medicine. There he built his own heart-lung bypass machine and employed it to support the first open-heart surgery in the United States west of the Mississippi River. That operation was performed at the Salt Lake General Hospital (SLGH, now the University of Utah Hospital) on an adult with an atrial septal defect. Nelson was the third surgeon in the United States to perform an open-heart operation successfully. Nelson was also the director of the University of Utah thoracic surgery residency program.

In March 1956, he performed the first successful pediatric cardiac operation at the SLGH, a total repair of tetralogy of Fallot in a four-year-old girl. He was at the forefront of surgeons focusing attention on coronary artery disease, and contributed to the advance of valvular surgery as well. In 1960, he performed one of the first-ever repairs of tricuspid valve regurgitation. His patient was a Latter-day Saint stake patriarch. He also provided the first surgical intervention for tricuspid regurgitation, a disorder that allows blood to flow backward into the right upper heart chamber. In an indication of his surgical skill, a 1968 case series of his aortic valve replacements demonstrated an exceptionally low peri-operative mortality. Later, he performed the same operation on future LDS Church president Spencer W. Kimball, replacing his damaged aortic valve. In 1985, Nelson along with his colleague, Conrad B. Jenson, performed a quadruple bypass surgery on the Chinese opera performer Fang Rongxiang [zh] (1925–1989). In 1981, Nelson held appointments as a visiting professor of surgery at the National Institute of Cardiology in Mexico City and the Catholic University in Santiago, Chile. In May 1982 he was a visiting professor at the Hospital de Clinicas in Montevideo, Uruguay.

In addition to his medical work, Nelson served frequently as a leader in The Church of Jesus Christ of Latter-Day Saints. In Minnesota, he served as what was then known as Sunday School Superintendent in his local congregation. In Washington DC, he was a counselor in the bishopric of the ward that Ezra Taft Benson (then an apostle) regularly attended while serving as Secretary of Agriculture to Dwight D. Eisenhower. In Massachusetts, Nelson was the secretary for the adult Aaronic priesthood organization in his Boston-area branch.

After returning to Salt Lake City, he served over youth groups, then a councilor in a bishopric, a stake high councilor, stake president, and the church's Sunday School General President. Nelson was called as an apostle by church president Spencer W. Kimball, whom he had served as a personal physician for many years. Nelson was sustained as a member of the Quorum of the Twelve Apostles and ordained as an apostle on 04/12/1984. He was ordained and set apart as church president on 01/14/2018. *Wikipedia* Addressing students At Brigham Young University devotional on September 09, 1984, Dr. Russell M. Nelson said: Our being here reminds me of those days when I was where you are now in your schooling. We had three important goals. One was to get married. Then, once married, our next goal was to get by financially. Then our goal was to get through. We got married when Sister Nelson was an undergraduate student and I was in my second year of medical school.

Because I was under legal age, parental consent was required. My father was very amused when I called him away from his work to sign for me so I could get a marriage certificate. With Sister Nelson's (and parental) help, we were able to make it through medical school after we each received our baccalaureate degree. I then informed her that it was customary to have a year internship. Following that I was determined to specialize, and I let her know that it would require additional training.

I'll confess to a bit of naivete. If we had known that the interval between my getting my doctor's degree and our finally going into practice would be twelve and a half years with six children added, we might not have been quite as enthusiastic in the beginning. So, I pay great tribute to her for her role in our partnership. I owe so much to her. Now I pray for the Spirit of the Lord to direct our discussion tonight.

I have entitled my remarks "Begin with the End in Mind." I suppose some of this comes from my surgical background. An elective incision is never made without planning to close it. The same principle is generally applicable in all fields, however. Track stars don't begin a race without knowing the location of the finish line. So, in your important race, I would plead for you to begin with the end in mind. To assist you in defining that end, I would ask you this simple question: What would you like said about you at your funeral? Or, if you were to write your own eulogy and you could have only three sentences (no big flowery speeches, please), what would you want to say?

If it's fair for me to ask that of you, it's fair for you to ask that of me. If I were to write what I hope might be said about me, those three sentences would include: I was able to render service of worth to my fellowmen, I had a fine family, and I evidenced unshakable faith in God and lived accordingly.

Some of you have already defined your goals. Some have even developed a system of priorities to give order to your interests and responsibilities. I applaud such discipline and think it's useful, but I believe that this ordering process may often be a little artificial. Rarely do we fragment the life that we live. It is not possible to influence one facet of our life without that affecting other aspects as well. So, in my own experience, I have preferred not to compartmentalize my interests, but to synergize them. Let me explain what I mean.

Nephi said, "I did liken all scriptures unto us, that it might be for our profit and learning" (1 Nephi 19:23). He was advising us to weave the fiber of scriptural wisdom into the fabric of our own being. King Benjamin taught this interrelationship: When ye are in the service of your fellow beings ye are only in the service of your God. (Mosiah 2:17) As I ponder serving God, I recognize that I cannot serve him without first serving the children that he has sent to bless our family. Then, as I ponder service to our children, I know I cannot serve them to the fullest without first serving and honoring my wife, the mother of those children. She is my highest priority. When we were married, we vowed that we would "seek first the kingdom of God and his righteousness" (see Matthew 6:33). Do you see how these goals and priorities all are indelibly intertwined? To say that your highest priority will be to your occupation or to your family or to the Lord is really much more difficult than it is to merge strengths and pursue those interests concurrently. One of the most remarkable things about these three objectives is that they all have one requirement in common. That requirement is education. The educational process is crucial for success in each objective and is never ending.

First, with regard to service of worth to mankind, I was introduced to you as a heart surgeon. But that really doesn't tell the whole story. When I started medical school, we were taught that one must not touch the heart, for if one did, it would stop beating. But I also pondered the scripture that tells us that "all kingdoms have a law given . . . And unto every kingdom is given a law; and unto every law there are certain bounds also and conditions" (D&C 88:36, 38). I believed sincerely the scripture that certifies: When we obtain any blessing from God, it is by obedience to that law upon which it is predicated. (D&C 130:21)

Knowing these scriptures while concentrating on the "kingdom" of and the blessing of the beating heart, I knew that even the function of this vital organ was predicated upon law. I reasoned that if those laws could be understood and controlled, perhaps they could be utilized for the blessing of the sick. To me this meant that if we would work, study, and ask the proper questions in our scientific experiments, we could learn the laws that govern the heartbeat.

In 1949 our group of researchers presented at the American College of Surgeons the report of the first successful use of the artificial heart-lung machine in sustaining the life of an animal for a thirty-minute period of time, without its own heart powering its circulation.

In the decade of the 1950s, successes in the animal laboratory were extended to human beings. Now, with many of those laws learned, the heartbeat can be turned off while performing delicate repairs on the damaged valves or vessels, and then turned on again—provided the laws are obeyed upon which that blessing is predicated. Over 200,000 (1984) open-heart operations are performed in this country annually, and many more worldwide, thereby extending life for many. But you should know that it was through the understanding of the scriptures and "likening" them to this area of interest, that the great field of heart surgery as we know it today was facilitated for me.

Turning now from service of worth to my fellowmen, the second sentence that I hope may be said of me at my funeral would be that I had a fine family. That's really a subject near and dear to my heart, and I won't try to treat it broadly except to say that Sister Nelson has brought into our family ten beautiful children. We have tried to treat them constantly with important scriptures: "Honor thy father and thy mother; that thy days may be long upon the land which the Lord thy God giveth thee" (Exodus 20:12). The importance of honoring parents extends beyond your own father and mother. This scripture implies that we honor the father and the mother of children that might yet be born to us…Part of honoring parenthood is honoring children. There is a great temptation to believe erroneously that our children are our possessions. They are not. They are sons and daughters of our Heavenly Father. Their spirits are eternal as are ours. The Lord said, "I have commanded you to bring up your children in light and truth" (D&C 93:40). This we have tried to do.

The third sentence that I hope I may merit at my funeral service is that my faith in God was unshakable. I do have a deep and abiding faith in him and his son, Jesus Christ. Education has increased that faith. As I have spent forty years of my life in the study of one of God's greatest creations, the human body, I know that this marvelous instrument is of divine origin. The anatomy, the physiology, the protective mechanisms, the healing powers—all are so well constructed and function so beautifully. It is as evident to me that they are the products of a divine creator as it must be for an astronomer to reach the same conclusion as he studies the endless phenomenon of the stars in the heavens.

Furthering education need not challenge, but should increase your faith. In fact, we have a religious responsibility to educate our minds. "The glory of God is intelligence"(D&C 93:36). We have a divine command to "obtain a knowledge of history, and of countries, and of kingdoms, of laws of God and man" (D&C 93:53). Similarly, the Lord exhorted us to "study and learn, and become acquainted with all good books, and with languages, tongues, and people"(D&C 90:15). The scriptures further admonish, "Learn wisdom in thy youth" (Alma 37:35, see also Proverbs 29:3). "Teach one another the doctrine of the kingdom. Teach ye diligently and my grace shall attend you"(D&C 88:77–78).

We all understand the importance of education. Perhaps now we should consider how to learn. May I suggest four steps to facilitate the learning process:

The first is to have a great desire to know the truth. As a teacher of surgery for many years, I have observed the differences in desires of individuals to learn. Before every operation there is an interval for scrubbing hands for a measured period of time. Some trainees have either been silent or have passed this time with trivial conversations that had no substance. Those with desire filled that time with questions. I observed that students with great desire know what they don't know and seek to fill those voids.

The second step would be to study with an inquiring mind. Again, I take this pattern from the scriptures. You remember that when the brother of Jared was preparing for a transoceanic migration, he realized there was no provision for light in the ships. So, he asked the Lord, "Shall we cross this great water in darkness?" The Lord gave an interesting reply: "What will ye that I should do that ye may have light in your vessels? . . . Ye cannot have windows, for they will be dashed in pieces; neither shall ye take fire with you. . . Ye shall be as a whale in the midst of the sea"(Ether 2:22–24).

The Lord could have told the brother of Jared what to do, but he was left to study this out in his own mind before proffering the solution. As a result, he selected sixteen stones and then asked the Lord to touch them that they might provide the light for their travel.

That same concept was again stressed in latter-day revelation, when the Lord told his servant, "You have not understood; you have supposed that I would give it unto you, when you took no thought save it was to ask me. But, behold, I say unto you, that you must study it out in your mind; then you must ask me if it be right"(D&C 9:7–8). Many of the revelations contained in the Doctrine and Covenants were given to the prophets only after profound study and thoughtful, focused inquiry of the Lord.

The third step is to apply or practice your learning in your daily lives. Those who have learned another language know how important that is. Even with great desire and study, mastery of a language comes only as it is applied to the daily situations of life.

The fourth and very important step in the learning process is to pray for help. I did not hesitate to communicate with the Lord in great detail, even about the technical steps in a new operative procedure that was to be performed. Often just the process of rehearsing it in my mind while engaged in prayer allowed divine direction for me to see a better way.

Now may I offer important words of warning: Learning, if misused, can destroy your goals. Let us consider some safeguards to protect you from such an undesirable end:

Your faith must be nourished. You are blessed at this university to do this by enrolling in religion classes. Enrich that faith additionally with private scriptural study and with exposure to other fine books, art, or music. Nourish the gifts of the Spirit on the same daily basis that you feed your physical body.

Choose your role model wisely. Before you endorse all of the teachings of any teacher, ask yourself if his or her faith is strong enough to be worthy of emulation. If it isn't, be very discriminating in what you learn from such an individual. Remember that the Bible, Book of Mormon, Doctrine and Covenants, and the Pearl of Great Price are the standards by which you should measure all doctrine.

Avoid poisons of faith such as sin, pornography, or barely abiding the letter of the law instead of embracing the ennobling spirit of the law. Remember, "The letter killeth, but the spirit giveth life" (2 Corinthians 3:6).

Many challenges will be put in your way. You will hear allegations that the Church is "anti-intellectual." When people make that statement, I am reminded of a common sight in the jungles of Africa. A bird, like the critic, will often perch on the uppermost part of an elephant. This bird pecks away at the hide of the stately animal, achieving temporary nourishment and position of eminence by virtue of this association. While the elephant doesn't need the bird, the bird needs the elephant for its place of prominence. Though the bird may peck, squawk, and smear, the elephant steadily pursues its course in seeming oblivion to its parasitic passenger.

Some of the greatest "intellectuals" have been those with the strongest faith. Socrates felt that the unexamined life is not worth living, so nothing was exempt from his questioning...Socrates never doubted the will of his personal God. He believed so much in freedom that he tied his own self-responsibility to that freedom. So deeply did he believe in the doctrine of immortality of the soul that although he might have prolonged his biological life by choosing exile, he submitted with complete serenity to the death sentence of the Athenian court.[3]

Lori Arviso Alvord in her anatomy lab: Standing in front of my cadaver I thought back on stories about this person and that person who had touched a dead thing, and the consequences that befell them. I thought about all the ch'iindis of all the dead people around me in that lab room. I looked at the faces of my classmates. They too looked slightly nervous and a little edgy. I think all medical students approach their first cadaver with some trepidation. I wondered if my classmates could read my face and see that I was feeling the bitter taste of fear rising in the back of my throat.

The zipper on the black bag was opened. I looked down, bracing myself. There below me was an older male of medium build. His skin was shriveled and toughened by formaldehyde, a slate-gray color that I'd never seen on a living person. At first glance, it was revolting and I struggled to quell my nausea. With its lifeless color, the cadaver almost appeared to be a plastic or rubber doll, with shapes that could have been human features at one time, but had ceased to be. Its nonhuman appearance helped me forget that this had once been a real, breathing home for a human soul. I shifted my gaze away from the corpse's face, and leaned hard against the table to still the dizziness.

The experience would have been much worse for a traditional Navajo. After all, I am half bilagcaana and come from a relatively modern family, and I knew I should set aside these beliefs as superstitions. But even for me the problem arose. As I glanced again at the gray, rubbery form that had once been a man, I thought: What will happen to me if I do this? By this time, my desire to become a doctor was very strong, as I am sure it is for all medical students. We were studying hard, training hard and had competed against difficult odds just to be admitted to Stanford's halls, which had their own kind of sacredness. There had been more than 4,000 applications for our coveted 86 spots. At this point, although a part of me was terrified of the next step forward, I knew there was no going back.

OK, I thought. This is what I want, the knowledge I acquire here is like that of a medicine man. I will be able to bring home a tremendous gift. And if I am good enough, my work could even fight processes that cause death. In the course of a career, I could help thousands of my people. Cast in this light, my decision became easier. I took a deep breath. Someone handed me a scalpel. I'm not afraid, I told myself. I'm not afraid. I reached down to the shape below me and slid the scalpel into the skin.[1]

Louis Pasteur made this statement on his reception into the French Academy: "The Greeks have given us one of the most beautiful words in our language, the word enthusiasm, which means 'a God within.' The grandeur of the acts of men is measured by the inspiration from which they spring. Happy is he who bears a God within!"

Begin with the end in mind. Shape your own destiny. Remember that the development of your career, your family, and your faith in God is your individual responsibility—for which you alone will be held accountable.[3]

1– *Cutting into sacred territory, Lori Arviso Alvord, MD – Elizabeth C VanPelt, 09/06/1999.*

2– *The Story of Self-Experimentation in Medicine, Lawrence K. Altman, MD, 1987.*

3– *Begin with the End in Mind, Russell M. Nelson, Of the Quorum of the Twelve Apostles, 09/30/1984.*

CHAPTER 5

GUINEA WORMS...

Medicine's ultimate goal is prevention, and the best prevention against a disease is, of course, to eradicate it so it can never harm anyone again. But only once in history have doctors been able to play symbolic taps for the death of a disease. In 1980 the World Health Organization declared smallpox eradicated after an army of its workers had used a derivative of a vaccine developed nearly two centuries earlier to wipe the viral disease off the face of the earth. Before that time, smallpox killed about one in four of its victims, scarred most survivors for life, and blinded others. Moreover, smallpox, like many other viral infections, could not be cured, nor could it be effectively treated once it came on. But it could be prevented.

The weapon against smallpox was a vaccine developed by Dr. Edward Jenner in 1796. Jenner's discovery became a model for all the immunizations that are used in medicine today: immunizations that mean children no longer risk choking to death from diphtheria or being brain damaged as a complication of measles or paralyzed from poliomyelitis; no longer are people in danger of getting "lockjaw" (tetanus) from stepping on a rusty nail; and many fewer babies are gasping from the severe paroxysms of whooping cough.

Edward Jener, an English country physician, took his cue from milkmaids who noted that people who came down with cowpox often escaped subsequent infection from smallpox. Jenner spent years developing a vaccine from matter derived from the sores of cowpox patients; along the way he was encouraged by John Hunter, who in 1767 contracted gonorrhea &/or syphilis not in the usual manner. These two diseases were among the most common ailments doctors treated in his era. He took pus from an infected patient and injected it into two places on his own penis in expectation of producing the same infection in himself. From this self-experiment, he did contract venereal disease and died at the age of sixty-five from third stage syphilis.

Jenner inoculated eight-year-old James Phipps with the cowpox matter; young Phipps got cowpox and recovered. Then in the and most crucial step, Jenner, on July 1, 1796, inoculated the boy with the smallpox virus. He repeated the inoculation about twenty times over the next two decades; Phipps did not get the disease.[1]

Nobel Prize-winning peacemaker Jimmy Carter (10/01/1924-12/29/2024) spent nearly four decades waging war to eliminate an ancient parasite plaguing the world's poorest people. Rarely fatal but searingly painful and debilitating, Guinea worm disease infects people who drink water tainted with larvae that grow inside the body into worms as much as 3-feet-long. The noodle-thin parasites then burrow their way out, breaking through the skin in burning blisters.

Carter made eradicating Guinea worm a top mission of The Carter Center, the nonprofit he and his wife, Rosalynn Carter, founded after leaving the White House. The former president rallied public health experts, billionaire donors, African heads of state and thousands of volunteer villagers to work toward eliminating a human disease for only the second time in history.

One of Carter's foremost achievements—"not for me, but for the people that have been afflicted," as he told ABC News in a 2015 interview—was the near-total eradication of Guinea worm, a vicious parasite passed on to humans by drinking stagnant, infected water in Africa and Asia. "Once you've seen a small child with a two or three-foot-long live Guinea worm protruding from her body, right through her skin, you never forget it," Carter wrote in a 1990 after visiting Ghana with his wife Rosalynn. He described walking through villages and witnessing hundreds of men, women and children in agony. "Nobody was doing anything about it, and it was such a spectacularly awful disease."

In 2015, as he suffered from cancer, the former president quipped to reporters that he'd like for the last Guinea worm to die before he did. It'd be the most exciting and gratifying accomplishment of my life, Carter commented in 2016. Even after entering home hospice care in February 2023, aides said Carter kept asking for Guinea worm updates.

When Carter died on December 29, 2024, at 100 years old, he had come tantalizingly close to realizing that wish. Thanks to the Carters' efforts, the worms that afflicted an estimated 3.5 million people in some 20 African and Asian countries when the center launched its campaign in 1986 are on the brink of extinction. Only 14 human cases were reported across four African nations in 2023, according to The Carter Center. The World Health Organization's target for eradication is 2030. Carter Center leaders hope to achieve it sooner. *AP 2024 and Smithsonian 2025*

According the CDC, Dracunculiasis, also known as Guinea worm disease (GWD), is an infection caused by the parasite Dracunculus medinensis. GWD is a neglected tropical disease (NTD) transmitted to people mostly by consuming unsafe water. Unfiltered drinking water from ponds or other stagnant surface water sources can contain near-microscopic crustaceans called copepods (tiny "water fleas") that are infected with Guinea worm larvae (immature forms of the Guinea worm).

People do not usually have GWD symptoms until about one year after infection. Then, a mature pregnant female worm full of larvae creates a blister on the skin through which she will emerge and expel her larvae when she comes in contact with water. A few days to hours before the worm, which can measure up to 3 feet (1 meter) in length, comes out of the skin, a person may develop fever, swelling, and pain in the area. Most worms come out of people's legs and feet, though worms can come out of other body parts, too. People in remote rural communities who have GWD often lack access to healthcare. When the adult female worm comes out of the skin, it can be very painful, disabling, and take a long time to remove. The emerging worm can cause a wound that may develop a secondary infection.

Anyone who consumes drinking water from a pond or other stagnant water source contaminated with infected copepods is at risk for infection. People's risk for disease can vary. People do not get immunity after GWD, which means they can get it again.

GWD transmission also has a seasonal pattern. Water contact triggers the Guinea worm to release a milky white liquid that contains hundreds of thousands of immature larvae into the water. In ponds and other stagnant water sources, these larvae are then consumed by copepods. People might become infected with Guinea worms by consuming unfiltered drinking water from such water sources containing infected copepods. People and animals might also become infected by eating certain aquatic animals (e.g., fish or frogs) that have swallowed infected copepods. People and animals infected with GWD can then spread the disease when the worm matures and is ready to emerge from the body if they enter ponds and other stagnant water sources that others drink from.

Guinea worm is a disease that has been prioritized for eradication by the World Health Organization. There were an estimated 3.5 million Guinea worm cases occurring annually in 20 African and Asian countries in 1986, but today, through the Guinea Worm Eradication Program (GWEP), only a handful of countries continue to have the disease.

GWEP undertakes several water-related and other measures to prevent GWD: 1-Surveillance and case containment; 2-Safe water practices, including distribution of cloth and pipe filters to remove copepods, and advocacy for installation or rehabilitation of safe drinking water supplies like borehole wells; and 3-Vector control of copepods by chemical means.

There is no drug to treat Guinea worm infection. Once part of the worm begins to come out of the wound, it is important that all of the worm is removed to prevent complications. Anti-inflammatory medicine can help reduce pain and swelling, and antibiotic ointment can help prevent infections. There is no vaccine to prevent Guinea worm infection. *CDC*

According to the State of Michigan Department of Natural Resources, the North American Guinea worms are nematodes found in numerous furbearing species in the U.S. and Canada. The human form of the disease, Dracunculus medinensis is <u>not</u> found in north America, but the life cycles are very similar and all are recognized under the common name Guinea worm disease. Two species of worms, D. insignis and D. lutrae, are recognized and the slender worms reside in the subcutaneous spaces of the legs of mammals, resulting in ulcerations in these affected areas.

D. insignis has been reported in the raccoon, mink, striped skunk, fox, muskrat, fisher, short-tailed weasel, opossum, badger, Bonaparte weasel and dog in the U.S. and Canada. Raccoons are the most favorable definitive host for D. insignis in North America. In Ontario, surveys found infections of D. insignis as high as 50% in raccoon and mink.

D. lutrae has only been reported in river otter in Ontario, New York, and Michigan. Eighty-eight percent of the river otter in Ontario surveyed in one year were infected with D. lutrae. In Michigan, dracunculosis has been diagnosed in raccoon, mink, red fox, river otter, fisher, pine marten, short-tailed weasel, and muskrat. The Guinea worm that infects man, Dracunculus medinensis, is <u>not</u>

found in North America and those present infect only wild mammalian species.

Gravid adult female D. insignis and D. lutrae are found in the subcutaneous space of the front and hind legs, thorax, abdomen, and groin. The worms are generally in the fascia in the tibial region of the hind leg. The anterior end of the viviparous female penetrates the dermis resulting in the formation of a blister. The blister soon ruptures and an ulcer forms. When the ulcerated area contacts water, the skin over the gravid female ruptures. First-stage larvae are liberated into the water and are ingested by suitable intermediate copepod hosts, the cyclops and possibly other species. The infected cyclops may contain from 1 to 23 larvae, but usually has only 4 or 5. After larval ingestion, the copepods may become lethargic and may live only 50 days. The first-stage larvae develop to the infective third-stage larvae in a few weeks.

A paratenic host, such as frogs (leopard frog, Rana pipiens, and green frog) or fish (rainbow trout, Salmon, and white sucker) may serve as an accumulator of the D. insignis and possibly D. lutrae infective stage larvae by eating the infected cyclops.

The accumulation of infective larvae maintains the high prevalence of the worm in the definitive hosts. The infective third-stage larvae probably remain viable in frogs for extended periods of time, so that large numbers of larvae can be ingested by eating a single frog.

The definitive hosts become infected by eating infected reservoir hosts or by drinking water containing parasitized cyclops. The infective larvae are released in the intestinal tract. The larvae penetrate the wall of the host's intestine and migrate through the body cavity to the connective tissues of the abdomen, thorax, and groin. In these preferred locations, the larvae mature, with the prepatent period usually being a year but possibly being as short as 77 days. Following maturity, the Guinea worms mate, and egg development in the female occurs.

The males and immature females remain in the above locations, but the egg-bearing females migrate to the legs with larvae developing within the eggs during the females' migration. Viviparous females may be found as early as 120 days post-infection in the infected animal's legs. After larval production, the exhausted female, in addition to the adult male and immature worms, may die and become calcified and resorbed by the host.

Transmission of D. insignis in raccoons is confined to only a few weeks of the year. Adult worms are usually patent in late spring or early summer thus corresponding with changes in the definitive host's food habits. Mink infections are not as seasonal as raccoon infections due to the mink's year-round feeding on aquatic life. Raccoons may serve as a reservoir host for this parasite and there is a higher incidence of infection with D. insignis in mink when raccoons share the same area. River otter probably would not show a seasonal infection rate because of their year-round food habits.

Externally, there is local hair loss and skin damage to the extremities due to self-inflicted trauma (scratching). These lesions are usually on the lateral surface of the carpal and tarsal regions of the legs.

There are no gross lesions in the subcutaneous space adjacent to the adult Guinea worms. Lesions are found on the extremities where the viviparous females reside. The skin over these worms is inflamed and hemorrhagic. Small, round, shallow ulcerations form when the female worms place their heads into the dermal layer of the skin. After larvae are released from the adult female worms, the ulcerations contain a purulent exudate and bacteria. Following the production of larvae, the female worm dies. The lesions heal rapidly; 14 to 21 days after the female dies and the only visible signs of an infection are yellow patches of necrotic debris in the subcutaneous tissues of the legs.

The adult female worms may be removed through the skin opening on the legs or by surgical dissection. Removal of the worms is very difficult and usually not done. Therefore, there is essentially no treatment.

In wild mammal populations, control would be impractical and unnecessary.

Ever since Fedcheko described the human form of the disease, Dracunculus medinensis', life cycle in 1870 and until 2014, only the waterborne route of Guinea worm transmission was considered in the epidemiology of the human Guinea worm. Guinea worm disease has classically been considered an anthroponosis, i.e., an infectious disease affecting exclusively humans. However, dracunculiasis is nowadays considered a zoonosis since several mammals, mainly dogs, act as reservoirs of the disease in several African countries.

In 2014, Eberhard and colleagues, in an attempt to give an explanation for the large number of infected dogs compared to the few scattered human cases in Chad (Africa), proposed a foodborne route of transmission, i.e., by eating aquatic paratenic/transport hosts—frogs and fish, respectively—harboring the infective larvae. Considering that the great success of the Guinea worm eradication program (from 3.5 million human cases in the 1980s to only 53 in 2020) has been achieved through the implementation of control measures only against waterborne transmission, the foodborne route seems to be only of anecdotal importance, at least in humans.

The classic waterborne route was recently evaluated in dogs. The experiment, groups of dogs were given drinking water containing different concentrations of copepods of similar size and species to those which can act as intermediate hosts for the infective Guinea worm larvae. The quantity of copepods ingested by the dogs was estimated and the probability of dogs becoming infected with sufficient male and female larvae to establish an infection was determined using field data on the prevalence of this parasite in wild copepods. According to their results, the authors of the study concluded that drinking water may be an unlikely route for dogs.

Consequently, the fact that, in accordance with the experiment carried out by Garret and colleagues, the waterborne route of transmission is unlikely for dogs leads to the assumption that the other possible route of acquiring Guinea worm infection, the food born route, i.e., by means of eating infected frogs and fish, should be considered to have a higher likelihood in order to explain the high rate of dog Guinea worm in Chad. *Front Vet Science*

Eli Wizevich, history correspondent for Smithsonian states: The dracunculiasis Guinea worms can infect a variety of animals: In 2020, 1,507 domestic dogs in Chad were found to have guinea worms. Dogs can become infected by drinking contaminated water or eating frogs that have swallowed infected copepods. In 2020, 61 domestic cats in Chad and three in Ethiopia were found to have guinea worms. In Ethiopia, a few baboons have been found to have guinea worms. In Raccoons and mink guinea worms can be found in the subcutaneous connective tissues of the legs of these animals.

Guinea worms are also known as Dracunculus insignis (See article MI Dept of Natural Resources above). The females are much longer than the males, producing ulcers in the skin of their host. When the worm matures, it can emerge from the body and spread the disease if the host enters stagnant water. Fish, should be considered to have a higher likelihood in order to explain the high rate of dog Guinea worm in Chad.

Jimmy Carter referenced Jesus in an interview with Playboy magazine and it cost the Democratic presidential nominee more than he could fathom in the moment. "I've committed adultery in my heart many times," Carter said, a quote that Playboy published weeks before the 1976 general election (president 1977-1981).

The article included other remarks related to Carter's faith — such as the importance of the separation of church and state, a conviction born of Carter's Southern Baptist upbringing — but the adultery comment opened a rift with Carter's kin in Christ.

That divide only widened after Carter's election that November and it fueled a fearsome counterattack to the president's progressive evangelicalism, even though the two sides shared certain core beliefs. That opposition, called the Religious Right, was instrumental in denying Carter a second term.

Carter was one of the most explicitly religious presidents in modern U.S. history. But his rise in politics from Georgia to the White House came during a transformative era in American Christianity. The rise of the Religious Right limited the influence of progressive evangelicalism in national politics, setting the stage for decades of cultural battles over issues such as abortion and same-sex marriage. Still, it didn't deter Carter from pursuing his progressive Christian ideals after he left the White House through teaching, funding initiatives abroad for health care and conflict resolution, and starting a coalition for Black and white Baptists. Carter died at age 100 and as the nation reflects on his legacy and specifically that of his religion, the religious movement and countermovement his presidency catalyzed is of equal importance to his lived faith.

He paid attention to people. If people think it was a theatrical show for many years for him to just use the church as a platform to speak, that is absolutely false.

The son of a church deacon who taught Sunday school and was baptized at 11, Carter experienced a religious reawakening in 1967 that became the basis for his social and political ethic. Following his 1966 defeat in Georgia's gubernatorial election, Carter came to realize his relationship with God was a very superficial one. He went on eye-opening mission trips to Massachusetts and Pennsylvania and continued to study theologians like Paul Tillich and Reinhold Niebuhr. It was clear that he knew his Bible and he read his Bible very seriously and consistently. It appears that shaped him in many ways personally but also politically throughout his career.

Carter's Playboy interview was a turning point, but not enough to cost him the presidency in November. Once in office, Carter's attendance at Sunday services at First Baptist Church in Washington and at the National Prayer Breakfast impressed Christian leaders who felt the president's faith commitment was authentic.

The Carters returned home to Georgia in 1981 and joined a congregation that splintered off from Plains Baptist Church, where Carter grew up attending. Carter began teaching weekly a Sunday school class at Maranatha. At one point, he decreased his teaching to once a month. Then, church members asked him to do it more often. There was such a demand for it that the church pleaded with him to do it twice a month, to see more visitors. And then of course, it was good for tourism, too, with a very small town of a population of 800 to 900 people.

Carter encouraged everyone who attended the Sunday school class to attend the church service that followed. Steele said in addition to their sincere interest in Sunday school attendees, both Carters also exhibited patience, staying after church to take pictures with visitors, sometimes for more than an hour.

Obviously, it was a big tourist attraction. On any given Sunday, they might have in excess of 500 people show up. There were some days where if you weren't in the parking lot by Saturday, there was a pretty good chance you weren't going to get a seat on Sunday morning for Sunday school.

Carter used his platform to reach people. He had a genuine interest in participants' spiritual growth and showed it by the way he interacted with them. His entire goal in that is to engage you and he always finished up with a challenge to you.[2]

A Plains Georgia native, Jimmy Carter, is the only United States Naval Academy graduate to be elected to the White House; he gave up his military career to save the family peanut farm; as a parent, Carter became involved in local politics when he served on an education board; he supported civil rights, which hurt his early political career in Georgia; and he became known as a budget cutter while in office.

Carter was a "dark horse" presidential candidate in 1976; the future President was tied for 12th in early polling, well behind former Alabama Governor George Wallace and former nominee Hubert Humphrey; and he used his image as a Washington outsider to defeat Gerald Ford in the general election.

The Carter presidency was a study in contradictions. President Carter played a key role in the Camp David peace accords, but he also struggled with Congress and the media. The Iranian Hostage crisis proved to be a significant factor in his 1980 loss to Ronald Reagan.

Carter's legacy grew after the 1980 loss. F. Scott Fitzgerald wrote, there are no second acts in American lives, but Carter's public career after the White House is an exception.

In 1982, he founded the Carter Center, which has played an active role in human rights and disease prevention issues globally. The Carters also helped publicize the Habitat for Humanity.

Carter received his Nobel Prize in 2002. He received the award "for his decades of untiring effort to find peaceful solutions to international conflicts, to advance democracy and human rights, and to promote economic and social development."

Harry Truman was Carter's favorite President. Carter told The Guardian in 2011 that he admired Truman for not trying to profit off his presidency.

In 2015, as he suffered from cancer, the former president Jimmy Carter quipped to reporters that he'd like for the last Guinea worm to die before he did. When Carter died on December 29, 2024 the Guinea worm still had a foothold and it is doubtful that it will ever become extinct. So far, only once in history has anyone been able to play symbolic taps for the death of a disease. In 1980 the World Health Organization declared smallpox eradicated after an army of its workers had used a derivative of a vaccine developed nearly two centuries earlier to wipe the viral disease off the face of the earth.

In November 2019, Carter led his last Sunday school class at Maranatha. The former president became ill shortly after the pandemic began, bringing his tenure as a Sunday school teacher to a close, though he continued to worship at Maranatha on Sundays. Carter's last Sunday school lesson focused on the "age-old question" of knowing where one's soul would spend eternity. Looking back now, how fitting was that?[2]

"Earlier in my life I thought the things that mattered were the things that you could see, like your car, your house, your wealth, your property, your office. But as I've grown older, I've become convinced that the things that matter most are the things that you can't see -- the love you share with others, your inner purpose, your comfort with who you are. The measure of a society is found in how they treat their weakest and most helpless citizens." *Jimmy Carter*

Shared at President Carter's funeral: "For I am persuaded, that neither death, nor life, nor angels, nor principalities, nor powers, nor things present, nor things to come, Nor height, nor depth, nor any other creature, shall be able to separate us from the love of God, which is in Christ Jesus our Lord." *Romans 8: 38-39*

1– *Who Goes First, Lawrence K. Altman, MD, 1987.*

2– Excerpts from: *The faith of Jimmy Carter: A born-again Christian who practiced his own version of progressive evangelicalism, Liam Adams Carla Hinton, USA TODAY NETWORK.*

CHAPTER 6

ANESTHETICS...

Smell is fundamental to our experience and linked with a variety of emotional responses. Some smells repel us, while some invite us in. They're a vital part of our world and our survival strategy. Without smell we become more depressed and, conversely, when we're depressed we can't smell as well. Smell seems to be the most confusing of our senses.

Different people react differently to the same odors, and they even identify them as coming from different things. Our scent scape does not seem to have a lot of objectivity, but our olfactory system has been very well-studied by scientists over the past century.

Our perception of scent is directly caused by specific chemicals in the air and our bodies are able to react to different chemicals in the environment. Many animals emit tiny traces of unique chemicals to communicate with each other. These chemical communication methods might be used to find prospective mates, learn who has been eating the best food, or maybe to ward off competitors and let scavengers know that an area is defended.

Human perception of smell is created by the interaction of scent molecules with the brain. The olfactory system works primarily by inhaling outside air in which scent molecules have been dissolved. These scent molecules then react with smell receptors on nerve endings in the olfactory epithelium near the top of our nose. The nerves send signals to the olfactory bulb, which is part of the brain. The olfactory bulb is connected to the rest of the brain a little differently than other senses. Unlike sight and touch, which are usually processed by the thalamus, smell bypasses the thalamus and goes directly to the amygdala and hippocampus, the brain's emotion and memory centers. As a result, it is very easy to create emotions and memories tied to smells, and often unavoidable.

Smell receptors are created by specific genes and bind to specific classes of scent-creating molecules. Some people may have "specific anosmia," a genetic condition that occurs when the gene for a receptor for one class of smell molecules isn't expressed so they can't perceive certain smells. For example: About half of the human population have "specific anosmia" and lack the genes to detect the smell of acetone. Acetone is a type of ketone, and it is the same fruity-smelling substance found in some nail polish removers. If the breath of a person with diabetes smells of acetone, this suggests that there are high levels of ketones in their blood. As the ketones build up, they increase the acidity of the blood. This can be toxic. When a person has diabetes, their body either does not make enough insulin or it cannot use insulin effectively. Usually, insulin breaks down glucose in the blood so that it can enter the cells and provide energy. If the body cannot get its energy from glucose, it starts burning fat for fuel instead. The process of breaking down fat for energy releases byproducts called ketones. Fortunately, I carry the gene to detect acetone. In most cases of ketoacidosis (high levels of ketones in the body) in cats or dogs I could diagnose diabetes during their physical exam by their acetone smelling breath.

The olfactory system is very sensitive to certain smells, able to detect concentrations of some molecules as low as one part in five billion (animals are much more sensitive to smells). The odor threshold for different smells varies considerably. It is extremely dependent on the tiniest changes in the chemistry of a smell molecule and the combination of incoming smells.

All scent-creating molecules have a few things in common. All of them are volatile, which means they tend to evaporate into the air at room temperature. Without this characteristic, they would be unable to get into the nose. Also, all scent molecules are capable of interacting with the organic carbon-based molecules that constitute smell receptors, which means that most of them are organic as well. Just like many other systems in the body, olfactory nerves are very sensitive to specific chemical configurations. Some people even like inhalant smells that are generally considered bad or even poisonous, like gasoline or paint fumes. The research is still being conducted, but there are two possible reasons for this. One is that perhaps gasoline evokes positive memories of road tripping or paint the memory of a good day's work. The other is that substances like gasoline and paint contain volatile organic compounds like benzene and toluene. When these chemicals enter the body they release dopamine and can cause a euphoric effect (in addition to raising the risk of cancer, neurological problems, and respiratory disease). So, these smells may be appealing or even addictive in a similar way to opiates, which also release dopamine.[1]

Inhalants are volatile substances that produce chemical vapors that can be inhaled to induce a psychoactive, or mind-altering, effect. Although other abused substances can be inhaled, the term "inhalants" is used to describe a variety of substances whose main common characteristic is that they are rarely, if ever, taken by any route other than inhalation. This definition encompasses a broad range of chemicals that may have different pharmacological effects and are found in hundreds of different products. As a result, precise categorization of inhalants is difficult. One classification system lists four general categories of inhalants — volatile solvents, aerosols, gases, and nitrites — based on the forms in which they are often found in household, industrial, and medical products.

Volatile solvents are liquids that vaporize at room temperature. They are found in a multitude of inexpensive, easily available products used for common household and industrial purposes. These include paint thinners and removers, dry-cleaning fluids, degreasers, gasoline, glues, correction fluids, and felt-tip markers.

Aerosols are sprays that contain propellants and solvents. They include spray paints, deodorant and hair sprays, vegetable oil sprays for cooking, and fabric protector sprays.

Gases include medical anesthetics as well as gases used in household or commercial products. Medical anesthetics include ether, chloroform, halothane, and nitrous oxide (commonly called "laughing gas"). Nitrous oxide is the most abused of these gases and can be found in whipped cream dispensers and products that boost octane levels in racing cars. Other household or commercial products containing gases include butane lighters, propane tanks, and refrigerants.

Nitrites often are considered a special class of inhalants. Unlike most other inhalants, which act directly on the central nervous system (CNS), nitrites act primarily to dilate blood vessels and relax the muscles. While other inhalants are used to alter mood, nitrites are used primarily as sexual enhancers. Nitrites include cyclohexyl nitrite, isoamyl (amyl) nitrite, and isobutyl (butyl) nitrite. Amyl nitrite is used in certain diagnostic procedures and was prescribed in the past to treat some patients for heart pain. Nitrites now are prohibited by the Consumer Product Safety Commission but can still be found, sold in small bottles labeled as "video head cleaner," "room deodorizer," "leather cleaner," or "liquid aroma."

Generally, inhalant abusers will abuse any available substance. However, effects produced by individual inhalants vary, and some users will go out of their way to obtain their favorite inhalant. For example, in certain parts of the country, "Texas shoeshine," a shoe-shining spray containing the chemical toluene, is a local favorite.

Although the chemical substances found in inhalants may produce various pharmacological effects, most inhalants produce a rapid high that resembles alcohol intoxication, with initial excitation followed by drowsiness, disinhibition, lightheadedness, and agitation. If sufficient amounts are inhaled, nearly all solvents and gases produce anesthesia — a loss of sensation — and can lead to unconsciousness.

Inhalants can be breathed in through the nose or the mouth in a variety of ways, such as—"sniffing" or "snorting" fumes from containers; spraying aerosols directly into the nose or mouth; "bagging" — sniffing or inhaling fumes from substances sprayed or deposited inside a plastic or paper bag; "huffing" from an inhalant-soaked rag stuffed in the mouth; and inhaling from balloons filled with nitrous oxide.

Inhaled chemicals are absorbed rapidly into the bloodstream through the lungs and are quickly distributed to the brain and other organs. Within seconds of inhalation, the user experiences intoxication along with other effects similar to those produced by alcohol. Alcohol-like effects may include slurred speech; the inability to coordinate movements; euphoria; and dizziness. In addition, users may experience lightheadedness, hallucinations, and delusions.

Because intoxication lasts only a few minutes, abusers frequently seek to prolong the high by inhaling repeatedly over the course of several hours, which is a very dangerous practice. With successive inhalations, abusers can suffer loss of consciousness and possibly even death. At the least, they will feel less inhibited and less in control. After heavy use of inhalants, abusers may feel drowsy for several hours and experience a lingering headache.

Evidence from animal studies suggests that a number of commonly abused volatile solvents and anesthetic gases have neurobehavioral effects and mechanisms of action similar to those produced by CNS depressants, which include alcohol and medications such as sedatives and anesthetics. A 2007 animal study indicates that toluene, a solvent found in many commonly abused inhalants — including model airplane glue, paint sprays, and paint and nail polish removers — activates the brain's dopamine system. The dopamine system has been shown to play a role in the rewarding effects of nearly all drugs of abuse.

Although the chemical substances found in inhalants may produce various pharmacological effects, most inhalants produce a rapid high that resembles alcohol intoxication, with initial excitation followed by drowsiness, disinhibition, lightheadedness, and agitation. If sufficient amounts are inhaled, nearly all solvents and gases produce anesthesia — a loss of sensation — and can lead to unconsciousness.

The chemicals found in solvents, aerosol sprays, and gases can produce a variety of additional effects during or shortly after use. These effects are related to inhalant intoxication and may include belligerence, apathy, impaired judgment, and impaired functioning in work or social situations; nausea and vomiting are other common side effects. Exposure to high doses can cause confusion and delirium. In addition, inhalant abusers may experience dizziness, drowsiness, slurred speech, lethargy, depressed reflexes, general muscle weakness, and stupor. For example, research shows that toluene can produce headache, euphoria, giddy feelings, and the inability to coordinate movements. Inhaled nitrites dilate blood vessels, increase heart rate, and produce a sensation of heat and excitement that can last for several minutes. Other effects can include flush, dizziness, and headache.

A strong need to continue using inhalants has been reported by many individuals, particularly those who have abused inhalants for prolonged periods over many days. Compulsive use and a mild withdrawal syndrome can occur with long-term inhalant abuse. A recent survey of 43,000 American adults suggests that inhalant users, on average, initiate use of cigarettes, alcohol, and almost all other drugs at younger ages and display a higher lifetime prevalence of substance use disorders, including abuse of prescription drugs, when compared with substance abusers without a history of inhalant use.

Inhalant abusers risk an array of other devastating medical consequences. The highly concentrated chemicals in solvents or aerosol sprays can induce irregular and rapid heart rhythms and lead to fatal heart failure within minutes of a session of prolonged sniffing. This syndrome, known as "sudden sniffing death," can result from a single session of inhalant use by an otherwise healthy young person. Sudden sniffing death is associated particularly with the abuse of butane, propane, and chemicals in aerosols.

Inhalant abuse also can cause death by: *Asphyxiation* — from repeated inhalations that lead to high concentrations of inhaled fumes, which displace available oxygen in the lungs; *suffocation* — from blocking air from entering the lungs when inhaling fumes from a plastic bag placed over the head; *convulsions* or *seizures* — from abnormal electrical discharges in the brain; coma — from the brain shutting down all but the most vital functions; *choking* — from inhalation of vomit after inhalant use; or *fatal injury* — from accidents, including motor vehicle fatalities, suffered while intoxicated.[2]

According to the Journal of Medicine and Life (04/15/2009), "the olfactory sense could have unbelievable attributes if we consider its capacity to modulate human behaviors. It has determinant roles in the evolution of human habitat, in the way of preparing food and, most important of all, in the social behavior. The odor is thought to be essential in defining human inner ego as an indispensable attribute of sophistication and complexity. The odor can even allow tracing the limits between professions, races, or diseases. Back in the ancient times, perfumes used to play a part in defining sexuality consciously contributing to the unconscious effect of pheromone–like chemicals on the vomeronasal organ.[2]

The smell is linked to taste and appetite in the same way emotions are associated with arts and normal social life requires intense participation of all the five senses in variable proportions, depending on the situation." It is not surprising that volatile inhaled substances were and are used for abuse and instrumental in developing the anesthetics used in medicine.

The first publicly demonstrated inhalation anesthetic of the modern era was *diethyl ether*. It was first synthesized in 1540 by Valerius Cordus, a German physician and botanist. Cordus called it "sweet oil of vitriol," because it was made by distilling ethanol and sulfuric acid, which was known as oil of vitriol at the time. In the 16th century it was observed that chickens exposed to ether went to sleep and then awakened, seemingly unharmed.

Diethyl ether is pleasant sweet smelling and mildly pungent; although it can be used for inhalational induction, an *ether* induction is very slow and risks laryngospasm. *Ether* is not a cardiac depressant and maintains the baroreceptor reflex, making it relatively safe in patients with septic shock.

Ether is still used as an anesthetic in some developing countries because of its low cost and high therapeutic index with minimal cardiac and respiratory depression, but its explosive flammability has eliminated its use in most developed nations.

Since *ether* is heavier than air it can collect low to the ground and the vapor may travel considerable distances to ignition sources. *Ether* will ignite if exposed to an open flame, though due to its high flammability, an open flame is not required for ignition. Other possible ignition sources include – but are not limited to – hot plates, steam pipes, heaters, and electrical arcs created by switches or outlets. Vapor may also be ignited by the static electricity which can build up when ether is being poured from one vessel into another.

Ether is sensitive to light and air, tending to form explosive peroxides. Ether peroxides have a higher boiling point than ether and are contact explosives when dry. To prevent the formation of peroxides in ether, it can be stored in a cool, dark place in tightly sealed containers. It turns into peroxides when exposed to air and temperature conditions. This process is called autoxidation and is caused by a free radical mechanism that incorporates two oxygen atoms from the air into the ether molecules.

Ether should be stored at lower than 78 degrees Fahrenheit. *Ether* was still being used when I first started work at Camden Pet Hospital, mostly an induction anesthetic for small rodents and to remove tape or help it stick to the fur and skin of patients. For induction, the animal was placed in a sealed glass container with a gauze soaked with *ether*. After loss of conscience, for maintenance, the patient's head was placed in a tube leading to a halogenated anesthetic gas and oxygen anesthetic machine. As a child *ether* was used as an anesthetic for a tonsillectomy. During induction, I remember the nurse asking me to imagine a merry go round spinning slowly and counting each horse as it went by. I don't remember *ether* having an objectional odor and I wasn't sick after the procedure. I mostly remember the promised vanilla ice cream since I was a good patient.

Not long before I joined the staff at Camden Pet Hospital, a veterinarian was inducing anesthetic using *ether* and took the lid off the glass induction container with a lit cigarette in his mouth. The *ether* ignited and he was "blown part way across the room." Because of this incident and the owner wanting to quite smoking, upon my arrival he announced to the staff that smoking was "against Dr. Hoge's religion" and there would be no more smoking in the building. In one sentence Dr. Hylton blamed me for stopping smoking in the building, informed them of my religion and embarrassed me in front of the entire staff. Also, whenever I opened the door of the treatment room refrigerator containing the *ether*, I would look away just in case there might be an electric arc setting off an explosion that might burn or blow glass in my eyes.

Nitrous oxide, one of several oxides of nitrogen, a colorless gas with pleasant, sweetish odor and taste, which when inhaled produces insensibility to pain preceded by mild hysteria, sometimes laughter and is known as laughing gas. Because inhalation of small amounts provides a brief euphoric effect, the substance has been used as a recreational drug. *Nitrous oxide* was discovered by the English chemist Joseph Priestley in 1772; another English chemist,

Humphry Davy, later named it and showed its physiological effect. *Nitrous oxide*'s potent analgesic properties can be useful in settings such as the dentist, obstetrical ward or emergency department. Its administration is often a 50% mixture of oxygen in these settings. Compared to other anesthetic agents, *nitrous oxide* causes minimal effects on respiration and hemodynamics. It leads to decreased tidal volume and increased respiratory rate but minimizes overall minute ventilation. *Nitrous oxide* leads to direct myocardial depression, but *nitrous oxide*'s sympathetic stimulation reduces this effect, and the net effect is minimal. Unlike other volatile anesthetics, *nitrous oxide* has no muscle relaxation properties. *Nitrous oxide* can cause diffusion hypoxia quickly following discontinuation of the agent. It is recommended that 100% flow rate of O2 for a few minutes after use be given to counteract the rapid dilution of O2 in the alveoli of the lungs.

The gas is also used as a propellant in food aerosols. In automobile racing, *nitrous oxide* is injected into an engine's air intake; the extra oxygen allows the engine to burn more fuel per stroke. It is prepared by the action of zinc on dilute nitric acid.

James Young Simpson, a successful obstetrician in Edinburgh, Scotland, was among the first to use ether for the relief of labor pain. He rapidly became dissatisfied with *ether* and sought a more pleasant, rapid-acting anesthetic. It was suggested that he might try *chloroform*, which had first been prepared in 1831. *Chloroform* has an ether-like odor and a slightly sweet taste. It's a colorless, volatile liquid that's also known as trichloromethane. To test this agent, Simpson and his friends inhaled it after dinner at a party in

Simpson's home on the evening of November 4, 1847. They promptly became unconscious and, when they awoke, were impressed enough to implement its use.

Knowledge of the anesthetic effects of *chloroform* spread rapidly, but very soon reports of sudden deaths mounted. The first fatality was a 15-year-old girl called Hannah Greener, who died in 1848. The opponents and supporters of *chloroform* were mainly at odds with the question of whether the complications were solely due to respiratory disturbance or whether *chloroform* had a specific effect on the heart. In 1911 experiments with animals showed that *chloroform* can cause cardiac fibrillation. Anesthetic fatalities were four times greater using chloroform vs ether.

Chloroform can be made from acetone which is used to make plastic, fibers, drugs, and other chemicals. It is also used to dissolve other substances. It occurs naturally in plants, trees, volcanic gases, forest fires, and as a product of the breakdown of body fat. It is present in vehicle exhaust, tobacco smoke, and landfill sites.

Unexpected observations led to the discovery of the next ether like smelling inhaled anesthetics to be used routinely, *ethyl chloride* and *ethylene*. *Ethyl chloride* is not found naturally, but it can be formed in soil systems by the microbial degradation of other chlorinated solvents. It was used as a topical anesthetic and counterirritant. Because ethyl chloride is so volatile, skin transiently 'freezes' when the agent is sprayed on it. It has been used as a local anesthetic for small incisions, tooth extractions, and needle punctures by spraying it on the surface of the skin, where its rapid evaporation produces a numbing sensation.

Natural sources of *ethylene* include both natural gas and petroleum; it is also a naturally occurring hormone in plants, in which it inhibits growth and promotes leaf fall, and in fruits, in which it promotes ripening.

Rediscovery as an inhaled general anesthetic came in 1894 general anesthetic. During the first half of this 19th century *ethyl chloride* was widely used but it never enjoyed universal acceptance by anesthesiologists and was abandoned.

Cyclopropane was synthesized in 1882 when investigators thought that a contaminant of a cylinder of propylene might have resulted in toxic reactions. Two kittens put in a jar with the contaminant, cyclopropane, were anesthetized and recovered uneventfully. *Cyclopropane* had several advantages. It was potent, had poor blood solubility, lacked irritant properties, and induced anesthesia quickly. It did not depress the heart; in fact, it increased blood pressure. However, it could explode, it caused the heart to sometimes beat irregularly, and it depressed breathing. In 1956, the Ministry of Health in the UK set up a working party to investigate fires and explosions associated with anesthesia and reported a total of 36 explosions and three deaths between 1947 and 1954.

These limitations and the advent of the nonflammable *halothane* eventually led to the abandonment of *cyclopropane*. However, as late as the 1980s, it continued to be used, especially in children, and in patients who needed support of their blood pressure. Eger remembers in the 1960s, promising volunteers that if they would breathe 10 breaths of 50% *cyclopropane* they would fall asleep by the tenth breath. He lied. They all fell asleep by the third breath.

The development of fluorinated hydrocarbon, sweet to ether like smelling, anesthetics began in the mid-20th century, with researchers exploring the potential of fluorine-containing compounds to create safer and more stable anesthetic agents, particularly after the concerns raised by the side effects of earlier options like ether and chloroform; the key breakthrough came with the introduction of *halothane* in 1956, which marked the widespread clinical use of fluorinated anesthetics, leading to further research and the development of newer agents like *enflurane, isoflurane, sevoflurane,* and *desflurane,* all with improved safety profiles and specific characteristics for different surgical procedures. At this juncture two trends increasingly influenced anesthetic practice, trends ensuring a persistent search for alternatives to *halothane* and *enflurane.* First, advances in anesthetic and surgical techniques, coupled with economic considerations, increased the demand for and scope of day case (patients being both admitted and discharged the day of surgery) surgery. By the 1980s, surgery was increasingly being performed on a day case basis, and in the US, by the 1990s, this increased to a majority. Second, obesity rates in prosperous nations steadily increased. Eventually, the rest of the world caught up with this epidemic of obesity. The increasing use of day case surgery and increasing girth of the population dictated a need for anesthetics that were eliminated rapidly to speed the rate of recovery. Those were not the only goals of the ideal anesthetic. Additionally, it should be non-flammable, lack toxicity (for both patient and operating room personnel), and have minimal cardiorespiratory effects. Also, it should be inexpensive.

Both *enflurane* and *halothane* fell short of the ideal.

Terrell's team synthesized more than 700 compounds in the 1950s and 60s, in pursuit of a better inhaled anesthetic. They synthesized the 469th compound in 1965, two years after having synthesized enflurane that was given the generic name, isoflurane. *Isoflurane* continued the trend towards a lower solubility and a greater resistance to metabolism. In animals, it had a good "anesthetic syndrome" without evidence of the convulsive activity seen with *enflurane*. It was stable to UV light and alkali, including soda lime (used to absorb CO_2 in anesthetic machines). It thus looked promising. However, the manufacturing process initially required purification by a large number of distillations to obtain the pure compound, and the expense of such distillations nearly led to the abandonment of *isoflurane*.[3]

I was trained in veterinary school (1971-1973) using *halothane* for anesthesia and we switched over to *isoflurane* in the 1990s. The drawback to halothane was the length of time it took for recovery which resulted in patients that had major surgery needing to be hospitalized overnight.

What I liked about *halothane*'s slow recovery rate was when we had dogs poisoned with metaldehyde contained in snail bait. Metaldehyde toxicosis includes seizures, muscle tremors, hyperthermia, gastrointestinal upset and uncoordinated movements. Treatment was primarily supportive care, including decontamination of the stomach by, if possible, inducing vomiting, IV fluids, anti-seizure medications and muscle relaxants (methocarbamol). If caught early the dog would have a good prognosis. However, if having seizures, the only option was to place them under a general anesthesia at high enough level to stop the seizures and periodically let them wake up until the seizures subsided. *Halothane* seemed made for the task. We would leave the pet under anesthetic for several hours, let them start to wake up periodically, and if seizures were noted, place them back on *halothane* and repeat the process. There was many a night I would drive back and forth to the hospital and check on dogs left under halothane to see if they could be taken off the anesthetic. I was never comfortable leaving an animal hooked up to an anesthetic machine even though an older colleague told me that he once forgot a dog was hooked up to *halothane* anesthetic and the next day the dog was fine. Good thing there was plenty of anesthetic in the canister and the oxygen tank servicing the anesthetic machine was full...True story? The story was never verified, I dared to leave a dog under anesthesia for only a couple of hours and I have made the waiting room bench a bed from time to time.

When I became owner of Camden Pet Hospital, ether was removed from the refrigerator and never used again in the practice. However, I periodically use ether in a chemical spray to help start my internal combustion electric generator when the power is out in our home. Out of habit? I still turn my head to the side to protect my eyes from potential eye damage.

1– *Why do bad smells smell good? Molekule, Vanessa Graham, 02/26/2021.*

2– *NIH National Institute on Drug Abuse, Nora D. Volkow, MD, July 2012.*

3– *A History of Inhaled Anesthetics, Edmund Andrews + other sources.*

CHAPTER 7

PROPOFOL...

K-pop idols operate within an environment marked by relentless demands and intense scrutiny. It is a world where the relentless pursuit of perfection isn't a mere goal—it's an expectation. K-pop idols are not just singers; they are all-encompassing entertainers. They must excel in singing, dancing and often acting, and this multifaceted talent requires hours upon hours of practice and training. These jam-packed schedules leave little room for personal time or rest as idols are constantly touring, recording, attending promotional events and making appearances on television. The K-pop industry also places a premium on physical appearance, and idols are expected to conform to specific beauty standards. This pressure can lead to unhealthy dieting and body image issues, all of which can take their toll on mental health.

Given these pressures, it is not surprising that some K-pop idols may seek refuge in substances that temporarily escape stress and scrutiny. A smaller dose of Propofol creates feelings of euphoria and tranquility, which can help with stress, while a full surgical-level dose induces a deep sleep with no residual "hangover." This can be very appealing to busy idols whose erratic sleep schedules often result in insomnia.

Propofol has been a controlled substance in South Korea since 2011, and illegal use is punishable with a hefty fine and potentially even a prison sentence. Despite this, there have been many high-profile cases involving K-pop idols using the "milk shot", as Propofol is called in Korea due to its milky, white appearance. Brown Eyed Girls' Member Gain was fined in 2021 for illegal Propofol use after a highly publicized case. Initially, Korean media had reported an unnamed singer, but Gain eventually came forward due to pressure. Gain initially came under police scrutiny after the arrest of a cosmetic surgeon who was jailed for 18 months for selling painkillers to patients. Gain's agency explained that her Propofol use was an attempt to self-medicate, but its explanation was notable for describing her as "reckless": Gain made a reckless choice due to severe depression and a sleep disorder. We feel a deep sense of responsibility for failing to help the singer, who has been in severe pain for year."

It is important to understand that Korea's classification of Propofol as a controlled substance resulted from Propofol abuse not seen elsewhere in the world. While this may be reassuring for other countries and suggest that similar legislative measures may not be immediately necessary elsewhere, it serves as a reminder to stay vigilant about changing drug use landscapes globally. It is also essential to recognize that legal penalties alone rarely solve the issue of drug misuse. South Korea's experience demonstrates that despite the criminalization of Propofol, the problem persists even 12 years after the legislation was passed. This highlights the importance of balancing legal consequences with robust rehabilitation and recovery services.

The case of Propofol and K-pop highlights so many topics which are front and center of the conversations around drug use, criminalization and treatment. It demonstrates that addiction can affect anyone, regardless of their wealth or success and reveals the role that stress, mental health and the pursuit of relief play in an individual's path towards substance misuse. Perhaps most importantly, it emphasizes the need for comprehensive strategies that encompass awareness, prevention, legal measures and, crucially, robust support for rehab and recovery.[1]

In the semi-distant past, patients had no choice but to be awake during surgery. Medical specialists were more valued for their ruthlessness and speed than their know-how. Without an existing way to control pain, both patients and physicians had to endure the terrifying scene of a surgical process. Therefore, finding agents that could ameliorate pain and induce loss of consciousness was a critical task.

While the quest to find these agents dates back to at least 4000 BCE, the term describing a state of temporary loss of awareness was introduced by the physician Oliver Wendell Holmes Sr. only in 1846. He coined the term "anesthesia" from the Greek words; "an" for without and "aisthēsis" for sensation.

Opium, acupuncture, mandrake leaves boiled in wine, coca leaves, and cannabis were all used to perform surgery and relieve pain. In the 1200s, people prepared sponges known as spongia somnifera by soaking a sea sponge in a mix of poppy and mandrake leaf extracts, dried them for storage. When it came time for use, the sponge was re-wetted. This concoction, when moist, could then be applied to patients' nostrils. While surgical procedures were somewhat possible, there was one caveat. The doses were often inconsistent due to the varying potency of the extracts, and patients often died.

Later, from the 1500s to 1800s, doctors explored volatile agents and gases. Volatile molecules like chloroform and ether — also known as "oil of vitriol" — easily evaporate, producing vapors that could be inhaled. Nitrous oxide — also known as laughing gas — and carbon dioxide were also used as anesthetics but required special equipment for delivery.

It was not until the mid of 20th century that scientists were able to make anesthetic molecules in a flask instead of extracting them from natural sources. The most prominent achievement was sodium thiopental, which was invented by medicinal chemists at Abbott. However, in the late 20th century, it was the resilience of John B. Glen that led to the development of one of the most common anesthetics used nowadays: a phenol derivative called propofol.[2]

Pure phenol is used in certain medical procedures and as an ingredient in numerous treatments and laboratory applications such as vaccine preservatives, sore throat sprays, and antiseptic soaps. Phenol is a type of organic compound. While toxic to consume on its own, it's available in tiny doses in many household products like mouthwash and spray cleaners. In its pure form, it may be colorless or white. It has a mildly sugary scent that might remind one of somewhere that's sterile, such as a hospital room. In limited quantities, it's available for several medical and health-related uses. Over time, pure phenol has been replaced by some of its derivatives as an antiseptic. One derivative is n-hexylresorcinol, which can be found in cough drops. The compound, butylated hydroxytoluene (BHT), replaced phenol as a food antioxidant.

Pure phenol is used in certain medical procedures and as an ingredient in numerous treatments and laboratory applications: Phenol can be injected into muscles to treat a condition known as muscle spasticity. This happens when the brain doesn't communicate properly with the spinal cord and nerves. It causes your muscles to become tight. Muscle spasticity can even interrupt the ability to walk or talk. It can be caused by conditions like Parkinson's disease, cerebral palsy, or brain trauma. A phenol injection helps limit the signals sent from your nerves to your muscles that cause contractions. This allows easier movement and less discomfort. This treatment is similar to getting a botulinum toxin A (Botox) injection. But phenol tends to be more useful for large muscles.

Phenol is commonly used in surgeries for ingrown toenails. It's used on more severe ingrown toenails that don't respond to other treatments. The phenol, in the form of trichloroacetic acid, is used to stop the nail from growing back. It is also used to penetrate through layers of skin to get rid of old or damaged skin.

Soap containing phenol-based compounds is often called carbolic soap. It's been used as an antiseptic during surgery since at least 1867. It was also a common fixture in state schools in England and Scotland until the 1980s. It's remembered by millions in the United Kingdom for its distinct smell and red streaks it left on bathroom sinks.

Carbolic soap is still widely used throughout the world. It's also a common tool used to assist countries who receive foreign aid from organizations like the Red Cross or Doctors Without Borders. It provides effective, low-cost hygiene to poverty-stricken communities.

Food and cosmetic preservatives. Phenol derivative butylated hydroxytoluene (BHT) is a common FDA-approved preservative used in cosmetics, and to keep food from going bad. It's safe to consume in small amounts. But some companies have removed BHT from their foods in response to public pressure.

Phenol liquid is often used in molecular biology with trichloromethane and chloroform to separate RNA, DNA, or proteins, and isolate them in the pure form. This process is known as liquid-liquid extraction. It's done by adding an equal amount of phenol and chloroform to a solution of cells or tissues.

The phenol-chloroform mixture separates molecules based on how soluble the tissue sample is in that solution. The pH level of phenol helps separate the DNA and RNA.

Plant-based compounds containing phenol are known to be antioxidants. This means that they can stop the reaction of free radicals with other molecules in the body, preventing damage to DNA as well as long-term health effects. Free radicals are molecules that have lost an electron and become unstable. This makes them prone to react with and damage molecules like DNA. Free radicals sometimes cause the molecules they react with to create even more free radicals. Antioxidant molecules are like a barrier between free radicals and healthy molecules: antioxidants replace the missing electron and render it harmless. Some notable phenolic antioxidants with proven health effects include: bioflavonoids, found in wines, teas, fruits, and vegetables; tocopherols, including vitamin E - found in many fruits, nuts, and vegetables; resveratrol, found in fruits, nuts, and red wine; and oregano oil - composed of many beneficial phenols like carvacrol, cymene, turpentine, and thymol.

Phenol-based compounds have been found to have some cancer prevention properties. Studies suggest that getting phenols from a diet heavy in plants containing phenolic compounds and foods fortified with phenols help strengthen the immune system and makes cells more resistant to cancer throughout the life cycle. Most of this research comes from animal models, but human studies are also promising. The complex structures of phenolic compounds appear to help make cancer cells more receptive to chemotherapy treatments.

Phenol may have its share of uses and health benefits, but it can also be toxic or cause long-term health effects if one is exposed to it in high amounts: Industrial phenol may increase the risk of heart disease. This may be partly due to exposure to many other industrial chemicals in addition to phenol; Consuming phenol in its pure form can damage your esophagus, stomach, intestines, and other digestive organs. It can be fatal if you have enough of it at one time; Don't put it on your skin. Pure phenol can damage your skin if it makes direct contact. This can include burns and blisters; Don't inhale it. Laboratory animals experienced breathing difficulties and twitching of muscles when they breathed in a lot of phenol for even a short period of time. Phenol has also been shown to cause systemic organ damage in laboratory animals; and, Don't drink it. Consuming water containing a lot of phenol can make muscles spasm and affect your ability to walk. Too much can be fatal.

In biochemistry, naturally occurring phenols are natural products containing at least one phenol functional one phenol group. Phenolic compounds are produced by plants and microorganisms. Organisms sometimes synthesize phenolic compounds in response to ecological pressures such as pathogen and insect attack, UV radiation and wounding. As they are present in food consumed in human diets and in plants used in traditional medicine of several cultures, their role in human health and disease is a subject of research:There are greater than 100 phenols that are germicidal and used in formulating disinfectants.[3]

The problem with anesthetics before propofol was that they were either too strong or they presented a delayed recovery after surgery. John Glen, a Veterinarian Anesthesiologist, helped develop propofol while working at AstraZeneca, then Imperial Chemistry Industries in the UK. It took four different formulations and 13 years before they developed a drug that was safe and could be sold on the market. The with anesthetics before propofol was that they were either too strong or they presented a delayed recovery after surgery. The most common side effects of synthetic anesthetic barbiturate, such as sodium thiopental, were slow breathing, nausea, sleepiness, headaches, cardiac arrhythmia, and the slow recovery of consciousness.

Propofol seemed to have barely any side effects. It was noted how quickly the research animals recovered after giving the anesthetic. A whole pen of pigs could be out cold one moment, and then digging into their food the next. They had mice trained to walk on little rods like tightropes and they regained their balance 3 minutes after waking up from propofol.

For a drug to serve as an ideal anesthetic, it contains dual properties. The drug needs to be fat-soluble to get into the brain, but it also needs to be water-soluble to be injected into veins. Propofol was not soluble in water, so it was overlooked initially. But in the 1970s, researchers developed a neat trick to "solubilize" propofol into water by adding of a surfactant that has a suitable pH range to prevent significant growth of microorganisms, creating a milky emulsion, hence the name "milk of amnesia."

The very first formulation was not successful. One of the ingredients known as cremophor, a component in castor oil, caused unexpected anaphylactic reactions. Scientists persisted and a few other formulations were tried but at the fourth time, the right formulation was obtained containing egg lecithin and soybean oil.

Forty years have passed and despite the success of propofol, little is known about how this anesthetic works. However, scientists have made progress toward understanding how propofol behaves at the molecular level. Propofol's main cellular target is the receptor GABAA in the brain. GABA-type receptors are channels located at the periphery of neurons that act as gates for ions to go in and out after binding of small molecules. When propofol binds to GABAA, the channel opens and negatively-charged ions flood the cell. This event can, in turn, block cell communication.

Propofol can also impact the function of the molecular motors called kinesins. These highly specialized proteins known as the "workhorse of the cell" transport cargo along the periphery of protein filaments called microtubules. Kinesins "walk" using these microtubules as paths to move along, attached by their heads. These heads are linked together through a short 14-amino-acid peptide chain or "neck linker." This neck connects to the stalk, an elongated region of kinesins that mediate cargo transport. Recent work showed that propofol interferes with kinesins' flexibility by sticking to one of their heads and to the neck linker. And there are more propofol targets that have not been explored in detail. Among them, voltage-gated channels in neurons, other regions pacemaker channels that induce rhythmic activity in heart and brain cells, and the receptor TRPA1 known to sense pain.

The most important missing information regarding how propofol (and any other anesthetics) act, is precisely how propofol binding to its cellular targets leads to loss of consciousness. So, it might take quite a while before the full spectrum of propofol action can be explained.[4]

Propofol (2,6-diisopropylphenol) is an intravenous sedative-hypnotic agent commonly used for the IV induction and maintenance of general anesthesia. It has a rapid-onset, provides a rapid recovery even after multiple bolus doses or continuous infusion, and has anti-emetic properties which decreases the incidence of post-operative nausea and vomiting. These benefits helped propofol become the most common IV induction agent in veterinary and human hospitals and clinics providing ambulatory anesthesia, where it is utilized as the IV induction agent in almost every modern general anesthetic.

Propofol acts on the GABAa receptor, potentiating its neuroinhibitory effect on postsynaptic neurons by hyperpolarizing them and inhibiting the generation of an action potential. The GABAa receptor is also potentiated by volatile anesthetic agents and is the receptor target of:

-Barbiturates are a class of drugs that act as central nervous system (CNS) depressants. They produce a wide range of effects, from mild sedation to deep anesthesia. The types of Barbiturates: Ultra-short-acting (e.g., thiopental, methohexital), short-acting (e.g., secobarbital, pentobarbital), intermediate-acting (e.g., amobarbital, butabarbital), and long-acting (e.g., phenobarbital, barbital). Medical uses: Sedation and hypnosis, anesthesia, anticonvulsant therapy, and preoperative anxiety reduction. Side effects:

Drowsiness, confusion, dizziness, impaired coordination, slowed breathing, addiction, and overdose (can be fatal). Abuse: Barbiturates are a Schedule II controlled substance in the United States due to their potential for abuse. They are often used recreationally for their sedative and euphoric effects. Withdrawal from barbiturates can be severe and life-threatening. Symptoms include seizures, tremors, anxiety, insomnia, and hallucinations. At Camden Pet Hospital, before propofol, we used barbiturates to induce anesthesia and still use pentobarbital as our primary agent for euthanasia.

- Benzodiazepines are a class of medications that act as central nervous system depressants. They are commonly used to treat anxiety, insomnia, seizures, and muscle spasms. Benzodiazepines enhance the activity of a neurotransmitter called gamma-aminobutyric acid (GABA). GABA has calming and relaxing effects, so benzodiazepines

WALTER R. HOGE, DVM

can produce sedation, drowsiness, and reduced anxiety.

Examples: Diazepam (Valium), Lorazepam (Ativan), Alprazolam (Xanax), Clonazepam (Klonopin), and Midazolam (Versed). Medical Uses: Anxiety disorders (e.g., panic disorder, social phobia); insomnia, seizures, muscle spasms and preoperative sedation. Side effects: Drowsiness, sedation, confusion, memory impairment, coordination problems, and dependence and addiction. They can interact with other medications, including alcohol, opioids, and antidepressants.

–   Neurosteroids increases both synaptic and tonic inhibition. They are endogenous regulators of seizure susceptibility, anxiety and stress that are synthesized in the brain, the adrenal glands, and the gonads. They have potent and selective effects on the GABA-A receptors.

–   Nonbenzodiazepines (Z-drugs), refers to a class of sleep medications that are not structurally similar to benzodiazepines but still act as sedatives, with the most common examples being zolpidem, zopiclone, and zaleplon, all of which have generic names starting with the letter "z" hence the "Z drug" moniker; they are primarily used to treat insomnia. Like benzodiazepines, they work by enhancing the activity of GABA neurotransmitter, promoting sleepiness. They are considered to have a better side effect profile compared to benzodiazepines, with shorter duration of action and less potential for daytime drowsiness. Z drugs can still cause side effects like dizziness, impaired coordination, and memory problems, especially when taken in high doses or combined with alcohol.

- Imidazoles are a group of compounds that can interact with gamma-aminobutyric acid (GABA) receptors. Some imidazoles act as agonists, while others act as modulators of GABA receptors. Imidazole compounds can have a variety of neurological effects, including improving cognition, reducing the risk of Alzheimer's disease, and promoting neural cell differentiation. Imidazole dipeptides, found in meat, can improve memory loss in the elderly and reduce the risk of Alzheimer's disease.

- Anticonvulsants, also known as antiepileptic drugs (AEDs), work by altering the balance of excitation and inhibition in the brain. They can work by blocking sodium channels, enhancing GABA activity, or affecting other neurotransmitters.

- Ethanol is used as a solvent, in the manufacture of other organic compounds, and as an additive to automobile fuel (a mixture known as gasohol). Ethanol is a major industrial chemical. The intoxicating portion in many alcoholic drinks, such as beer, wine, and distilled spirits, is ethanol.

Depending on the drug and dose, potentiation of the various GABA receptor subtypes produces sedative, anxiolytic, anticonvulsant, amnestic, hypnotic, and/or euphoric effects.

First reported in 1973, propofol was the agent selected after John Glen, a Veterinary Anesthesiologist substituted phenol compounds for anesthetic properties superior to sodium thiopental and methohexital, the barbiturate IV anesthetics that had been in use since 1934. Pure propofol is a yellowish oil at room temperature. Easily dissolved in organic solvents, propofol's poor solubility in water (150 mcg/L) required the use of a carrier vehicle to enable IV injection of doses suitable to produce general anesthesia. In 1981, clinical trials of propofol which had been ongoing for four years were halted due to anaphylactoid reactions. Despite the desire by the manufacturer to discontinue the development of propofol, its discoverer John Glen suspected the adverse reactions were not due to the drug, propofol, but the vehicle carrier, Cremophor EL, which is made from polyethoxylated castor oil. He began to investigate other suitable vehicle carriers, and after several years of research, and improvements in lipid emulsion technology, produced the current propofol macroemulsion. This lipid emulsion is composed of soybean oil, egg yolk fat (lecithin) and glycerol in water. Glycerol is a natural component of fats and oils (triglycerides). Clinical trials began in 1983, and successful outcomes in these clinical trials led to the approval of Diprivan (propofol) in 1989.

The lipid emulsion consists of 0.15-0.3 ☐m droplets of soybean oil which provides the lipid environment in which propofol resides in high concentration. The soybean oil-propofol droplets in water, which would otherwise coalesce into larger droplets of oil and eventually separate into water and oil phases, are stabilized by the egg yolk lecithin, which imparts a net negative charge to the surface of the oil droplets, making an emulsion which is stable for several years. It is these oil droplets, which scatter visible light, that give the propofol macroemulsion its white appearance.

Although this propofol emulsion was exceptionally successful as an IV general anesthetic agent, it did have some drawbacks that some believed could be ameliorated by altering the constituents of the emulsion. These included pain on injection in 10-30% of patients, and concerns of potential bacterial growth in the nutrient rich emulsion. EDTA was added to the propofol emulsion in 1996 to inhibit bacterial growth after several postoperative infections were suspected to be caused by propofol. EDTA is used in medicine to prevent blood samples from clotting and to remove calcium and lead from the body. It is also used to keep bacteria from forming a biofilm. It is a type of chelating agent. Further investigations of these infections, found the likely source of the postoperative infections to be extrinsic contamination of the propofol resulting from poor (non-sterile) handling techniques.[5]

Michael Jackson was born on August 29, 1958, in Gary, Indiana, to a large and musical family. When he was five years old, he joined four of his older siblings in their band The Jackson 5 and eventually became the group's frontman. Under the unrelenting — and frequently violent — eye of their father, Joe, the boys in The Jackson 5 became a success in the early 1970s with hit songs like "I Want You Back" and "I'll Be There."

However, Michael Jackson also started to make a name for himself on his own. In 1972, he released his first solo album for Motown, Got to Be There, and showed off his acting chops in the cult classic film The Wiz (1978). Then, in 1979, Jackson released his first solo album for Epic Records, Off the Wall, which became the best-selling album of the entire year.

But everything really changed in the 1980s. Then, Jackson released his album Thriller (1982) and his now-iconic "Thriller" music video the next year. The album became the best-selling album in world history, eventually selling 70 million copies, and the music video arguably heralded the MTV era. Jackson's incredible dance moves, including the "moonwalk," also led Los Angeles Times critic Robert Hillburn to deem Jackson the "King of Pop." As Jackson became a bigger star, however, troubling rumors about him began to bubble to the surface. Some concerned his ever-changing appearance, especially his skin, which had started to lighten before the world's eyes. And some were far more serious. In the 1990s, Michael Jackson started facing allegations that he'd molested young boys.

By the 1990s, Michael Jackson's appearance had dramatically changed from his early days of fame. His brown skin had become noticeably whiter, almost translucent. Jackson addressed the rumors about his skin in a 1993 interview with Oprah Winfrey, telling her he had a skin disorder called vitiligo. "It is something I cannot help," Jackson said during the interview, claiming that he'd only used makeup to fix blotchiness caused by vitiligo and never bleached his skin. "When people make up stories that I don't want to be who I am, it hurts me. It's a problem for me. I can't control it. But what about all the millions of people who sit in the sun to become darker, to become other than what they are. Nobody says nothing about that."

Bill Whitfield, began his role as Jackson's bodyguard in December 2006, revealed that the King of Pop was deeply affected by the child sexual abuse allegations that had haunted him for years. These accusations first emerged in 1993 and resurfaced in 2005, leading to a highly publicized trial that ended in Jackson's acquittal. However, the emotional toll from these events left Jackson reclusive and profoundly changed. Whitfield stated that he was sad a lot, things were different and he had just come off facing a couple of trials. Initially uncertain about the truth of the allegations, Whitfield grew to believe in Jackson's innocence after observing his interactions with his children and others close to him. Despite being cleared of the charges, Jackson struggled to recover from the damage to his reputation and the intense public scrutiny.

In 2009, Jackson announced his "This Is It" tour, which was intended to mark his triumphant return to the stage. However, as rehearsals progressed, Whitfield noticed a decline in Jackson's health. He was a little more frail than normal, he was doing a lot of rehearsing. I could tell it was weighing on him. He was definitely stressed out, and stress can be a killer. Whitfield expressed deep sorrow that Jackson was not able to fully clear his name and restore his legacy before his death. He believed that the allegations and the ensuing trials left a lasting impact on Jackson, both emotionally and publicly.

Michael Jackson was more than $500 million in debt in 2009 when he died ahead of a planned concert tour, according to new court documents. The deep financial hole the "King of Pop" found himself in was detailed in a petition the executors of his estate filed Friday in Los Angeles County Superior Court stating that: "At the time of Michael Jackson's death, Michael Jackson's most significant assets were subject to more than $500 million of debt and creditors' claims, with some of the debt accruing interest at extremely high interest rates, and some debt in default."

On June 24, 2009, Michael Jackson attended rehearsal as normal. The tour was set to begin the next month at London's O2 Arena, and Jackson rehearsed until about midnight. After that was done, he hugged his dancers, thanked his crew, and returned to his Los Angeles home. There, Jackson — who had long suffered from insomnia and was having an especially difficult time sleeping in recent months — told his personal doctor, Conrad Murray that he needed rest. In the early hours of June 25, 2009, Murray gave Jackson a series of drugs that were meant to help him sleep, including the anti-anxiety medication lorazepam, the sedative midazolam, and Valium.

Murray later told investigators that he initially resisted Jackson's requests for propofol, an anesthetic that Murray had given the singer before (even though it's not meant to be used outside of hospital or clinic settings). As the morning hours stretched on, however, Murray relented. Mere moments later, Murray realized that Jackson was not breathing. He said he made multiple attempts to resuscitate him, as did first responders who arrived at the home. But it was too late — Michael Jackson died after suffering cardiac arrest brought on by acute propofol intoxication. Eight months after Michael Jackson's death, investigators charged Conrad Murray with involuntary manslaughter. In 2011, Murray was found guilty and sent to prison where he served two years of a four-year jail sentence.[6]

Let me see, why do you think Michael Jackson died from propofol intoxication – or was it just the propofol? 1-He was given lorazepam with potential side effects of loss of consciousness; 2-Midazolam can have serious side effects, including respiratory depression; 3-Valium CNS depression that can cause shallow breathing and sleepiness; 4-Propofol can cause respiratory depression and lead to decreased in the body's ability to respond to low oxygen levels, apnea (reduced breathing rate), bradypnea (slow heart rate), or hypercapnia (a medical condition where there is an excessive amount of carbon dioxide ($CO2$) in the blood); and 5-Doctor Murray left Jackson for (mere moments?) and realized he was not breathing.

You make the call. All I know is that before propofol was given to an animal for anesthesia at Camden Pet Hospital; they were allowed to breath pure oxygen for several minutes, propofol was given to effect and an endotracheal tube placed before they were placed on the anesthetic machine.

1– *The dark side of K-pop success, Primrose Lodge, 01/25/2025.*

2– *How scientists developed the most popular anesthetic used today, without totally knowing how it works The "milk of amnesia"…, U.of Saskatchewan, Chemical Biology, Josseline Ramos-Figueroa, 08/19/2021.*

3– *Health Line, Phenols, medically reviewed by Alan Carter, Pharm.D, Tim Jewell, updated on January 26, 2019.*

4– *Julia A Licholai, Neurobiology, Brown University.*

5– *A Brief History of Propofol…, Paul Azzopardi MS, DDS, 02/08/2021.*

6– *"King of Pop," Michael Jackson, 06/27/2024.*

CHAPTER 8

ONE OF MANY SINS...

On August 16, 1977, Elvis Presley "The King" was found dead on his bathroom floor in Memphis, Tennessee. Despite his physician's insistence and the assertions of the original medical examiner that drugs played no role in his death, later examination revealed this was absolutely not the case. Through his toxicology reports, medical examiners found that he actually had traces of 14 drugs in his system, 10 of which were present in significant quantities. These primary 10 substances include:

Codeine and *morphine* opioids that are used for pain and sedation.

Methaqualone is a barbiturate-like sedative and hypnotic medication that is more commonly known by its brand name, Quaalude. This central nervous system depressant was popular for recreational use in the 1970s and 1980s. It was first synthesized in India in 1951 while scientists were conducting research on finding new antimalarial medications. By 1965, it was the most commonly prescribed sedative in Britain. An overdose could lead to nervous system shutdown, coma and death. Additional effects are delirium, convulsions, hypertonia, hyperreflexia, vomiting, kidney failure, coma, and death through cardiac or respiratory arrest.

During the 1980s, the apartheid regime in South Africa ordered the covert manufacture of a large amount of Quaalude as part of a secret chemical weapons program known as Project Coast. Details of this activity came to light during the 1998 hearings of the post-apartheid Truth and Reconciliation Commission.

Actor Bill Cosby admitted in a 2015 civil deposition to giving Quaalude to women before allegedly sexually assaulting them. Film director Roman Polanski was convicted in 1977 of sexually assaulting a 13-year-old girl after giving her alcohol and methaqualone.

Valium, and *N-Desmethyldiazepam*) are known as he benzodiazepine (BZDs) and possess psycholeptic, sedative, hypnotic, anxiolytic, anticonvulsant, muscle relaxant, and amnesic actions, which are useful in a variety of conditions such as alcohol dependence, seizures, and insomnia.

Naturally occurring BZDs were first detected in mammalian tissues in 1986. For years, naturally occurring BZDs were found in mammalian organisms mostly confined to post mortem CNS material. The plant Erythrina velutina Willd (Fabaceae plant) also contains BZDs.

Ethclorvynol is not a benzodiazepine, carbamate, or barbituric aid derivative. Its molecular structure is considerably simpler and was popular in the mid-1990s as a sedative and a hypnotic medication for treating insomnia.

Pentobarbital, phenobarbital, and *butabarbital* cause sedation and are used to treat anxiety, insomnia, seizures and an anesthetic. They were discovered from the synthesis of barbituric acid in 1864, by German chemist Adolf von Baeyer. This was done by condensing urea (urine) with diethyl malonate (which occurs naturally in grapes and strawberries as a colorless liquid with an apple-like odor, and is used in perfumes. It is also used to synthesize other compounds such as artificial flavorings, vitamin B1, and vitamin B6). No substance of medical value was discovered, however, until 1903 when two German scientists discovered that barbital was very effective in putting dogs to sleep.

Ethinamate is a short-acting sedative-hypnotic medication used to treat insomnia. Like many such similar medications, the regular use of ethinamate can result in the development of drug tolerance in a patient. Nevertheless, the medication itself is generally no longer effective after using it for greater than 7 days. Structurally, it does not resemble the barbiturates, but it shares many effects with this class of drugs. The depressant effects of ethinamate are generally milder than those of most barbiturates.

These drugs found in Presley's body are very addictive and should have never been mixed. As demonstrated in his death, significant doses can result in depression of the nervous system to the point of suppressed breathing and heart rate enough to be fatal. Further, the amount of codeine found in his body alone was over 30 times higher than the recommended dose.

All of the drugs found during autopsy were prescription medications rather than street drugs like heroin. While it's not impossible to purchase these kinds of medications illegally, especially for a celebrity with deep pockets, evidence indicates that Presley was offered many of these medications legally.[1]

Addiction is defined as a chronic, relapsing disorder characterized by compulsive drug seeking and use despite adverse consequences. It is considered a brain disorder, because it involves functional changes to brain circuits involved in reward, stress, and self-control. Those changes may last a long time after a person has stopped taking drugs. Addiction is a lot like other diseases, such as heart disease. Both disrupt the normal, healthy functioning of an organ in the body, both have serious harmful effects, and both are, in many cases, preventable and treatable. If left untreated, they can last a lifetime and may lead to death.

In general, people take drugs to produce intense feelings of pleasure. This initial euphoria is followed by other effects, which differ with the type of drug used. For example, with stimulants such as cocaine, the high is followed by feelings of power, self-confidence, and increased energy. In contrast, the euphoria caused by opioids such as heroin is followed by feelings of relaxation and satisfaction.

To feel better, some people who suffer from social anxiety, stress, and depression start using drugs to try to feel less anxious. Stress can play a major role in starting and continuing drug use as well as relapse (return to drug use) in patients recovering from addiction. Others feel pressure to improve their focus in school or at work or their abilities in sports. This can play a role in trying or continuing to use drugs, such as prescription stimulants or cocaine.

Adolescence is a developmental period during which the presence of risk factors, such as peers who use drugs, may lead to substance use. When they first use a drug, people may perceive what seem to be positive effects. They also may believe they can control their use. But drugs can quickly take over a person's life. Over time, if drug use continues, other pleasurable activities become less pleasurable, and the person has to take the drug just to feel "normal." They have a hard time controlling their need to take drugs even though it causes many problems for themselves and their loved ones. Some people may start to feel the need to take more of a drug or take it more often, even in the early stages of their drug use.

Even relatively moderate drugs use poses dangers. Consider how a social drinker can become intoxicated, get behind the wheel of a car, and quickly turn a pleasurable activity into a tragedy that affects many lives. Occasional drug use, such as misusing an opioid to get high, can have similarly disastrous effects, including impaired driving and overdose.

The initial decision to take drugs is typically voluntary. But with continued use, a person's ability to exert self-control can become seriously impaired. This impairment in self-control is the hallmark of addiction. Brain imaging studies of people with addiction show physical changes in areas of the brain that are critical to judgment, decision-making, learning and memory, and behavior control.

No single factor determines whether a person will become addicted to drugs. As with other diseases and disorders, the likelihood of developing an addiction differs from person to person. In general, the more risk factors a person has, the greater the chance that taking drugs will lead to drug use and addiction. Protective factors, on the other hand, reduce a person's risk. Risk and protective factors may be either environmental or biological. Risk factors include aggressive behavior in child hood, lack of parental supervision, low peer refusal skills, drug experimentation, availability of drugs, and community poverty. Protective factors include self-efficacy (belief in self-control), parental monitoring and support, positive relationship, good grades, school anti-drug policies, and neighborhood resources.

Biological factors that can affect a person's risk of addiction include their genes, stage of development, and even gender or ethnicity. Scientists estimate that genes, including the effects environmental factors have on a person's gene expression, called epigenetics, account for between 40 and 60 percent of a person's risk of addiction. Also, teens and people with mental disorders are at greater risk of drug use and addiction than others.

The home environment, especially during childhood, is a very important factor. Parents or older family members who use drugs or misuse alcohol, or who break the law, can increase children's risk of future drug problems. Friends and other peers can have an increasingly strong influence during the teen years. Teens who use drugs can sway even those without risk factors to try drugs for the first time. Struggling in school or having poor social skills can put a child at further risk for using or becoming addicted to drugs.

Although taking drugs at any age can lead to addiction, research shows that the earlier people begin to use drugs, the more likely they are to develop serious problems. This may be due to the harmful effect that drugs can have on the developing brain. It also may result from a mix of early social and biological risk factors, including lack of a stable home or family, exposure to physical or sexual abuse, genes, or mental illness. Still, the fact remains that early use is a strong indicator of problems ahead, including addiction.

Smoking a drug or injecting it into a vein increases its addictive potential. Both smoked and injected drugs enter the brain within seconds, producing a powerful rush of pleasure. However, this intense high can fade within a few minutes. Scientists believe this powerful contrast drives some people to repeatedly use drugs to recapture the fleeting pleasurable state.[2]

Among Elvis Presley fans there is little middle ground concerning George Nichopoulos – "Dr Nick" – who prescribed thousands of doses of various drugs for Presley during the singer's final years, but was acquitted of being criminally responsible for his death in 1977. He was vilified by many, while others praised him as a sane voice who attempted to steer Elvis away from his sundry bad habits.

"The King" was 42 when he was found on the floor of a bathroom at Graceland; Nichopoulos signed the death certificate. He ruled that Presley died of cardiac arrhythmia caused by heart disease and hypertension. However, doubts about the case began to swirl at once. The pathologist who conducted the autopsy thought the combination of more than a dozen drugs found in Presley's body was lethal. But the medical examiner determined that the drugs were not in concentrations high enough to kill. He ruled that Presley died of cardiac arrhythmia caused by heart disease and hypertension, though doubts about the case began to swirl at once.

In 1980 Dr Nick was charged with prescribing excessive amounts of drugs to Presley, Jerry Lee Lewis and other patients. Prosecutors showed that in the final seven months of Presley's life he prescribed more than 10,000 pills, including sedatives, amphetamines and narcotics. Nichopoulos also admitted that he had borrowed nearly $300,000 from Presley, but denied that the loans affected his judgement.

On tour, Nichopoulos took along three locked suitcases filled with drugs. He explained that he was the "team physician" for nearly 150 people on Presley's payroll and that the drugs were not exclusively for the singer. Nichopoulos was acquitted and returned to his medical practice in Memphis. But the Tennessee Board of Medical Examiners later charged him with prescribing too many drugs to those patients and revoked his medical license in 1995.

He was briefly a road manager for Jerry Lee Lewis, and later worked in the disability benefits office of Federal Express into his 80s. He later helped organize an exhibit of his Elvis memorabilia, including his medical bag, examination instruments, pill bottles and guns, but the venture ended in a welter of legal wrangling. George Constantine Nichopoulos, physician: born Ridgway, Pennsylvania 29 October 1927; married Edna Sanidas (three children); died Memphis 24 February 2016.[3]

The Old Testament is filled with good examples to emulate and bad examples to avoid. What makes it especially applicable, however, is its stories of good people who often try to do what is right but also make mistakes. King David is one such example.

The prophet Moroni said, "Give thanks unto God that he hath made manifest unto you our imperfections, that ye may learn to be more wise than we have been" (Mormon 9:31). We can apply this same principle to King David's life.

We do not glorify the mistakes he made, but thankfully we can learn from them. King David was foreordained to accomplish great things. And as a young man he had great zeal for the Lord and rose to great heights. But foreordination is no guarantee. Rather, it is an opportunity that depends upon faithfully living the gospel. As Elder Neal A. Maxwell (1926–2004) explained: "God foresaw the fall of His beloved David but did not cause it. (See D&C 132:39.) Sending for Bathsheba was David's decision."

President Thomas S. Monson (1927–2018) said, "David commenced well the race, then faltered and failed to finish his course." David's failure, however, did not come all at once but by degrees. The story of David and Bathsheba begins with the Israelite army fighting a battle against the Ammonites at Rabbath-Ammon, modern-day Amman, Jordan. But the account adds what turns out to be an ominous detail: it was the time of year "when kings go forth to battle ... but David tarried still at Jerusalem" (2 Samuel 11:1). Kings were expected to lead their armies into battle, but David decided to stay home instead.

Elder Hartman Rector Jr. of the Seventy encouraged Church members to "be where you should be when you should be there." Whether it is attending Church meetings, helping with a service project, or magnifying callings, we should always fulfill our covenant responsibility to be in the right place, at the right time, doing the right things. Being "anxiously engaged in a good cause" (D&C 58:27) can safeguard us against many temptations, because, as President Gordon B. Hinckley (1910–2008) taught, "idleness leads to evil."

One evening, King David "walked upon the roof of the king's house: and from the roof he saw a woman washing herself; and the woman was very beautiful to look upon. And David sent and inquired after the woman" (2 Samuel 11:2–3). In Jerusalem, there are often comfortable evening breezes, and even today people will go out on the roof to cool off. David's palace was probably on the crest of a densely populated hill, today called the City of David, where it would have been common to see others below on their roofs.

However, as President Dallin H. Oaks, First Counselor in the First Presidency, taught, David "allowed himself to look upon something he should not have viewed." Another pivotal mistake was that when David found out Bathsheba was married, he did not let the issue go. The king knew Jehovah had commanded Israel to honor marital vows with complete fidelity (see Exodus 20:14, 17), yet "David sent messengers, and took her" (2 Samuel 11:4).

How could such a great hero, so favored by the Lord, have made such misguided choices? In his younger days, "David behaved himself wisely in all his ways; and the Lord was with him" (1 Samuel 18:14). Yet in the face of temptation, David gave in to lustful desire. Modern revelation again teaches us that "he that looketh upon a woman to lust after her shall deny the faith, and shall not have the Spirit" (Doctrine and Covenants 42:23). The loss of the companionship of the Spirit certainly hindered David's ability to choose wisely.

Elder Bruce C. Hafen of the Seventy observed that David "somehow developed too much confidence in his own ability to handle temptation. He was tragically willing to flirt with evil, and it ultimately destroyed him." A better course of action would have been to follow the example of Joseph of Egypt, who, when confronted with temptation by Potiphar's wife, wisely "got him[self] out" (Genesis 39:12). As President Spencer W. Kimball (1895–1985) counseled: "The time to protect against the calamity is when the thought begins to shape itself. Destroy the seed and the plant will never grow."

His judgment impaired by the loss of the Spirit, David then committed adultery with Bathsheba and conceived a child out of wedlock (see 2 Samuel 11:4–5). As Alma explained, sexual immorality is "an abomination in the sight of the Lord; yea, most abominable above all sins save it be the shedding of innocent blood or denying the Holy Ghost" (Alma 39:5).

Upon learning that Bathsheba was pregnant, the king compounded the tragedy by trying to hide his sin. David summoned Bathsheba's husband, Uriah, who was in the Israelite army fighting against the Ammonites. When Uriah arrived in Jerusalem, David twice tried to convince him to go home and be with his wife so that everyone would think that the child was Uriah's. In stark contrast to David, however, Uriah refused to spend time at home while his fellow soldiers were at war. (See 2 Samuel 11:5–13.) If there are any heroes in this story, Uriah the Hittite is one of them. Though not an Israelite by lineage, Uriah's faithfulness to the Lord is manifest by his name ("My light is Jehovah" in Hebrew) and by his actions.

David's situation went from bad to worse. Modern revelation teaches that when a priesthood holder—as King David was—attempts to cover his sins, "the Spirit of the

Lord is grieved; and when it is withdrawn, Amen to the priesthood or the authority of that man" (Doctrine and Covenants 121:37). The loss of the companionship of the Spirit as well as of his priesthood authority continued to erode the king's capacity to make righteous decisions. It was while in this diminished spiritual state that David arranged for the murder of Uriah. Ironically, Uriah carried the letter containing his own death sentence back to the battlefield, where he died at the hands of the Ammonite soldiers. (See 2 Samuel 11:14–17.)

David's downfall was not determined by one fatal mistake but rather a series of increasingly unwise and selfish decisions. It is important to remember that at any time during this devastating progression, David could have chosen to humble himself and seek repentance. Tragically, however, David admitted his guilt only after he was confronted by the prophet Nathan (see 2 Samuel 12:13). And while the Lord offers forgiveness to those who fully repent, He does not necessarily remove the negative consequences of sinful behavior. As President Ezra Taft Benson (1899–1994) taught, "It is better to prepare and prevent than it is to repair and repent."

One of the central lessons for us from the story of David and Bathsheba is the importance of the Holy Ghost and its role in helping us make good choices. Nephi taught that if you "receive the Holy Ghost, it will show unto you all things what ye should do" (2 Nephi 32:5), thus helping us to be in the right place at the right time to avoid temptation. By extension, the Holy Ghost can also show us what we should not do, giving us courage to flee temptation when we are confronted by it.

David's poor choices progressively hindered his ability to be filled with and use the precious gift of the Holy Ghost. In our own lives, it is critical that we live worthy of the companionship of the Spirit so that this precious gift may help us navigate the difficult roads of life.[4]

Question asked on Dr. Laura Schlessinger's radio program: "I have heard you mention repentance many times on your radio program, especially when people are trying to decide whether to forgive someone else or themselves. You have talked about the four R's required for repentance. I'm always driving in the car when you are doing that part and can never stop to write it down. Could you do this here, please?" – Los Angeles, CA.

Dr. Schlessinger: I do talk to many callers who are confused on this issue of forgiveness. Some imagine that they have to forgive and forget and just move forward with somebody who has done something bad or wrong to them or someone else, in spite of the fact that the wrongdoer has never owned up or apologized.

Check the Scriptures and you'll see that repentance is a constant requirement from the prophets and from God. The qualities of repentance, getting back on track, are the four R's: The first is responsibility: We must recognize that we have done wrong. The second is regret: We must have true remorse for doing wrong and for the pain and problems we've caused. The third is resolve: We must be committed never to repeat the act regardless of the temptations or situation. The fourth and probably the most difficult is to repair the damage we've done, or at least do what we can to apologize directly to the injured party.

When someone goes through these four R's with sincerity, I believe you have the obligation to forgive even if the trust is not yet re-established. And, as to that trust, there is an old Arabic saying: "Forgive, but tie up your camel."[5]

In retrospect, the role of drugs was obvious in Presley's death, despite his doctor's efforts to cover up his abuse and his odd stance as an anti-drug advocate (self justification?). To this end, even the original autopsy listed cardiac arrest as a cause of death. However, this was quickly refuted by the results of a more thorough investigation, which highlighted the astounding cocktail of drugs he had consumed in the hours before he died.

In spite of the shock his death caused, those who knew Presley's life likely weren't surprised. He was hospitalized in 1973 for pethidine addiction (an opioid – brand name Demerol) and overdosed twice on barbiturates in the same year. By the end of his life, he was also very overweight and allegedly suffered from numerous complications of drug addiction, including glaucoma, liver damage and high blood pressure.

George Nichopoulos was Presley's physician from 1970 to 1977. He began working with Presley to address saddle pain before getting caught up in prescribing an unnecessarily large number of drugs. He fell into the same trap that led to David's downfall. It was not determined by one fatal mistake but rather a series of increasingly unwise and selfish decisions. It is important to remember that at any time during this devastating progression, David (or Dr. Nick) could have chosen to humble themselves and seek repentance. Tragically, however, David admitted his guilt only after he was confronted by the prophet Nathan (see

2 Samuel 12:13). And while the Lord offers forgiveness to those who fully repent, He does not necessarily remove the negative consequences of sinful behavior.

Dr. Nick didn't appear to have had a "God Talk" with a prophet, or been influenced much, if any, by the Holy Spirit during his life, or suffered the negative consequences of sinful behavior and humbled himself enough to seek repentance. He did not recognize any guilt and his public responses concerning the death of Presley were: As Dr. Nick put it: "Presley felt that by getting drugs from a doctor, he wasn't the common everyday junkie getting something off the street...No one understands that Elvis was so complicated, I worked so hard just to keep things together and then they turned the tables and decided I was to blame...I once refused to give him drugs, Presley shot me, wounding me slightly...My patients, the ones I didn't kill, were very faithful...They just never stopped going after me, they always wanted a scapegoat for Elvis's death...I worked very hard trying to do all the right things with Elvis...I don't regret any of the medications I gave him. They were necessities."[1,3]

1– *The 10 Drugs That Were in Elvis Presley's System When He Overdosed – and Other Revelations, FHE Health, Kristina Robb-Dover, 04/20/2024.*

2– *NIH, National Institute on drug abuse, Facing Addiction in America: The Surgeon General's Report on Alcohol, Drugs, and Health, Modified with permission from Volkow et al. 1993.*

3– *Independent, Washington Post, Doctor George Nichopoulos: 03/04/2016.*

4– *What We Can Learn from King David's Fall, Frank F. Judd Jr. Ass Prof Ancient Scripture BYU, 10/218.*

5– *R's of repentance: Deseret News, Dr. Laura Schlessinger, 05/08/1998.*

CHAPTER 9

DIURETICS...

Diuretics, as therapeutic agents that act on the kidney to increase salt and water excretion, have a relatively short history. On the other hand, the very reason for which diuretics were developed, i.e., mobilization of excess body fluids, has a long history which dates back to the beginnings of medicine. No history of diuretics would be complete without some consideration of this long prelude, which is particularly important for an appreciation of the wonders that diuretics have accomplished and the essential niche they now occupy in therapeutics.

The agonal picture of volume overloaded patients drowning in their dropsy (edema), after prolonged suffering and invalidism, has been a matter of human sympathy and medical concern since the earliest days of recorded history. "Flooding of the heart," the ancient Egyptians termed it, and shrouded in the mist of antiquity are the first musings on its treatment. Among the celestial cures recorded on the pillars of the Aesklepion at Epidaurus is that of a Spartan girl, Arete, who suffered from dropsy and asked the god for relief. Aesculapius cut off her head, turned her upside down until the fluid ran out, and then replaced her head. A cure, the same records indicate, that could not be repeated!

A great reformer Thomas Sydenham, 1675, writes in a treatise on Gout and the Dropsy: "With respect to the evacuation of the water it is well worth observing, that weak purgatives (to promote bowel movements) do more mischief than good in dropsical cases ... of all diseases the dropsy requires the roughest and quickest purgatives ... With respect to purging for the cure of dropsy, great care must be had to carry off the water as speedily as the strength will permit; it being proper to purge every day, unless great weakness, or the too violent operation of the purgative, should require a day or two to be interposed. For if purging be used only at distant intervals (though the last purge brought away plenty of water) we shall allow time for the fresh collection of water and by such a delay instead of accomplishing the cure, leave it unfinished....There are other cases, likewise where the waters are not to be discharged by vomiting or purging; for instance, in weak constitutions and hysteric subjects (emotional or exaggerated reactions), they cannot be evacuated by purgatives, and much less by vomitives, but are to be carried off by diuretics."

Relevant changes that were occurring for the treatment of heart disease prompted, George Wallis, editor of the 1863 edition of Sydenham's text on dropsy to make the following annotation on the use of digitalis: I was convinced of the superior efficacy of this medicine over any other in the present practice, in a dropsical case at Hampstead; a lady had long labored under visceral obstruction, which at last brought on a dropsy, an anasarca (generalized edema) united with ascites, and tympany; squills, pariera brava, alkaline salts, etc. were tried in vain; at last the digitalis purpurea was given two grains twice a day, for 3 days she passed considerably more water than she had done for 10 or 14 days before, notwithstanding the different diuretics which had amongst been tried to produce this effect, and I am persuaded that the digitalis purpurea is the first and most certain of the class of diuretics.[1]

Digoxin is a type of medicine called a cardiac glycoside and it's the only medicine of its kind. It is used to improve the strength and efficiency of the heart, or to control the rate and rhythm of the heartbeat. This leads to better blood circulation and reduced swelling of the hands and ankles in patients with heart problems. Digoxin is used much less commonly now than in the past because newer, more effective medicines for heart failure and certain heart problems, such as arrhythmia and atrial fibrillation, are now available. The drug digitalis comes from the dried leaves of the common poisonous foxglove plant, Digitalis purpurea. It's been used to treat heart failure for over 200 years.

Mechanical means of removing blood (leeches, bloodletting, cupping, lancing), also came to be used in the therapy of dropsical patients. Once again, their use stemmed from the notion that diseases resulted from humors generated by inflammation in the system and that blood removed from the proximity of the site that was painful or the organ considered to cause the disease would remove the noxious humors and provide cure.

Leeches had been used as early as 400 CE for dropsy and were especially in vogue during the latter part of the 18th and early 19th centuries. To appreciate how much blood could be removed one needs to consider the number of leeches applied (usually 10-30) and that when fully gorged each leech could contain about one-half to one ounce of blood. To increase the quantity of blood removed the tail was snipped or salt and vinegar sprinkled on the leech. Leeches were considered particularly useful in children or the physically weak, who could not stand the harsher bloodletting.

Drainage of subcutaneous edema fluid by incision, and later by the insertion of Southey's tubes, were terminal drastic measures fraught with danger. Hippocrates had warned of the problem in one of his aphorisms: "In dropsical persons, ulcers forming on the body are not easily healed." With the advent of lancing time proved him right. Many an unfortunate patient succumbed to the complications of incisions to relieve edema, none so famous as Samuel Johnson (1709-1784). Johnson, who had been incapacitated for months by his terminal dropsy, had been lanced for the removal of edema. On the morning of December 13,1784, he lanced himself and cutting very deep bled to death that night. His autopsy revealed an enlarged heart, an atrophic left kidney, and an enlarged right kidney. The latter was secondary to nephrolithiasis and the former to an aortic valve defect.

During the 1800s it became clear that dropsy (extensive edema, ascites, pleural effusions) was not a single disease, but a late feature of failure of the heart, liver or kidneys. For around 2,000 years treatment was based on purgatives, bleeding, sweating, and other means to make the body lose fluid.

Mercurous chloride (Hg_2Cl_2), an inorganic mercury-containing compound, Calomel, was found to have diuretic properties in 1520. A white tasteless compound, it was used especially as a component of laboratory electrodes, as a fungicide, and formerly in medicine as a purgative. More of a laxative than a diuretic, it was notably toxic. However, in the 17-1800s it was still a standard treatment, often used in combination with the laxative plant extract squills, or digitalis. Some use of Calomel has been reported as late as 2019.

Organic mercury compounds became used to treat syphilis and other infections in the late 1800s. In 1919, it was observed that a patient with heart failure having a diuresis when treated. These were weak effects by modern standards, but pharmaceutical companies immediately sought to develop less toxic derivatives. Intravenous use, in particular, was associated with significant toxicity, as the use of calomel had been previously.

Despite 40 years of supportive observations, the central role of salt retention was only fully accepted after it was found in 1941-2 to relieve of edema by limiting salt intake to less than 1g/day in patients with heart failure, and that they had limited ability to excrete higher salt loads. This was strengthened by demonstrations that high blood pressure could be lowered by extreme salt restriction at around the same time. Oral cation exchange resins to bind sodium in the gut had a temporary therapeutic life, but the observations guided pharmaceutical company efforts to develop drugs that caused renal salt loss.

In 1937 it was noted that the new antibiotic Sulfanilimide caused metabolic acidosis through inhibiting renal carbonic anhydrase. It helps the body eliminate waste, reduce acidosis and maintain fluid balance - it also causes diuresis in patients resistant to mercurial compounds. Acetazolamide, introduced in in 1954, was more potent. It retains a few niche indications, including use in altitude sickness.

Sharp and Dohme pharmaceutical company set up a notable renal program in 1943, aiming to manipulate renal tubular function pharmaceutically. They produced PAH (a pulmonary atrial hypertension drug), probenecid (to preserve penicillin levels in blood, treatment for gout and hyperuricemia – high levels of gout), and in 1955 showed that Chlorothiazide increased excretion of sodium and chloride. The drug, marketed in 1958, was a landmark development. Thiazides proved much better at relieving edema, with few side effects, and they also lowered blood pressure, with randomized BP trials reporting real treatment benefits in 1967 and 1970. The search for more potent compounds in the 1950s led to the discovery of first ethacrynic acid and later furosemide (1959). Furosemide was released in 1964, ethacrynic acid the year after. They are given to help treat fluid retention (edema) and swelling that is caused by congestive heart failure, liver disease, kidney disease, or other medical conditions. It works by acting on the kidneys to increase the flow of urine. All the new diuretics caused undesirable potassium loss, so there was a search for agents to rectify that, including returning to drugs shelved earlier for the same reason. Spironolactone (1961) and Triamterene (1964) were followed by Amiloride (1968). Both work by directly blocking sodium channels on the apical membrane of epithelial cells in the distal convoluted tubule and collecting ducts of the kidney, preventing sodium reabsorption and thus promoting the excretion of sodium and water while minimizing potassium loss, making it a potassium-sparing diuretic; essentially, it inhibits sodium transport without significantly affecting potassium secretion.

While some relief must have been obtained by ancient modes of therapy, their effectiveness perhaps can be best gleaned from a recounting of the death of Heraclitus (540-480 B.C.E.): "He became so misanthropic that he withdrew and went off to live on herbs and plants in the mountains. But when this diet made him more edematous, he returned to the city and consulted the doctors, asking them about his condition in the form of a riddle: Could they change the wet weather into a drought? Since they did not understand, he shut himself up in a stable, hoping to cure himself and dry up the water by the heat of manure, with which he covered himself. To no avail—he ended up dead of it at age sixty."

Looking back over this prelude to the history of diuretics, a history as ancient as the earliest civilizations, it is remarkable that hardly any of the diuretics used today are older than the First World War. By the time that World War II started, only four drugs were accepted as effective agents to increase urine flow: caffeine, a mild diuretic at best; digitalis, a powerful agent but effective only in heart failure; mercury, which despite its improvement as an organo-mercurial, remained potentially a toxic one; and acidifying agents, whose utility was questioned by most. 80 years ago, Southey's tubes began their journey draining fluids from the body, to eventually become a curious historical artefact. In just one decade, edema and salt retention became treatable, transforming the care of heart failure, kidney and liver disease, and hypertension, through deliberate manipulation of kidney handling of electrolytes. Dialysis and kidney transplantation also has become of age in the same decade.

History of Diuretics, Heart Failure, Baylor College of Medicine, last update 11/12/2023: History of Nephrology, The invention of diuretics: and Google Search…

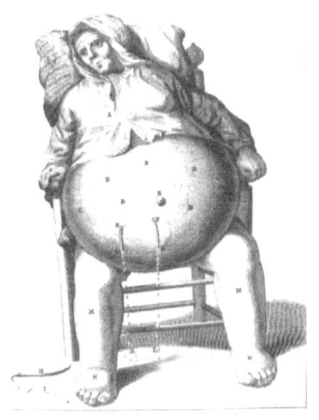

CHAPTER 10

CALCIUM BLOCKERS...

Sodium (Na+) and potassium (K+) are essential minerals that play a critical role in the functioning of the nervous system, primarily by facilitating the transmission of electrical impulses along nerves through a process called action potential, which relies on the movement of these ions across the neuron's cell membrane via a mechanism called the sodium-potassium pump; essentially acting like a tiny battery powering the nerve signals.

The sodium-potassium pump actively pumps sodium ions out of the neuron and potassium ions into the neuron, creating a concentration gradient which is crucial for generating electrical signals. When a neuron receives a signal, sodium channels open, allowing sodium ions to rapidly flow into the cell, causing a depolarization (electrical change) which generates the action potential.

Following the influx of sodium, potassium channels open, allowing potassium ions to move out of the cell, restoring the resting membrane potential and preparing the neuron to fire again. Proper balance between sodium and potassium levels is vital for normal nerve function.

Imbalances can lead to neurological issues like muscle weakness, irregular heartbeat, and even seizures.

Calcium is one of the most important and common minerals in the body. Most of the body's calcium is stored in the bones, but calcium is needed in the blood as well. The calcium in the blood helps nerves work, helps make your muscles squeeze together so they can move, helps blood clot and helps the heart working properly. A low level of calcium in the blood (hypocalcemia) can hinder the body's ability to perform these important functions. Calcium is a major element in the bones that makes them strong.

If one doesn't consume enough calcium in the diet, the body takes calcium store in the bones to use in the blood, which can weaken them. Hypocalcemia happens when there are low levels of calcium in the blood, not the bones. The levels of calcium in blood and bones are controlled by two hormones called parathyroid hormone and calcitonin. Vitamin D also plays an important role in maintaining calcium levels because it's needed for absorption of calcium. Hypocalcemia can affect people of all ages, including infants. The age at which someone could develop hypocalcemia usually depends on the cause. For example, if an infant has hypocalcemia, it's often because of a genetic disorder. Healthcare professionals and researchers have not yet determined how common hypocalcemia is. This is likely because hypocalcemia is usually a side effect of other health issues.

People who have mild hypocalcemia often have no symptoms (are asymptomatic). The symptoms of hypocalcemia depend on if it's mild or severe. Symptoms of mild hypocalcemia can include muscle cramps, especially in the back and legs and brittle nails, dry skin and more coarse hair.

If left untreated, over time hypocalcemia can cause neurologic (affecting the nervous system) or psychologic (affecting the mind) symptoms, including: 1-Confusion, memory loss, irritability or restlessness, depression or hallucinations. 2-Tingling in the lips, tongue, fingers and/or feet. 3-Muscle spasms in the throat that make it difficult to breathe (laryngospasm). 3-Stiffening and spasms of the muscles (tetany) and seizures. 4-Abnormal heart rhythms (arrhythmia) and congestive heart failure.

Most of the time, hypocalcemia is an issue with the parathyroid hormone (PTH) levels and/or vitamin D levels are involved with the cause of hypocalcemia. This is because PTH helps control the level of calcium in the blood and vitamin D helps absorb calcium. Several health conditions and disorders can cause hypocalcemia. The three most common causes of hypocalcemia include: 1-Hypoparathyroidism: this happens when the parathyroid glands (four small pea-sized glands behind the thyroid in the neck) don't make enough parathyroid hormone (PTH). Low levels of PTH cause low levels of calcium in the body. It can also be an inherited disorder or from having one or more of the parathyroid glands or the thyroid gland surgically removed. 2-Vitamin D deficiency: Vitamin D helps absorb calcium properly, so a lack of vitamin D in the body can cause low levels of calcium in the blood (hypocalcemia). Vitamin D deficiency can be caused by an inherited disorder or by not getting enough sunlight or not consuming enough vitamin D. 3-Kidney failure (renal failure): Hypocalcemia in chronic renal failure is due to an increased level of phosphorus in your blood and decreased renal production of a certain kind of vitamin D.

The stretch reflex, "knee-jerk", represents the best-known and longest studied neural circuit. Unlike sensory circuits, for example in the visual system, the stretch reflex connects an external input to a behavioral output, both mechanical in nature, and is thus easily demonstrable without technical equipment. It provides an extremely reliable input—output relationship —hence, our view of the "knee-jerk" reaction as the epitome of automatic behavior. Yet, the underlying physiology of this stretch reflex is not so simple.

Indeed, it consists of an extensive chain of events, characterized by many conversions between mechanical, electrical and chemical forms of energy. The stretch reflex invokes the burgeoning fields of excitation—secretion coupling and excitation —contraction coupling.

The chain of causality between a tap on the tendon and the subsequent knee jerk is now understood in considerable detail. At three stages—two electro-chemical synapses and one electro-mechanical transducer—electrical impulse spread is linked to the flow of calcium ions, and, in one way or another, that flow of $Ca2+$ is controlled by $Ca2+$ channels. These $Ca2+$ channels do not function in isolation—rather, they work in coordination with other varieties of ion channels, notably, voltage-gated sodium and potassium channels, as well as ligand-gated channels controlled by the neurotransmitters glutamate and acetylcholine (acetylcholine and glutamate act as both neurotransmitters and neuromodulators. As neuromodulators, they change neural information processing by regulating synaptic transmitter release, altering baseline membrane potential and spiking activity, and modifying long-term synaptic plasticity). But the critical and specific role of Ca2+ channels in signal transduction is unique: in every instance, the conversion of an electrical signal to a chemical message requires the activation of Ca2+ channels. This is a nearly universal rule in excitable cells.

In a typical cell, the concentrations of Na+ and K+ on both sides of the membrane are in the millimolar range, so a much larger flux of ions would be needed to produce a proportional change in concentration; thus, the ion fluxes that generate Na+ and K+ spikes are not sufficient to deliver an ion-encoded message. Moreover, calcium has an additional advantage for signaling, in that receptor proteins that respond efficiently to Ca2+ ions could be readily utilized because calcium's divalent charge provides the energy needed to help drive large conformational changes. Finally, inasmuch as Ca2+ is a "hard" ion, it satisfies a more sharply defined set of requirements for high-affinity binding than a soft ion such as Mg2+, thereby favoring highly specific interactions.

Calcium (Ca2+) signaling plays a crucial role in the control of neuronal function and plasticity. Changes in neuronal Ca2+ concentration are detected by Ca2+-binding proteins that can interact with and regulate target proteins to modify their function. Members of the neuronal calcium sensor (NCS) protein family have multiple non-redundant roles in the nervous system.

Calcium has a major role in neurons as the trigger for neurotransmitter release. In addition, many other aspects of neuronal function are regulated by changes in intracellular free Ca2+ concentration. Rapid exocytosis of neurotransmitter-containing synaptic vesicles is activated by a local increase in Ca2+ concentration at the presynaptic active zone within 10s of microseconds through the action of the Ca2+ sensor synaptotagmin. In other Ca2+ -the regulated events require more changes in neuronal Ca2+ concentration and are activated over longer time scales and the changes can persist for minutes to days. In part the specificity of the effects of Ca2+ on neuronal physiology is determined by the magnitude, kinetics and spatial localization of the Ca2+ signal. The transduction of changes in Ca2+ concentration requires Ca2+-binding proteins and these can contribute to the overall specificity of Ca2+ signaling.

Calcium channel blockers (CCBs) are a type of drug that prevents calcium from entering the muscle cells of the heart and blood vessels. This relaxes the blood vessels, which allows blood to flow more easily and lowers blood pressure. CCBs are also known as calcium antagonists. The discovery of calcium channel blockers (CCBs) began in the 1960s with the study of coronary dilators:

1959: Arunlakshana and Schild published a paper that outlined a quantitative procedure for defining the action of antagonists. This paper became known as "The Schild plot".

1963: The cardiac effect of calcium withdrawal was mimicked by a new compound, later named verapamil.

1969: The term "calcium antagonist" was given to a new drug designation.

1975: The first dihydropyridines were discovered. (Dihydropyridines are a class of molecules derived from a chemical structure which is a cyclic compound with two hydrogen atoms added to a pyridine ring; they are most commonly known as calcium channel blockers, primarily used to treat high blood pressure and are found in various synthetic compounds, not naturally occurring in a single source). They are a type of calcium channel blocker (CCB) that works by blocking calcium channels in the walls of blood vessels, which causes blood vessels to widen and reduces blood pressure. Dihydropyridines bind to and block voltage-gated L-type calcium channels in the smooth muscle cells of blood vessels. These channels open in response to electrical signals, and regulate the amount of calcium that enters muscle cells. Calcium in muscle cells causes contractions, so blocking the channels reduces contractions and causes vasodilation. Dihydropyridines can also cause the vascular endothelium to release nitric oxide (NO), which contributes to the vasodilation effect.

Dihydropyridines are used to treat high blood pressure and angina, a type of chest pain caused by a lack of oxygen to the heart muscle. They have a relatively small effect on the heart.

1980s: CCBs began to be used globally.

2000: Controversy surrounding the approval of calcium channel blockers (CCBs) primarily stemmed from concerns about their potential to increase the risk of myocardial infarction (heart attack) in certain patients, particularly when using short-acting formulations, which can cause significant blood pressure fluctuations, leading to adverse cardiovascular events; this concern was further amplified by early studies showing increased mortality in post-myocardial infarction patients taking high doses of short-acting nifedipine.

Subsequent large-scale clinical trials with newer, longer-acting CCBs have largely mitigated these concerns, demonstrating their efficacy in treating hypertension and angina with a more favorable safety profile when used appropriately. The controversy over the safety of CCBs trial was settled in 2002.

In recent years, rapid progress in the fields of Ca2+ channel structure, function, diversity and regulation can be attributed to several key factors. 1-Investigators have approached the study of calcium channels from many angles, ranging from hardcore biophysics and biochemistry to clinical perspectives. 2-Even with the advent of improved technologies, and the availability of a veritable cornucopia of potent, selective Ca2+ channel drugs, the field would not have experienced such a rapid rate of progress without a shift in the prevailing attitudes of the individual investigators. The sharing of information and resources between scientists has greatly contributed to the speed of new discoveries. In earlier times, compartmentalization stood as a barrier to collaborative discovery. As Rodolfo Llinαs put it in a 1983 letter: "We need to unify our fields a bit more. Nature seems to be trying to tell us something and we continue stubbornly to think that muscles and nerve cells are not next of kin." Thankfully, this wish for unification has now largely been realized, and we now understand a great deal more about what nature can tell us about Ca2+ channels, their diversity, and their critical roles in cellular processes.

The dihydropyridine, tetrahydropyridine, and piperidine ring systems are found in numerous natural and synthetic compounds. Tetrahydropyridine and piperidine, both cyclic nitrogen-containing compounds, exhibit a wide range of biological actions, including potential anti-inflammatory, antioxidant, antimicrobial, anticancer, and analgesic properties, with many derivatives currently investigated as drug candidates due to their diverse pharmacological effects depending on the substituents attached to the ring structure; with piperidine derivatives often showing antihypertensive, neuroprotective, and antibacterial activities, while tetrahydropyridines are explored for their potential as insecticides and antimalarial agents.

Since their inception, heterocyclic compounds (some or all the atoms are joined in a ring) have become a pillar of medicinal and chemistry research. These compounds (and many others) look to be repurposing themselves for the future. Nature is stubbornly telling us that all of God's creations are interlocked together making life on our Earth possible. God has revealed the path for discovery of nature's secretes in Matthew 7:7-8: "Ask and it will be given to you; seek and you will find; knock and the door will be opened to you. For everyone who asks receives; the one who seeks finds; and to the one who knocks, the door will be opened." I'm certainly grateful that scientists kept knocking at natures door long enough to find the calcium channel blockers (CCBs) in time for them becoming available when I began needing them!

A Brief History of Calcium Channel Discovery, Landes Bioscience, Richard W. Tsien and Curtis F. Barrett, Go to: : Landes Bioscience; 2000-2013& several Googled references...

CHAPTER 11

THE STATINS...

The discovery of statin medications during my life time has helped millions of people escape the horrors of the buildup of plaque in the arteries, heart disease and early death. They lower cholesterol levels in the blood by inhibiting the production of cholesterol in the liver and are taken by millions of people, like me. The story of the development of statins is told by Dr. Endo: I (Akira Endo) was born into a rural farming family in northern Japan, in Akita, where I lived for 17 years with my extended family, including my grandparents. My grandfather, who had an interest in medicine and science, was a great home teacher to me. Thanks to his influence, I became fascinated with mushrooms and other molds, and at the age of 10.

In 1957, I joined a pharmaceutical company in Tokyo, where I was assigned to one of the applied microbiology groups. I worked toward developing a new pectinase that hydrolyzed viscid pectin contaminated wines and ciders. In 1958, I found a grape-parasitic fungus to be a potent producer of such an enzyme. One year later, this new enzyme was commercialized. I then purified it and elucidated its properties.

At this point, I became interested in cholesterol biosynthesis and I eventually worked in New York on the role of phospholipids in an enzyme system involved in the synthesis of bacterial cell wall lipopolysaccharides from 1966 to 1968. While living in New York, I was very surprised by the large number of elderly and overweight people, and by the rather rich dietary habits of Americans compared to those of the Japanese. In the residential area of the Bronx where I lived, there were many elderly couples living by themselves and I often saw ambulances going to take an elderly person who had suffered a heart attack to the hospital. At that time, coronary heart disease was the main cause of death in the United States. The number of patients with hypercholesterolemia, a precursor to coronary heart disease, was said to exceed 10 million.

In 1784, French physician-chemist François Poulletier was the first to obtain pure cholesterol from gallstones. Some thirty years later they named it cholesterine (solid bile in Greek: chole for bile and stereos for solid). The exact molecular formula of cholesterol was accurately established in 1888 and the proof of the structure of cholesterol was obtained 1932.

During the 19th century, arteriosclerosis was well recognized, but its etiological and pathological significance had not been established. The hypotheses explaining it ranged from disturbed arterial metabolism to adherent blood clots that gradually changed into arteriosclerotic plaques. The first hint that cholesterol was related to atherosclerosis goes back to 1910, when it was reported that atherosclerotic plaques from aortas of human subjects contained over 20-fold higher concentrations of cholesterol than did normal aortas. Three years later, rabbits fed pure cholesterol were found to produce marked hypercholesterolemia and severe atherosclerosis of the aorta. This was the first experimental production of atherosclerosis. At that time, however, these findings were largely rejected or at least not followed up.

Serious research on the role of cholesterol in human atherosclerosis did not really get underway until the 1940s, due to a prevailing view that the disease was a simple consequence of aging and could not be prevented. The genetic connection between cholesterol and heart attacks was first made in 1939 when it was found that several large families in which high blood-cholesterol levels and premature heart attacks together were an inherited trait. In addition to studies with animal models, the genetic studies strongly suggested a causal relationship between cholesterol and atherosclerosis and coronary heart disease.

In the early 1950s, the epidemiologic study of the cholesterol-coronary connection was unfolded by using a newly developed ultracentrifuge to separate plasma lipoproteins by flotation. They found not only that heart attacks correlated with elevated levels of blood cholesterol but also that the cholesterol was contained in low density lipoprotein (LDL). They also observed that heart attacks were less frequent when the blood contained elevated levels containing high density lipoprotein (HDL).

The epidemiologic connection between blood cholesterol and coronary atherosclerosis was firmly established by physiologists who showed the incidence of heart attacks in 15,000 middle-aged men followed for 10 years was linearly proportional to the blood level of cholesterol. It provided the first solid and unarguable evidence that individuals with higher blood cholesterol levels at the time of the baseline examination were more likely to experience a myocardial infarction in the subsequent years of follow-up. It also showed that the risk was increased by a number of other factors such as high blood pressure and smoking. The clinical interest in cholesterol led to an intense effort in the 1950s to determine the pathway by which cholesterol was synthesized in the body.

Cholesterol in the body can be derived from what is absorbed from the diet and from what is synthesized in the body, mainly by the liver. The former type is supplemented by the latter if the required levels are not met, but if the former type of "exogenous" cholesterol reaches its required level, the synthesis function of the liver is suppressed to prevent excessive production of cholesterol.

Feedback suppression of cholesterol synthesis in the liver by dietary cholesterol is mediated through changes in the activity of HMG-CoA reductase (an enzyme that controls the rate cholesterol is produced).

In humans, cholesterol produced in the liver exceeds what is absorbed from the diet, even when a large quantity of cholesterol is ingested. These findings suggested that the inhibition of HMG-CoA reductase would be an effective means of lowering plasma cholesterol in humans. The development of HMG-CoA reductase inhibitors, also known as statins, are drugs that lower cholesterol levels by blocking the enzyme the body uses to produce cholesterol. They are used in conjunction with diet and exercise to treat high cholesterol and prevent cardiovascular disease.

As evidence grew that high blood cholesterol levels were linked to heart disease, scientists in both academia and industry began searching for drugs to lower blood cholesterol. In the 1950s and 1960s, many companies were searching for molecules that would block one of the 30 steps in the synthesis of cholesterol. Many molecules homologous to intermediates along the pathway were synthesized. Some molecules were effective in animals, but none of those were effective at the clinical level. In 1959, the first cholesterol-lowering agent was found that inhibited cholesterol synthesis. However, it was withdrawn from the market in the early 1960s because of serious side effects, including cataracts. It inhibited the final stage in the cholesterol synthetic pathway, resulting in the accumulation of other sterols (any of a group of naturally occurring unsaturated steroid alcohols, typically waxy solids) which can cause cataracts.

The cholesterol-lowering properties of nicotinic acid (vitamin B3), discovered in 1955, is a nutrient in the vitamin B complex that the body needs in small amounts to help some enzymes work properly and helps skin, nerves, and the digestive tract stay healthy. Nicotinic acid is found in many plant and animal products. At that time, nicotinic acid was the only drug effective in lowering both cholesterol and triglycerides. Cholestyramine, an anion-exchange resin, acts by binding bile acids within the intestinal lumen, thus interfering with their reabsorption and enhancing their fecal excretion. It was highly effective in the treatment of many patients with hypercholesterolemia, but unfortunately, it is not tolerated by all patients. Up until this time there were no ideal agents in terms of efficacy or safety.

After Dr. Endo returned to Tokyo in 1968, he had the opportunity to work on a project of his own choosing. Antibiotics were shown to inhibit many different kinds of enzymes, not only in bacterial cells but also in mammalian cells. Although no metabolites that inhibited any enzymes involved in cholesterol synthesis had been isolated previously, he speculated that fungi like molds and mushrooms would produce antibiotics that inhibited HMG-CoA reductase. Inhibition of HMG-CoA reductase (also called statins) would thus be lethal to these microbes.

As HMG-CoA was too expensive to use for determining the inhibitory activity of thousands of samples, they searched for microbial culture broths that inhibited the incorporation of acetate into non saponifiable (means to convert something into soap, or to hydrolyze a fat with alkali to form soap and glycerol) liquid. The active broths were then tested for their ability to inhibit lipid synthesis. Culture broths that were active in the first assay but not active in the second determination were suspected to contain a compound (or compounds) that inhibited the early stages in the cholesterol synthetic pathway.

Antibiotics were shown to inhibit many different kinds of enzymes, not only in bacterial cells but also in mammalian cells. Although no metabolites that inhibited any enzymes involved in cholesterol synthesis had been isolated previously, we speculated that fungi like molds and mushrooms would produce antibiotics that inhibited HMG-CoA reductase. Inhibition of HMG-CoA reductase (also called statins) would thus be lethal to these microbes. In the mid-summer of 1972, we found a second active culture broth of blue-green mold, Penicillium, which was isolated from a rice sample collected at a grain shop in Kyoto. This mold is similar to the blue-green molds that contaminate fruits, like oranges and melons. It took one year to isolate the active principles from the culture broth. Finally, in July 1973, these metabolites showed potent activity to inhibit cholesterol synthesis both in vitro and in vivo. HMG-CoA reductase is the rate-controlling enzyme in cholesterol synthesis. The goal know was to find an inhibitor of HMG-CoA reductase (the first one found was called compactin).

To move the compactin project on, it was essential to show that compactin was active in lowering plasma cholesterol in experimental animals. In the early spring of 1976, a pathologists who were keeping laying hens for research purposes, agreed to a joint research project to evaluate compactin using the hens. The experiments were a great success. The plasma cholesterol of laying hens that received compactin decreased by 50% after one month. We were also able to confirm the profound cholesterol-lowering effects of compactin in dogs and monkeys. These results defined compactin as a candidate for a new type of drug. So, the 'Compactin Development Project' - including pharmacologists, pathologists, toxicologists, organic chemists and microbiologists—was launched in August 1976.

At the end of the 1970s, the findings showing the dramatic effects of compactin in dogs and monkeys inspired many pharmaceutical companies to begin searching for another statin. Researchers confirmed test findings and were astonished at the potency of the drug. They set out to find its own statins and in February 1979 isolated a statin very similar to compactin in chemical structure, called mevinolin, from the fungus Aspergillus terreus.

Lovastatin was given FDA approval to become the first commercial statin in September 1987. It was followed by a new statin, simvastatin and pravastatin and launched it in 1989. Four synthetic statins were subsequently developed. Today the most popular statin is atorvastatin (Lipitor®).

Statins have now been tested in many large-scale clinical trials, involving 90,000 subjects who were followed for 5 years. The results in all these studies have been consistent: treatment with statins lowers plasma LDL levels by 25–35% and reduces the frequency of heart attacks by 25–30%. It is said that the percentage reduction in coronary events would be even more dramatic if the treatment were longer and if statin therapy were started earlier. No major adverse effects of lowering cholesterol were noted in any of the studies. The remarkable safety of statins derives from their unique mechanism of action. The statins are the largest selling class of drugs currently taken by patients throughout the world.[1] Fungi are very diverse groups of organisms encompassing a wide range of life forms, from single celled to very complex multicellular organisms. They can be microscopic or present large fruiting bodies with underground systems that extend for miles. About 100,000 species have already been identified, but scientists estimate a vast number of species are yet to be cataloged, with the total number ranging from 0.8 to 3.8 million species.

Some species can be detrimental to humans, animals and plants, such as mildews, canker, ringworm or thrush. However, due to its vast diversity, fungi occupy different niches in nature and are responsible for important ecosystem services, which benefit humans and the overall ecosystem. Fungi are an important part of soil biodiversity, and this diverse group of organisms can help tackle global challenges. Fungi are closely interlinked with vegetation and carbon and nutrient cycling. As a result, they are major drivers of soil health and carbon sequestration, among other ecosystem functions. Fungi are heterotrophic organisms; therefore, they rely on photosynthetic carbon to produce energy, and some species get this carbon from plant root exudates. Together, plants and fungi capture carbon from the atmosphere and store it into the soil for decades if not hundreds of years. This process improves soil fertility.

Fungi have the ability to transform nutrients in a way that makes them available for plants. Some fungi are decomposers which mean that they break down plant and animal debris, thus cycling nutrient and increasing their availability in the soil. They can also propel nitrogen fixation and phosphorus mobilization, two of the main nutrients required for plant development and productivity. Fungi are important contributors to the soil carbon stock. They play a major part in the carbon cycle through the soil food web. Decomposers cycle carbon from litter and dead plant material, while other species living in mutual symbiotic association with plant roots (i.e., mycorrhizal fungi), provide more stable stocks of carbon.

Some mushrooms are commonly found in the diets of many people around the world. These edible mushrooms are rich in nutrients such as vitamin B, C and D, fiber, minerals including potassium, phosphorus, calcium and they are also a good source of protein. In fact, many mushrooms rank above vegetables, because of their protein content. For that reason, edible mushrooms are considered a good substitute for meat in vegetarian/vegan diets and in diets of people who don't have access to meat.

Fungi are used for the production of beer, cheeses and even chocolate. In the case of chocolate, the fungi are used to ferment cacao beans to make them sweeter and more palatable to humans.

In addition, edible mushrooms can be cultivated using agricultural waste, they don't depend on fertile soil and don't compete for resources with other food crops. Therefore, mushroom cultivation can reduce agriculture waste while increasing food supply, farmers' income and generating new employment opportunities.

Six percent of edible mushrooms possess medicinal properties, which can help prevent diseases and boost the immune system. Fungi are amazing producers of natural products. They are crucial to the health and the well-being of people throughout the world. They are excellent producers of hydrolytic enzymes, biofuels, organic acids, polysaccharides, and secondary metabolites such as antibiotics, anticancer drugs, hypocholesterolemic agents, immunosuppressants, and others.

Fungi have been found to help degrade various pollutants from the environment, such as plastic and other petroleum-based products, pharmaceuticals and personal care products, and oil. Some of these substances are persistent toxins, which mean that they take a long time to break down in the environment and accumulate in humans and other species, presenting adverse effects on organisms. Therefore, fungi can act as a powerful tool to reduce environmental pollution. Studies show that some fungi species can help in ecosystem restoration by advancing reforestation in degraded soils and act as pest control seeing that some species are pathogens of arthropods or nematodes. Mycelium, which is the root structure of mushrooms are now being used to replace unsustainable materials, such as plastic, synthetic and animal-based products. The products from Mycelium are biodegradable and require less water and land resources to be produced. Some of the mycelium-based products already in the market include packaging, clothes, shoes, sustainable leather, skincare products and others. *UN Decade on Restoration &others…*

Statins were developed from a fungus, called blue-green mold, found in a rice sample collected at a grain shop in Kyoto. This mold is similar to the blue-green molds that contaminate fruits, like oranges and melons. Finding the competitive inhibitor of HMG-CoA reductase, and compactin was indeed a wonderful gift from nature made available for man. Their final step took them only one year to isolate the active principles from a culture broth. For more than three decades scientists had been attempting to find a way to lower cholesterol and help prevent cardiovascular disease.

Still, many people who could benefit from the drug don't take it. Statins have a role in people's health under the right circumstances, yet, those who can benefit from statin therapy sometimes avoid it because they misunderstand how the drug works, including the nature and frequency of side effects, as well as the larger role statin therapy can take in managing their longer-term health.

Statins work to lower the production of low-density lipoproteins (LDL), or "bad" cholesterol, by blocking an enzyme in the liver that helps make cholesterol. High LDL levels can create plaque buildup in the arteries, which can block blood flow, and raise the risk of a heart attack or stroke.

The benefits of statins go beyond just lowering LDL cholesterol. Statins have anti-inflammatory properties, and inflammation is a known contributor to plaque buildup. Also, statins help prevent plaques from breaking open and releasing chemicals that stimulate blood clot formation, which is the cause of most heart attacks. Anyone who has coronary artery disease or other arterial disease caused by plaque buildup should be on a statin, even if the person has a normal cholesterol profile. Statins also can benefit otherwise healthy people with elevated LDL cholesterol levels and those with a 10-year risk of cardiovascular disease. Even people with lower LDL cholesterol levels should consider taking a statin if they have other risk factors, such as diabetes, a family history of heart disease before age 55, smoking, or high blood pressure.

Many people avoid statins because they fear possible side effects of statins. The most common side effect is achy muscles, and some people report feeling less energetic, weak, or tired, all of which may cause them to exercise less or at lower intensity. Yet, studies have shown that most often these side effects are not actually caused by the statin.

One rare, but potentially serious, side effect of statins is widespread muscle damage causing high levels of a muscle enzyme that can lead to kidney injury. The symptoms are pain in various muscles, weakness, and dark urine.

If this occurs, stop taking the drug and call your doctor immediately.[2]

Since my stroke from high blood pressure, I take my statin medication on a daily basis along with six other drugs and am glad I feel the way I do and am still alive. Most all these pharmaceuticals weren't available during my parents' life and finding the competitive inhibitor of HMG-CoA reductase, and compactin was indeed a wonderful gift from nature made available for man. It's wonderful that there are some human beings that "never give up" working with microbes that we detest, fear and flee – yeast, molds and fungi…

1– *Pro Jpn Acad Ser B Phys Biol Sci, A historical perspective on the discovery of statins, 05/11/2010.*

2– *Don't be afraid of statins, Havard Health Publishing, 10/19/2023.*

CHAPTER 12

SYMPATHETIC NERVOUS SYSTEM...

In 1918 a Dr Oliver entered into the Physiology lab at the University College London and approaches Edward A Schafer with an instrument he had invented with which he claimed to be able to measure, through the unbroken skin, the diameter of a living artery, such as the radial artery at the wrist. He appears to be using his family in his experiments and a young son was the subject of a series of studies where by Oliver injected extracts of various animal glands under the skin. In particular, with the statement that injection under the skin of a glycerin extract from calf's adrenal gland was followed by a definite narrowing of the radial artery. Professor Schafer is said to have been entirely skeptical, and to have attributed the observation to self-delusion. Dr Oliver, however, was persistent; he … suggested that, at least, it would do no harm to inject it into the circulation, through a vein, a little of the adrenal extract, which he produced from his pocket. So, Professor Schafer makes the injection, expecting a triumphant demonstration of nothing, and finds himself standing 'like some watcher of the skies, when a new planet swims into his ken', watching the mercury rise in the manometer with amazing rapidity and to an astounding height. *Wikipedia*

The parasympathetic nervous system is part of your autonomic nervous system. It could be called your "automatic" nervous system, as it's responsible for many functions that you don't have to think about to control. This can include control of your heart rate, blood pressure, digestion, urination and sweating, among other functions. While the sympathetic nervous system controls your body's "fight or flight" response, your parasympathetic nervous system helps to control your body's response during times of rest. Its job is usually to relax or reduce the body's activities. Because of the signals it carries, the rhyming phrases "rest and digest" or "feed and breed" are easy ways to remember what your parasympathetic nervous system does.

The parasympathetic nervous system can have the following effects: 1-It constricts the pupils to limit how much light enters the eyes. It also makes changes that can help improve close-up vision, and causes tear production. 2-It makes glands in the mouth produce saliva, and glands in the nose produce mucus. This can be helpful with digestion and breathing during times of rest. 3-It tightens airway muscles and ultimately reduces the amount of work your lungs do during times of rest. 4-It lowers your heart rate and the pumping force of the heart. 5-It increases the rate of digestion and diverts energy to help digest food. It also stimulates the pancreas to make and release insulin, helping the body break down sugars into a form the cells can use. 6-It relaxes the muscles that help you control when peeing (urinate) or pooping (defecate). 7-It influences some of the body's mating behaviors.

The sympathetic nervous system takes the lead when safety and survival are at risk "flight or fight", but this system's actions can strain body systems when it's over used. Because these two systems offset each other, they help maintain balance in the body.

As mentioned, the sympathetic and parasympathetic nervous systems are parts of the autonomic nervous system. The autonomic nervous system is a subsystem of the peripheral nervous system, which is all the nervous tissue in the body excluding your brain and spinal cord. The parasympathetic nervous system uses four of the 12 cranial nerves. These are nerves that connect directly to the brain: 1-Three of those four only involve your senses and glands connected to your eyes, nose and mouth. 2-The fourth, vagus nerve, connects to part of your mouth and also extends down through your neck to your chest and abdomen. The vagus nerve makes up about 75% of the parasympathetic nervous system overall, connecting to the heart, lungs and other vital internal organs. Farther down, 31 spinal nerves connect directly to the spinal cord, but the parasympathetic nervous system only uses some of them in the lower part of your spine. This sends signals to the bladder and bowels to relax during urination and defecation. The parasympathetic nervous system's components are similar to those found in other parts of the nervous system. The neurons are the main type of cell present and they can generate and receive signals.

Adrenaline (epinephrine) and noradrenaline (norepinephrine) are both hormones that are primarily associated with the sympathetic nervous system, which is responsible for the "fight or flight" response in the body, meaning they are released during stressful situations to prepare the body for immediate action. Adrenaline is mainly secreted by the adrenal medulla (the inner part of the adrenal gland) as a hormone, while noradrenaline acts as the primary neurotransmitter of the sympathetic nerves, causing effects like increased heart rate, blood pressure, and alertness.

The adrenal cortex is the outer layer of the adrenal gland and produces hormones that regulate salt balance, blood sugar, and sex hormones; essentially, the medulla handles immediate stress responses, while the cortex manages more long-term bodily functions.

Catecholamines are a group of neurohormones that act as chemical messengers in the body. They are produced by the adrenal medulla and brain and include: epinephrine (adrenaline), norepinephrine (noradrenaline), and dopamine. Research began with the discovery of adrenaline in the adrenal glands in the late 19th century, followed by the identification of noradrenaline as a neurotransmitter in the sympathetic nervous system in the mid-20th century; later, it was established that dopamine is a distinct neurotransmitter in the brain, paving the way for understanding its role in movement disorders like Parkinson's disease and psychiatric conditions like schizophrenia.

"Alpha and beta blockers" are a class of medications that work by blocking the effects of the hormones adrenaline and noradrenaline at specific receptors in the body, primarily used to treat high blood pressure (hypertension) by relaxing blood vessels and slowing the heart rate; "alpha blockers" target alpha receptors, while "beta blockers" target beta receptors, and some medications may block both types depending on their selectivity. The key points about alpha and beta blockers: 1-Both alpha and beta receptors are part of the sympathetic nervous system, which controls "fight or flight" responses; by blocking these receptors, the drugs counteract the effects of adrenaline, leading to relaxation of blood vessels and a slower heart rate. 2-Alpha blockers are primarily used to treat conditions related to urinary tract obstruction, like enlarged prostate, as they relax muscles in the bladder neck, improving urine flow. 3-Beta blockers are commonly used for hypertension, angina (chest pain), arrhythmias (irregular heartbeat), heart failure, and migraine prevention. 4-Some alpha and beta blockers selectively target specific receptor subtypes, while others block multiple types, which can lead to different side effects.

The history of alpha and beta blockers is a century-long journey that includes the discovery of receptors, drug development, and clinical trials began in 1897. Beta-blockers are widely used in clinics today and have revolutionized cardiovascular therapies. They are also used by musicians, public speakers, actors, and professional dancers to avoid performance anxiety, stage fright, and tremor.[1]

Life's rhythms and demands are often challenging and require intense physical and psychological efforts in order to be sustained. An individual reacts to physical and mental strain that is potentially health threatening by activating interconnected neuroendocrine circuits. This response allows the body to face and deal with the challenge and re-establish homeostatic equilibrium. If the individual perceives a noxious stimulus as too intense, or its duration as too long, he may fail coping with it, and incur maladaptation. In this case, the stress response does not resolve into a state of balance (either similar or new, i.e., adapted, compared with the state before stress hits), neuroendocrine parameters remain altered, and illness may ensue.

It is clear that stress has both a physical (objective) and a psychological (subjective) component: the latter, depends on the individual perception of its predictability and controllability. The way a person can anticipate a certain stressor and then control it, largely defines the resulting stress response, how promptly and efficiently it is activated promoting adaptation, and how fast it is turned off once equilibrium has been recovered.

The time course of the stress response, characterized by measurable neuroendocrine and behavioral indexes, thus reveals whether a destabilizing stimulus is manageable, or conversely, cannot be handled and consequently becomes harmful. This implies that not all stimuli that elicit strong neuroendocrine responses are real stressors, but only those that exceed the individual's ability to change and adapt.

Cortical centers in the brain sense a disturbing stimulus and respond by activating pathways through the limbic system: The limbic system is a group of interconnected brain structures that help regulate your emotions and behavior. The structures (also known as components or parts) of the limbic system work together with other brain regions by processing memory, thoughts and motivations, then tells body how to respond. The limbic system stimulates peripheral networks, including the sympathetic–adrenal–medullary axis and the renin-angiotensin system, and later the hypothalamic–pituitary–adrenal (HPA) axis. A cascade of events follows that results in the orchestration of a complex response. Adrenaline and other hormones, and neuropeptides are produced and regulate cardiovascular and metabolic functions (inducing, for instance, increases in heart rate, breath frequency, glucose release) for a prompt response concerted to overcome the challenge.

If the distressing stimulus persists, the HPA axis (hypothalamic-pituitary-adrenal axis) kicks in to sustain the immediate reaction mediated by the centrally activated peripheral systems. The HPA response starts with the hypothalamus delivering corticotropin-releasing hormone to the pituitary and culminates with the stimulation of the adrenal cortex by the pituitary-derived adrenocorticotropic hormone to produce glucocorticoids (GCs). Most organs and tissues, including sympathetic nerves, immune cells and several brain regions express GC receptors and are responsive to GCs induced by stress. Consequently, these hormones participate in the regulation of disparate stress-associated processes, from the modulation of cardiovascular effects and the immune function, to the eventual dampening of the stress response through inhibition of the HPA axis when adaptation is attained.

In situations in which the stressor is overwhelming and cannot be resolved, stress becomes chronic. In this case, the GC-dependent negative feedback mechanism that controls the stress response does not work, GC receptor resistance develops, and the systemic levels of the molecular mediators of stress remain high, compromising the immune system and damaging in the long-term multiple organs and tissues.

When considering the numerous cellular targets of the chemical mediators of stress, one would expect that protracted, stress-dependent neuroendocrine dysregulation may damage directly or through functional circuits practically all organs and tissues. To clarify this assumption and identify the biochemical pathways significantly impaired by chronic stress to the extent of producing illness, researchers have on one hand searched for putative morphological tissue alterations associated with stress, and on the other analyzed the molecular mechanisms of action of the main stress hormones.

It has been shown that chronic stress is linked to macroscopic changes in certain brain areas, consisting of volume variations and physical modifications of neuronal networks. For example, several studies in animals have described stress-related effects in the prefrontal cortex (PFC) and limbic system, characterized by volume reductions of some structures, and changes in neuronal plasticity due to dendritic atrophy and decreased spine density. These morphological alterations are similar to those found in the brains of depressed patients examined postmortem, suggesting that they could also be at the basis of the depressive disorders that are often associated with chronic stress in humans. This hypothesis is supported by imaging studies that evidenced structural changes in the brain of individuals suffering from various types of stress-related disorders, such as those linked to severe traumas, major negative life events or chronic psychosocial strain. In particular, atrophy of the basal ganglia and significantly reduced gray matter in certain areas of the PFC in subjects afflicted with long-term occupational stress. In general, the consequences of these alterations in a brain region can expand to other functionally connected areas, and potentially cause those cognitive, emotional and behavioral dysfunctions that are commonly associated with chronic stress, and that may increase vulnerability to psychiatric disorders.

The understanding of the molecular circuits that underlie brain architectural changes and medical conditions linked to chronic stress is just at the beginning. Research in this area has centered primarily on the signaling functions of those molecules that are directly induced by stress through the activation of the sympathetic-adrenal-medullary and HPA networks, focusing on their possible cellular targets. Since receptors for stress neuropeptides and hormones are broadly expressed in immune cells, most studies have concentrated on the effects of stress on the immune system (IS). In fact, psychological stress can induce the acute phase response commonly associated with infections and tissue damage, and increase the levels of circulating cytokines and of various biomarkers of inflammation. In fact, the interlink between the stress response and inflammation elicited by the IS can be explained from the evolutionary perspective by considering that the stress response is an adaptive process developed by co-opting the IS mechanisms of defense, sets in motion a neuroimmune circuit that stimulates the IS to mount a protective reaction intended to prevent damage, repair it and restore homeostasis.

This neuroimmune communication is bidirectional because the cytokines produced by stress-stimulated immune cells also convey a feed-back to the nervous system, further modulating the release of stress hormones in the brain, as well as brain activity that regulates behavior and cognitive functions. In a situation of chronic stress, the neuroimmune axis can be overstimulated and breaks down, thus causing neuroendocrine/immune imbalances that establish a state of chronic low-grade inflammation, a possible prelude to various illnesses.

Diseases whose development has been linked to both stress and inflammation include cardiovascular dysfunctions, diabetes, cancer, autoimmune syndromes and mental illnesses such as depression and anxiety disorders.

The recognition that chronic stress can cause serious diseases has intensified research to determine the biochemical perturbations that compromise homeostasis to a degree that prevents spontaneous recovery. The picture is very complex because chronic stress appears to affect organ and system functions at multiple levels. Yet, it is by pinpointing specific biochemical processes affected by chronic stress that it will be possible to envisage solutions to stimulate resilience and control stress-dependent diseases.

It is clear that in the case of illnesses caused by heightened occupational stress, priority should be given to preventive interventions with the purpose of creating and maintaining work conditions respectful of human physiological, emotional and social needs: in other words, the work environment should stimulate growth and productivity while supporting each individual in their challenges. Elements like discordant interactions with coworkers and superiors' demands beyond formal agreements, that are quite common in very competitive work environments, can sharpen tensions and exaggerate the psychosocial strain to the point of causing illness, yet they usually remain overlooked and uncontrolled.[2]

Reading the details about the use of Dr Oliver's son to conduct experiments made me think about my father's respect and interest in the professor's work he observed during his graduate studies. I remember him being thrilled when I decided to attend graduate school and pursued Animal Science. Tongue in cheek, I'm even not so sure that he wouldn't have been honored including me in some of his studies if he continued doing research and teaching as a career.

Even though I also did not pursue research and teaching as a career, I have found myself often still thinking about the scientific method and doing little experiments here and there. 1-Two observations I made for over a year on the medium and average number of shirt sleeves I needed to turn inside out after being washed or dried. 2-A Geiger counter daily study on nuclear half-lives (nuclear decay) following surgical placement of radioactive pellets into my prostate for cancer. 3-At this current moment in my life, I'm monitoring urine indices (dipstick) on a daily basis after taking an over-the-counter medication twice daily (a more refined/higher dose form [phlorizin] is often used as a secondary prescription when metformin is not keeping blood glucose in check) that is supposed to flush glucose into the urine. My goal is to see if it may help reduce my A1C – along with an experiment I've been doing for several years that is supposed to be doing the same thing - chromium and cinnamon.

So far, during my experiments, I haven't gotten into trying to figure standard deviations, a measure of how dispersed the data is in relation to the mean. A low, or small, standard deviation indicates data are clustered and I could predict consistent results of my studies.

It's probably not too late to try another proven experiment, if it's done before diabetes has taken over my body - reducing carbohydrates in my diet and exercise more may help. Love of sweets and arthritis makes me look to a probable better solution – if only I can get my primary care physician to agree. For me, if my A1C worsens, I would like to try the newly developed Semaglutide (GLP-1) medication. It is an injectable drug used to treat type 2 diabetes, help with weight loss and promises that there are many new positive findings on their way. It seems to have even more health promises than even the "wonder drug" I am now taking - metformin. Think of it – one stick of a needle about every week and utopia. "Eat your sweets and stay on the couch" with continued health, slower aging changes and a longer life expectancy. There are even current studies that GLP-1 drugs may become available in a pill form. Adding it to my six daily prescription pills would be less effort and pain.

I found a poem, author unknown, that I think pretty much summarizes why in my 70s I began to recognize aging symptoms from arthritis, prostate cancer, stroke and high blood pressure. I've always wanted to credit it to my inherited gene pool, but I'm sure my life's habits especially including many fears and anxieties along the way, have helped it along even though the stressors mostly became "so what's".

First, I was dying to finish my high school and start college.

And, then I was dying to finish college and start working.

Then, I was dying to marry and have children. And,

I was dying for my children to grow old so…

I could go back to work.

But, then I was dying to retire.

And, now I am dying.

And suddenly I realize I forgot to live…

Please don't let this happen to you. Appreciate your current situation and enjoy each MOMENT…Old Friend. LIFE'S TRAVELS…YOUR CALL!

Despite this tale being reiterated many times about experiments conducted on Dr Oliver's son, it is not beyond doubt. It has been stated by faculty at the University College that there has been shown some surprise that the constriction of the radial artery was measurable in 1918. Of Oliver's descendants, none recalled experiments on his son. The report of subcutaneous injections contradicts the concerned parties. Oliver: "During the winter of 1893–4, while prosecuting an inquiry as to … agents that vary the caliber of … arteries … there was found that the administration by the mouth of a glycerin extract of the adrenals of the sheep and calf produced a marked constrictive action on the arteries." Schafer: "In the autumn of 1893 there called upon me in my laboratory at University College a gentleman who was personally unknown to me.

… I found that my visitor was Dr. George Oliver, [who] was desirous of discussing with me the results which he had been obtaining from the exhibition by the mouth of extracts from certain animal tissues, and the effects which these had in his hands produced upon the blood vessels of man." Systemic effects of orally given adrenaline are highly unlikely, so details of the canonical text may be legend. *Wikipedia*

However, it is a wonderful story and true or false, I am grateful that even though the research history of alpha and beta blockers began in 1897 that they came along in time for my graduation date in high school, 1964. They are widely used in clinics today and have revolutionized cardiovascular therapies – one of them is currently on my prescribed list of medications.

1– *Parasympathetic Nervous System (PSNS), Cleveland Clinic, last review 06/06/2022.*

2– *The effects of chronic stress on health: new insights into the molecular mechanisms of brain–body communication, Future Sci OA, Agnese Mariotti, 11/01/2015.*

CHAPTER 13

PHLORIZIN, GLUCOSE AND PEE...

Phlorizin, as a flavonoid from a wide range of sources, is gradually becoming known for its biological activity. Phlorizin can exert antioxidant effects by regulating the IL-1β/IKB-α/NF-KB signaling pathway. At the same time, it exerts its antibacterial activity by reducing intracellular DNA agglutination, reducing intracellular protein and energy synthesis, and destroying intracellular metabolism. In addition, phlorizin also has various pharmacological effects such as antiviral, antidiabetic, antitumor, and hepatoprotective effects. Based on domestic and foreign research reports, this article reviews the plant sources, extraction, and biological activities of phlorizin, providing a reference for improving the clinical application of phlorizin.

Phlorizin is the glucoside of phlorizin, which belongs to the dihydrochalcone class of flavonoids. The leaves of the tea pear are rich in dihydrochalcones, which are traditionally used in the treatment of liver diseases. They can be used as an alternative hepatoprotective agent to prevent and treat liver damage caused by acetaminophen (APAP). Dihydrochalcones from Lithops polystachyon prevent cisplatin-induced nephrotoxicity in mice via mitogen-activated protein kinase pathway-mediated apoptosis.

Phlorizin is mainly found in the young leaves, rhizomes, and apple fruits of apples, sweet tea, and other tissues. In addition, phlorizin has multiple health-promoting effects, including cardiovascular protection, antiviral, antioxidant, and antidiabetic activity. Multiple studies have found that phlorizin can inhibit the sodium–glucose transporter system (SGLT1) on the small intestinal epithelial mucosa and block intestinal glucose absorption by improving insulin sensitivity and glucose uptake. In addition, phlorizin has a good inhibitory effect on tyrosinase and can prevent certain skin diseases. Therefore, this article reviews the sources, extraction methods, and biological activities of phlorizin to provide a theoretical basis for subsequent research on phlorizin.

The main natural source of phlorizin is Malus plants, specifically apple leaves. Apple leaves are a by-product of apple fruit production and show promise as a source for extracting phlorizin. Phlorizin is primarily found in non-edible parts of the apple tree, such as leaves, branches, root bark, seeds, and immature fruits. Among these parts, the highest concentration of phlorizin is found in the fruit. Apple leaves contain significant amounts of phloretin and its glycoside phlorizin, ranging from 5.4% to 14% of the leaf's dry weight. The phlorizin content in leaves is not greatly influenced by factors like apple variety or harvest period, making it relatively stable over time and across different apple varieties. Phlorizin is a flavonoid compound that is naturally present in the human diet. It is also found in other food sources like apples, tea, red wine, onions, pomegranate fruit, polygonum, peaches, plums, canine roses, grapes, cranberries, and crabapples.

In recent years, extensive research has been conducted on the pharmacological activity of phlorizin, particularly in exploring its potential pharmacological mechanism through its antioxidant effects. Oxidative stress is a common feature of many diseases, including cardiovascular disease, cancer, and diabetes. The antioxidant effect of phlorizin has been widely studied and is considered an important aspect. The screening of natural bioactive substances with anti-aging properties is currently a trending research topic. Through its antioxidant effects, phlorizin can improve the biochemical indicators of aging mice, regulate apoptosis-related proteins to inhibit apoptosis (programmed cell death), and modulate the signaling pathways to exert antioxidant effects. Phlorizin, is a plant compound with important pharmacological activities, exhibits significant antioxidant capacity and cytoprotective effects. It achieves this through the regulation of antioxidant enzyme activity, inhibition of oxidative stress-related signaling pathways, and other mechanisms.

Previous studies have reported on the bacterial inhibitory activity of phlorizin. Phlorizin has demonstrated the ability to inhibit various Gram-positive and Gram-negative bacteria, including Staphylococcus aureus, Listeria monocytogenes, and Salmonella typhimurium. However, the specific inhibitory mechanism of phlorizin against bacteria remains unclear. The inhibitory mechanism of phlorizin on bacteria is believed to involve intracellular

DNA agglutination, reduced intracellular protein and energy synthesis, and disruption of intracellular metabolism. Phlorizin nanofibers are highly promising materials for wound dressings in future clinical applications, as they meet various requirements of the wound healing process, possess antibacterial effects, and demonstrate potential as effective candidates.

Phlorizin has been found to have antiviral effects. In one study on the effect and mechanism of phlorizin on treating a significant global disease, bovine viral diarrhea virus, they found a promising new dietary strategy for controlling BVDV both in vivo and in vitro. Also, phlorizin hinders Zika virus infection by using an interfering cellular glucose that reduces infection titers. These studies may serve as a valuable foundation for the development of antiviral drugs. Anticancer discoveries have provided a theoretical basis and potential for utilizing phlorizin as a natural food or pharmaceutical ingredient in the treatment of esophageal cancer. Numerous studies have also demonstrated the inhibitory effects of phlorizin on the growth of various types of other cancer cells, including human leukemia, bladder cancer, rat mammary adenocarcinoma, mouse melanoma, and human leukemia cells. However, despite the extensive research on phlorizin's anti-cancer properties, it is characterized by poor solubility in lipids and water, an unclear target of action, and limited efficacy.

Phlorizin exerts its anti-tumor effect by regulating cell proliferation and apoptosis processes, inhibiting the proliferation of tumor cells by blocking the progression of the cell cycle and thereby inhibiting the division and growth of tumor cells. Additionally, phlorizin promotes the apoptosis (cells death) of tumor cells, inhibits their survival and spread by regulating apoptosis-related signaling pathways. Phlorizin's ability to regulate cell growth and death is crucial to its anti-tumor effect.

In summary, phlorizin exerts its anti-tumor effect by regulating cell proliferation and apoptosis processes, inhibiting the proliferation of tumor cells. It also regulates the expression of cell cycle-related proteins, blocking the progression of the cell cycle and thereby inhibiting the division and growth of tumor cells. Additionally, phlorizin promotes the apoptosis of tumor cells and inhibits their survival and spread by regulating apoptosis-related signaling pathways. Phlorizin's ability to regulate cell growth and death is crucial to its anti-tumor effect. Also, Phlorizin docosahexaenoate, a novel fatty acid ester of plant polyphenols, inhibits the formation of spheroids and exhibits cytotoxic effects in breast cancer stem cells.

Phlorizin has been utilized for over 100 years due to its various biological activities, including antioxidant properties and liver protection. It has been reported that phlorizin can alleviate oxidative stress, maintain the activity of endogenous antioxidant enzymes, preserve normal nerve cell morphology, and enhance cognitive ability and memory in D-galactose-induced mice. Furthermore, studies have suggested that there are anti-aging and liver-protective effects.

Phlorizin has been reported to have significant inhibitory effects on damage caused by ultraviolet B (UVB) irradiation in nude mice, including erythema, epidermal thickening, and skin shedding. Furthermore, phlorizin has been found to enhance the self-repair ability of normal human keratinocytes and fibroblasts. Overall, research findings include the beneficial effects of phlorizin in various areas such as skin loss resistance, cerebral ischemia resistance, colitis improvement, myocardial ischemia resistance, and memory enhancement

The medicinal phlorizin dihydrochalcone demonstrates numerous biological activities, such as antioxidant, antibacterial, antiviral, antidiabetic, antitumor, and hepatoprotective properties. Its common biological activities and potential mechanisms, presenting new opportunities for the utilization of phlorizin. Phlorizin, a dihydrochalcone compound, has a slight sweet taste and can be used as a food additive in the food industry. At the same time, it has good moisturizing properties and strong antioxidant capacity, and it also shows great market application prospects in skin care products. With the deepening of research, the biological activity of phlorizin is gradually being understood. The various biological activities it exhibits have strong appeal in the medical field. Soon, phlorizin may occupy a larger market in the food, cosmetics, and pharmaceutical fields.[1]

Existing treatments are helping many people with diabetes live healthier lives, but there is still an urgent demand for new diabetes medications. Many years of research have enhanced understanding of diabetes and its effects on the body, including its role in kidney damage. Likewise, research into how the kidneys function has led to a better understanding of how the kidney manages glucose (sugar) and fluid in the body. Collectively, this research has led to the discovery of a new class of drugs that targets the kidneys to help control blood glucose in people with diabetes.

Glucose is a sugar that serves as the body's chief energy source. For those with diabetes, their cells have difficulty using glucose properly, leading to hyperglycemia (high blood glucose). Some people with type 2 diabetes can control their condition with physical activity and diet, while others require diabetes medications. As the disease progresses, many require injections of insulin, a hormone which helps the body utilize glucose. Existing diabetes drugs can help people with diabetes maintain their blood glucose levels in a healthy range, reducing their chances of complications later in life. However, these existing treatments sometimes carry side effects (such as hypoglycemia, or low blood glucose) and/or restrictions that can limit their usefulness. Moreover, even with the expanded choice of treatments now available, meeting recommended blood glucose level targets can be challenging.

From many years of research, another approach to reducing blood glucose levels emerged: a new class of diabetes drugs, called SGLT2 inhibitors, that allows the kidneys to dispose of excess blood glucose in the urine. Clinical studies in people with type 2 diabetes have shown that these medications can safely and effectively lower blood glucose levels and improve glycemic control.

Every day, a healthy adult's two kidneys, each about the size of a fist, together filter 120 to 150 quarts of blood. Blood carrying wastes enters the kidneys, and the kidneys' millions of filtering units, called nephrons, filter that blood in a two-step process. First, blood passes through the glomerulus, a structure which keeps blood cells and larger molecules, such as proteins, in the blood, while allowing wastes and excess fluid to pass through. The filtered fluid then passes through the tubule, which reclaims needed minerals and glucose, sending them back to the bloodstream. Wastes and extra fluid continue on to the bladder as urine. In this way, the kidneys maintain blood's healthy composition, keep levels of electrolytes such as sodium and potassium stable, and (through fluid management) contribute to healthy blood pressure.

The kidneys play an important role in managing glucose levels in the body. Because glucose is small enough that it can pass through the glomerulus, it will end up in the urine if it is not reclaimed or "reabsorbed." Because the body uses glucose as fuel, losing significant amounts of glucose in the urine would be wasteful for a healthy person. To prevent this loss, healthy kidneys in people without diabetes recapture virtually all the filtered glucose and return it to the bloodstream.

After the blood is filtered through the glomerulus, the filtered fluid (or "filtrate") moves on to the tubule, where glucose reabsorption takes place. In the tubule wall, one side of each cell faces the filtrate and the other faces the circulation. In this way, tubule cells can act as both sensors monitoring the components of the filtrate, and conduits that can move materials from the filtrate back into the blood. The filtrate flows over the tubule cells, and transport proteins on the tubule cell surface recapture the glucose, much like workers plucking items from a conveyor belt. Glucose is transported into the tubule cells and then pumped out the other side, back into the blood.

The kidneys' glucose reabsorption system is optimized to work best when blood glucose concentrations are in a normal range. In people with poorly controlled diabetes, who have increased blood glucose levels, this system begins to break down. The amount of glucose in the blood exceeds the kidneys' ability to recapture it, and some glucose continues through the tubules and is lost in the urine, a condition called glucosuria.

Until recently the exact details of how kidney cells reabsorb glucose were unknown. The first clue as to how the kidneys accomplish this task was discovered in the early 1980s by researchers who noticed differences in glucose transport capacity throughout the rat kidney tubule: the early part of the tubule could absorb more glucose more quickly than the downstream part of the tubule. Understanding of how this worked on the molecular level emerged from studies of how glucose from food is absorbed by the cells lining the intestine. Researchers studying the cells lining the intestine discovered the gene for the intestinal glucose transport protein. The protein belonged to a new class of glucose transporters called sodium-glucose cotransporters, or SGLTs. The intestinal transport protein was named SGLT1. Scientists then found a second, closely related protein, SGLT2. Both SGLT1 and SGLT2 are responsible for glucose transport in the kidney.

SGLT1 and SGLT2 are proteins on the cell surface of the tubule cells. Both reclaim glucose from the kidney filtrate, moving glucose together with sodium into the tubule cells, where they can then be returned to the blood. SGLT2 is found earlier in the tubule and is a very high-capacity glucose transporter, while SGLT1 is found later in the tubule and is a lowercapacity transporter. Thus, filtered glucose will first encounter SGLT2 before encountering SGLT1. SGLT2 is responsible for 90 percent of the total glucose absorption as urine is made, while SGLT1 is responsible for the remaining 10 percent. In addition to the kidney and intestine, SGLT1 is also found in many other tissues of the body.

Because of their key role in glucose reabsorption, the SGLTs, particularly SGLT2, were promising drug targets to alter blood glucose levels. Healthy kidneys can reabsorb up to 180 grams (roughly 0.40 pounds) of glucose per day. If a medication could safely block SGLT2 activity and encourage the kidneys to pass that glucose out with the urine rather than reclaim it back into the blood, the thought was that it might be a solution to persistently high blood glucose levels. In fact, a condition called familial renal glucosuria or FRG has already been demonstrated in nature (FRG is a genetic disorder characterized by the persistent presence of glucose in the urine [glucosuria] despite normal blood sugar levels, meaning there is no underlying hyperglycemia, and no other signs of kidney dysfunction; it is caused by mutations in the SLC5A2 gene which affects the reabsorption of glucose in the kidney tubules). This condition is caused by changes in the gene coding for SGLT2, resulting in reduction in SGLT2 activity. This reduced activity prevents most glucose in the filtrate from being reclaimed, and people with FRG lose significant amounts of glucose in the urine. Interestingly, for reasons that are not entirely understood, this condition does not seem to cause hypoglycemia or any serious side effects. Therefore, researchers investigated if SGLT2 inhibitors would be a safe and effective way of treating people with diabetes?

By the time the SGLT proteins were discovered, an SGLT inhibitor called phlorizin had been studied for over 150 years, although only in recent decades have scientists discovered its mechanism of action. Phlorizin came from the root bark of the apple tree. As published by PubMed: Diabetes has been acknowledged since ancient times. However, it was only during the late 1800s that we realized that the primary organ for blood glucose regulation was the pancreas that produces two hormones (insulin which decreases blood glucose & glucagon which increases blood glucose). The 20th century witnessed insulin purification, which revolutionized the treatment of diabetes; this was followed by the development of oral antidiabetic drugs, gliflozins being the latest class. Unique cardio and reno-protective effects separate them from other oral antidiabetic drugs.

Researchers isolated a crystalline glycoside called phlorizin from the bark of apple trees while working at their boss's nursery. Their discovery was published in German in 1835. After a half century, it was decided to administer phlorizin to dogs. They observed increased urination followed by glucose in the urine and postulated that phlorizin affected the kidneys. In 1887, they reported that phlorizin also induced glucosuria in people with diabetes. They also found that phlorizin causes several gastrointestinal side effects and has a poor oral bioavailability. Eventually, phlorizin-based drug trials were initiated and a drug called gliflozin was approved in 2014. The impact of these agents on heart failure and chronic kidney disease seems independent of their antidiabetic properties. More than 100 years after its original discovery, descendants of phlorizin have become a stable medication for the control of diabetes. They are considered a commonly used medication for type 2 diabetes, often prescribed as an add-on therapy alongside metformin when other medications aren't effectively controlling blood sugar levels, but it's generally not considered the first-line treatment, with metformin typically being the most widely prescribed initial medication for diabetes.[2]

In 2022-2023 the FDA approved two new phlorizin-based oral medications (one tablet / one liquid) for once daily treatment of diabetes in cats. What is important to consider regarding them is they are NOT indicated for cats that have already been treated with insulin. These are not drugs meant for treating cats who are insulin-dependent diabetics and neither drug is indicated if a cat has symptoms of diabetic ketoacidosis (DKA). Both drugs increase the risk of DKA as well as euglycemic DKA in cats. Just like DKA, euglycemic DKA is a life-threatening emergency that is characterized by euglycemia (normal range blood glucose), metabolic acidosis, and ketoacidosis. Unlike DKA, euglycemic DKA may be overlooked due to the absence of hyperglycemia. Very careful screening of cats who are being considered for treatment with either of these drugs is imperative. Prior to initiating treatment, the veterinarian should ensure the cat is alert, active, eating, and drinking. The veterinarian should conduct a physical examination, obtain a medical history, CBC, serum chemistry, serum fructosamine (*See Gila Monster chapter for A1C vs fructosamime*), and urinalysis including evaluation for ketonuria.

Laboratory values or physical assessment that indicates the presence of ketones, DKA, kidney or liver disease, or recurrent urinary tract infection (UTI) would preclude the use of either of these medications.

If there is a delay of more than a week between diagnosis of diabetes mellitus and initiation of either of these medications, the veterinarian should re-evaluate the cat with a full physical examination and updated history to ensure the cat still meets the criteria described above. A delay of more than a week between diagnosis and starting medication may increase the risk of developing diabetic ketoacidosis since the cat's diabetes would be untreated during this period.

Also crucial is diligent monitoring regardless of the duration of or the response to treatment, and the ability to and how to promptly recognize and intervene if there are serious and life-threatening adverse reactions. Sudden onset of loss of appetite, anorexia, lethargy, dehydration, or weight loss should indicate the medication should be immediately discontinued and the cat should be assessed for DKA.

What is important to consider regarding the medications is that they are NOT indicated for cats that have already been treated with insulin. These are not drugs meant for treating cats who are insulin-dependent diabetics and neither drug is indicated if your cat has symptoms of diabetic ketoacidosis (DKA). Both drugs increase the risk of DKA as well as euglycemic DKA in cats. Just like DKA, euglycemic DKA is a life-threatening emergency that is characterized by euglycemia (normal range blood glucose), metabolic acidosis, and ketoacidosis. Unlike DKA, euglycemic DKA may be overlooked due to the absence of hyperglycemia. Sudden onset of loss of appetite, anorexia, lethargy, dehydration, or weight loss should indicate the medication should be immediately discontinued and the cat should be assessed for DKA.

For caregivers who are uncomfortable with needles, it is an alternative treatment. It is easier to find someone willing to care for the cat if an insulin injection is not involved or blood glucose testing is not needed. (The need for home testing is not mentioned in any of the manufacturer's materials. However, it is encouraged to do home testing.) The cost appears to be less expensive than insulin. Based on studies, there appears to be a lower potential for hypoglycemia.

Diarrhea is the most common adverse reaction to both drugs. They should be discontinued in cats that develop diarrhea that is unresponsive to conventional treatment. Approximately 20 – 30% of cats have persistent excessive urination and/or water intake that can be a risk factor for dehydration-induced DKA. Cats should be evaluated for concurrent disease including pancreatitis, infectious disease, urinary tract infection, neoplasia, hypersomatotropism (acromegaly), elevated creatinine values that may indicate kidney disease and weight loss.[3]

See chapter on Gila Monsters: Glucagon-like peptide 1 (GLP-1) is an incretin hormone secreted by L cells in the intestines in response to luminal nutrients, bacterial products, and secondary bile acids. GLP-1 acts as an "early warning system" to prepare the body for the nutrient load, particularly glucose that is about to arrive. It increases insulin secretion by sensitizing beta cells in the pancreas to glucose stimulation and decrease glucagon release by alpha cells. GLP-1 analogs have the highest therapeutic potential in diabetic cats however, the effects of GLP-1 analogs have been documented primarily in rodent models. The concern is that with GLP-1 analogs, diabetes is detected with the onset of clinical signs and symptoms which occur after there is widespread beta cell loss. Since GLP-1 maximized the function of the remaining beta cells, the use of this therapy may be limited to cats whose diabetes has been detected quite early. Based on the existing research, these drugs need to be combined with insulin to achieve glycemic control in cats.

The phlorizin-based oral medications to control diabetes in cats came out about a year before my retirement. Like any new medication, I was hesitant to begin using it until reports emerged of success or failure from other veterinarians using it on their client's pets. Also, with the requirement of close monitoring, diabetic ketoacidosis, urinary infections, dehydration etc. meant that there could be dire consequences using the product.

I really like the recently developed Gila monster incretin hormone injection that has become so popular treating humans for diabetes and weight loss. An injection once a week and it can give man a new lease on life. Also, it may in the near future become a pill that you only need to swallow it with water.

Two concerns in cats: Clinicians will need to be monitoring blood on a regular basis to diagnose diabetes before too many pancreas beta cells are lost and some cats diagnosed as diabetic can revert back to normal. Diabetic remission occurs when a cat maintains a normal glucose level for more than four weeks without insulin injections or oral glucose regulating medications. Not all cats go into remission, but those that do may stay that way for months or years. But for cats, it's actually curable in many cases, with as many as 90% achieving diabetic remission in the first few weeks after diagnosis.

According to current medical knowledge, type 2 diabetes in a man has never been considered "cured" as there is no known cure for the disease; however, some individuals can achieve a state of remission through significant lifestyle changes like weight loss and exercise, where they may no longer need medication to manage their blood sugar levels. Also, there is no cure for type 1 diabetes, but there have been some promising developments in research and clinical trials. A pancreas transplant or a transplant of the cells that produce insulin is the only known cure for type 1 diabetes. However, the shortage of organs makes this an option for only a small percentage of people with the disease. In December 2021, an Ohio man who participated in a clinical trial appeared to be the first person to be cured of type 1 diabetes. The man's body was able to control its own.

Stem cell therapy is a promising treatment option for type 1 diabetes. Clinical trials have shown that stem cells can be used to develop regenerative therapies for diseases that are currently incurable.

Other treatments for type 1 diabetes include insulin therapy, diet, and exercise.

1– *Phlorizin, an Important Glucoside: Research Progress on Its Biological Activity and Mechanism, Molecules, 05/29/2024.*

2– *Story of Discovery: SGLT2 inhibitors: harnessing the kidneys to help treat diabetes, updates, 06/09/2016. Research Update June 9, 2016.*

3– *Info New Treatments for Feline Diabetes, discussion 'Feline Health & Main Forum, last edited 02/28/2024.*

CHAPTER 14

METFORMIN...

Ever wonder why certain medications are called "wonder drugs"? Sometimes it's because of the tremendous health benefits the drug provides for a particular condition, like insulin for type 1 diabetes or antibiotics for pneumonia. Or, it might be because the drug is good for many different conditions: aspirin has often been called a wonder drug because it can relieve pain, treat or prevent cardiovascular disease, and even prevent cancer.

Could metformin be joining this list? It's approved in the US to treat type 2 diabetes when used with diet and exercise by people ages 10 and older. But in recent years, interest has grown regarding the potential "repositioning" of it to prevent or treat a variety of other conditions, including aging. Yes, aging. If that's true, wonder drug might be an understatement.

The history of metformin goes back hundreds of years. In Europe, the medicinal herb Galega officinalis was popular for digestive health and to treat urinary problems and other ailments. In 1918 a scientist discovered that one of its ingredients, guanidine, could lower blood sugar.

Medicines containing guanidine, such as metformin and phenformin, were developed to treat diabetes. But they fell out of favor due to serious side effects caused by phenformin, and by the discovery of insulin.[1]

Drug "repositioning", that is, the use of a drug in an indication other than the one for which it was initially marketed, is a growing trend. Its origins lie mainly in the attrition experienced in recent years in the field of new drug discovery. Despite some regulatory and economic challenges, drug repositioning offers many advantages, and a number of recent successes have confirmed both its public health benefits and its commercial value. Some examples of "repositioned" medications are:

As mentioned above, aspirin became the world's bestselling drug and the first synthetic over-the-counter drug in 1915. It is an everyday painkiller for aches and pains such as headache, toothache and periodic pain. It can also be used to treat colds and flu-like symptoms, and to bring down a high temperature. Aspirin has also been "repositioned" as a blood thinner used for cardiovascular diseases and strokes and help to prevent cancer.

Meloxicam is a nonsteroidal anti-inflammatory drug (NSAID) and was patented in 1977 and approved for medical use in the United States in 2000. It is approved to relieve the symptoms of arthritis (juvenile rheumatoid arthritis, osteoarthritis, and rheumatoid arthritis), such as inflammation, swelling, stiffness, and joint pain. However, this medicine does not cure arthritis and will only help as long as it is taken. While research is ongoing, there is currently no established evidence that meloxicam can be "repositioned" to promote hair growth; in fact, some studies indicate that it may even be associated with hair loss as a rare side effect.

Celebrex (celecoxib) was patented in 1993 and approved by the FDA on December 31, 1998. It became available for medical use in 1999. Celecoxib is another nonsteroidal anti-inflammatory drug (NSAID) used to treat mild to moderate pain and help relieve symptoms of arthritis (osteoarthritis, rheumatoid arthritis, or juvenile rheumatoid arthritis), such as inflammation, swelling, stiffness, and joint pain. It has also been "repositioned" to help treat and prevent cancer in a number of ways, including: 1-Some research suggests that celecoxib may reduce the risk of bowel cancer. 2-Small clinical studies have shown that celecoxib can prevent the growth of polyps in patients at high risk of colorectal cancer. 3-A clinical trial found that patients with stage 3 colon cancer and PIK3CA mutations who took celecoxib after surgery lived longer and had longer disease-free survival. 4-Celebrex can help make checkpoint inhibitors more effective by targeting a protein that helps cancer cells escape the immune system. 5-Celebrex can inhibit tumor growth by blocking enzymes needed for cell growth. And, 6-It can reduce the formation of drug resistance. Celebrex has been used in clinical trials for a number of cancers, including colon, breast, lung, prostate, stomach, and head and neck. The mother of my children was diagnosed with stage 4 colon cancer, also known as metastatic cancer, which is the most advanced stage of cancer. It indicates that the cancer has spread beyond its original site to other parts of the body, such as the lymph nodes, bones, liver, lungs, or brain. She was placed on Celebrex and passed in 2003 (2 ½ years after diagnosis).

Thalidomide was originally developed as a sedative in the 1950s. It was marketed as a non-barbiturate hypnotic that could produce deep sleep without hangover or risk of dependency. It was later used to treat a variety of conditions, including: colds, flu, nausea, and morning sickness in pregnant people. It was popular because it was widely available, inexpensive, and accessible without a prescription. However, it was later discovered to be a teratogenic drug that caused birth defects in children of mothers who took it during pregnancy. Thalidomide has now been "repositioned" for use in combination with dexamethasone to treat multiple myeloma. This medicine is also used to treat moderate to severe new lesions of leprosy and as maintenance treatment to prevent and keep erythema nodosum leprosum (skin lesions of leprosy) from coming back.

Sildenafil, the chemical name for Viagra, was originally developed in 1989 to treat hypertension (high blood pressure) and angina pectoris (chest pain caused by heart disease) During clinical trials, researchers noticed that sildenafil was more effective at causing erections than treating angina. The FDA approved "repositioning" sildenafil for treating erectile dysfunction in 1998. It became the first oral treatment for erectile dysfunction in the United States. It is also has been found affective when used to treat pulmonary arterial hypertension. However, it can interact with anti-anginal or anti-hypertensive agents to cause potentially fatal hypotensive crises. *Google Search*

Metformin was rediscovered decades later and approved as a treatment for diabetes in Europe in the 1950s. It wasn't until 1995 that the FDA approved it for use in the US. It has since become the most widely prescribed medication for people with diabetes who cannot control their blood sugar through diet and exercise alone.

Since the approval by the FDA of metformin and its wide use, it has been known that it does more than just help lower blood sugar in people with diabetes. It also has been used to treat much more than helping lower blood sugar. It also offers them cardiovascular benefits, including lower rates of death due to cardiovascular disease. And it sometimes helps people with diabetes lose excess weight. Metformin may also have health benefits for people who don't have diabetes. Doctors have long "repositioned" the use of metformin by prescribing it off-label — that is, to treat conditions outside its approved use, including:

1-Prediabetes. People with prediabetes have elevated blood sugar that isn't yet high enough to qualify as diabetes. Metformin may delay the onset of diabetes or even prevent it among people with prediabetes. 2-Pregnant women may develop elevated blood sugar that returns to normal after delivery. Metformin can help control blood sugar during pregnancy in such women. 3-Polycystic ovary syndrome (PCOS). This disorder tends to affect young women whose ovaries develop multiple cysts. Menstrual irregularities and fertility problems are common. Although the results of clinical studies are mixed, metformin has been prescribed for years for women with PCOS to help with menstrual regulation, fertility, and elevated blood sugar. 4-Antipsychotics are powerful medications prescribed for psychiatric diseases such as schizophrenia. One common side effect is significant weight gain. Metformin may lessen weight gain among some people taking these drugs.

In addition, researchers are investigating the potential of metformin to lower the risk of cancer in persons with type 2 diabetes. These include cancers of the breast, colon, and prostate. 6-Lower risks for dementia and stroke. Some studies have noted less cognitive decline and a lower rate of dementia, as well as a lower rate of stroke, among people with diabetes taking metformin compared with those who were not taking it. 7-Slow aging, prevent age-related disease, and increase lifespan. Preliminary studies suggest that metformin may actually slow aging and increase life expectancy, possibly by improving the body's responsiveness to insulin, antioxidant effects, and improving blood vessel health.

Because the vast majority of research regarding metformin included only people with diabetes or prediabetes, it's unclear whether these potential benefits are limited to people with those conditions, or whether people without diabetes may derive benefit as well.

The safety profile for metformin is quite good. Side effects include nausea, stomach upset, or diarrhea; these tend to be mild. More serious side effects are rare. They include severe allergic reactions and a condition called lactic acidosis, a buildup of lactic acid in the bloodstream. The risk for this is higher among people with significant kidney disease, so doctors tend to avoid prescribing metformin for them.

The bottom line: Metformin is a first-line treatment for type 2 diabetes, according to current diabetes guidelines. It's relatively inexpensive and its potential side effects are well understood. If a person has diabetes and needs metformin to help lower their blood sugar, its other potential health benefits are a wonderful — not harmful — side effect. And if one doesn't have diabetes, its role in preventing or treating diseases, and possibly even slowing aging and extending life expectancy, is much less clear.[1]

After suffering from a stroke, the medical profession finally have me "under their power". I currently have eleven doctors listed that care for my health needs – enough to field a football team (thank goodness us old folks have Medicare). One of the first things they confronted me with was a blood test called an A1C. A1C stands for glycated hemoglobin. It is a measurement of the average blood sugar level over the past two to three months. When blood sugar (glucose) levels are high, it attaches to hemoglobin, a protein in red blood cells. The A1C test measures the percentage of hemoglobin that is glycated (attached to glucose). A higher A1C level indicates higher average blood sugar levels that can be a sign of prediabetes, diabetes, and poorly controlled diabetes. Normal A1C Levels: Less than 5.7%: Normal, 5.7% to 6.4%: Prediabetes, and 6.5% or higher: Diabetes. The A1C test is an important tool for diagnosing and monitoring diabetes. It can help individuals and healthcare providers track blood sugar control and make necessary adjustments to treatment plans. *Google search*

When my primary physician approached me about taking metformin, I "repositioned" myself, and asked him a question that clients often asked me when caring for their pets: "What would you do if it were your pet?" Of course, I asked him what he would do if metformin was recommended for his health. His answer, "I'm currently taking metformin and you are awful young to risk diabetes." I appreciated him believing 78 was a young age and that he recommended a drug that not only may help me from becoming a diabetic and that its other "repositioned" benefits might help me age slowly and have an extended life expectancy.

    1– *Is metformin a wonder drug? Harvard Health Publishing, Robert H. Shmerling, MD, 04/08/2024.*

CHAPTER 15

GILA MONSTERS...

In 2017, the U of Utah natural History Museum relates this legend: Southern Utah is home to a creature that could have stepped straight out of ancient Greek mythology: a 35-pound monster with poisonous, fetid breath; impenetrable, armored skin; and a bite that is always fatal. Adding insult to injury, it takes either the sunset or a clap of thunder to release its deadly bite. It's the dreaded Gila monster, Heloderma suspectum, and like Greek mythology, people once believed all of those "facts," but now we know them to be myths.

The Apache people believed that the Gila monster's breath was lethal, while the Seris and Yaquis believed in the healing power of its hide. Reputable publications like Scientific American in 1890 published facts such as, "The breath is very fetid, and its odor can be detected at some little distance from the lizard. It is supposed that this is one way in which the monster catches the insects and small animals which form a part of its food supply—the foul gas overcoming them.

More surprising is the tale of Mormon pioneers in Utah who believed that Gila monster oil taken from their fatty flesh had supernatural powers. An account from the June 16, 1881, Tombstone Epitaph recounts how the pioneers would send Gila monsters they killed to St. George where they would be processed in a huge boiler for three days and the oil skimmed off the top. It continues: Mormons stricken with remorse congregate from different parts of Utah Territory to this (St. George) temple during the conference. Then may be seen the oil, which is religiously preserved, cast on the water by the officiating bishop, while poor, deluded men and women avail themselves of its efficiency—as they imagine—by entering this tank and bathing in it, thus believing by so doing they are entitled to a corner in heaven.

Not monsters at all, Gila monsters are one of the few species of venomous lizards on the planet. These carnivores are classified as near threatened, and they are native to Arizona, California and Mexico. Gila monsters are black, patterned along their backs with contrasting pink or orange. In the southern subspecies, the reticulated Gila monster, the light markings are broken up to form a reticulated pattern. In the northern subspecies, the banded Gila monster, the light markings generally form an unbroken band across the back. The largest lizard native to the United States, Gila monsters can measure up to about 22 inches (56 centimeters) in total length and its name comes from the Gila River, where the lizards are common.

Gila monsters are desert dwellers, living near washes and arroyos and in semiarid rocky regions of desert scrub or grasslands. Gila monsters also seem to prefer rocky foothills and avoid open flats and agricultural areas. They can live at elevations up to 5,000 feet (1,500 meters). They normally live 20 or more years in human care, though the record is 36 years.

The Gila monster is one of only a small number of venomous lizards (including the Mexican beaded lizard, the Komodo dragon and some Australian species). It can bite quickly and hold on tenaciously. Rather than injecting venom through hollow fangs like venomous snakes, Gilas have enlarged grooved teeth in their lower jaw where venom glands are located. When they bite, their powerful jaws chew the venom secreted near the teeth through capillary action along the grooves in these teeth. Gila monster venom is about as toxic as that of a western diamondback rattlesnake. However, a relatively small amount of venom is introduced in a Gila bite. Because it often attaches itself firmly to its victims, there are reports that Gilas at times must be forcibly disengaged from bite victims.

Gila monsters most often raid nests to prey on small birds and eggs. They also catch small mammals, lizards, frogs, insects and carrion. They can eat up to one-third of their body weight in one meal.

Their large size means they can store more energy than smaller lizards. They store fat both in their tails and their bodies. Their low metabolic rates and ability to eat large meals combined with their capacity to store fat, make frequent searching for food unnecessary. Therefore, Gila monsters often stay hidden underground. It has been suggested that Gilas can consume all the calories they need for a year in three or four large meals. Their top speed is 1.5 miles per hour (2.4 kilometers per hour).

They are diurnal, but most active in the morning. Gila monsters spend most of their lives hidden below the ground. Most of their aboveground activity occurs in three months in the spring. They are usually solitary animals, but do gather in communal areas in the spring for mating. Gila monsters have a home range of about 1 square mile (1.6 square kilometers). They mate in the spring, which is also when food is most abundant. In late April to early June, courtship and male-to-male combat takes place. Females lay two to 12 leathery eggs that spend the winter below ground and hatch the next spring after 120 to 150 days. Hatchlings are about 6 inches (15 centimeters) long and are miniature replicas of their parents. Hatchlings are on their own immediately. *Smithsonian Magazine*

In a 2024 article, Scientist Scott Tavers in Forbes Innovation Science, explains the dangers of Gila Monster venom: Unlike most of the world's lizards, the Gila monster venom allows it to fend off predators despite its lack of agility. They've lived in the Sonoran Desert for millions of years, adapting over time to an increasingly arid environment and evolving to store water for survival in the hot, dry Arizona summers.

Most venomous creatures use their venom to capture their prey. Gila monsters are very large, slow-moving and they don't need to envenomate the small prey they eat. The Gila monster's venomous bite evolved solely for self-defense purposes against predators such as coyotes, owls, and hawks. They don't aggressively attack or lunge at people and unless provoked bites are very rare.

In March of 2024, a 34-year-old man from Lakewood, Colorado died after being bitten by one of his pet Gila monsters, which he owned illegally. This incident is particularly notable because, prior to this, there were no confirmed fatalities from Gila monster bites after 1930. Following the bite, the man immediately exhibited symptoms typical of venom exposure: vomiting, losing consciousness and ceasing to breathe. Despite being rushed to the hospital, he succumbed to his condition days later. The exact cause of his death remains uncertain, with speculation about whether an allergic reaction to the venom or the venom's inherent toxicity was the fatal factor.

According to a 2018 case study of a 41-year-old man who fully recovered from a Gila monster envenomation, bites can lead to two types of venom effects: local and systemic. The local effect happens right where one is bitten, causing severe pain, swelling and a tingling sensation. If the venom affects the whole body, which is more serious, one might experience a dangerous drop in blood pressure and swelling in the airways, making it hard to breathe.

A 2021 review based on 22 cases of Gila monster envenomation found that three life-threatening conditions can be at play: 1- Angioedema. This is swelling similar to hives, but it occurs under the skin instead of on the surface. It is particularly dangerous when it causes the throat or respiratory pathways to swell, leading to difficulty in breathing or even blocking the airway completely. 2- Significant fluid losses. This refers to the body losing a lot of fluid through diarrhea, vomiting and sweating. This can lead to a drop in potassium levels in the blood (hypokalemia) and sometimes a condition called metabolic acidosis, where the body produces too much acid or the kidneys aren't removing enough acid from the body. 3- Atrioventricular conduction disorders. These are problems with the electrical signals in the heart, which can mimic the symptoms of cardiac ischemia (a condition where the heart muscle doesn't get enough oxygen from the blood). It affects the heart's ability to pump blood effectively.

Despite these potentially life-threatening effects, there is no antivenom available. The lack of antivenom for Gila monster bites does not imply that venomous lizards are more dangerous than venomous snakes, for which antivenoms for many species exist. The rarity of Gila monster envenomation and low fatality rate may contribute to the lack of antivenom. Incidents involving Gila monster bites are exceedingly uncommon, especially when compared to snake bites, which are a significant global health issue, killing between 81,000 to 137,000 humans each year.

What does the Gila monster have that humans don't have? The key to more effortless weight-loss. It turns out the venom of this small, Southwestern lizard played a critical role in developing a whole new class of anti-obesity drugs, called GLP-1s. One of the newest GLP-1s is called semaglutide. It is sold under the brand names of Ozempic and Wegovy and has been taking Hollywood by storm. The rising demand and shortages for these types of drugs is because they mimic key hormones that tell us to feel full. But before semaglutide became the darling shot of Hollywood, scientists discovered that compounds in the venom of Gila monsters could help drug developers make better diabetes medications than they'd ever had before.

Researching Gila monster saliva really began with Daniel Drucker a scientist and endocrinologist at the University of Toronto who has dedicated his career to understanding the universe of hormones in the body, which do everything from regulating appetite to helping with digestion. His curiosity about the Gila monster led to a call with a zoo in Utah. In 1995, Drucker had a lizard shipped from Utah to his lab and began experiments on the deadly venom. Ten years later, a synthetic version of a hormone in the venom became the first medicine of its kind approved to treat type 2 diabetes.

It was in the early 1990s when government researcher Dr. John Eng discovered the special hormone in Gila monsters' venom. The hormone is quite similar to a hunger-regulating hormone humans harbor in the small intestine, which helps control blood sugar levels. In people, it's called glucagon-like peptide-1. In Gila monsters, Eng named it exendin-4. Exendin-4 degrades more slowly than the human form of GLP-1, lasting for hours instead of minutes. That means it's a much better model for drug development, since it wouldn't be practical to take a drug dozens of times a day.

At first, Eng tried to point this remarkable feature of Gila monster spit out to pharmaceutical makers and the government. He shopped his idea around at the Department of Veterans Affairs, where he worked at the time, as well as several different pharmaceutical companies, but didn't have much success. In the end, he patented the molecule in 1995, and licensed the discovery to a now-defunct biotech startup called Amylin.

Amylin used Eng's Gila monster research to create a synthetic hormone, called extenatide. Extenatide was approved by the Food and Drug Administration (FDA) in 2005 to treat type 2 diabetes. It's still used by hundreds of thousands of children and adults with diabetes today. Extenatide was the very first GLP-1-mimicking drug. It ushered in a whole new class of diabetes medications that are arguably safer, and more effective, than previous treatments were. More recently, GLP-1s have been designed to also target obesity.

Today's GLP-1s work to help people lose weight because they mimic a hormone the small intestine makes naturally, which regulates hunger in several different key ways. When a patient's blood sugar levels are high, GLP-1 drugs send signals to their pancreas to secrete more insulin — but the hormone-mimicking doesn't stop there. GLP-1s also send signals to a person's brain, telling their body to feel fuller with less food. Finally, GLP-1s slow down digestion, changes the way a person's body turns food into energy.

Over the years, people have turned to extreme and unlikely interventions to try to lose weight, from jaw wiring, laxatives, and vagotomies to lap band operations and fen-phen, a "miracle" diet drug that was ultimately recalled. Fen-Phen was a combination of Pondimin (fenfluramine), Redux (dexfenfluramine), and phentermine. It was considered a miracle diet pill that suppressed appetite and increased calorie burning. However, the FDA removed the drug from the market in 1997 after finding that it caused heart defects and rare lung diseases. A lawsuit was filed by patients who experienced heart defects after taking Fen-Phen. The lawsuit alleged that American Home Products failed to warn consumers and physicians of the risks associated with the drug. A settlement was open to all who took Fen-Phen, regardless of whether they filed a lawsuit. The settlement became final in 2002.[1]

The new once a week injectable treatment from a Danish pharmaceutical company that had hired many leading diabetes and obesity scientists as consultants, is poised to more safely help many people control health-threatening diabetes and obesity. The drug's most common side effects — nausea, diarrhea, constipation, and vomiting — were mostly short-lived. The adverse reactions might be caused by how the drug differs from the naturally occurring peptide hormone: The hormone acts mostly locally and degrades quickly, while the medicine works mainly on the brain and is designed to stick around in the body. That's where the nausea, vomiting probably derive from.

Yet many people with obesity may not seek out semaglutide, and doctors may not prescribe it to them — not only because of the dangerous history of weight loss medications, but also because of a persistent bias and stigma around a disease that now afflicts nearly half of Americans. Obesity is still widely viewed as a personal responsibility problem, despite scientific evidence to the contrary. And history has shown that the most effective medical interventions, such as bariatric surgery – currently the gold standard for treating obesity – often go unused in favor of dieting and exercise, which for many don't work.

Bariatric surgery reduces the size of the stomach, limits how much food a person can eat, and changes the body's ability to digest food. This can lead to changes in appetite, metabolism, and feelings of fullness. Bariatric surgery can help with weight loss and improve or resolve many obesity-related diseases, such as type 2 diabetes, heart disease, and sleep apnea. Studies show that bariatric surgery can reduce the risk of early death by 30–50%).[1]

October 24, 2024, NBC News reported that recent preclinical evidence suggests that GLP-1s also protect against neurodegeneration, and neuroinflammation (pain). In addition, it is used to treat obesity, type 2 diabetes, cardiovascular diseases, chronic effects of smoking, and alcohol drinking - all of which are risk factors for Alzheimer's disease. Novo Nordisk 's blockbuster diabetes drug Ozempic may reduce the risk of developing Alzheimer's disease, suggesting its potential to delay or prevent the memory-robbing condition, according to a study released.

During my 50 years of companion animal veterinary practice obesity was a subject often discussed during a dog or cat's life. Obesity in dogs and cats can lead to a range of health issues including joint problems like osteoarthritis, increased risk of diabetes, respiratory difficulties, heart disease, decreased lifespan, higher risk of certain cancers, complications during anesthesia, and reduced mobility due to excess weight putting strain on joints and muscles; essentially impacting their quality of life significantly.

I first confronted pet obesity with Bernie, a miniature dachshund I had rescued while attending Purdue University Veterinary School. I started him on a commercial prescription weight loss diet that he refused to eat. I finally resorted to using some of the advice I recalled being given by our pediatrician for our young children: Be patient, it can take time before a pet is willing to try a new food. Don't force, pressure, or yell - it can make the situation worse. Give praise when your pet is interacting with the food, even if it's just looking at it or smelling it. Prepare the food in different ways and mix other foods the pet likes with the food. I finally resorted to the "I'll give him only this food and he will eat it or starve himself to death" mentality. I offered him the food and he refused it on a daily basis. I began to feel guilty that Bernie might really "starve himself to death" and one morning told myself that if he hadn't started to eat the diet when I came home from work – I would place him back on a regular diet and he could reach the goal he seemed to desire, "be the fattest wiener dog in the world when he took his last breath." You may have guessed it. When I got home, he had finally started to eat the special diet.

Companion animal obesity has emerged as a significant veterinary health concern globally, with escalating rates posing challenges for preventive and therapeutic interventions. Obesity not only can lead to immediate health problems but also contributes to various comorbidities affecting animal well-being and longevity, with consequent emotional and financial burdens on owners. While past treatment strategies have shown limited success, recent breakthroughs in human medicine present new opportunities for addressing this complex issue in companion animals. These drugs, originally developed to treat type 2 diabetes in humans and subsequently repurposed to treat obesity, have demonstrated remarkable weight loss effects in rodents, non-human primates and people.

Additionally, newer drug combinations have shown even more promising results in clinical trials. Despite current cost and supply challenges, advancements in oral and/or extended-release formulations and increased production may make these drugs more accessible for veterinary use. Thus, these drugs may have utility in companion animal weight management, and future feasibility studies exploring their efficacy and safety in treating companion animal obesity are warranted.

The ongoing rise in companion animal obesity rates may involve genetics, diet and lifestyle habits. Factors such as age, sex and surgical sterilization also contribute to obesity, emphasizing the multifactorial nature of the condition and its association with behavioral factors and feeding practices. However, the single most important factor contributing to pet obesity is the owner's underestimation of their pet's body condition and misconception of what an animal at a healthy weight looks like.

Additionally, there is a clear association between owners' overweight/obesity and the weight status of their pets, emphasizing the interplay between human and animal health. This bidirectional impact of obesity in both human and animal health reinforces the One Health concept, which emphasizes the interdependence of the health of humans, animals and the environment and advocates for therapeutic strategies that consider the diverse factors influencing this epidemic.

Obesity not only poses immediate health risks including high blood pressure and breathing difficulties, but also contributes to the development of various comorbidities, such as type 2 diabetes, heart and liver diseases, osteoarthritis and cancer. Obesity-related comorbidities contribute to diminished animal well-being, which imposes emotional and financial burdens on pet owners. Additionally, obesity leads to profound consequences on animal longevity, and a negative correlation between obesity and lifespan has been demonstrated in both cats and dogs.

Current treatment of companion animal obesity involves a multifaceted approach with dietary management and behavioral modifications. This includes a controlled calorie intake through balanced diets, and encouraging physical activity, underscoring the necessity of collaborative efforts between veterinarians and pet owners associated with comprehensive strategies to address the complexities of companion animal obesity. However, the alarming rates of obesity worldwide make it clear that present strategies have not been effective.

One reason for the failure of current pet obesity treatments is the lack of owner compliance. Low compliance has been interpreted to result from an insufficient understanding of the importance of addressing pet obesity by the owners, especially when the benefits are unclear or long-term, and from the central role that feeding plays in emotional and social interactions between owners and their pets, especially dogs. In communicating with owners, veterinarians must highlight not only the impact of obesity on overall health and lifespan but especially short-term health improvements and financial benefits to increase treatment adherence. In this sense, the most appealing reason from the owners' perspective for the prevention and treatment of obesity may be to avoid the development of type 2 diabetes (T2D), a debilitating chronic disease commonly occurring in cats that is treated with expensive and laborious therapeutics. Most patients with T2D will die prematurely within 2 years of their diagnosis due to the inability of owners to follow therapeutic protocols. Recently, the assessment of glycosylated hemoglobin (A1C) and glycated proteins (fructosamine) have been optimized so that feline pre-diabetic conditions can be successfully diagnosed and treated before disease onset. Therefore, pre-diabetic cats would especially benefit from weight loss in terms of significantly reducing their risk for T2D…

Added: Both Hb A1C and fructosamine are blood tests used to monitor blood sugar levels, but while A1C reflects average blood glucose over a longer period (2-3 months), fructosamine provides a shorter-term picture of glucose levels over the past 2-3 weeks, as it measures glycated proteins in the blood rather than glycated hemoglobin which A1C measures; essentially, they are both indicators of glycemic control but with different timeframes, making fructosamine useful in situations where rapid changes in blood sugar need to be monitored. A1C is typically used for routine diabetes management, while fructosamine might be preferred in situations like rapid insulin adjustments, pregnancy, or when there are concerns about red blood cell turnover affecting A1C accuracy (e.g., sickle cell anemia). Although they both measure blood sugar levels, A1C and fructosamine results may not perfectly align, and the correlation between them can be influenced by factors like albumin levels. Diabetic dogs and cats are usually monitored by using fructosamine levels…

In contrast, several obesity drugs are available for human use, and a promising new generation of drugs has recently been approved by the FDA and adopted widely. Why are these drugs already available to humans but these or similar drugs are not used in companion animals? The lack of weight loss drugs targeting pets may represent a substantial and overlooked opportunity for the veterinary market.

Consider the incretins that are approved for humans and developed from Gila monster venom discussed above. The incretins are a new class of anti-obesity and anti-type 2 diabetes drugs, called GLP-1s. As is often the case, the origins of the current clinical treatments for obesity can be traced back to basic science discoveries that initially did not appear to have any clear relationship to body weight regulation or obesity. The incretin effect, which indicated that a GI hormone(s) could increase insulin secretion from pancreatic β-cells, was demonstrated experimentally in 1964; the first hormone responsible for the incretin effect, GIP, was identified and sequenced in the early 1970s; and a second incretin, GLP-1, was identified in 1987; the first GLP-1-based drug, was approved for T2D treatment in humans in 2005.

Initial Phase 1 and 2 clinical trials indicate that orally active forms of these types of drugs produce weight loss in humans comparable to that obtained with injections, suggesting they can be effectively administered orally. The availability of orally active versions of these drugs and the newer drugs in development would likely facilitate their use in animals such as dogs and cats, as it would avoid ongoing owner injections of the animals.[2]

Weight-loss drugs like Ozempic may decrease your risk of developing 42 health conditions, but increase your chance of experiencing 19 others, according to one of the most comprehensive studies-of-its-kind to date. Glucagon-like peptide 1 receptor agonists (GLP-1RAs) have become increasingly popular over the past decade for the treatment of type 2 diabetes and obesity, with versions like Ozempic and Wegovy becoming household names. These drugs help treat diabetes by promoting the release of insulin and helping to reduce blood sugar levels. But they have also been linked to weight loss, potentially by slowing down the digestion of food and curbing appetite. In 2024, Wegovy also received regulatory approval in the U.S. to treat heart disease, although the exact mechanism-of-action is unclear. Evidence is additionally emerging to suggest that GLP-1RAs may help prevent the onset of conditions such as Alzheimer's disease and help patients to manage others like substance-use disorders. However, concerns have also been raised regarding the negative side effects of taking GLP-1RAs, including reports of gastrointestinal issues.

Now, in a new study, scientists have compiled what they say is the clearest ever picture of the effectiveness and risks associated with taking GLP-1RAs. In the study, researchers assessed the impact of taking GLP-1RAs on the health of 215,000 people with type 2 diabetes over around four years. They then compared these effects to a control group of more than one million individuals who received different types of anti-diabetic drugs. Data on all participants was obtained from the U.S. Department of Veteran Affairs.

Overall, the researchers found that GLP-1RAs have many beneficial effects, some of which were previously recognized. For instance, those who took GLP-1RAs had a 9%, 8% and 12% reduced risk of having a heart attack, deep vein thrombosis and Alzheimer's, respectively, compared to controls. They were also less likely to develop substance-use disorders, including alcohol-use disorders and cannabis-use disorders (both an 11% lower risk), as well as having a 12% lower risk of experiencing bacterial infections. These effects may somehow be linked to both the health benefits of physically losing weight, as well as other effects of GLP-1RAs in the body, such as reducing inflammation and influencing reward signaling in the brain.

However, these benefits did not come without risks, the researchers observed. For example, GLP-1RAs also increased people's odds of developing gastrointestinal issues such as abdominal pain (12%), plus low blood pressure (6% higher risk) and arthritis (11% higher risk).

"We tend to think of drugs as being surgically designed to do only one thing, but the reality is, it's almost never like this."[3]

> "I walk through the grass in my bare feet.
> – There is something special there.
> Something that no man has or will
> ever create – the spark of life.
> All plants and animals carry their own
> history – their genetic code.
> Nature is always true, can be unforgiving
> and grave – the rules never change.
> Man makes the rules that are ever changing
> – seeming only fair for those in power.
> I place my love and trust in nature – it has
> never hurt when I abide by the rules.
> Man promotes pride, and agitation – nature gives
> my soul peace and harmony..." *WR Hoge*

A few weeks ago, a friend of mine called and asked if I could come over to his house and inject a medication prescribed him by his doctor. It appears that his physician felt that he was "too fat" and a pre diabetic. I told him that I would help him with the injection if he had written information I could review before the event. He later texted me that his wife had done the deed.

Yesterday, my wife and I fasted for 12 hours and submitted ourselves to a lab full of phlebotomists to take blood for our next doctor's appointment. Part of our lab work was to evaluate our A1C. We are both on metformin to help prevent type 2 diabetes and if our A1Cs advance beyond a certain limit – our doctor may call us "too fat", approaching diabetes, and have us pick up at the pharmacists a pen like object full of a GLP-1 medication for injection in our bodies. If this is the case, my hope is the oral form of GLP-1 has been made available.

As the 2025 Hollywood awards season kicked off with the Golden Globes on Sunday night, so too did another round of jokes, speculation and sponsorships linking the industry to the use of GLP-1 medications for weight loss. Comedian Nikki Glaser, host of the 2025 Golden Globe Awards ceremony, dove right in at the start of her opening monologue: "Good evening, and welcome to the 82nd Golden Globes—Ozempic's biggest night," she began. The wisecrack, of course, is a nod to the rumors of the rampant off-label, purely cosmetic use of drugs like Novo Nordisk's Ozempic and Wegovy, and Eli Lilly's Mounjaro and Zepbound by celebrities hoping to slim down for roles or red-carpet appearances, contrary to the meds' approved uses to treat only those who are clinically overweight or obese, or who have Type 2 diabetes.

"GLP-1's seems to be too good to be true. Since you're using it – Can't take my eyes off of you.

You've become like Heaven to touch and I want to help inject that drug in your butt.

At long last, carnal and devilish love has arrived. I thank God for this stuff and that we're both still alive.

Pardon the way that I stare – There's nothing like GLP-1's to compare. Even though it sometimes leaves us weak without words left to speak. I need you baby to help warm the lonely night and rub my feet..." *Adapted from: Can't Take My Eyes off You song, Carly E. Simon*

Those rumors reached such a fever pitch last year that Lilly took it upon itself to produce a pair of commercials calling out that off-label use. One of the ads seemed to take aim specifically at the practice in Hollywood: It began airing shortly before the 2024 Academy Awards and said, "Some people have been using medicine never meant for them, for the smaller dress or tux, for a big night, for vanity. But that's not the point. People whose health is affected by obesity are the reason we work on these medications. It matters who gets them."

"Son of a gun. You walked into the party like you were walking onto a yacht - Your hat strategically dipped below one eye, your scarf it was apricot, you had one eye in the mirror, as you watched yourself gavotte. You probably think this song is abought you – You're so vain.

You had me several years ago when I was still quite naïve – not knowing that you were taking GLP-1 and those needle scares weren't to control your highs and lows. No, this song is not about you – it's about some people taking the medicine never meant for them.

You, the special ones, wanting the smaller dress or tux, for a big night, for vanity – taking away the GLP-1 from the people whose health is affected by obesity they've worked on these medications for.

You probably think this song is about you - You're so vain (so vain)

Don't you don't you, don't, don't you know – you're so vain.

It's the GLP-1 you're taking from them in need – You're so vain (so vain)"

Adapted from: You're So Vain song by Carly Simon

1– *We wouldn't have Ozempic without Gila monsters — their hunger-regulating venom inspired weight-loss drugs, Hilary Brueck, 03/22/2023.*

2– *Advances in Drug Treatments for Companion Animal Obesity, Biology, 05/11/2024.*

3– *Ozempic-style drugs tied to more than 60 health benefits and risks in biggest study-of-its-kind, LifeScience, Emily Cooke, 01/19/2025.*

CHAPTER 16

SNAKE ISLAND AND THE GOLDEN LANCEHEAD SNAKE...

The Golden lancehead snake, scientifically known as Bothrops insularis is one of the most venomous snakes in the world. The snake is endemic to the Ilha de Queimada Grande Island, popularly known as Snake Island. The island, situated about 90 miles off the coast of the Brazilian state of Sao Paulo, covers an area of 110 acres. Snake Island consists of tropical and subtropical moist forests, shrubs, and open spaces. At first glance, the island seems like one of those tropical destinations everyone dreams about. However, the island is home to thousands of venomous snakes that inhabit the island, making it one of the most dangerous places on earth. Golden lancehead snakes present on the island are also not safe on the island because they face threats from poachers, habitat degradation, and diseases. In the last 15 years, their population has declined by nearly 50% by some estimates. The species is currently listed as critically endangered by the International Union for Conservation of Nature.

Experts believe that a bite from the lancehead snake on a human carries a 7% chance of death. Even with treatment, humans still face a 3% chance of dying. Venom from the snake is likely to cause brain hemorrhaging, kidney failure, intestinal bleeding, and necrosis of muscular tissue. Lancehead viper venom is hemotoxic, which means that it destroys red blood cells, disrupts blood clotting, causes organ degeneration, and tissue damage. The venom thus helps digest the prey before the snake swallows it. The venom is also known to have neurotoxic properties, meaning that it can cause muscle paralysis, respiratory difficulty, and death. Chemical analysis of the snake's venom indicates that it is five times more potent than that of its mainland cousin, Bothrops jararaca. The venom also acts faster than that of its cousins. There are several legends about fatalities on the island. One such tale tells of a fisherman who strayed and decided to search for bananas on the island, his body was discovered days later in his boat, with snake bite marks on it. From 1909 to the 1920s, there were a few people who lived on the island to run its lighthouse. According to other local tales, the islands last lighthouse keeper and his entire family died after numerous snakes slithered through the windows of his home and attacked them. Operations at the lighthouse have since been automated and only require annual maintenance services from the Brazilian Navy. The island is also currently uninhabited, and adventure travel to the island is not allowed by the authorities. However, a few scientists are allowed on the island to study the snakes. The scientists also occasionally milk golden lancehead snakes for their venom, which is used in developing medication.

Golden lancehead snakes feed on perching migratory birds that stopover at the island and lizards. There are also incidents of cannibalism among the snakes. Golden lancehead newborns and younger snakes feed on invertebrates. Scientists believe that about 11,000 years ago, a rise in sea levels gradually separated the Ilha da Queimada Grande Island from mainland Brazil, leading to the isolation of the species. The snakes, therefore, evolved over thousands of years on a different path compared to their mainland cousins. A lack of ground predators meant that they reproduced rapidly. However, the only challenge was that the island also lacked ground prey. The snakes, therefore, slither up the trees to hunt migratory birds. Golden lancehead snakes also evolved one of the most potent venoms in the world that kill prey almost instantly.[1] On the mainland of Brazil, chemical analysis of the snake's venom indicates that it is five times less potent than its cousin that lives on Snake Island. Even so, an average of 29,000 snakebite cases are reported each year, resulting in approximately 120 fatalities and around 600 cases with curable sequelae, excluding unreported cases. Among venomous snakes, the Viperidae family, particularly the subfamilies Crotalinae (including snakes of the genera Crotalus, Bothrops, and Lachesis), are noteworthy. Bothrops snakebites cause systemic reactions, including severe blood clotting disorders such as disseminated intravascular coagulation. Complications such as hypotension and hypovolemic shock can lead to fatalities. Severe local reactions comprising edema, pain, hemorrhage, and necrosis are common, often resulting in substantial tissue loss and potential limb amputations.

The only effective treatment for snakebite envenomation is specific antivenom. Despite its efficacy in reducing lethality and reversing systemic effects, antivenom inadequately addresses local reactions, which cause severe sequelae. This deficiency is due to the rapid onset of these local actions and the fact that antivenom cannot reverse established or triggered damage or neutralize endogenous mediators involved in the process.[2]

In the early 1980s, hypertension conferences were routinely enlivened by the poisonous Brazilian viper, Bothrops jararaca. With its striking zig-zag markings and aggressively protruding tongue, images of the snake were a welcome break from graphs and tables in presentations about captopril — the first of the angiotensin-converting enzyme (ACE) inhibitors, whose effects on blood pressure mechanisms mimicked those of the snake's venom. When the cardiovascular juggernaut alighted in Sao Paulo, Brazil, for a major congress in 1984, there was even an opportunity for delegates to visit a snake farm and see the beast in all its glory.

The discovery of the ACE inhibitors and the creation of captopril was one of the really great advances in cardiovascular medicine, alongside beta blockers, calcium channel blockers and statins. ACE inhibitors work by blocking the activity of an enzyme called angiotensin-converting enzyme (ACE), which prevents the conversion of angiotensin I into angiotensin II, a potent vasoconstrictor; by inhibiting this conversion, ACE inhibitors effectively relax blood vessels, leading to lowered blood pressure and improved blood flow throughout the body. When captopril arrived, there was a lot of excitement and a feeling that acting on the renin-angiotensin system was going to be a very important step forward.

ACE was identified as the enzyme responsible for the conversion of angiotensin I to the vasoconstrictor substance, angiotensin II, in the mid-1950s. In 1968, studies showed that peptides from the Brazilian viper's venom inhibited the activity of ACE from dog lung. Researchers at the time were wary about the finding because at the time the renin-angiotensin system was thought to play a role only in the most serious "malignant" hypertension. However, it was decided that there was enough clinical interest to proceed with trying to develop synthetic ACE inhibitors that were orally active.

Between 1970 and 1973, Squibb scientists randomly tested about 2,000 chemical structures for ACE inhibitor activity but could not find what they wanted. Their luck changed in 1974, when they decided to follow up some newly published research on an inhibitor of carboxypeptidase A

— an exopeptidase thought to have a similar active site to ACE. Then, 60 compounds and 18 months later, they had captopril, and early clinical studies confirmed its antihypertensive effects.

The 1981 launch of captopril brought fresh headaches for Squibb as a battery of papers and letters started to appear reporting serious hypotensive effects of the high doses of captopril that were initially recommended. It was found out that the original dose-ranging studies for captopril were carried out during the rebound phase of drug resistance seen in many patients after the first dose, unrecognized at the time of the studies. As a result, the recommended doses were far higher than necessary.

Even when the doses of captopril that were used in the 1980s started to come down, some patients experienced a first-dose hypotension and, when it became clear that ACE inhibitors had a role to play in heart failure, the need to resolve the issue of dosing and hypotension took on a new urgency. It was discovered that there is greater activation of the renin-angiotensin system in heart failure patients because of the use of diuretics, and so the same dose of ACE inhibitor produces a much greater effect than in hypertensive patients. While most hypertensive patients could cope with feeling a little dizzy, the combination of low blood pressure, deteriorating renal function and increased plasma potassium could result in arrhythmias and deaths in heart failure patients.

By the mid-80s, captopril had a rival in the longer-acting Merck ACE inhibitor enalapril, which initially appeared to have a better side effect profile as well as an easier dosing schedule. However, as with captopril, the launch dose of enalapril appears to have been too high, and reports of severe hypotension after the first dose in heart failure patients led to recommendations that initiation of all ACE inhibitor treatment should be carried out under strict medical supervision. A serious question mark hung over the future of ACE inhibitors, at least in heart failure.

The outlook for ACE inhibitors changed dramatically in 1987 when a study showed a 31 per cent reduction in mortality at one year in patients with severe heart failure who were treated with enalapril. Dropping the dose of enalapril in high-risk patients reduced the problem of hypotension to acceptable levels. The trial was stopped early by the data and safety monitoring board of the study and the triallists were called to a meeting. They were pretty furious but, when the results were presented to them, there was spellbound silence. There had never been such a significant reduction in heart failure mortality in a major trial.

Further trials produced equally impressive results in less severe disease. In a September 1992 issue of the New England Journal of Medicine, the Survival and Ventricular Enlargement (SAVE) trial reported a 20 per cent reduction in mortality in heart attack patients with left ventricular dysfunction treated with captopril, and the Studies of Left Ventricular Dysfunction (SOLVD) trial showed a 29 per cent reduction in heart failure and deaths in patients with asymptomatic left ventricular dysfunction.

As it became clear that ACE inhibitors saved lives, there was renewed effort to find a way of administering them safely to heart failure patients. Admitting every patient to hospital for a test dose was impractical and expensive. On the basis of a comparison of large fixed doses of captopril and enalapril, which showed that the longer acting drug produced more prolonged hypotensive effects, a system was introduced for administering a small test dose of the short-acting captopril and, if all went well, increasing the dose or switching to enalapril.

It was all a nonsense because doctors now take the opposite view, that the longer acting ACE inhibitors, such as lisinopril (benazepril) and perindopril, which are currently in use, have a slower onset of action and are therefore less likely to cause problems than a fast onset, shorter acting drug. What really mattered was the dose, and the need to start on a reasonable dose and move up gradually rather than starting high and reducing the dose, as tended to happen in the US. In 1999, the Assessment of Treatment with Lisinopril and Survival (ATLAS) study provided the evidence needed to support this approach, showing that maintaining patients on low doses of ACE inhibitor was unlikely to achieve the survival benefits seen in the earlier outcome studies, but that there was little advantage of using high doses over intermediate doses.

Before ACE inhibitors, heart failure patients were treated with bed rest, digoxin and diuretics. Now, they are put on an exercise program and treated with a cocktail or diuretics, ACE inhibitors, beta blockers and other medication. As a result, patients have better control of symptoms, there are fewer admissions to hospital, and there is a reduction in mortality. The gloomy side is that heart failure is becoming more common as patients get older and more survive heart attacks. ACE inhibitors contributed to the improvement in outlook, but they haven't provided a cure.[3]

Golden lancehead snakes are in very high demand in the black market. Wealthy animal collectors from around the world are particularly interested in the species due to their uniqueness. Overzealous scientists, eager to make medical breakthroughs, also drive the high demand on the black market. The island is therefore frequented by wildlife smugglers keen to cash in on the lethal vipers. Experts estimate that a single golden lancehead snake can go for between $10,000 and $30,000, which is an attractive sum of money for the poachers. Research suggests that the illegal removal of individuals from the island could be a reason behind the decline of the golden lancehead population.

Poaching is particularly harmful to the species since it targets the largest and thus the oldest individuals, which are also the most reproductively mature. Targeting such older snakes means that fewer snakes in the population reach old age classes leaving higher proportions of younger snakes. Studies also reveal that body size is usually positively related to the ability of producing an abundance of offspring (fecundity), especially in female reptiles. A decline of older and larger individuals could, therefore, lead to a drop in fecundity, which negatively affects population growth Conservationists are also concerned about habitat destruction on mainland Brazil. Although the snake island is miles away, many of the birds that arrive on the island (a primary source of food for the snakes) originate from mainland Brazil. The golden lancehead snake preys on two out of 41 migratory birds that seasonally arrive on the island. The tyrant flycatcher is the most common prey among adult pit vipers. The bird is found on the coast of southeastern Brazil towards the end of the wet season (austral summer). Low numbers of tyrant flycatcher birds making stops on the island in the corresponding season results in low survival rates of the snake population due to a scarcity of food. Prey availability also affects reproduction. Golden lancehead snakes have lower breeding frequency than the B. jararaca species found on the mainland, which enjoys relatively higher prey availability rates. The observation indicates that there is a close relationship between prey availability and population trends. Migratory birds, therefore, help maintain a delicate balance on the island's ecosystem. Land clearing and the destruction of forests on mainland Brazil essentially robs migratory birds of their natural habitat leading to a decline in the bird population, which consequently affects the delicate balance on the island. Such human-made destructions have led to a steep decline in the number of migratory birds making stopovers on the island, which means less food for the snakes.

The Brazilian Navy has also been accused of destructive vegetation clearing around the lighthouse. Such activity negatively affects the habitat on the island, which consequently affects the snake population. Since the species is only found on the island, any alteration of its environment can have potentially devastating effects on the snake population.[1]

Before ACE inhibitors, heart failure patients were treated with bed rest, digoxin and diuretics. Now, they are put on an exercise program and treated with a cocktail or diuretics, ACE inhibitors, beta blockers and other medication. As a result, patients have better control of symptoms, there are fewer admissions to hospital, and there is a reduction in mortality. The gloomy side is that heart failure is becoming more common as patients get older and more survive heart attacks. ACE inhibitors contributed to the improvement in outlook, but they haven't provided a cure.[3]

We should give thanks to the poisonous Brazilian viper, Bothrops jararaca, with its striking zig-zag markings and aggressively protruding tongue from Snake Island for its poisonous venom and the persistence of scientists developing ACE inhibitors for folks like me. My particular brand is Benazepril taken with a concoction of five other medications to control my blood pressure.

And, if you ever find yourself stranded on snake island, your best bet is to avoid the forests and stay on the rocky shore, where you're unlikely to bump into a golden lancehead. If you venture into the forest, watch out for vipers overhead and on the ground. Edible plants and animals are limited, but you could eat one of the snakes (if you can catch it). Just be sure to remove the head, where the venom glands are located, and bury it in the ground away from your camp, before you attempt to skin and cook it. Remember many a man has been bitten by a "dead snake." There is a saying that "snakes don't die until after sunset." People in the know say this is a common folklore myth, meaning it is not true; once a snake is killed, it is dead regardless of the time of day, and the idea that it would stay alive until sundown is simply a superstition. However, even with the head cut off the body continues to move and it is very creepy removing the skin and cutting it up when it is still moving.

If you suffer a golden lancehead bite, you'll need to get medical attention very quickly: the venom can kill in under an hour, although only around seven per cent of people die. The island is patrolled by the navy, so a speedy rescue isn't impossible.[4]

1– *Venomous Golden Lancehead Of Brazil's Snake Island: Why It Must Be Left Alone? World Altas, 12/05/2019.*

2– *Understanding Bothrops jararaca Venom, Biomedicines, 03/26/2024.*

3– *Landmark drugs, Jenny Bryan, 04/17/2009.*

4– *Snake Island: The bizarre true story of Earth's most venomous isle, BBC Science Focus, Claire Asher, 11/1/2023.*

CHAPTER 17

CRUISING WITH THE DEVIL'S BREATH...

Devil's Breath, also known as scopolamine or hyoscine, is a tropane alkaloid that's used to treat various medical issues like nausea, vomiting, motion sickness, and even muscle spasms. All alkaloids are organic and naturally occurring compounds with at least one nitrogen atom, and tropane alkaloids (TAs) are specific a class of alkaloids that contain over 200 known compounds and form a tropane ring system.

Cocaine, as well as hyoscyamine/scopolamine, can pass through the blood-brain barrier and cause dose-dependent hallucination and psychoactive effects. Conversely, calystegines are newly discovered TAs that have not been shown to have the same effect, though not enough research has been done to confirm this.

"Devil's Breath" is scopolamine in powdered form. While scopolamine is sometimes used in the medical community to treat postoperative nausea and vomiting (PONV) and motion sickness, it also has dangerous potential side effects and a history of criminal uses. In various parts of the world, criminals use scopolamine-rich seeds to incapacitate their victims.

Devil's Breath is made from several plant species. One of these is called Brugmansia, also known as "Angel's Trumpet" for its large, trumpet-shaped flowers. While they're native to South America, they're also ornamental plants that are popular across the United States and other parts of the world since they're both elegant and fairly easy to care for.

Angel's Trumpet, however, contains various belladonna alkaloids, which include atropine, hyoscyamine, and scopolamine (Devil's Breath). The roots and seeds of Angel's Trumpet have the highest concentrations of alkaloids, though ingesting the raw flowers, smoking the dried leaves, or drinking tea brewed using any part of the plant can cause serious side effects. Because it's so widely available, young adults often use Angel's Trumpet for recreational purposes as a hallucinogen.

Scopolamine is also found in Datura stramonium (Jimsonweed), Scopolia carniolica, and Hyoscyamus niger (henbane), all of which produce toxic belladonna alkaloid compounds as a form of self-defense.

Scopolamine is listed by the World Health Organization (WHO) as an "essential medicine" due to being both effective and low-cost. While high doses of scopolamine can lead to harmful side effects, this anticholinergic drug can also be used to treat various conditions. With professional medical supervision and proper dosing, scopolamine can help treat: 1-gastrointestinal spasms, 2-Chemotherapy nausea, 3-asthma attacks, 4-depression, 5-excessive sweating,

6-smoking cessation therapy, 7-nausea and vomiting after surgery under general anesthesia, transdermal scopolamine is the most common method of administering the drug.

Transdermal medications are given in the form of a patch directly on the skin. Scopolamine is usually applied behind the ear, and it will take a few hours to start working. For surgery, a doctor may the patch placed on the evening before.[1]

Diary from my friend Terri: 11/15/2024. We were starting into the Atlantic Ocean on a cruise and with the information that there was going to be larger waves, Bob asked me to put a patch behind his ear. Just to make the day interesting, Bob later tried to get up from bed and ended up rolling onto the floor face down between the beds with half his body on the bed & night stand. His back was hyper extended. He couldn't get traction with his feet and I couldn't lift him up.

I ended up calling the medical staff and they sent a young man to help lift him up. Turned out it took two men to get him back onto the bed in a sitting position. The doctor came and checked him out. They put Neosporin on his rug Rashed knees and replaced the beds that had been moved. After they left, he wanted to sit in the chair he had chosen as his. I helped him navigate to that. He read a little and decided to go to the restroom. I got him there and he was able with a lot of help to get back into bed. His leg muscles were just not working at all. I hoped things would get better in the morning.

The next time he tried to get to a standing position from the toilet, he ended on the floor again. So, after another 2 hours of struggle I called the EMT's again. Once they got him onto the bed, the head EMT noticed the patch behind Bob's and asked how long he had been wearing it. At that point it was about 8 hours. He suggested that we remove the patch and the doctor said that she agreed and that the only medication they recommended for sea sickness was the pill.

The doctor mentioned that people using the patch or the bracelet sometimes made them feel like they were having a stroke. I had noticed that when Bob was talking, he had some very strange mouth movements. So, we removed the patch. About 3 hours later he had better control of his leg muscles but still needed help sitting up in bed so he could then stand up.

The next day, we spent time reading, I went to breakfast, then back to the room. We rested and then both went to the restaurant and had a nice lunch. This became a very difficult time for me because Bob began hallucinating minute by minute. We are out in the Atlantic Ocean sailing south along the Argentinean coast, it was very concerning as Bob had been hallucinating a lot. So far, he had seen a black cat come through a secret door near Bob's chair and exit through a closed sliding door onto our balcony, a man was walking his dog, a baby seal on the deck outside our balcony, three men using hula hoops then going inside a cage to practice baseball. He thought there was a very young, very small blonde who is a member of the crew but who is sleeping in our room.

We went downstairs to ask a couple of questions from the guest services desk on the first floor and he tried to tell the lady we were talking to about this strange young lady sleeping in our room. He is totally confused about this trip, expected Tom and his wife to join us on board and worried that Tom didn't know our room number. I hoped this is just another reaction to the patch which was removed from his body the day before.

Two days from removing the patch, Bob is still sure there is a blonde in our room and that he did see a black cat. We spent most of today in our room. After a rest we went to have "Tea". I had caffeine free black tea and shared the tiny gluten free sandwiches and biscuits with Bob. He wasn't interested in tea. He is sure his hallucinations are not hallucinations, but he appears to not be having any more so hopefully we are done with that.

As a side note, he still remembers his hallucinations but now acknowledges that they are, indeed, hallucinations. *Personal correspondence & written article*

The old saying 'red as a beet, dry as a bone, blind as a bat, hot as a hare, mad as a hatter' is often quoted when describing the autonomic effects of drugs that block the muscarinic cholinergic system. These effects may be subtle or dramatic, yet can be overlooked or discounted as a natural consequence of old age. Elderly patients can be particularly sensitive to the anticholinergic action of drugs (like scopolamine) because of physiological and pathophysiological changes that often accompany the aging process. The use of multiple drugs, a common finding in older patients, may result in pharmacodynamic and pharmacokinetic drug interactions that heighten anticholinergic effects.

While the classic anticholinergic problems of decreased secretions, slowed gastrointestinal motility, blurred vision, increased heart rate, heat intolerance, sedation and possibly mild confusion, may be uncomfortable for a younger patient in relatively good health, these effects can be disastrous for older patients. Even the most common peripheral anticholinergic complaint of dry mouth can reduce the ability to communicate, predispose to malnutrition, promote mucosal damage, denture misfit or dental caries, and increase the risk of serious respiratory infection secondary to loss of antimicrobial activity of saliva. Mydriasis and the inability to accommodate will impair near vision and may precipitate narrow angle glaucoma in predisposed patients, but less obviously could lead to an increased risk of accidents, including falls. Somatic complaints of constipation and urinary hesitancy, could, in the presence of anticholinergic challenge, result in fecal impaction or urinary retention. Cardiac effects may be poorly tolerated. Increases in heart rate may precipitate or worsen angina. Finally, thermoregulatory impairment induced by anticholinergics, which block the ability to sweat, may lead to life threatening hyperthermia. Central anticholinergic effects range from sedation, mild confusion and inability to concentration to frank delirium. Even mild effects can reduce function and increase dependency. At any level of care, the loss of independence increases the caregiver burden, costs, and most importantly, can negatively affect quality of life. Many age-related and disease-related conditions may predispose elderly patients to anticholinergic drug toxicity. Careful attention to anticholinergic effects when prescribing drugs, patient education, regular review of the entire drug regimen, and familiarity with the signs and symptoms of anticholinergic toxicity will help to reduce the risk of drug-induced problems.[2]

Alcohol and scopolamine should not be consumed together as they can interact and cause serious side effects. Scopolamine is a medication used to prevent motion sickness and nausea. It works by blocking acetylcholine, a neurotransmitter that plays a role in muscle contractions and other bodily functions.

Alcohol is a central nervous system depressant that can affect coordination, judgment, and reaction time.

When alcohol and scopolamine are consumed together, they can potentiate each other's effects, leading to: Increased drowsiness, Blurred vision, Dizziness, Confusion, Slowed breathing, and Impaired coordination. This can increase the risks of falls, accidents, and overdose. This information was found on Google and provided for general knowledge and informational purposes only, and does not constitute medical advice.

Motion sickness is a common ailment that can cause bothersome symptoms when traveling by car, air or sea. Many people are now exploring natural remedies for symptoms of motion sickness. Anti-nausea bands may offer a natural alternative to medications. An anti-nausea band is a band that usually has a small, round plastic button. These bands are designed to be worn around the wrists, close to the creases between the end of the forearm and the beginning of the hand, with the button pressing against the skin on the underside of each wrist. Anti-nausea wrist bands are also known by other names, such as motion sickness bracelets, sea sickness bands, travel bands and motion sickness wrist bands.

The round button on the wrist band presses on an acupressure point that, according to traditional Chinese medicine, may relieve nausea and vomiting, regardless of the cause. You can also choose to press on the specific point for 2–3 minutes with your thumb. The efficacy of wrist bands for motion sickness is still unclear. Some scientific research studies have investigated whether acupressure helps with nausea and vomiting. More research is needed to understand if using wrist bands for nausea is as effective as standard anti-nausea drugs. Because many pregnant women prefer nondrug alternatives to manage minor health concerns, there has been interest in the use of nausea bracelets during pregnancy. Although some research indicates that acupressure doesn't help with morning sickness, some women report anti-nausea wrist bands to be helpful.

Side effects associated with motion sickness bands are generally considered to be mild. Local skin reactions, mild discomfort and swollen wrists have been reported in some studies. Follow the product instructions carefully and monitor for any signs of redness or skin breakdown near the wristband. If any skin irritation, pain or swelling occurs, remove the bands immediately.

Acupressure, either done by your own hands or with the help of wrist bands, may or may not help with various kinds of nausea. There are no known risks of trying wrist bands for nausea associated with motion sickness, pregnancy and chemotherapy.[3]

Alternative oral over the counter medications to prevent motion sickness come in two varieties: Dramamine is a brand name product that contains the active ingredient dimenhydrinate, which is an antihistamine. Meclizine is also an antihistamine but is generally less sedating. In fact, meclizine is the active ingredient in another Dramamine product, Dramamine Less Drowsy Formula. It is also the active ingredient in Bonine. So, to discuss the difference between meclizine and Dramamine, one needs to focus on the difference between meclizine and dimenhydrinate.

Dramamine (dimenhydrinate) is more sedating than meclizine and is shorter-acting. It lasts around 4-6 hours per dose compared to around 12 for meclizine. Studies show that Dramamine (dimenhydrinate) is likely more effective for treating motion sickness than meclizine. You may recognize diphenhydramine as it is the active ingredient in Benadryl. Dimenhydrinate is over 50% diphenhydramine by weight and therefore, the bulk of its effects comes from that. Dramamine is actually two molecular compounds attached to each other. Diphenhydramine is classified as a sedating antihistamine. Specifically, it is further classified as an ethanolamine antihistamine. Ethanolamine antihistamines are known for their strong anticholinergic effects, which can cause: 1-drowsiness, 2-dry mouth, 3-dry eyes and 4-constipation. While many of these anticholinergic effects are undesirable, they also help to relieve motion sickness by inhibiting stimulation of the inner ear. *Google*

In Terri's diary: "The doctor mentioned that people using the patch or the bracelet sometimes made them feel like they were having a stroke": Appears to be incorrect concerning the use of bracelets causing symptoms of having a stroke. In fact, "there are known risks of using the patch and more research is needed to understand if using wrist bands for nausea is as effective as standard anti-nausea drugs."

Bob's side effects from wearing the patch have been documented and being in his 80s, it appears that it would be good advice for him to not use the patch. Especially, if he were going to mix alcohol with scopolamine.

Maybe these cruise ships should have an information warning about alcohol and the patch when they are making all the effort to promote "all you can drink alcohol packages" for their guests. I know that when we sign up for the "soda packages," our consumption is in hopes we can get "more than our money's worth."

Many years ago, scout leaders Rich Hoge and Ron Simons, got all excited about taking their Scout Troop to Santa Cruz from San Jose on a deep-sea fishing trip. They got up before the light of day and took a baker's dozen of teenage boys to the dock. Rich warned them that, even though they were still sleepy, they should sit erect where they could see the sky line and lessen their chances of getting motion sickness from the rocking movement of the waves.

Motion sickness occurs when there is a lot of motion, such as on a boat, car, airplane, or amusement park ride, and usually affects women and children more frequently. It happens when the brain cannot make sense of all the information it is receiving from the inner ears, eyes, and other body parts, such as the muscles of the arms and legs. As a result, susceptible individuals experience motion sickness (car sickness, seasickness, or airsickness) and frequently feel sick to the stomach. They can also have other symptoms, such as vertigo.

As you might have guessed, when we reached the fishing area, most of the boys were asleep in the bottom of the boat. That day: Most made attempts to fish, some vomited and they all complained until the boat was safely ashore. At our next scout meeting, there was a unanimous vote to never "do deep-fishing again" - And we never did.

1– *What Is Devil's Breath (Scopolamine)?*

2– *Drugs Aging, The problems of anticholinergic adverse effects in older patients, 07/03/1993.*

3– *Do wrist bands for motion sickness work? Updated by Julie McDaniel, MSN, RN, CRNI, August 2024.*

CHAPTER 18

SAVING LIVES BY BREATHING UP THEIR BUTT...

At the end of James Cameron's 1989 underwater thriller The Abyss, oil rig diver Bud Brigman, played by Ed Harris, dons an experimental diving suit in which instead of air he breathes a special oxygenated liquid. This allows him to avoid the lethal effects of extreme water pressure and descend to the bottom of a deep ocean trench to defuse a nuclear warhead. While certainly a memorable plot device, surely such a technology is pure science fiction, right?

Well, not as much as you might think. The breathing fluid depicted in the film, oxygenated perfluorocarbon, actually exists, and while scenes with the diving suit were filmed with Ed Harris holding his breath, an earlier scene in which a rat is immersed in breathing fluid was filmed for real. While The Abyss is certainly the most famous depiction of liquid breathing, the technology has been experimented with for over a century, and while it might not be quite ready for use in deep-sea diving, it may have lifesaving applications in the field of medicine.

The first experiments with liquid breathing were conducted shortly after the First World War, when doctors began investigating the use of oxygenated saline solutions to help heal the lungs of soldiers damaged by poison gas. But it was not until the height of the Cold War in the late 1950s that research truly began in earnest, as the US Navy sought ways of allowing sailors to escape a sinking submarine without suffering from decompression sickness.

Decompression sickness, also known as The Bends, is a condition that results from breathing air at pressure. As a diver descends and the water pressure increases, more and more Nitrogen from the air becomes dissolved in their tissues. If they then ascend too rapidly to the surface, the sudden drop in pressure causes this Nitrogen to come out of solution, forming tiny bubbles that can cause severe joint pain, air embolisms, strokes, and death. Consequently, divers must ascend slowly and make frequent decompression stops to allow Nitrogen to be gradually released from the body.

But if instead of air a diver or escaping submariner could breathe an oxygenated liquid, then the pressure inside and outside the lung would be equal, preventing Nitrogen buildup and the need to decompress. Liquid breathing would also help reduce or eliminate other hazards of deep diving, including Nitrogen Narcosis or "Rapture of the deep", an alcohol-like intoxication caused by breathing Nitrogen under pressure. Oxygen itself also becomes dangerous below a certain depth, a phenomenon known as oxygen toxicity. To avoid these effects, divers use various breathing gas mixtures such as Heliox or Trimix which dilute the Oxygen and Nitrogen with Helium. But even this only works up to a point, as below around 160 metres breathing Helium induces severe tremors and other neurological effects known as High Pressure Nervous Syndrome. As a result, the deepest any diver breathing pressurized gas has been able to descend is 701 meters – and even then only in a land-based diving chamber.

In 1962 a team lead by Dr. Johannes Klystra at Duke University succeeded in getting mice and other small animals to breathe an oxygenated saline solution pressurized to 160 atmospheres – the high pressure being necessary to dissolve sufficient oxygen in the fluid. But while respiration was sustained in this manner for around an hour, the animals died soon after of respiratory acidosis – AKA carbon dioxide poisoning. This revealed one of the major shortcomings of liquid breathing which has plagued researchers ever since: while breathing fluid can easily deliver sufficient oxygen to the body, it is far less efficient at removing exhaled carbon dioxide. In order to prevent acidosis, the average human would have to move 5 liters per minute of breathing fluid through their lungs while resting and 10 liters per minute to perform any sort of physical activity – a flow rate human lungs are not capable of sustaining for any length of time. Any practical fluid breathing system would thus have to actively pump fluid in and out of the lungs, like the mechanical ventilators used in hospitals.

In 1966 American researchers Leland Clark and Frank Gollan made a breakthrough in liquid breathing research by replacing Klystra's oxygenated saline with an exotic liquid called perfluorocarbon (PFC). First developed as part of the Manhattan Project during the Second World War, PFC is a colorless liquid composed of the elements carbon and fluorine. The bond between these two elements is among the strongest in nature, making PFC unreactive and biologically inert. It has twice the density of water but a quarter the viscosity and can hold nearly 20 times as much oxygen and carbon dioxide as water – properties which make it ideal as a breathing fluid. Clark and Gollan's early experiments involved simply immersing rats and mice in oxygenated PFC and allowing them to breathe naturally. While the high density of the fluid made breathing difficult, the animals were able to survive fully immersed for up to 20 hours without any ill effects. Larger animals required the use of forced ventilation to prevent carbon dioxide buildup, but experiments on anaesthetized dogs further demonstrated the viability of PFC as a breathing fluid.

Clark and Gollan's work on PFC was soon taken up by Klystra, who between 1969 and 1975 conducted one of the most comprehensive studies on liquid breathing in history, using both animals and humans as test subjects. In the course of this research, US Navy diver Francis J. Falejcyk became the first human to breathe both oxygenated saline and PFC. Despite receiving no medication except for local anaesthesia to facilitate intubation, Falejcyk did not find the experience overly uncomfortable, though they encountered difficulty draining the fluid from his lungs and he developed pneumonia as a result.

In 1971 Falejcyk delivered a lecture on his experiences which was attended by a then 17-year-old James Cameron, inspiring him to write a short story that would eventually become the screenplay for The Abyss. Klystra's research concluded that a human could breathe PFC for up to an hour without suffering carbon dioxide poisoning provided they didn't overly exert themselves, making liquid breathing a viable method for escaping a sinking submarine. For more physical applications, Klystra also experimented with emulsions of PFC and Sodium Hydroxide which could more readily absorb carbon dioxide from the bloodstream. Ultimately, however, none of these techniques ever saw practical use in real world scenarios. The Navy SEALs reportedly experimented with liquid breathing in the early 1980s, but found breathing PFC so strenuous that several divers suffered rib sprains and fractures from the effort during testing exercises.

One proposed solution to the acidosis problem is to fit divers with a venous shunt device that scrubs carbon dioxide directly from the bloodstream. Unfortunately, the medical and logistical issues inherent in such a device are fairly obvious, and liquid breathing still has a long way to go before it becomes a viable technique for deep-sea diving. It may, however, have an important role to play in medicine, especially in the care of premature infants.

Our lungs contain around a half a billion alveoli, tiny sacs of tissue through which oxygen is absorbed into the bloodstream. To prevent these from collapsing in on themselves like a wet paper bag, the body produces a substance called pulmonary surfactant, a mixture of lipids which reduces the surface tension of water and allows the alveoli to remain open. Premature babies, however, are incapable of producing sufficient amounts of surfactant, and as soon as they are born most of their alveoli collapse, making it difficult for them to breathe. While traditional mechanical ventilators have been used for decades to help premature infants breathe, the high pressures produced by these machines can severely damage their delicate lungs. But by flooding the lungs with breathing fluid, liquid ventilation recreates the conditions found in the womb and allows the alveoli to open up, greatly increasing gas exchange. The technique also provides a convenient means of administering medication directly to the lungs.

Neonatal liquid ventilation was first pioneered by J.S. Greenspan at Temple University Hospital in Philadelphia, who in 1989 placed 13 premature infants on liquid ventilators for between 24 and 96 hours. All were successfully weaned back to breathing air, and of the 13 these 11 showed marked improvement in lung function, though six later died of causes unrelated to the experiment. A similar study conducted by R.B. Hirschl in 1995 on 19 adult, pediatric, and neonatal patients similarly confirmed the viability of liquid ventilation, with 11 of the 19 patients surviving with improved lung function.

However, the equipment required to carry out full liquid ventilation was found to be overly complex and expensive, so in 1991 B.P. Fulman developed a simpler technique known as partial liquid ventilation, or PLV. In PLV, the lungs are only partially filled with breathing fluid, the rest being supplied with air via a regular mechanical ventilator. This allows the breathing fluid to open up around 40% of the lung's alveoli while allowing for more efficient removal of carbon dioxide. Another proposed technique involves administering breathing fluid as an aerosol mixed with air or oxygen, which produces similar results while being far more comfortable for patients than breathing straight fluid.

And in 1995 Mike Darwin and Steven Harris demonstrated the application of liquid breathing to the induction of therapeutic hypothermia. This refers to the cooling of the human body following cardiac arrest to slow the onset of brain and other tissue damage. By perfusing the lungs with chilled PFC, Darwin and Harris achieved a cooling rate of 0.5 degrees Celsius per minute – faster than any existing technique. As a result of these and other breakthroughs, the FDA has granted liquid perfusion "fast-track" development status in order to bring this potentially lifesaving technology to patients as quickly as possible.[1]

The concept of liquid ventilation has been investigated for more than 40 years. The basic principle of liquid ventilation is to fill the lung with perfluorocarbon up to a volume equivalent to functional residual capacity... (Perfluorocarbons (PFCs) are odorless, non-corrosive, colorless liquids with low surface tension and a considerable density difference with air. Their density is almost double that of water, and they are highly stable and miscible with biological fluids. In terms of chemical composition, they are hydrocarbons in which fluorine replaces most or all of the hydrogen atoms, and, occasionally, other halogen atoms are present in their structure. These substitutions change the physical properties of these compounds. The element with the highest electronegativity is the fluorine. As a result, the carbon-fluorine bond in these compounds is powerful and polar, but it does not result in water solubility because the molecule is ultimately non-polar. All PFC molecules can dissolve vast quantities of gas. Besides oxygen, these compounds can dissolve up to four times as much CO_2 compared to oxygen) ...Following this first step of filling the lung with PFCs, the lung is ventilated using either PFC (total liquid ventilation) or gas (partial liquid ventilation). Animal studies have shown that compared to conventional mechanical ventilation, liquid ventilation improves gas exchange and pulmonary compliance, and reduces secondary lung injury. One of the suggested mechanisms is the use of atelectatic and consolidated (dependent) lung regions, thereby reducing the use of normal intra pulmonary areas of the lungs.

For technical reasons clinical application of liquid ventilation has mainly focused on partial liquid ventilation. Despite the promising animal data, studies in adults, children, and newborns have failed to show clear benefits of partial liquid ventilation compared to conventional mechanical ventilation. Based on these results several ongoing trials have been stopped and placed on hold. It is unclear if and when trials in newborn infants will be continued.

Despite these disappointing results partial liquid ventilation is also investigated for other purposes. It may play a future role as an adjunctive therapy for open lung ventilation, facilitating the use of atelectatic lung regions. Secondly, animal and human data have proposed a role for partial liquid ventilation for the induction of lung growth in congenital diaphragmatic hernias.

Total liquid ventilation is still in the preclinical phase, but as some of the technical aspects of device design and technique are refined, we can expect this mode of ventilation to enter the clinical arena in the near future.[2]

Continuous positive airway pressure (CPAP) therapy is one of the most effective treatments for obstructive sleep apnea (OSA), a sleep-related breathing disorder. CPAP therapy uses a device that delivers a steady stream of humidity warmed pressurized air through the nose &/ or mouth to keep the airway open and prevent breathing disruptions.

Both COVID-19 and OSA affect breathing, so it's natural for questions to arise about how using a CPAP affects the risks of COVID-19 infection, whether CPAP can be used to treat the complications of COVID-19, and how people with OSA safely used their CPAP during the pandemic.

Fortunately, using CPAP therapy was associated with lower rates of COVID-19 in people with OSA. Adherence to CPAP therapy generally requires using the device for at least four hours per night no less than five nights per week, though even those who only use their CPAP device for a few hours per night may have a lower risk of infection than those who do not use CPAP therapy at all.

Many people who were admitted to the hospital with Covid-19 had low levels of oxygen in their blood, a condition called respiratory failure. When this occurs, doctors have several options they can use to hopefully improve blood oxygen levels: The use of a mechanical ventilator involves intubating a person by inserting a plastic tube into their windpipe and having a machine move air into and out of their lungs. This is an invasive treatment, and the risks of complications makes it not the best option for everyone who needs supplemental oxygen. According to the CDC, the risk of severe outcomes is increased in people of all ages with certain underlying medical conditions and in people who are 50 years and older. Despite the progress achieved in supportive care, the mortality rate of acute respiratory distress syndrome (ARDS) in ICU is still high (35–40%) and it increases with the severity of hypoxemia (27% in mild, 32% in moderate, 45% in severe ARDS.

Mechanical ventilation requires specific equipment, which was a concern at the beginning of the pandemic when ICU beds and the equipment was limited. As a result, doctors have explored the use of more available CPAP therapy equipment and other non-invasive treatments to address low oxygen levels. *CPAP as a Treatment for COVID-19, Jay Summer*

Enteral ventilation via anus (EVA) is an enema-like procedure to deliver oxygen to the body through the distal gut. This is a provocative idea and those first encountering it will express astonishment. Yet, as the potential clinical role is considered and the data is examined, EVA emerges as a promising therapy deserving scientific and medical interest. Initial perception of EVA is likely to parallel that of fecal microbiota transplant for recurrent *Clostridium difficile* infection which not long ago was deemed untenable for "practical and aesthetic reasons," but now has less stigma as data supporting effectiveness are overwhelming… "When the microbiome in the digestive tract is taken over by disease causing microbes that antibiotics, change of diet or other methods fail, doctors are reaching out more and more to inoculating the intestinal tract with new microbes - much like farmers share rumen fluid in cows. How do they do that – they basically feed you with human poop that hopefully does not contain parasites or microbes that can act as pathogens.

In human medicine, using poop to restore normal microbiomes in the GI tract has been around since the fourth century. Chinese medicine appears to be the first documentation of using fermented fecal material and giving it to patients who have diarrhea and showing it helps improve symptoms. There has been little human scientific literature written until about 2010,2012. Inoculating the GI tract with poop is called Fecal Microbial Transplantation (FMT) and you take fecal material from a healthy donor and put that fecal material into a diseased recipient. The poop can be administered in a lot of different ways. Most commonly it's given via an enema, as a slurry during an endoscopic exam and more products for oral FMT are becoming available. There are frozen products where a capsule is filled with feces and given orally, but there's also lyophilized products where feces is freeze dried and encapsulated. It can be stored at room temperature and taken orally.

But it's really taking that fecal material and in that fecal material are all those great microbes, and it's not just bacteria, that's what we tend to talk about, but it's that whole microbial community and that microbial community then has the opportunity to engraft or take up a niche or a home within the new recipient. And there is a lot of encouragement that FMT can be used in human and animal medicine to help cure or help prevent disease.

In 1976 I started practice at Camden Pet Hospital. I'm certain the owner Dr. Hylton, having been a large animal practitioner, was very familiar with the procedure of transplanting the rumen contents from a healthy cow to one with digestive problems. He taught me how to apply the principle of fecal microbial transplantation (FMT) by taking feces from a healthy cat, placing it into a pill capsule and giving it by mouth to a cat with untreatable diarrhea. And, I saw cats actually return to have normal bowel movements.)" *pgs. 53-64 book II Thoughts on my Thoughts, W.R. Hoge, DVM.*

...The concept of EVA as a therapy that employs the distal gut to aid failing lungs is not the first example of repurposing tissue barriers to replace failing organs. In kidney failure, peritoneal dialysis repurposes the abdominal peritoneal membrane to replace the function of failed kidneys. Peritoneal dialysis involves instillation and exchange of fluid into the abdominal peritoneal cavity to cleanse the blood and is now more common in some countries than traditional hemodialysis. It should also be noted that development of peritoneal dialysis required iterative efforts over many years, and if EVA ultimately reaches the intensive care unit, the work in this issue will be marked by historians as a key scientific contribution.

Why is a therapy like EVA needed? Acute respiratory failure can require mechanical ventilation to support impaired respiratory drive or inadequate gas exchange in the lungs. For most patients, mechanical ventilation is adequate for delivery of oxygen and removal of carbon dioxide from circulation. However, in some situations faced by first responders, mechanical ventilation is not available. Further, the Covid-19 pandemic has demonstrated that mechanical ventilators are a finite resource. Even if mechanical ventilation is available, in severe disease gas exchange may be impaired to the degree that oxygenation is inadequate. Faced with this situation, extracorporeal membrane oxygenation is a technology that can temporarily replace the functions of the heart and lungs: providing forward flow of blood and gas exchange using an external apparatus. Yet extracorporeal membrane oxygenation has inherent risks, requires significant outlay of human labor and financial resources, and therefore availability is limited. A therapy such as EVA could occupy the niche created when mechanical ventilation is unavailable or inadequate.

Using small and large animal models with acute hypoxia it has been shown that EVA has the potential for a meaningful degree of oxygen delivery. First, they assessed oxygen delivery with gas EVA in a mouse model and reported that it required mechanical abrasion of the gut mucosa to be effective. Next, they demonstrated an alternative liquid EVA approach that improves arterial oxygenation and extends survival without requiring mucosal abrasion. Promising results are also reported using a porcine model in which mean improvement in oxygenation after EVA enema persists for 18.7 min. Thus, in current form, this therapy requires repeated cycling of fluid, and the potential of EVA is a short-term treatment of hypoxia.

The liquid EVA that has been used in studies are perfluorocarbons (PFC) which are a class of hydrocarbon with hydrogen atoms replaced by fluorine that endows the inert liquid with a remarkable oxygen carrying capacity. Early work in the 1960s describe dramatic experiments in which anesthetized mice survive hours submerged in such a liquid. Newer generation perfluorochemicals were developed as blood substitutes and ultimately tested in a phase III clinical trial that showed decreased transfusion requirements in patients undergoing cardiovascular surgery. However, increased rates (compared with control) of cardiovascular events (40% versus 30%) and digestive system events (7% versus 2%) tempered enthusiasm, and a separate phase III trial was suspended due to concern for adverse neurologic outcomes. EVA should not be dismissed based on prior experience with perfluorochemicals as blood substitutes because it would remain confined to the gut lumen. To their credit, the authors measured PFD in circulation in a rat model and found them below the lower limit of detection.

It must be remembered, however, that the models of acute hypoxia in this study do not fully reflect the complex multisystem insults experienced by critically ill patients that add infection, inflammation, and hypoperfusion. It is important to discover how long EVA can be used and if the mucosal barrier of the distal gut can tolerate prolonged repurposing.

The time is right to bolster the footing of EVA given its translational potential. The pandemic has highlighted the need to expand options for ventilation and oxygenation in critical illness, and this niche will persist even as the pandemic subsides. While EVA is a new concept, it takes advantage of decades of work developing perfluorochemicals as blood substitutes.[3]

Thoughts on my thoughts to consider this: Modify a Foley type catheter that has a channel (lumen) with two ports (balloon port and fluid drainage port) on one end and a balloon that is distal to the drainage eyes (not proximal as seen in diagram) on the other end. There would also be an expandable balloon at the drainage end of the catheter proximal to where the balloon port and drainage port come together. The proximal rectal expandable balloon would be used to block fluid material from going forward into the small intestines and stomach areas/and fecal material from passing into the large intestine. The distal rectal expandable balloon would trap fluid in the large intestine and prevent fluid from passing out the rectum. The balloons would also be used to control pressure of the enteral ventilation via anis (EVA) solution.

There would also be a short open at each end catheter (not pictured) that would lead from outside of the rectum beyond the distal expandable balloon into the perfluorochemicals EVA solution trapped in the large intestine. It would be used to remove the EVA solution and recycle it into a collection chamber where it could be monitored, cleansed, CO_2 removed, oxygenated, warmed and with controlled pressure forced back into the large intestine.

The apparatus would act much like a CPAP machine. Instead of providing "continuous positive air pressure" (CPAP), it would be providing "continuous positive EVA solution pressure" (CPEP). Warming and recycling using a controllable steady pressure. Instead of preventing interrupted sleep and helping to maintain safe oxygen and CO_2 levels via the lung tissue – CPEP would help maintain proper oxygen and carbon dioxide levels by using the blood vessel rich lining tissue of the large intestine. Patent a design with me anyone? Instead of Foley catheter, it could be called the modified Hoge EVA stabilization system.

So, while James Cameron won't be able to reach the Marianas Trench without a fancy submarine for some time to come, he can at least take comfort in the fact that the technology which so inspired him as a teenager may one day save many lives. On the other hand, his inspired movie may have sparked the interest that will pave the way for the development of EVA that will more practically one day save millions of lives with the Hoge EVA stabilization system.

1– *Can Humans Breathe Liquid Like in The Abyss? Gilles Messier, 08/13/2021.* August 13, 2021 *Gilles Messier.*

2– *Neonatal Mechanical Ventilation, Mechanical Ventilation, C. van Kaam, 2008.*

3– *Enteral ventilation via anus: You can hold your breath, Med – CellPress, Caleb J. Kelly, 2010.*

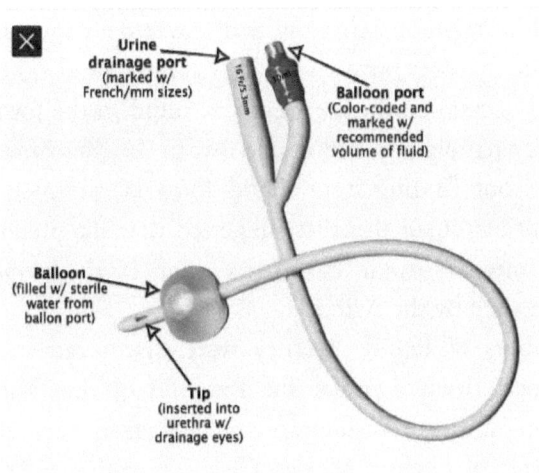

CHAPTER 19

MERCURY – GOOD AND BAD...

In 2015, a team of archeologists discovered a large quantity of liquid mercury beneath the Mexican pyramid. There are several occasions where mercury is found in the form of a powdery red pigment called cinnabar in the Mesoamericans' tombs, but finding it in liquid form is extremely rare. Ancient astronaut theorists suggested that the presence of liquid mercury might have been a part of the propulsion system used by the Aztecs.

Traces of liquid mercury were discovered in three chambers situated under the Pyramid of the Feathered Serpent at the Teotihuacan archaeological site, 50 km northeast of modern Mexico City. Excavating the tunnel at the site unsealed in 2003 after 1,800 years, they found strange artifacts near the tunnel's entrance such as jade figurines, seashells, jaguar remains, and a box filled with carved shells and rubber balls.

It is believed that the discovery of liquid mercury could be a representation of the underworld where the dead resided, probably the remains of the kings. The Aztecs called the ancient site a "City of the Gods." There is no record of when the city was built, but it flourished as early as 400 BC and became a most powerful and influential place by 400 AD. It is estimated that around 100,000 to 200,000 people lived there and built giant monuments such as the Temple of Feathered Serpent and the Pyramids of the Sun and the Sun Moon.

Mesoamericans used cinnabar to create liquid mercury to decorate jade objects and apply it to the dead bodies of their royal members. There are three other sites in Central America where mercury was found, but not at such a large scale beneath the Temple of the Feathered Serpent.

The many structures that still stand in Teotihuacan appear to be encoded with advanced mathematical and cosmic principles, and the layout precisely mirrors the positions of the planets in our solar system. Modern excavations at the site have unearthed discoveries of liquid mercury, walls lined with mica (mica powder is a naturally occurring mineral dust often used in makeup foundations, as filler in cement and asphalt, and as insulation material in electric cables), and strange golden spheres containing unknown substances–all of which are out of place in the ancient world. Could these artifacts be the remnants of an alien society? Perhaps even an extraterrestrial spaceport?

Mercury is a very toxic element that humans can be exposed to in several ways. Its exposure can cause headaches, chills, fever, chest tightness, coughs, hand tremors, nausea, vomiting, abdominal cramps, diarrhea, etc. Although scientists are puzzled about what had been discovered under the Aztec pyramid, ancient astronaut theorists believe the mercury found at the Quetzalcoatl temple may have a direct connection with the feathered serpent god that came down from the sky.

Liquid mercury was not only found in Teotihuacan, according to old Indian texts, it was once part of the propulsion system which extraterrestrials used for their flying machines. Some people believe that in India around 7000 years ago, the people knew how to create Vimanas (flying machines) to traverse the sky and beyond using a technology that NASA is still trying to harness today. There are references in ancient Vedic texts that cite Vimanas that could fly in air, water, and land. They mention various propulsion including mercury propulsion.

Many legends say the Nazis went through these ancient Sanskrit texts to build their flying machine. The future spacecraft engine planned by NASA uses mercury bombardment units powered by solar cells. The mercury propellant is vaporized, fed into the thruster discharge chamber, ionized, converted into plasma, and accelerated through small openings to pass out of the engine at velocities between 1200 to 3000 kilometers per minute. But, so far NASA is successful only producing one pound of thrust which is inadequate. But, supposedly 108 years ago a Sanskrit scholar of Bombay was able to use the knowledge to produce sufficient thrust to lift his aircraft 1500 feet into the air. It is suggested the mercury in the chamber of the feathered serpent pyramid might depict the presence of a physical craft that was actually a spacecraft. there at some point.

A similar case of the use of mercury can be found in China where there is a funerary of 8,000 life-sized

Terra-Cotta Warriors and Horses. Researchers could not scale the massive underground structures due to high levels of mercury writings but, like the Aztec story of Quetzalcoatl coming down from the sky, the Chinese have a legend of the Yellow Emperor descending from heaven on a dragon. It is believed that the dragon was a spacecraft that could cover vast distances in a short time period. According to an ancient astronaut theory, the Aztecs and the Chinese received hidden secrets of mercury that allow them to create a mercury river for the extraterrestrials or their gods.[1]

Almadén is a town and municipality in the spanish province originally a Roman, and later, a Moorish mining settlement, the town was captured by the Christians in 1151. The mercury deposits of Almadén account for the largest quantity of liquid mercury metal produced in the world. Almadén mine stopped working in 2002, due to the European mercury mining prohibition. In 2006, the mine opened to the public who can visit the first level, 160 ft underground.

The geology of the area is characterized by volcanism. Almadén is home to the world's greatest reserves of cinnabar, a mineral associated with recent volcanic activity, from which mercury is extracted. From antiquity, cinnabar was used to make the pigment vermillion. In the Islamic era, furnaces capable of extracting mercury from the cinnabar were installed. The mines of Almadén exported mercury throughout the entire Mediterranean basin.

Two German bankers administered the mines during the 16th and 17th centuries in return for loans to the Spanish government. Mercury became very valuable in the Americas in the mid-16th century due to the introduction of amalgamation, a process that uses mercury to extract metals from gold and silver ore. The demand for mercury grew, and so did the town's importance as a center of mining and industry. Most of the mercury produced at this time was sent to Seville, then to the Americas.

The dangerous working conditions of the mines made it difficult to find willing laborers. As the demand for mercury grew, convict labor was introduced. The danger of death or sickness from mercury poisoning was always present. Twenty-four percent of convicts died before their release dates, most often because of mercury poisoning. Nearly all prisoners experienced discomfort due to mercury exposure and most of the men working at the furnaces. Convicts were also forced to bail water out of the mines. These men escaped the dangers of mercury exposure but suffered exhaustion on a daily basis. A group of four men, even the sick, had to bail out 300 buckets of water without rest. Those that could not meet this quota were whipped.

People abducted for slavery, mainly from North Africa, were purchased directly from slaveholders to work alongside the convicts. The enslaved people purchased to work in the mines at Almadén were those considered less desirable, unwanted by their slaveholders for various reasons, so were much cheaper than others on the market at the time. Purchasing enslaved people at the usual market price would have been uneconomic. By 1613, the enslaved outnumbered convicts by a two-to-one ratio.

Safer mining technology was introduced in the last quarter of the 18th century, and free laborers began to take an interest in the mine again. By the end of the century, free workers had replaced most of the slave labor. The penal establishment at Almadén was closed in 1801.

In 1835, the mine was leased indefinitely to the bank of N M Rothschild & Sons. The price paid was high, but one of the Rothschild family firms had previously purchased the quicksilver mine in now Slovenia from Austria; creating a monopoly on mercury, until the discovery of mercury in New Almaden California (within one mile of where I live). Volume was expanded and the metal sold at a substantial markup returning a substantial profit to both Spain and the firm. In 2000, the mines closed due to the fall of the price of mercury on the international market. *Wikipedia*

The New Almaden Quicksilver Mines - established in 1847 and named for the famous mines of Almaden, Spain - were once the richest mercury mines in North America. New Almaden mercury was used in sluice boxes during the California Gold Rush to amalgamate with gold. Between 1850 and 1875, miners extracted a total of 46 million pounds of liquid mercury from ore taken from the New Almaden Mines.

The mine and its villages flourished under the 20-year directorship of James Randol, who took over as general manager in 1870. Under Randol's orderly discipline the community became a mining town unlike any other in the state, somewhat resembling a beneficent feudal society. The residents' health, wealth, cultural and social lives were taken care of by company-sponsored organizations that the progressive but authoritarian Randol set up. After his retirement in 1892 the mine began to decline. Ore yield dropped off by more than half by the turn of the century. In 1912 the Quicksilver Mining Company declared bankruptcy and closed the mine. In 1974 the County of Santa Clara purchased the hills area for development as a county park.

Mercury was refined from cinnabar, a reddish rock found in the hills at New Almaden. Crushing then roasting the cinnabar to extract the mercury leaves a waste product called calcines. Miners left calcines and other mining rubble in heaps, often adjacent to the streams. Mercury-containing sediment now washes from these heaps into the streams and reservoirs, making its way to the San Francisco Bay.

The most dangerous form of mercury is not liquid mercury, the well-known quicksilver valued by miners, but a compound called methylmercury. When mercury sits in the sediments of oxygen-poor waters of lakes and wetlands, bacteria produce this potent neurotoxin from the mercury. It is taken up by algae, then it concentrates as it moves from algae, to zooplankton, to prey fish, to predator fish, and finally to humans. To protect the public from the dangers of eating contaminated fish, warning signs near local ponds and reservoirs instruct anglers not to eat their catch.[2]

In 1976 my family moved to Almaden Valley less than a quarter of a mile from the New Almaden Road that leads to the mercury mines and villages. My scout troop visited the museum and some of the areas around the deserted mine. I learned that the metal produced in the mine was important for extracting gold during the California Gold Rush and we weren't supposed to fish or eat contaminated fish in the area.

The history of mercury as a medicine—and awareness of its toxicity in higher quantities—goes back to antiquity in Egypt and China. Qin Shi Huang, a Chinese emperor of the third century BC, whose physicians fed him large amounts as the key to immortality, reportedly went mad and suffered an early death at age 49. Even in the end, he was a believer; he was buried in a bejeweled tomb with mercury pools, which to this day cannot be opened because of concerns of toxic contamination.

Cinnabar (mercury sulfide), the ore from which most pure mercury is extracted, has had a place in Chinese traditional medicine for sedation for over 2000 years. It was widely used by the classical Greeks and throughout the Western world through medieval times for a variety of conditions including melancholy, venereal diseases, parasites, trachoma (chlamydia bacteria that get into eyes and can cause blindness), and constipation. Mercury turned the stools black, and it was thought that this resulted from removing an excess of bile, one of the four 'humors' of the body (black bile, yellow bile, phlegm and blood), whose appropriate balance was believed to be important to health. On the contrary, toxic doses can cause difficulties with vision and hearing, kidney complications, peeling skin, itching or burning feelings of the limbs due to nerve damage, and memory disturbances; up to three-quarters of patients may display various degrees of depressive symptoms.

Both topical and oral forms of mercury were a mainstay in the treatment of syphilis, which had become widespread in Europe by the end of the fifteenth century. Calomel, a mercury chloride preparation, was in widespread use from the sixteenth until the twentieth century, as a cathartic, as well as for syphilis, typhoid fever, mumps, and a variety of other conditions. The administration for syphilis was immortalized in a famous saying: "A night with Venus, and a lifetime with mercury."

Mercury had a place in the popular imagination as well. In Jules Verne's 1871 novel 20,000 Leagues Under the Sea, the submarine Nautilus was powered by batteries containing mercury in combination with sodium from seawater.[3]

The story of mercury being used in hat making is an unexpected one. By the 17th century, the growing demand for hats necessitated mass production, and being a milliner became a lucrative business. During the 19th century, felt hats, in particular, became very popular in North America and Europe.

Hat makers started experimenting with a variety of production methods, including the use of camel hair. Over time it was found that hair soaked in camel urine was far easier to work with. The nitrogen in the urine worked to disrupt the fur's chemical bonds.

The breakthrough that led to the use of mercury happened in France when workers started to use their own urine rather than camel urine. Crucially, it was noticed that one workman was consistently producing a superior felt. What was it in his urine that was having this magical effect? It turned out that he was being treated with a mercury compound for syphilis. He was taking mercurous chloride (calomel) as medicine. As a result, people started using an orange-colored compound known as mercuric nitrate $Hg(NO_3)$ in place of urine to produce superior felt.

Turning the fur into a finished hat was a complicated process. Usually, with cheaper fur, a solution of mercuric nitrate was applied to toughen the fibers and allow them to mat together more efficiently. This process is called carroting because the fur would turn orange afterward.

Hat makers had to use beaver, rabbit, or hare fur to produce high-quality felt. Beaver fur has natural serrated edges, making this step unnecessary and a preferred fur for making hats. But given its scarcity and cost, cheaper furs that required carroting had to be used.

After carroting, the fibers were shaved off the skin and made into felt. The felt was later dipped in a boiling acid solution to harden and thicken it. The barbs on the raw fibers of the fur lock together much like Velcro interlocks. The last step was to shape the hat by steaming and then ironing it. During this process, hat makers typically worked in shops that were not adequately ventilated. Consequently, the vapors would concentrate and over time and the workers would breathe in the mercury compound, leading to mercury poisoning.

Mercury poisoning is also known as erethism, mad hatter disease, or mad hatter syndrome. It's a neurological disorder that damages the brain and produces changes in behavior. Its physical symptoms include loss of teeth, uncontrollable trembling, excessive drooling, loss of coordination, and slurred speech. Its mental symptoms include memory loss, irritability, depression, anxiety, mood swings, and difficulty thinking clearly. In some extreme cases, the victims also experienced hallucinations, delusions, and extreme paranoia. Workers were suffering tremendously and could do nothing about it.

Consequently, mercury poisoning was widespread in the city. People referred to this ailment as The Danbury Shakes. Near the end of the 19th century, Hatter's Shakes also became a term to describe the intense muscle spasms and tremors seen in hat makers.

Most of us are familiar with a character known as the Mad Hatter. This eccentric man was featured in Lewis Carroll's 1865 novel Alice's Adventures in Wonderland and his behavior may have been a reference to the frequent neurological and psychiatric symptoms appearing in Victorian hat makers, who used mercuric nitrate in the process of making felt from fur.[4]

Since 1865 Stetson Hats has been the powerhouse of hat manufacturers credited with the creation of the American cowboy hat. John B. Stetson founded the company with only $100. He rented a small room, purchased all the necessary tools and $10 in fur; that's all it took and that's what they use to this day. The hats are still made from raw fibers of fur but mercury or urine is not part of the process. Mercury products were widely used during both world wars, both as components of cartridge primers and blasting caps, but also as wound antiseptics. Organic preparations of mercury were developed in the 1920s and widely given as diuretics until the advent of thiazides in the 1950s. Mercurochrome, an organic preparation, was a common over-the-counter antiseptic and is still used in some parts of the world though no longer in the U.S. Thiomersal, a mercury-based preservative, widely used in vaccines, became a subject of controversy and was removed from children's vaccines in the U.S. in 2001.

Today, concerns are still raised about the health consequences of the accumulation of mercury in the body. Among these have been reports of mood changes in dentists exposed to low levels of mercury while working with dental amalgams, and disorders of the cardiovascular and immunological systems, as well as depression, in patients receiving them. Although a 2013 treaty among 145 countries was designed to greatly limit the commercial use of mercury, it is still widely used illegally in gold mining in the third world, where it has been associated with developmental and neurological disorders.[3]

One of the world's richest biodiversity hot spots is Peru's Madre de Dios, a region of the Amazon nestled at the base of the Andes mountains. When Jacqueline Gerson, Ph.D. biogeochemist student at Duke University, first traveled there in 2017, she found herself on a boat headed downstream through the forest. As the riverbanks passed by, she observed a scenic shift. At first, she found it was beautiful, primary old-growth forest, lots of birds, lots of different wildlife. As she continued downstream … first she noticed these rocks that as she kept going, there were pile after pile after pile, and then she noted seeing some deforestation.

She was witnessing the signs of changes made to the environment in a traditional and nonmechanized way, and small-scale gold mining. Unlike large-scale industrial operations with fleets of dump trucks and excavators, workers here use basic tools or their own hands to extract ore. These informal gold-mining efforts are so prolific in Madre de Dios that they support at least half of the region's economy. Lush tracts of Amazonian rainforest are torn down to make way for mining operations, leaving behind mounds of sediment and pits that fill the water. The small-scale miners mix mercury into riverbank sediments that contain flecks of gold. This produces a gold-mercury amalgam that can easily be separated from the muck and then burned to isolate the gold. But that burning also releases fumes of mercury into the open air.

Globally, people unleash more tonnes of mercury into the air each year, from coal combustion plants, waste incineration facilities, cement production sites, mining operations and other sources. Artisanal (made in limited amounts in a traditional way) and small-scale gold mining generates more than $1/3^{rd}$ of these mercury emissions, making it the leading anthropogenic source.

In the environment, bacteria convert the element into the more toxic methylmercury, which bioaccumulates more readily in wildlife and people. Exposure to large amounts of mercury can wreak havoc on the central nervous system, digestive tract and kidneys, leading to seizures, blindness, sleep loss, memory loss, headaches, muscle weakness or even death.

Unsurprisingly, mercury levels in the air correlated with the proximity to mining. But water shed by leaves in the forest canopy, known as throughfall, offered a more complicated picture. The denser the canopy, the more concentrated the mercury in the throughfall, with the highest levels showing up in a conservation area called the Los Amigos Biological Concession. The mercury levels in the throughfall at Los Amigos are the highest loads of any location known on the globe. It was a surprise to find this in one of the most remote areas in the world. The large leaves in the mature forest canopy work like quicksilver collectors, providing wide surfaces for airborne mercury to gather on, accumulate and later be washed to the ground by rain. If you have a mining community surrounded by old-growth forests, that's where you're going to see high loads of mercury.

And it wasn't just the leaves. The mining contaminated wildlife too. Mercury levels in feathers from three songbird species with varied diets were on average two to three times higher at Los Amigos than at another old-growth forest located far from mining. Throughfall and shed leaves deliver mercury to the soil, where the contaminant gets methylated by bacteria and consumed by plants and animals (including man).

To help spread gold miner's awareness of the dangers of mercury fumes, the researchers distributed locally made devices called retorts that reduced miners' exposure to mercury fumes. Surveys showed that the work they did helped: The portion of respondents who reported believing that mercury was dangerous increased from 83 to 94 percent, and the percentage of individuals using retorts at least sometimes went up from 3 to 64 percent.[5]

Amalgam has been used for many years for restorations, commonly known as fillings. Prior to 1900 many compositions were tried but few were successful when placed in the oral environment. Around 1900, small amounts of copper and occasionally zinc were added. Zinc acts as a scavenger because it prevents oxidation of the other metals in the alloy during the manufacturing process. Zinc accomplishes this by combining readily with oxygen to form zinc oxide. Amalgam restorations made from this balanced formula were reasonably successful and its longevity increased.

To fabricate an amalgam filling, the dentist uses a mixing device to blend roughly equal parts (by mass) of shavings of a silver-base alloy with mercury until the shavings are thoroughly wetted. The silver alloy typically contains copper, tin and zinc. The zinc is mostly consumed during melting and lost as oxide.

The dentist packs the plastic mass, before it sets, into the cavity. The amalgam expands over 6-8 hours on setting. Dental amalgam does not bond to the tooth structure and is bacteriostatic.

Concerns have been raised about the potential for mercury poisoning with dental amalgam when used in a dental filling. Major health and professional organizations regard amalgam as safe but questions have been raised and acute but rare allergic reactions have been reported. Critics argue that it has toxic effects that make it unsafe, both for the patient and perhaps even more so for the dental professional manipulating it during a restoration. A study by the Life Sciences Research Office found that studies on mercury vapor and dental amalgam provided insufficient information to enable definitive conclusions.[3]

Mercury is a neurotoxin. It's also bio-accumulative, which means it's absorbed by the body at a faster rate than the body can remove it. The most common way to get mercury poisoning is through eating contaminated seafood. That is why the Minamata Convention on Mercury in 2013 is one of the very few instances where the governments of the world came together pretty much unanimously and ratified a treaty. The U.N. treaty named for a city in Japan whose residents suffered from mercury poisoning from a nearby chemical factory for decades. Because mercury pollutants easily find their way into the oceans and the atmosphere, it's virtually impossible for one country to prevent mercury poisoning within its borders. Mercury is an intercontinental pollutant and required a global treaty.[6]

Mercury is a naturally occurring element that can be found in the environment from geological deposits mainly of cinnabar; fuels in raw materials like coal, crude oil, and other fossil fuels; volcanic eruptions release into the atmosphere; weathering rocks; or undersea vents.

Mercury can also be released by humans into the environment through burning of coal and other fossil fuels for energy; burning mercury-contaminated waste; mining for mercury, gold and other metals; or making chlorine (using a cell process, also known as the Castner–Kellner process, for producing chlorine and sodium hydroxide (NaOH) or potassium hydroxide (KOH) that uses mercury as a fluid electrode.[6]

Currently, mercury is used to produce electrical and electronic goods, industrial chemicals, dental preparations, medicines, mercury batteries, thermometers, and atomic plants. Permits for mercury use in fluorescent lighting and dental amalgams are being phased out.

In 2018, an employee at Apollo Fusion approached the Public Employees for Environmental Responsibility (PEER), alleging that the Mountain View, CA based space startup was planning to build and sell thrusters that used mercury propellant to multiple companies building low Earth orbit (LEO) satellite constellations. Four industry insiders ultimately confirmed that Apollo Fusion was building thrusters that utilized mercury propellant. Insisting that the composition of its propellant mixture should be considered confidential information, the company still withdrew its plans for a mercury propellant in April 2021.

Apollo Fusion wasn't the first to consider using mercury as a propellant. NASA originally tested it in the 1960s and 1970s with two Space Electric Propulsion Tests (SERT), one of which was sent into orbit in 1970. Although the tests demonstrated mercury's effectiveness as a propellant, the same concerns over the element's toxicity that have seen it banned in many other industries halted its use by the space agency as well.

Were it not for mercury's extreme toxicity, it would actually make an extremely attractive propellant. Apollo Fusion wanted to use a type of ion thruster called a Hall-effect thruster. Ion thrusters strip electrons from the atoms that make up a liquid or gaseous propellant, and then an electric field pushes the resultant ions away from the spacecraft, generating a modest thrust in the opposite direction. The physics of rocket engines means that the performance of these engines increases with the mass of the ion that you can accelerate.

Mercury is heavier than either xenon or krypton, the most commonly used propellants, meaning more thrust per expelled ion. It's also liquid at room temperature, making it efficient to store and use. And it's inexpensive compared to other fuel sources.

In 2019, studies showed that the use of mercury for propellants of low earth orbit constellation satellites would result in about 3/4[th's] of the mercury eventually ending up in the oceans. In 2022, the United Nations adopted a provision to phase out the use of mercury as a satellite propellant by 2025.[6]

Camden Pet Hospital was required to have an "in case of emergency" check off list posted near each exit door.

It contained an arrowed map of all exit routes from the building, fire extinguisher locations, proper vacating of occupants including hospitalized animals, and outside meeting locations. There was also a check off list containing items such as: turning off oxygen tanks, closing all doors and windows, emergency phone numbers, location of reporting forms for OSHA (Occupational Safety & Health Administration) – Workman's Compensation – Camden's insurance. Also, since at the time only mercury thermometers were available, the list included the location of the Mercury Spill Safety Kit.

The Mercury Spill Safety Kit contained mercury amalgamation powder that converts elemental mercury into a solid, stable zinc amalgam that's safer and easier to handle than pure mercury. It also helped to prevent hazardous mercury vapors from being released into the air. When sprinkled over a mercury spill, the powder binds with the mercury to create the amalgam. The amalgam can then be collected and disposed of. Sponges were to be used to collect the mercury from vertical or overhead surfaces. The kits were recommended for schools, hospitals, laboratories, warehouses, factories, and chemical plants that use liquid mercury. Mercury spill kits also typically included safety items like goggles and gloves, as well as cleanup items like wipes, a dust pan, and a disposal bag.

My friends in Blackfoot, Idaho used to break open thermometers and collect the mercury. We then "polished" old coins and made them look "brand new" by rubbing them with the metal. When mercury dropped to the floor it shattered into many small silvery liquid pieces that reminded me of hot splashes of solder dripping onto a work bench - except the solder would quickly harden (soldering is a process that joins two or more metal pieces together using a filler metal called solder that contains combinations of lead, copper, silver, antimony &/or bismuth. The solder is melted and applied to the metal parts, and then allowed to cool and solidify, creating a strong mechanical and electrical bond). We would rub a coin containing silver over the mercury spill area trying to absorb it onto the coin.

And yes, we ate a lot of potatoes growing up in Idaho but never pushed "polished" coins into the spuds to remove the mercury. To end this article on mercury I would like to quote some coin collector's comments I found, portions of which I can imagine being written by one of my grandchildren or from my experiences:

"My grandfather tried to "polish" a few silver coins using mercury - he essentially made an alloy that no collector will touch because of toxicity. I am looking at the phase diagram of silver and mercury and I am thinking that it is telling me that short of total melt-down there is no simple temperature way to separate these metals. Does anyone have any experience with this? How can I clean the mercury off these nice old silver coins?

Reply: "Boy - you do have a problem. And I must admit it is one I have never heard of. One thing for sure - you need to be careful - mercury can be quite dangerous. Now then - first of all it is unlikely that the coins have much collector value left. Polishing them with even a plain cotton cloth can greatly damage the coins. But putting mercury on them and then polishing them? I don't know if they can be saved. But I'll see if I can at least give you an idea. Only handle the coins when wearing latex gloves so your skin cannot absorb any of the mercury. This next part may sound crazy - and I won't guarantee that it will not harm the coins even more - but it will get the mercury off. Take a raw potato and cut a small slit into it - slide the coin into the slit until it is completely inside the potato. Leave it there for about 24 hrs. The potato will absorb the mercury and should leave the coin clean. Then take the coin and give it a LONG rinse under running water - don't drop it. Then rinse the coin in distilled water - lay it on a cloth and allow to air dry. And make sure to dispose of the potatoes in such a way that no one or an animal can eat them. Cutting them up and putting them down the garbage disposal seems best - but if you do - make sure you throw away the knife you use. I suggest you try this with 1 coin. After your cleaning is complete - then you can have a coin dealer examine the coin and see if he is interested. Second reply: "Back in the good old post WWII days, school kids used to break thermometers to get the mercury out, so they (we) could play with it. It's characteristic of being liquid at room temperature made for some fascinating effects! One common use was to shine up silver coins by rubbing the mercury on the coin (yes Virginia, small change was made of silver in those days), all without knowledge that we were exposing ourselves to potential brain-damage. Come to think of it, maybe that's why I'm obsessed with coins in my dotage (a state or period of old age especially when accompanied by mental decline)."

1– *Liquid Mercury Found In Ancient Mexican Pyramid: A Fuel For Alien Spacecraft? Emily Frost, Smithsonian, 06/08/2024.*

2– *Guide to San Francisco Bay Area Creeks, The Legacy of the Mercury Mines.*

3– *Psychopharmacology, Heavy Metal Blues: The History of Medicinal Mercury, 01/31/2024.*

4– *Why Mercury was Used In Hat Production, hatrealm, Taylor James, 02/04/2024.*

5– *A biogeochemist is tracking the movements of toxic mercury pollution, Science News, Nik Ogasa, 09/23/2024.*

6– *U.N. Kills Any Plans to Use Mercury as a Rocket Propellant, Michael Koziol, IEEE Spectrum, 04/19/2022.*

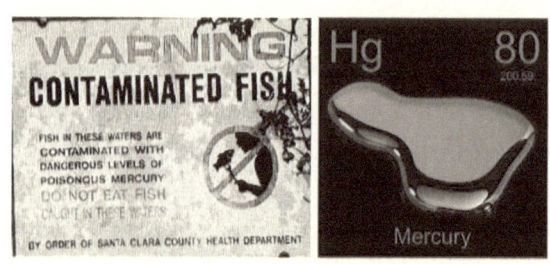

CHAPTER 20

HOOKWORMS ANYONE...

Poliomyelitis kills by suffocation and attacking motor neurons in the spinal cord, weakening or severing communication between the central nervous system and the muscles. The ensuing paralysis means that the muscles that make it possible to breathe no longer work. Polio existed in isolated outbreaks around the world for millennia, but it didn't become epidemic until the 20th century – helped, ironically, by improvements in sanitation. Poliovirus enters the body through the mouth, via food or water, or unwashed hands, contaminated with infected fecal matter.

Until the 19th century, almost all children would have come in contact with poliovirus before the age of one, while they still enjoyed protection from maternal antibodies transferred from mother to baby during pregnancy. However, as sanitation improved, children were less likely to come into contact with poliovirus as babies; when they encountered it as older children, their immune systems were unprepared.

At its peak in the 40s and 50s, the virus killed or paralyzed at least 600,000 people annually worldwide.

1952 saw the largest single outbreak of polio in US history – mostly in children. In places where outbreaks occurred, families sheltered in fear at home with the windows shut. All kinds of public gathering places closed. Human interactions were laced with uncertainty.

The mother was usually passing enough immunity from polio to her child during pregnancy to last until the child was exposed to enough virus in the environment to stimulate its own immunity (like receiving a vaccine). The phrase "cleanliness is next to godliness" is a saying that conveys the importance of cleanliness in a person's life. It's often used as a reminder to wash or clean up. In the case of polio, cleanliness did not lead to godliness – it turned out too often leading to polio. The child was not exposed to enough virus from the environment to stimulate its own immunity. Polio virus is shed by infected people (usually children) through feces and nasopharyngeal secretions, where it can spread quickly, especially in areas with poor hygiene and sanitation systems. Immunity from natural exposure to a disease is known as the "hygiene hypothesis". (See *Thoughts on my Thoughts, Book II,* Walter R. Hoge)

According to the American Academy of Allergy, Asthma & Immunology (AAAAI), it has long been known that an over active immune system can result in allergies and asthma that tends to run in families. Also, children where one or both parents have an allergic disease, it is more likely they will develop these conditions. Fortunately, following some of the principles of the hygiene hypothesis, there are steps that may delay or possibly prevent allergies or asthma from developing. The hygiene hypothesis is a theory that suggests that a lack of microbial, parasitic or food exposure in early life may increase the risk of developing allergies and asthma. This theory is based on the idea that natural infections and microbial exposures may help immunize against these conditions. Food allergies can cause problems ranging from eczema to life-threatening allergic reactions. Common triggers include peanuts, tree nuts, cow's milk, egg, soy, wheat, sesame, fish, and shellfish. Infants with a sibling or at least one biological parent who has allergic conditions are at risk for developing food allergy, especially if they already exhibit allergic symptoms of atopic dermatitis, allergic rhinitis or asthma. Restricting a mother's diet of specific allergens during pregnancy and while breast-feeding, when a child is otherwise well, is not routinely recommended as a means to prevent food allergies. Most recent information indicates there is no significant allergy prevention benefit to your baby if you avoid highly allergenic foods during this time. Breast milk is the ideal way to nourish your infant. It is least likely to trigger an allergic reaction, it is easy to digest and it strengthens the infant's immune system. Especially recommended for the first four to six months, it may possibly reduce early eczema, wheezing and cow's milk allergy. For infants at risk for food allergy where the mother is unable to breast feed, hydrolyzed infant formulas are recommended as hypoallergenic substitutes over cow's milk and soy formulas. Between four to six months of age begin implementation of the hygiene hypothesis by introducing single-ingredient infant foods. Typically including fruits (apples, pears and bananas), vegetables (green vegetables, sweet potatoes, squash and carrots) and cereal grains (rice or oat cereal) one at a time. Food can be introduced this way every 3 to 5 days as appropriate for the infant's developmental readiness. This slow process gives parents or caregivers a chance to identify and eliminate any food that causes an allergic reaction. Egg, dairy, peanut, tree nuts, fish and shellfish can be gradually introduced (in appropriate forms) during the same four to six month window after less allergenic foods have been tolerated. In fact, delaying the introduction of these foods may increase your baby's risk of developing allergies. Since some airborne substances may trigger allergy or asthma symptoms, reducing contact with these substances early in life may delay or prevent allergy or asthma symptoms. Research for this is clearest with dust mites. The relationship between early life exposure to animals and the development of allergies and asthma is somewhat confusing and there are many factors to consider. Previous evidence suggested that children exposed to animals early in life are more likely to develop allergies and asthma. More recent research seems to show that early exposure to animals (cats and dogs in particular) may actually protect children from developing these diseases. Newer research also suggests children raised on farms develop fewer allergies and asthma. Consistent exposure to allergens can reduce or eliminate allergy symptoms. And, lifestyle shifts, such as spending more time indoors or moving to a new region, can improve allergy symptoms. Allergies can change over time, and some people may outgrow them. About a quarter to a third of children outgrow their childhood allergies. Adults may see their symptoms improve and as people age, their immune function declines, which can lead to a less severe immune response to allergens. Some allergies may fade again in the 50s and beyond.

Some people may build up a tolerance to their triggers, especially with pet allergies. However, adults may also develop new allergies due to increased exposure to environmental allergens. Allergy symptoms may also worsen due to an aging immune system and other chronic health conditions.

Both hay fever and asthma are good examples of conditions caused by overactive immune systems. Our immune system is typically viewed there to defend us against all manner of invasions. Without it, we would struggle to survive, as even the most innocuous bug could kill us. Overactive immune cells can start to attack innocuous substances, such as reacting to pollen in the air, or even turn on the body's own cells as in autoimmune conditions. Diseases caused by a hyperactive immune system (hyper immunity) in humans include: allergies (like asthma, hay fever), autoimmune diseases (like lupus, rheumatoid arthritis, type 1 diabetes), inflammatory bowel disease (Crohn's disease, ulcerative colitis), eczema, vasculitis, Sjögren's syndrome, and certain types of hypersensitivity pneumonitis; essentially, conditions where the immune system overreacts to foreign substances or attacks the body's own tissues. It's even thought that some of the fatalities caused by covid-19 infection results from an attack of the immune system on the body's own lung cells. Hyper immunity diseases also occur in animals.

So why should our immune system have this propensity to get out of control and damage our bodies in this way? It's becoming increasingly clear that a major part of the answer is worms. For quite some time, epidemiologists have noticed that diseases such as asthma, hay fever and autoimmune conditions are much more prevalent in the affluent Western world than in poorer countries such as sub-Saharan Africa and India. When they looked into potential causes for this, one difference really stood out: the prevalence of parasitic worms, which are ubiquitous in less developed countries, but much rarer in Europe and most of the USA. Interestingly, there is growing experimental evidence from studies in mice that the presence of these worms acts against the development of disorders caused by overactive immunity.

One possible explanation for this is known as the hygiene hypothesis. Parasitic worms, just as any parasite, have to battle constantly with the host to prevent the body removing them. To do this, they have evolved an arsenal of chemicals that they use to suppress the body's immune system to prevent them from detecting and killing the worms. The hygiene hypothesis supposes that throughout human history, the majority of the population was infected with parasitic worms most of the time. As a result, our immune system had to evolve so that it was strong enough to battle other infections whilst being dialed down by the parasitic worms – just as you might turn your headphones up when on a noisy train. When you step off the train onto a quiet platform, suddenly the noise of the headphones feels deafening. In the same way, when there are no parasitic worms around, the immune system is too strong and liable to attack anything in sight, resulting in the symptoms of asthma or autoimmunity.

This is a beautiful theory and presents an immediate idea for a cure for these diseases. If only it were that simple. Parasitic worms are far from harmless inhabitants of the body – as they can cause potentially fatal diseases; in addition, they impose a constant burden on the body's resources leading to malnutrition and fatigue. So instead, the major prize is to work out what the parasitic nematodes make in order to dampen down the immune system. If we could figure this out, then we could use it as a drug to treat allergies, asthma and autoimmune disorders.

Scientists became interested in the possibility that some parasitic worms might be secreting types of RNA molecules, known as microRNAs. They are tiny segments of RNA that have important roles in the development of many different types of cells, including immune cells. MicroRNAs exert their function by pairing to specific target messenger RNAs (mRNAs) and causing these to be shut down. This enables microRNAs to repress a very specific set of genes. However, many RNAs, like the sequence that is the same in worms, flies and humans, the infected host can't block. RNA is also quite unstable and the environment inside the host's body has a lot of enzymes that chop up (degrade) RNA.

The challenge for the parasite in getting microRNAs to the host cells, however, is considerable. The worm would have to export the microRNAs from inside its own cells and then get them into the cells of the host. But the journey for a lonely RNA molecule between two cells is perilous. RNA is intrinsically quite unstable and the environment has a lot of enzymes that chop up RNA. However, pioneering work discovered a potential solution to this degradation problem. It found that parasitic worms release microRNAs encased in "vesicles"- delivery vehicles that bud off from the cell thus enclosing their cargo in a protective membrane.

The second problem is one of delivery. It was a challenge to understand how the worm could be made to produce enough vesicles, containing microRNAs, to deliver enough vesicles to affect the host cells. Once they get into the cell there was also the question of how they would be able to incorporate themselves into the host system of gene repression. To do this, it was decided to use a species of parasitic round worm called *Trichinella spiralis*. This worm was chosen because of its very unusual lifecycle. Larval worms infect muscle cells of a variety of mammalian species, including humans. There they remain as larvae, potentially for many years, until the host is predated on. The larvae are released when the meat is digested in the predator's stomach and triggers their development into adults. The adults frantically mate in the intestine and release new larvae. The larvae burrow into the intestine and migrate to muscle cells. Once they reach the muscle, they enter the muscle cell where they remain until the next predation event.

The adult is extracellular, in the intestine, and the larvae are intracellular in the muscle. Both have developed an immune system that the host doesn't recognize, either within the muscle cell or within the intestine. This finding may lead to ways that MicroRNA can be used to pair with specific target messenger RNAs (mRNAs) and cause immune cells to be shut down – resulting in preventing hyper immunity diseases.[1]

Greyhound racing in the United States is coming to a close. Since the peak of dog racing in 1985, state laws have led to the closure of racetracks across the country.

After Florida's tracks closed at the end of 2020, and Iowa and Arkansas' closed by the end of 2022, only two active commercial racetracks will remain—both in West Virginia. These closures are occurring from reduced attendance, the increase availability of more cassinos, stigma from past doping dogs and fixed races, and public outcry of animal abuse.

Even though they are superb athletes with great endurance that can run an average of 39 miles per hour, they are also fragile. For example, they have very little body fat and a thin hair coat which makes them susceptible to hypothermia. They are also prone to stress fractures of their feet and legs from the forces placed on them while running on a circular track. There is concern about what will happen to greyhounds that are retired from a race track. Most are retired by 3-4 years of age and their normal life expectancy is 12-15. There have been accusations of selling retired dogs for research and illegal killing of thousands of them.

The greyhound breed goes back in history over 4000 years. The ancestors of the modern greyhounds were used for hunting in ancient Egypt, the Arab world, Persia and in the Greco-Roman epoch. In the 5th century a Greek soldier Xenophon who was Socrates' pupil wrote a manual on hunting with dogs. Fast hunting dogs were a prized possession of pharaohs, kings and ancient aristocracy. The hunting breed was even mentioned in the Bible – Proverbs 30-31 "A lion which is strongest among beasts, and turneth not away for any; a greyhound; and he goat also; and a king, against whom there is no rising up."

The modern history of greyhound racing started in 19th century England when somebody came up with an idea of a circular racing course. That idea was met with great enthusiasm from the public. They could conveniently sit on the stands and watch the dogs running around circular racing tracks chasing a mechanical rabbit. In 1912 an inventor by the name of Owen P. Smith perfected the mechanical lure by making it electrically powered. It became easy to control the speed of the lure keeping the rabbit always at a close distance in front of the dogs. (see *Thoughts on my Thoughts,* Walter R. Hoge) In 2017 another event occurred that has put further strain on the greyhound breed – worms.

Ray Kaplan, a parasitologist and veterinarian then at the University of Georgia, started receiving e-mails from colleagues around the U.S. asking for help with resistant parasitic infections in dogs. The parasites were hookworms, a group of roundworm species that target animals and humans.

Through a series of studies published over the past few years, Kaplan and his colleagues traced the origin, evolution and spread of drug-resistant hookworms in dogs. Their findings implicate the greyhound racing industry in the rise of these superparasites. Once a national pastime, greyhound racing is now nearly extinct in the U.S. But it may have left a dangerous legacy that poses a risk to all dogs. The researchers' discoveries also offer a cautionary tale for the management of human parasite infections.

Parasitic roundworms are ubiquitous in the animal kingdom. Hookworms are named for their hook-shaped mouthparts, which they use to latch on to a host's intestinal wall and feed on its blood. In dogs, the most common species is *Ancylostoma caninum*. Adult hookworms live in the gut, and their eggs are spread through feces. Dogs can get infected when they come into contact with the larvae while walking or playing in contaminated areas or when they ingest larvae-ridden feces.

A. caninum infection is known by veterinarians to be potentially fatal for puppies. The worms consume so much blood that young animals can die from blood loss. A puppy is also at risk because high numbers of larvae can pass through the milk of its infected mother.

Hookworm is typically treated with one of three classes of antiparasitic drugs: benzimidazoles, macrocyclic lactones or tetrahydropyrimidines. To find out whether dog hookworms are resistant to any of these drugs, Kaplan began a series of laborious in vitro and in vivo tests on hookworm samples from three dogs with stubborn infections, including one greyhound named Worthy.

Greyhounds are notorious for developing resistant hookworm infections. For years veterinarians blamed this tendency on A. *caninum's* ability to lie dormant in its host's tissue and remerge after the original infection had cleared, a phenomenon known as larval leak. But Kaplan's initial results, published in 2019, showed that the worms in the three dogs he tested were resistant to all three main classes of drugs used to treat hookworm infections.

These findings, along with the greyhound's hookworm reputation, led Kaplan to suspect something was happening on greyhound farms. What he found on further investigation was the perfect combination of factors to promote the evolution of drug resistance.

In the early 1990s greyhound racing in the U.S. was at its peak. In 1993 greyhounds were competing at dozens of tracks throughout 19 states, and the National Greyhound Association reported that 39,139 new dogs were born on greyhound farms that year. The sport began to decline in the early 2000s because of pressure from animal welfare organizations and the decision by many states to ban it. By 2020 the number of new greyhounds born on farms had dropped to 4,898 a year. Today dog racing is illegal in 42 states, and just two tracks remain active, although roughly 100 breeding farms are still operating.

During their heyday greyhound farms raised hundreds of dogs at a time and treated them regularly with dewormers—regardless of whether they had an active infection—to keep them in peak health. This practice is exactly what you don't want to do if you want to avoid resistance.

Constant drug exposure means any worms that survive have a reproductive advantage and dominate the next generation. Moreover, the exercise pens for these dogs are set up on sand or dirt, which can be the perfect habitat for developing hookworm larvae. After dogs defecate in the pens, the hookworm eggs hatch, and the larvae eventually molt, reaching their infective stage within five to 10 days. Thus, every day when the greyhounds go out to run, they are exposed to resistant hookworm larvae from other dogs, and they seed the environment with resistant hookworms of their own.

To confirm that hookworm drug resistance was originating on greyhound farms, Kaplan carried out a second study, published in 2021, in which he sampled worms from two greyhound adoption kennels in Birmingham, Ala., and Dallas, Tex., and an active racing kennel in Sanford, Fla. The results replicated what Kaplan had found two years earlier: hookworms on the farms had high levels of resistance to all three drug classes. In the 2021 study of greyhound farms, DNA from 99 percent of the samples sequenced had one of the three resistance mutations.

The presence of drug-resistant hookworms at greyhound farms posed a threat to the pet population. As the racing industry began its decline in the early 2000s, organizations sprang up to rehome the dogs, leading to thousands of greyhounds being adopted across the country in the past two decades. Greyhounds infected with drug-resistant hookworm could pass the parasites to other pet dogs. Vets didn't pay much attention to hookworm infections in dogs, because there weren't that many cases. When doctors did see them, they prescribed drugs, but little follow-up occurred, and persistent infections were blamed on larval leak.

Then dog parks started gaining in popularity. Between 2009 and 2019 the number of such parks in the 100 largest U.S. cities increased by 74 percent. These spaces provide the perfect environment for the spread of parasites. As many as 500,000 hookworm eggs can be left in a single dropping from an adult canine, and once eggs and larvae are present in a park, it is nearly impossible to get rid of them. Two studies from 2020 and 2021 found that dogs visiting dog parks had a 70 percent higher prevalence of hookworm infections compared with the overall population.

Having established that greyhound farms were generating drug-resistant hookworms and that at least some pet dogs were infected with them, Kaplan needed a way to determine just how common the superparasites had become in the general dog population. After sequencing fecal samples known to contain hookworms procured from diagnostic labs in Tennessee, Massachusetts, Illinois and California, the researchers were shocked. They found that one of the known resistance mutations was present in 49 percent of the fecal samples, and a novel mutation, which they confirmed also conferred resistance, was present in 31 percent. These results, suggest that roughly 50 percent of dogs in the U.S. with hookworm infections are carrying worms resistant to benzimidazole drugs. Although genetic screens for drug resistance are not possible for the other drug classes, Kaplan thinks it is likely that some of the worms will also be resistant to them.

The rise of drug-resistant hookworm in dogs serves as a warning of what could happen with other species of roundworms that infect humans. Several serious, neglected tropical diseases in humans are caused by roundworms; including river blindness, lymphatic elephantiasis and ascariasis. Because these worms are genetically similar to dog hookworms and are treated with the same drugs, they can develop similar mutations that confer drug resistance. For the past decade public health officials, nongovernmental organizations and pharmaceutical companies have carried out mass drug administration programs in communities affected by the worms that cause these diseases. They have delivered millions of doses of antiparasitic drugs, mainly to children, who suffer the most from morbidity and developmental delays caused by heavy worm infections, with great success. Lymphatic elephantiasis was deemed eradicated in several countries after such programs were implemented.

Already there are reports of the same benzimidazole-resistance mutations appearing in human roundworms. The drugs alone cannot eliminate parasites, and, as the greyhound example shows, drug resistance can appear in one population and easily spread to others.[2]

In the British Medical Journal in 1989, Dr. David P. Strachan posited a scientific theory called the hygiene hypothesis. According to the theory, many modern diseases have gotten out of hand and are rapidly growing in industrialized western countries because of chlorinated drinking water, vaccines, antibiotics and the sterile environment of early childhood. Moreover, it is theorized that since we have become so good at preventing infections, we have upset the internal balance and ecology in our bodies. One missing element of hyper-clean and sterile environments is that our inflammatory responses do not function as they should. Parasites and bacteria play a symbiotic role in preserving our health.

In the late 1980s, Nottingham University medical professor David Pritchard made a trip to Papua New Guinea. While there, he found that many of the natives were infected with the *Necator americanus* hookworm. Hay fever and asthma were uncommon in spite of the huge amounts of allergens occurring naturally in that tropic environment. Pritchard wondered if the hygiene hypothesis might explain why there were so few cases of autoimmune diseases in the tropics. In 2004, after years of research, the immunologist-biologist wanted to test his findings: that certain parasites can improve the immune system's defense against allergies, and possibly more serious autoimmune illnesses. Circumventing the inevitable years of red tape, Pritchard used himself as the first test subject, injecting 50 hookworms under his skin. He was able to deduce that only 10 hookworms were necessary for future test subjects. Later, another colleague, Dr. Rick Maizels of Edinburgh University, confirmed Pritchard's research and subsequently identified the process. Maizels found that the white T-cells in the blood regulate immunity responses, and the hookworms cause an increase in white T-cells.

Hookworms typically infiltrate a human host when larvae, hatched in human excrement, penetrate the soles of the feet, enter the bloodstream, travel through the heart and lungs, and are swallowed when they are coughed up. It is estimated that in underdeveloped countries about 740 million people are infected. Hookworms can cause anemia and speed up the process of malnutrition and stunt growth in children.

On average, hookworms measure about 1 cm long and can survive about five years latching on to the intestinal wall, siphoning off tiny amounts of blood, and — this is the crucial part — regulating the volume of immune responses. They mate inside the host, with females laying up to 30,000 eggs per day — up to 50 million eggs during a lifetime — which pass out in feces.

Hookworms cannot and do not replicate in the gut, are not infectious, and are limited to maturation only in the small intestine. In small numbers doctors consider them to be harmless, and are easily eradicated with hygienic practices, parasiticides, and possibly antibiotics.

As a last resort from health issues, Jasper Lawrence from Santa Cruz, CA wrote: "My life had declined … with asthma. Modern medicine seemed to have nothing to offer me except palliative drugs. … I felt there wasn't a choice for me. Then I read about the Pritchard and Maizels' studies, everything immediately made sense to me. It seemed to me that in our obsession with cleansing and sterility, with the eradication of parasites we had thrown the baby out with the bath water. The central idea is that our bodies have an internal ecosystem. One of the ironies of this, to me, was that everyone is concerned about biodiversity in the outside world and saving the rainforest, but we've also screwed up the biodiversity inside us."

Lawrence immediately began a process to try to get accepted as a participant in one of several ongoing university studies investigating the therapeutic use of hookworm and whipworm parasites. In spite of his best efforts, he was declined. Lawrence reasoned that infecting himself was a last resort but worth a try. He heard that the African country of Cameroon was a paradise for hookworms, and a large number of people there were infected. He immediately began a campaign to poll his friends involved in the medical profession.

He sent them all the research and asked them their opinion. They all said the same thing: "Yes, it appears safe, but I would not advise you to do this; you need to wait 20 or 30 years for all the studies to come in, for a molecule to be identified and a drug to be tested. But Lawrence wasn't about to wait. Instead, he made the trip to Cameroon and spent the next two weeks walking around barefoot in public latrines in an attempt to infect himself with hookworms.

After he returned home to Santa Cruz, Lawrence had no idea if he had succeeded. At the end of the incubation period, six or eight weeks, Lawrence hoped to have embryos in his feces. He sent his stool samples to a lab for confirmation and they came back negative.

Lawrence was later shocked when he accidentally discovered his symptoms had abated. He also discovered that the reason the lab results came back negative was because the labs did not know what they were looking for, since hookworms are uncommon in humans in the United States.

Lawrence followed up on participants involved in the clinical trials in the UK. Several of the participants had gone into a lasting remission. That gave him an idea. Lawrence consulted his friends in the medical field about finding a medically viable way to produce sterile, safe hookworm eggs in small packets that he could sell over the internet to infect interested people. He developed a kit and began selling them with five years of treatments, including support services, for $3,900. He justified the cost by comparing the cost of multiple sclerosis drugs that can easily surpass $150,000 a year.[3]

I had allergies during my youth and they became severe enough while attending veterinary school that I received allergy shots. They were and still are the most commonly used and effective form of allergy immunotherapy for the treatment of allergic conditions affecting the nose and eyes (allergic rhino-conjunctivitis), ears (allergic otitis media), lungs (bronchial asthma) as well as for severe insect sting allergy in the human being.

The skin prick test, also known as a scratch test, is the most common type of skin test used to determine what is causing allergies. A small amount of suspected plant and animal allergens are individually placed on the skin and the allergist scratches the skin to introduce the allergen into underlying tissues. A positive reaction to an allergen, such as a red bump or hive, usually appears within 15–20 minutes. A concoction of the positive allergens is placed into a solution and injected subcutaneously at various times and strengths. The strength of the injection is increased over time in hopes the patient will develop resistance to the allergens. The goal of these allergy shots is to use the principle of the "hygiene hypothesis" by encouraging the body to become insensitive to the allergens (immunotherapy).

Immunotherapy failed and I was encouraged by the allergist to pursue a different profession, stay away from environmental allergens and hope not to develop asthma. I ignored his advice, lived with mostly a stuffed-up nose or worse allergy symptoms until into my 50s and overcame most allergies. However, I still take antihistamines on a daily basis. For years, whenever I had an allergy attack the spot where I had received the allergy injections would form a large itchy red spot for a few days. I believe I had successfully received hypo immunity from most of my allergies by the principle of the hygiene hypothesis – from exposure to the environmental demons of allergens that had plagued my body.

Using the principle of the hygiene hypothesis to cause immune cell shut down, has shown some success attempting to prevent hyper immunity diseases. The article cited above, using *Trichinella spiralis* worms MicroRNA to pair (attach) with specific target messenger RNAs (mRNAs) and causing hypo immunity appears to be a step in the right direction.[1] Dogs were successfully vaccinated against infection with the dog hookworm, Ancylostoma caninum, by vaccination with third-stage larvae (L3) that have been attenuated with ionizing radiation. Subsequently, varying levels of vaccine efficacy have been reported for the major antigens secreted by hookworm L3 in murine (rodent) hosts and dogs. Despite encouraging levels of protection with larval antigens, only partial reductions in fecal egg counts and adult worm burdens have been reported, which suggests that an ideal hookworm vaccine might require a mixture of recombinant proteins that targets both the larval and blood-feeding adult stages of the parasite.[4]

Two recently developed products, Cytopoint (injection) and Apoquel (pill), uses a monoclonal antibody that attaches to interleukin-31, a protein that triggers dermatitis in dogs. This prevents the protein from binding to nerve receptors in the skin, reducing the itch response (causing immune cells to shut down). Skin prick or scratch tests are well on their way to extinction as a tool in treating dogs for allergies (works some in cats – not labeled for use). Maybe someday soon humanoids can swallow a pill or be given an injection once a month to shut down immune cells.

A recombinant vaccine is made using recombinant DNA technology to insert DNA from a virus or bacterium into cells, which then produce an antigen that stimulates an immune response. The process is as follows includes: A small piece of DNA from the virus or bacterium is inserted into the DNA of bacterial or yeast cells, the cells express the antigen, and the antigen is purified from the cells.

Monoclonal antibodies are laboratory-made proteins that are used to treat and diagnose a variety of diseases, including cancer. They are designed to bind to specific targets in the body, such as antigens on the surface of cancer cells. They can be used alone or to carry drugs, toxins, or radioactive substances directly to cancer cells. Monoclonal antibodies are produced by cloning a unique white blood cell, and all subsequent antibodies are derived from that parent cell.

The monoclonal antibodies, Cytopoint and Apoquel, were both developed to treat itchiness and inflammation in dogs caused by allergies. They are used for short- or long-term treatment of atopic dermatitis in dogs of any age. They can be used together to treat intermittent flare-ups of pruritus. Some say that the combination of the two medications is often the best option for dogs with difficult-to-manage allergies. Both can have side effects, and neither inhibits skin or serum allergy testing.

The results from Kaplan's work with Greyhound's resistant to hookworm infections and expanded studies, it appears that roughly 50 percent of dogs in the U.S. with hookworm infections are carrying worms resistant to benzimidazole drugs. Although genetic screens for drug resistance are not possible for the other drug classes, Kaplan thinks it is likely that some of the worms will also be resistant to them.

The rise of drug-resistant hookworm in dogs serves as a warning of what could happen with other species of roundworms that infect humans. Several serious, neglected tropical diseases in humans are caused by roundworms; including river blindness, lymphatic elephantiasis and ascariasis. Because these worms are genetically similar to dog hookworms and are treated with the same drugs, they can develop similar mutations that confer drug resistance. For the past decade public health officials, nongovernmental organizations and pharmaceutical companies have carried out mass drug administration programs in communities affected by the worms that cause these diseases. They have delivered millions of doses of antiparasitic drugs, mainly to children, who suffer the most from morbidity and developmental delays caused by heavy worm infections, with great success. Lymphatic elephantiasis was deemed eradicated in several countries after such programs were implemented.

Already there are reports of the same benzimidazole-resistance mutations appearing in human roundworms. The drugs alone cannot eliminate parasites, and, as the greyhound example shows, drug resistance can appear in one population and easily spread to others.[2]

The modern Greyhound is very similar in appearance to an ancient breed of sighthounds that goes back to the Egyptians and Celts. Dogs domesticated by hunters with long, slender bodies and deep chests, appear in temple drawings from 6,000 BC found in present-day Turkey.

The Whippet is a dog breed that originated in England in the 19th century and is descended from Greyhounds, Italian Greyhounds, and Terriers. It was originally bred to chase rabbits for sport, and was known as the "poor man's racehorse" in England. The breed's history is complex, and there are several theories about how it came to be. Some say the Whippet was bred from runt Greyhounds, while others believe it was a cross between Greyhounds and Spaniels. They also have slender bodies and a deep chest for endurance running. The Whippet is a medium-sized sighthound, with a close, smooth coat that is usually gray, tan, or white. It can run up to 35 miles per hour and is known for being quiet and even-tempered.

The Manchester Terrier rose from the experimental breeding of a Whippet and a cross-bred terrier to produce a new, energetic ratting dog. The new breed was very successful and by the mid-19th century Manchester, England was well known for its "Rat Terrier", thus earning the breed's name, the Manchester Terrier. These sight hounds have slender bodies, a deep chest, erect ears and resemble a Doberman Pinchers in color and markings. Our family dog, BeBe, is a Manchester Terrier and we always keep her on leash. Being a terrier, anything she sees that moves she will chase. When four months of age, she caught an unsuspecting Flicker wood pecker in midair, ran around our house two times throwing the bird up towards the sky several times and catching it before reaching the ground. During her final lap around the house, she ran into an open door and laid down in the living room with the dead prey in her mouth.

We should not have been surprised because Manchester Terriers were used like cock or pit bulls to fight in Europe arenas during the 1800 & 1900s for betting. In this case, the Manchester Terriers were used to show how many rats they could individually kill in an allotted time. They even collected the rats from the countryside because they fought harder than the "lazy city rats". One champion weighed 5.5 pounds and a woman's diamond bracelet was used as her collar.

During his research at the University of Pittsburgh Medical School, Dr. Jonas Salk discovered a potential vaccine for polio. When they needed healthy human test subjects, Salk volunteered himself and his entire family for a vaccine trial. The filial gamble paid off. Everyone tested positive for antibodies against the virus. He refused to patent the vaccine, and never received financial compensation for his discovery. (When Edward R. Murrow asked Salk who owned the patent on the vaccine, Salk responded with one of his most famous quotes: "Well, the people, I would say. There is no patent. Could you patent the sun?")

At the turn of the 20th century, August Bier developed a method for spinal anesthesia. It involved injecting cocaine into the cerebrospinal fluid. To test its effectiveness, Bier enlisted himself. During the experiment, a mix-up left Bier with a hole in his spine leaking cerebrospinal fluid (the brain and spinal cord have a surrounding protective layer of cerebrospinal fluid (CSF). CSF contains nutrients that your brain can use. The CSF layer also supports and cushions your brain and spinal cord from sudden movements. The effect is similar to putting a grape inside a jar. If the jar is empty and you give it a good shake, you'll bruise or damage the grape. That's what would happen to your brain if you had no CSF. But if you fill the jar with water and then shake it, the water slows down how fast the grape moves and cushions it, preventing damage. The primary symptom of a spinal fluid leak is a low-pressure headache that worsens when sitting up and improves when lying down). Bier's assistant stepped in to take his place in the study. Once the assistant was properly numb, Bier kicked his shins, bludgeoned and burned him, plucked out his pubic hairs, and mashed his genitals. The assistant felt nothing—a success the two celebrated by drinking excessively that evening.

In 1929, in the basement of the Eberswalde Hospital in Germany, surgical resident Werner Forssmann inserted a ureteral catheter tube into his elbow, feeding it through a vein up to his heart. He used a mirror as his assistant, since he had restrained his nurse to the operating table. He then took an x-ray of his chest to determine that the catheter had indeed made it to the right atrium. Instead of praise, Forssmann was met with condemnation by medical ethicists. This rejection led him to abandon cardiology for urology, but he was later honored with the Nobel Prize in 1956.

While at the Medical Pneumatic Institute of Bristol, UK, Humphry Davy studied gases. Through a series of self-experiments with oxides of nitrogen, Davy created what is known today as laughing gas. Though his initial attempts were meant to reproduce the pleasurable effects of opium and alcohol, Davy would ultimately recommend the use of nitrous oxide as an anesthetic. His recommendation would not be heeded until long after his death, but nitrous became an instant hit at fashionable parties.

Swiss chemist Albert Hoffman was researching the fungus ergot for a pharmaceutical company when he discovered lysergic acid. His initial tests were inconclusive, but Hoffman decided to retest a synthesized version of the acid. In April 1943, he ingested 25 milligrams of a substance he called LSD-25 in his lab. Legend has it, on his bike ride home, his eyes were opened up to a brave new hallucinogenic world. To this day, LSD enthusiasts observe April 19 as "Bicycle Day." Hoffman would continue to experiment with LSD until his death at 102.

After witnessing a devastating yellow fever epidemic in 1793, Stubbins Ffirth hypothesized the viral hemorrhagic disease was not contagious. To prove his thesis, he tested the disease's characteristic black vomit. On himself. This included, but certainly was not limited to, pouring vomit into his open cuts or onto his eyeballs, drinking infected black vomit by the glassful, and stewing up to his waist in a veritable sauna of vomit. He would later rub blood and urine on his body as well, but ultimately avoided infection. In his 1804 book A Treatise on Malignant Fever; with an Attempt to Prove Its Non-Contagious Nature, he declared yellow fever not contagious. (Later researchers discovered that it was contagious, but only through bites from infected mosquitos.)

In 1982, Professor Marshall and Dr Warren, succeeded in cultivating a previously unknown bacterial species – later named Helicobacter pylori – from several biopsies. They found that the organism was present in almost all patients with gastric inflammation, duodenal ulcer, or gastric ulcer. Marshall was unsuccessful in developing an animal model, so he decided to experiment upon himself. In 1984, following a baseline endoscopy which showed a normal gastric mucosa, he drank a culture of the organism. Three days later he developed nausea and achlorhydria. Vomiting occurred and on day 8 a repeat endoscopy and biopsy showed marked gastritis and a positive H. pylori culture. At day 14, a third endoscopy was performed and he then began treatment with antibiotics and bismuth. He recovered promptly and thus had fulfilled Koch's postulates for the role of H. pylori in gastritis. For their work on H. pylori, Marshall and Warren shared a 2005 Nobel Prize. Today the standard of care for an ulcer is treatment with an antibiotic. And stomach cancer — once one of the most common forms of malignancy — is almost gone from the Western world.

Dr. Robert Lopez, a veterinarian from Westport, New York, intentionally infested himself with ear mites from infected animals in 1993. He wrote about his experience in the Journal of the American Veterinary Medical Association. Lopez's experience included: Taking a sample from a cat's ear with ear mites and placing it in his own ear, experiencing severe itching, to the point where he couldn't sleep, hearing scratching and moving sounds as the mites explored his ear canal, and experiencing a cacophony of sound and pain as the mites traveled deeper toward his eardrum. Lopez repeated the experiment twice to see if it was typical. He was awarded the 1994 Ig (immunoglobulin) Nobel Prize in entomology for his work.

In 2004, after years of research in Papua New Guinea, immunologist-biologist David Pritchard wanted to test his findings that certain parasites can improve the immune system's defense against allergies, and possibly more serious autoimmune illnesses. Circumventing the inevitable years of red tape, Pritchard used himself as the first test subject, injecting 50 hookworms under his skin. He was able to deduce that only 10 hookworms were necessary for future test subjects. By taking this bold step, Pritchard may have opened a door in research where by a way might be found to not only help control hyper immune diseases, but also find a way to stimulate animal and man's biosystems to recognize and destroy the hookworm as other foreign invaders such as microorganisms. He may go into the annuals of science as the one instrumental in saving the Greyhound, Whippet and my BeBe's progeny (the Manchester Terrier).

As for Lawrence's business of selling hookworms through the mail, it grew slowly but steadily for the next three years. His reception on the internet was extraordinary. Nearly all of the feedback was positive. To his misfortune, an unknown bureaucrat decided to classify it (his product) as a pharmaceutical. He had hoped the U.S. Food and Drug Administration would stay out of it, or classify his product as a supplement. In November, the FDA visited his California home warning him he was under investigation. He had not been charged, but Lawrence got spooked and fled the United States. In exile, Lawrence still sells his product but is hyper-vigilant and does not keep a permanent address.[3]

1– *MRC Laboratory of medical sciences, Why catching a parasite might be the best thing for your allergies, 07/03/2020.*

2– *"Dead Heat", Bradley van Paridon, Scientific American Magazine, 329 #6, p. 44, June 2023.*

3– *Man infects self with hookworms to treat severe allergies, KSL.com Utah, Mel Borup Chandler, 06/25/2012.*

4– *The Journal of Infectious Diseases, Volume 189, Issue 10, 05/152004 May 2004.*

CHAPTER 21

COVID, US AND THE ANIMALS...

The earliest reports of a coronavirus infection in animals occurred in the late 1920s, when an acute respiratory infection of domesticated chickens emerged in North America. The infection of new-born chicks was characterized by gasping and listlessness with high mortality rates of 40–90%. The virus was then known as infectious bronchitis virus (IBV). In the late 1940s, two more animal coronaviruses, one that causes murine [rat] encephalitis (MBD) and mouse hepatitis virus (MHV) that causes hepatitis in mice were discovered. It was not realized at the time that these three different viruses were related.

Human coronaviruses were discovered in the 1960s when scientists collected a unique common cold virus in 1961. The virus could not be cultivated using standard techniques which had successfully cultivated rhinoviruses, adenoviruses and other known common cold viruses. In 1965, a novel virus was successfully cultivated by serially passing it through organ cultures of human embryonic trachea. The isolated virus when intranasally inoculated into volunteers caused a cold and was inactivated by ether which indicated it had a lipid envelope. They isolated and grew the virus in kidney tissue culture, designating it 229E. A research group was able to isolate another member of this new group of viruses using organ culture and named it OC for organ culture. Like IBV, MBD, and MHV, the novel cold virus OC43 had distinctive club-like spikes when observed with the electron microscope.

The IBV-like novel cold viruses were soon shown to be also morphologically related to the mouse hepatitis virus. This new group of viruses were named coronaviruses after their distinctive morphological appearance. Other human coronaviruses have since been identified, including SARS-CoV in 2003, HCoV NL63 in 2003, HCoV HKU1 in 2004, MERS-CoV in 2013, and SARS-CoV-2 in 2019. There have also been a large number of animal coronaviruses identified since the 1960s. *Wikipedia*

During the outbreak of COVID-19 [the global spread of the disease caused by SARS-CoV2 (Severe Acute Respiratory Syndrome-Covid Virus 2)] took place at the end of 2019 in Wuhan, China. After infection of more than 120,000 people and the death of almost 5,000, the World Health Organization announced it as a global controllable pandemic. In April of 2020, the number of cases exceeded 2 million and the infection was spread over more than 180 countries. Human coronaviruses (HCoVs) were on the origin of not only the current pandemic, but also of the SARS and MERS epidemics, which infected and took the lives of thousands of people. Virologic and genetical studies confirmed that bats have been transmission hosts for both of the viruses, which were further spread by civets and dromedaries. Recent studies suggest that specific types of animals can be the source of different coronaviruses: bats for alpha- and beta-CoVs, avian for gamma- and delta-CoVs, and rodents for the ancestor of the beta-CoVs lineage.

The infection is not exclusive to wild animals and there are many known strains that affect livestock and pets. Symptoms caused by coronaviruses depend on the type of strain; they may include gastrointestinal ailments (diarrhea, vomiting, anorexia), respiratory ailments (dyspnea, coughing, wheezing) and others. The animal origin of the novel coronavirus led to a discussion about the possible transmission of the disease by contact with pets. A common fear that raised even more after the confirmation of the SARS-CoV2 in a tiger in the Bronx zoological garden. The World Health Organization faced those concerns stating the lack of evidence on the spreading of the novel coronavirus from pet animals to people.

The empirical observations showed that the presence of pets may have a positive impact on the course of COVID-19. Anecdotal evidence seems to persuade that veterinary doctors are rarely affected with COVID-19. Also, Dr. Sabina Olex-Condor, a Spanish physician in Madrid, suggested in an interview that the mild course is more frequent in patients owning pets.

The possible positive effect of pet-ownership can be considered if the presence of the animal coronaviruses is high across the pet population. Therefore, studies were made of papers presenting the occurrence of the animal coronaviruses. Analysis focused on dogs, for two reasons: 1) they are the most common species taken as home pets and canine coronaviruses can be transmitted easily to humans via droplets. Feline coronaviruses are also detected in cats, but their symptoms are mainly related to the gastrointestinal tract or are the causative agent of uncommon and usually fatal, aberrant immune response to viral infection FIP (Feline Infectious Peritonitis), but transmission animal-to-human is highly limited.

The correlation between pet-ownership and the presence of a mild course of COVID-19 has not been able be to established as a possible explanation to this observation. It suggested that the re-emerging contact with animal coronaviruses may lead to the stimulation of the immunological system, thus creating an effective response to SARS-CoV-2 infection.

Conclusions to the study: Canine respiratory coronaviruses occur often among dogs. Ownership of a pet can lead to the contact with dogs' coronaviruses. Re-occurring contact with dogs' coronaviruses might stimulate the human immunological system, and provide an effective response to SARS-COV-2.[1]

Although cats can get infected with SARS-CoV-2 from human beings, the possibility of cat-to-cat (under natural circumstances) and cat-to-human transmission is less likely to occur as they lack the capacity to facilitate the onward transmission of the virus. Therefore, extensive epidemiological investigations should be conducted among the cats living in geographic areas with a high prevalence of SARS-CoV-2 in humans to confirm the role played by domestic cats in the ongoing pandemic.

According to Totton et al. (2021), the following two essential criteria must be met to demonstrate the cat-to-human transmission of SARS-CoV-2:

The individual should undergo an effective quarantine period, followed by negative PCR and serologic testing that eliminates the potential for undetected SARS-CoV-2 infection.

The individual must remain isolated from all other sources of SARS-CoV-2 from the start of the effective quarantine period, through exposure to the infected cat, development of symptoms, and diagnosis.

Despite limited evidence of cat-to-cat SARS-CoV-2 transmission (only in experimental conditions) and lack of evidence on cat-to-human transmission, it should not be forgotten there is a possible role that could have been played by the domestic cats in disease dissemination. At the time of this study; evidence indicates that cats play a limited role in COVID-19 epidemiology, and pets are probably dead-end hosts of SARS-CoV-2 and pose negligible risks of transmission to humans.

Therefore, in terms of the magnitude of infection and potential to transmit SARS-CoV-2 to humans, our surveillance efforts should mainly focus on mustelids (especially minks, ferrets, and others) for early detection and control of infection. This will help ensure that SARS-CoV-2 will not get established in the wild animal population of these susceptible species. We agree with Dr. Passarella Teixeira on the possibility of domestic and feral cats acting as an urban reservoir, subsequently transmitting the virus to human beings. However, it is less likely that such a phenomenon will be reported even if it has occurred due to the efficient and extensive human-to-human transmission of SARS-CoV-2.[2]

Veterinarians, in their day-to-day work, have direct contact with both animals and their owners, which in the time of a pandemic exposed them to a high risk of contracting the (SARS-CoV). The SARS-CoV coronavirus, like MERS-CoV and human coronaviruses that cause colds, belongs to β-coronaviruses that have a similar structure. The group also includes animal coronaviruses such as Bo-CoV (bovine coronavirus) and Cr-CoV (canine coronavirus).

The coronavirus that causes respiratory disease in dogs has a strong antigenic relationship with the coronaviruses that cause human colds. Presumably, Cr-CoV is a bovine virus (Bo-CoV) that crossed the interspecies transmission barrier and adapted to the dog. Canine coronavirus is also spread through humans, who may be passive carriers of Cr-CoV.

At least 40% of the human population has lymphocytes that are responsive to SARS-CoV-2 coronaviruses. It is suspected that they owe this immunity to a previous infection with other coronaviruses that cause the common cold. This is possible because pathogens – like some vaccines – can cause cross-reactivity. It is suspected that these lymphocytes were produced in the body after an earlier cold caused by coronaviruses. The immune response from the common cold coronavirus against SARS-CoV-2 may be associated with a protein called spike, found on the surface of all of these microbes. They are slightly different in each type of coronavirus, but have a common component, the S2 subunit.

This subunit differs slightly among different coronaviruses, but the human body's immune mechanisms do not seem to distinguish them. This applies at least to b-coronaviruses that cause colds, as well as SARS, MERS and COVID-19 diseases.

Moreover, the coronavirus genome encodes for approximately four structural and sixteen non-structural proteins. The spike proteins (S-proteins) are structural proteins that recognize and attach to ACE2 located on the cell membrane of the airways' epithelia and lung parenchyma. Scientists sequenced the SARS-CoV-2 amino acidic sequence and compared it to the sequences derived from other animal coronaviruses. The analysis showed that the resemblance of the whole sequence between SARS-CoV-2 and Cr-CoV is 36.39%.

This is another reason why veterinarians were tested for canine coronavirus and not, for example, feline coronavirus (which belongs to α-coronaviruses and has lower antigenic compatibility with SARS-CoV-2). We assumed, in accordance with the literature, that such a high antigen similarity between SARS-CoV-2 and Cr-CoV may be the cause of the phenomenon of antigenic mimicry and trigger an immune response based on the cross-reactivity.

Although veterinarians may be exposed to the canine Cr-CoV coronavirus, we did not detect the presence of the canine coronavirus in any of the veterinarians we studied. None of the veterinarians had a significant increase in T lymphocytes, which could be an effective defense against SARS-CoV-2.[3]

Those who've dodged COVID-19 may have a newly discovered immune response to thank. In a study that intentionally infected volunteers with the coronavirus, participants with elevated activity of a little-studied immunity gene called HLA-DQA2 didn't get a sustained infection after exposure to SARS-CoV-2. The study offered an unprecedentedly detailed look at how the immune system responds to the coronavirus, and how variation in that response could explain why some people get sick while others don't.

The results stem from a challenge trial: At the height of the pandemic in 2021, scientists in the United Kingdom exposed 36 young, healthy unvaccinated volunteers who'd never gotten COVID-19 to the virus through their noses. While the initial goal was to establish how much virus it takes to kick-start an infection, 16 of the participants underwent more extensive testing. Researchers tracked the actions of a wide range of immunological players in the blood and lining of the nose, both before and after exposure, allowing a detailed view of when and where different players spur into action.

Initially, biologists thought they were wasting experiments on people that they didn't actually infect. But later, they realized they'd stumbled across a "unique opportunity" to understand how some people who got an infectious dose of the virus managed to fend it off. It's unclear how many people have dodged COVID-19. The most recent estimate from the U.S. Centers for Disease Control and Prevention suggested that by the end of 2022, nearly 1 in 4 Americans hadn't caught the virus.

Challenge trials are controversial, as some experts question the ethics of deliberately infecting people with a pathogen. But it can't be underplayed how valuable this kind of information is. It's rare that we get to see a snapshot of what's actually happening in early infection during challenge trials that can track people from the moment they encounter the pathogen.

Participants who didn't get sick in a 2021 trial fell into two categories. Seven individuals never tested positive for the virus, while three got transient infections in their nose that their bodies quickly shut down, so they never got sick. In the former group, researchers detected widespread, but subtle, changes in immune cells called monocytes and MAIT (mucosal-associated invariant T cells). The transiently infected individuals mounted a robust immune reaction, known as an interferon response (group of signaling proteins made and released by host cells in response to the presence of several viruses), in their noses within a day of exposure. Interferons help signal a viral threat, attracting cells that fight the infection.

By contrast, people who got sick took about five days, on average, to marshal the same interferon response in their noses, giving the virus time to proliferate and spread. The discrepancy suggests that swift, localized activity at the site of infection may help prevent SARS-CoV-2 from getting a foothold.

Surprisingly, sick participants' blood showed interferon activity before their noses did. That's the exact opposite of what was hypothesized, given that the virus was delivered via the nose. The immune system is capable of sensing that something is happening and relaying this to the body before the cells that are actually affected know about it.

Among those who didn't get sick, scientists aren't sure why some got briefly infected and others didn't. But before exposure, both groups exhibited elevated activity of the gene HLA-DQA2 in specialized immune cells that help alert the immune system to pathogens, compared with people who developed symptoms. They aren't sure exactly what this gene does, though previous research linked it to milder COVID-19 outcomes. We may eventually be able to predict who is susceptible to infection just by looking at their gene signature for this particular gene.

A lot has changed since these challenge trials were conducted in 2021. Virtually everyone has some immunity to SARS-CoV-2 from infection or vaccination, meaning most people's immune responses would likely differ from those traced here. A larger, more diverse study population — for instance with people of different ages — also, could show more varied responses.

For whatever reason, folks who have this different constellation of immune cells present in the nose prior to infection may be able to mount an immune response more quickly. If so, it's a lucky break for those people. In a sense, the study was also a lucky break for researchers. Subsequent challenge trials have struggled to infect volunteers, given virtually everyone has some immunity to COVID-19 now. That's what makes this study so unique. We'll hopefully never be in the position to do this kind of study for SARS-CoV-2 again.[4]

The virus responsible for COVID-19 is now widespread in wildlife. A recent study in the US identified exposure rates of up to 60 percent in some species. The take-home message is the virus is ubiquitous, studies found positives in many common backyard animals.

Testing almost 800 nasal and oral swabs from animals in rehabilitation centers or that were trapped and released in the wild, the researchers identified six different species with antibodies indicating they'd been infected with SARS-CoV-2 at some point.

Most of the infected species are common across North America and the researchers think it's likely that wildlife exposure to the virus is widespread. However, they found no evidence of SARS-CoV-2 being transmitted back to humans from wildlife. Sites with high human activity had three times the prevalence of viral antibodies in animals, suggesting that, as with most diseases, humans are doing the majority of the spreading. It is believed that humans pass on twice as many viruses to other animals as we receive from them.

As humans rarely come into physical contact with wildlife, the researchers suspect most wildlife exposure to SAR-CoV-2 occurs indirectly through trash and wastewater. The species found to have been infected included eastern cottontail rabbits, racoons, eastern deer mice, Virginia opossums, groundhogs, and eastern red bats. Not all species showed symptoms of the virus or viral shedding when tested in laboratory conditions.

There results highlight that evaluating the importance of each species in the context of a broader community of hosts will be critical for controlling future zoonotic disease risk. Multiple animals tested positive for current infections at the same sites within four days of each other, suggesting animal-to-animal transmission is occurring.

The virus' affinity is to infect humans. However, exposure of the virus to animal results in adapting and possible mutating to thrive in new hosts. The concern is a sylvatic cycle developing where the virus mutates enough to sustain itself in wild animal populations and has the potential of becoming a source of new mutations with potential risks for humans.

Analyzing 126 blood samples, the researchers found most of the strains in the wildlife were the same as those found in humans. But they did detect one previously unreported mutation in the virus taken from an opossum. This mutation may make it easier for the virus to avoid our current treatments.

These findings highlight the need for continued COVID-19 surveillance and further research to understand the virus's movements within and between species. It will be important to continue to sequence variants from wildlife as well as humans to assess if SARS-CoV-2 is adapting to new wildlife hosts.[5]

I believe it was during an immunology class in veterinary school where I heard the comment: "Considering the hyper immunoglobulins produced in your body from exposure to infectious diseases from domesticated animals, wildlife and close client contact over the years – your hyperimmune blood may be more valuable than the professional services you perform."

Passive immunotherapy is one of the alternatives to be further explored for treating coronavirus infections. It has been used in medical practice for some years and stands out as a possibility in the current pandemic scenario. It is a treatment that aims at inducing rapid immunity in a short time and is extremely relevant as a therapy of choice in a pandemic.

Over the years, the use of antibodies for antiviral treatments has grown from therapy with hyperimmune sera, evolving into the use of polyclonal and monoclonal antibodies. Passive immunization treatments aim to increase the patient immune response, preventing the disease from progressing to more severe conditions. This strategy has been used recently in European countries affected by COVID-19 as adjunctive therapy to antivirals, and other medications, as it acts directly on viral neutralization, preventing disease progression. The highlights among these biotechnological products are intravenous immunoglobulins, convalescent plasma, monoclonal antibodies, nanobodies, and hyperimmune sera.

Intravenous immunoglobulins are obtained from healthy donors, with a high titer of specific antibodies against the target agent. They are used in the treatment, for example, of autoimmune, and coronavirus diseases. Convalescent plasma is collected from individuals cured from the infection of interest. The plasma must be purified, and free from infectious agents, and can be administered to patients with more severe conditions, such as in COVID-19. It is worth mentioning that this therapy has already been used to treat infections such as influenza and cytomegalovirus. However, despite the potential, its main limitation is the number of available donors that have high antibody titers for coronavirus.

Monoclonal antibodies are antibodies selective for a specific viral antigen and are homogeneous, produced by a single clone of B cell. As the SARS-CoV-2 is an RNA virus, it may mutate and become resistant, which is a great disadvantage to the use of these antibodies. Currently, many studies in this area involve protein S, which is present on SARS-CoV-1 and SARS-CoV-2 and can be used in treatment for both of these. These antibodies can be administered in association with other drugs or as monoclonal antibody cocktails.

Nanobodies are active fragments of antibodies (single monomeric variable domains) that, in recent years, have been extensively explored for the treatment of poisoning by venomous animals, bacteria, and parasitic zoonoses. They can recognize antigens and have been studied for therapies against, for example, influenza virus, MERS-CoV, and Congo hemorrhagic fever virus. They are quite thermally stable, easy to reproduce in prokaryotic systems, specific, and can be humanized so they have potential as therapeutic tools.

Since the 19th century, polyclonal immunoglobulin therapies have been widely used. They are made with pools of human or animal donor serum with high neutralizing titers. Hyperimmune serum contains polyclonal antibodies, which can be used therapeutically to treat viral infections. They are concentrates of heterologous immunoglobulins, formed by intact IgG molecules or digested Fab, and F(ab')2 fractions.

The initial studies on polyclonal immunoglobulin therapies date back to 1891 with Émile Roux, in which hyperimmune horse serum was used successfully to treat tetanus, bubonic, and pneumonic plague. In 1894, hyperimmune sera from animals were used to treat cases of accidents with venomous animals. Subsequently, this therapy with hyperimmune serum against specific venoms became established and uses equine plasma as a source of polyclonal antibodies. Some countries already have a high production of hyperimmune serum against the rabies virus. The serum is used prophylactically in cases of human accidents involving animals with or suspected of carrying the rabies virus. Good results of this treatment have resulted in researchers studying this same therapy against influenza, and Ebola. Pre-clinical studies with the Ebola virus, H5N1 influenza virus and SARS have shown very promising results.[6]

During my wife's two-week recovery from Covid-19 for the fourth time, I began to wonder why I hadn't suffered the ravages of this disease. When she and I tested positive for the first time, I was dressed and ready to go to work. I quarantined myself for five days without symptoms. It's been that way all four times except recently I tested negative. I never felt ill – only side effect was loss of taste for approximately two months. It helped me appreciate how older people can lose their desire for food. Increased spice, salt and sugar on my food helped encourage me to eat. I especially desired semi sweet dark chocolate.

I was able to find the reference cited above: "Doctor Sabina Olex-Condor, a Spanish physician in Madrid, suggested in an interview that the mild course is more frequent in patients owning pets." So, I contacted associates and clients that I knew had direct contact with cats and asked them about their families experience with covid. I chose cats because it has been shown that dogs can spread their own respiratory disease and most dogs in my area don't come in contact with wild animals (including feral cats) on a regular basis, like indoor/outdoor cats do.

Six families, including mine, and a total of twelve people. The results were:

- 1 with moderately severe disease and four incidences of infection (dog & cat home exposure).
- 2 with moderately severe disease, one event, boyfriend & a husband (home exposure to pets).
- 1 may have had covid while working in South Dakota for two months?
- 2 moderate cases (home exposure cats).
- 3 mild cases of covid. (cattery breeders & veterinary technician). Two had some loss of taste.
- 2 tested positive but showed no symptoms. (veterinarian and staff member) One had loss of taste for about two months.
- 1 did not have covid (was not tested)?

It definitely appears to be that some of us folks for whatever reason, have this different constellation of immune cells present in the nose prior to infection that may be able to mount an immune response more quickly. It may be that you are lucky enough to have elevation of the gene HLA-DQA2 circulating in your body to stimulate immunity. Or you may have been exposed enough to less pathogenic covid virus' enjoying the contact with your dog or cat enough to become resistant to covid-19 virus. I may have been extra lucky being exposed during my career to dogs, cats, rabbits, birds, chinchillas, gerbils, hamsters, wildlife, at times pet exotics (ferrets, wild squirrels, a skunk, raccoons, a wild piglet etc.), as well as clients that have been exposed to their sick with coronavirus companion animals.

I just might have some of that hyperimmune blood flowing through my veins that was more valuable to me than my professional services during the pandemic. Don't tell anyone – at my age I'm fearful sharing a pint or two of my blood may "be the straw" that accelerates my decline.

From my research and little investigation, I strongly suspect animal exposure has something to do with it. I just hope wildlife doesn't turn the tables with another virulent coronavirus to contend with.

1– *Do pets protect their owners in the COVID-19 era? Med Hypotheses, 09/12/2020.*

2– *SARS-CoV-2 infection in domestic and feral cats: current evidence and implications, Vet Q., 08/18/2021.*

3– *Cent Eur J Immunol. 2022; 47(3): 275–279, Could veterinarians be immune to contracting SARS-CoV-2? 10/04/2022.*

4– *Some people have never gotten COVID-19. An obscure gene may be why, ScienceNews, Jonathan Lambert, 08/10/2024.*

5– *Virus Behind COVID-19 Now Rampant in Wild Animals, Study Finds, Health, Nature Communications, Tessa Koumoundouros, 08/11/2024.*

6– *Int Immunopharmacol. Covid-19 and Hyperimmune sera: A feasible plan B to fight against coronavirus, 2021 Jan; 90: 107220.*

CHAPTER 22

CATS AND TOXO...

Regardless of size and form variations, all cats look alike, and they are easily recognized as members of the Felidae. The cat-like ecomorph is consistent throughout the felid species, and is one of the most conspicuous among the families of the order Carnivora. Many cat species are quite distinguishable by differences in their body mass and color pattern. However, the variations in their skeletal design are less evident, as well as the ecomorphological implications associated with these.

Although cats show several ecological particularities along their distribution in many biomes worldwide, they are consistently successful hypercarnivores. Both big and small cats show similarities on their hunting strategy: it starts with prey stalking, followed by a variable range sprint, and then they capture their prey with the anterior limbs and claws, holding it for the fatal neck bite. Usually, this attack injures the spinal cord, but some large cats bite the throat in order to suffocate the prey.

It appears that nature has found a perfect working design and behavior in Felidae – it works and has changed little over the millennia.[1]

Since house cats (Felis catus) were domesticated over 9000 years ago, humans have introduced them across much of the world. Today, cats inhabit all continents, except Antarctica, and have been introduced to hundreds of islands, making them amongst the most widely distributed species on the planet. Because of this cosmopolitan distribution, cats have disrupted many ecosystems to which they have been introduced. Specifically, cats spread novel diseases to a range of species including humans, out-compete native felids and other medium sized carnivores or omnivores, threaten the genetic integrity of wild felids, prey on native fauna, and have driven many species to extinction. As a result, free-ranging cats (i.e., owned or unowned cats with access to the outdoor environment) are amongst the most problematic invasive species in the world.

One attribute that has allowed cats to be successful invaders is their generalist diet. Cats are opportunistic predators and obligate carnivores that can survive on preformed and metabolic water in food for months. Furthermore, cats have evolved to survive only on animal tissue and have a set of specific nutritional adaptations as carnivores. Specifically, cats have a limited ability to regulate enzymes of amino acid metabolism, and an inability to use plant material for conversion to amino acids and vitamins. Hence, while cats consume plant material, they are dependent on meeting their energetic demands through consuming a high protein diet. As a result of these physiological needs and behavioral attributes, cats are known to depredate and scavenge a wide variety of animals.

Dietary analyses have been carried out for cats around the world for well over 100 years, with many studies revealing that either birds or small mammals are the dominant prey items, often depending upon the ecosystems in which the studies were conducted. Such dietary differences across studies are likely in part a reflection of differences among locations in prey availability. Hence, while widely distributed species are commonly found in cat diets [e.g., house mouse (Mus musculus), house sparrow (Passer domesticus)], this is more a reflection of study location and prey distribution and abundance, rather than diet preference. However, recent findings suggest cats continue to hunt particular species of prey, even when these prey species become scarce, and that they can exhibit individual variation in hunting behavior. Furthermore, cats scavenge carcasses of animals, including animals larger than they can kill, and consume spoiled and wasted food left by people, which allows them to exploit these resources and exist in a wide range of ecosystems and potentially at greater densities. However, scavenging is not the dominant source of food for cats due to their high energetic needs.[2]

Invasive species pose a direct threat to the survival of Hawaii's native wildlife and the health of unique island ecosystems. Biodiversity on the remote volcanic islands in the Hawaiian archipelago evolved in total isolation over many millennia. Today, Hawaii is recognized as the endangered species capital of the nation, and is a global extinction hotspot. The high extinction rate can be attributed, in large part, to the introduction of non-native species. Because none of their natural predators exist in Hawaii, invasive species such as the coconut rhinoceros beetle, feral pigs, feral cats, ungulates, rosy wolf snails, and countless plant species, successfully outcompete the native species for resources such as prey, space, and nutrients. Invasive species also transmit and serve as reservoirs for introduced diseases that native Hawaiian species never evolved protections against.

The damage done by invasive species can be found throughout the entire Hawaiian island chain, but the effects are magnified on the most densely populated island of Oahu. Perhaps the most injurious species, at-large cats, have proven to be an extraordinary regulatory and management challenge in Hawaii and throughout the world. Cats are believed to have been introduced in the Hawaiian Islands from sailing ships that arrived in the early to mid-1800s. In the absence of predators, they quickly established feral colonies throughout the islands and just as quickly became a significant threat to native wildlife.

At-large cats have been determined to be responsible for the extinction of 33 species and are considered to be a principle threat to 8% of critically endangered birds, mammals, and reptiles worldwide. At-large cats disrupt Hawaii's ecological balance by predating native wildlife, including ground nesting seabirds such as the Newell's shearwater, Hawaiian petrel, and Laysan Albatross.

They also play a pivotal role in spreading a zoonotic disease called Toxoplasmosis. The combination of the direct predation and disease caused by at-large cats pose one of the greatest threats facing Hawaii's endemic species including marine mammals, and has become the leading cause of disease related mortality for the endangered Hawaiian monk seal.

At-large cats include feral and abandoned cats, and cats that are permitted to roam freely outside. While many other species can be infected by Toxoplasma, it cannot complete its life cycle to produce the infectious stage that is deposited in the environment (these species are called intermediate hosts). Although Toxoplasma can infect many different species it disproportionately impacts the health of mammals, including humans and marine mammals.

Domestic cats are the only definitive host species present in Hawaii, and therefore the only animals that can shed the infectious oocysts into the environment in their feces. These microscopic oocysts contaminate the environment where they can be ingested by wildlife, and sometimes even humans, causing infections in those intermediate hosts. While ingestion of oocysts is the most common route of infection, Toxoplasmosis can also be contracted by eating undercooked meat of intermediate hosts, such as feral pigs, deer, goats, and other mammals.

Toxoplasmosis is the leading cause of disease related death in Hawaiian monk seals and is one of the two leading threats to the survival of this endangered species. Toxoplasmosis has been linked to fatal organ failure and brain damage in monk seals and other marine mammals, to reproductive failure in domestic and wildlife species, and to declines in terrestrial and aquatic wildlife populations.

But if cats live on the land, how does Toxoplasma infect marine mammals? At-large cats deposit oocysts throughout the environment in their feces. The oocysts are washed into streams, waterways, ground water, and storm water systems and then flushed into the ocean. Heavy rainfall also contributes to the widespread distribution of toxoplasma oocysts throughout the ecosystem, as water makes its way from mountain tops to the sea. Once oocysts are introduced into the marine ecosystem, monk seals may ingest them directly or, like many other marine mammals, they may be exposed by eating contaminated or infected prey.[3]

Marine species constitute a very diverse group of animals with global distribution, mostly along coastal regions or habitat. The human population density in coastal areas greatly increased during the recent decades and zoonotic pathogens can be transmitted to humans directly or indirectly from marine animals. Thus, the health of marine mammals can substantially influence human's well-being.

Toxoplasmosis, caused by the intracellular protozoan Toxoplasma gondii, is a zoonotic infection with felids as definitive hosts, and a wide range of homoeothermic (warm blooded) vertebrates as intermediate hosts. Pregnant women and immunocompromised patients are at a higher risk for developing the clinical disease with harsh outcomes, including congenital toxoplasmosis (hydrocephalus, chorioretinitis, and cerebral calcifications) and life-threatening encephalitis.

Understanding T. gondii transmission routes in wild, free-ranging marine mammals is problematic. There are three possible routes by which marine animals could become infected with T. gondii, including: ingestion of oocysts, ingestion of bradyzoites in tissue cysts of other intermediate hosts or vertically. Oocysts are shed via cat feces into the environment, which can readily infect several animal species. Small T. gondii oocysts show remarkable

317

resistance to common disinfectants and remain alive in moist surroundings, even when exposed to a vast range of salinity and temperature conditions. This environmental tolerance leads to a fast and extensive dispersal of infection, particularly following heavy rainfalls. The runoff originated from rainfalls alongside wastewater outfalls being likely contaminated with stray/feral cat fecal material make a huge depot of infective oocysts, which are usually discharged into a water body, i.e., sea and ocean, posing potential risk of T. gondii infection in those species dwelling in marine habitats. In another way, marine animals acquired infection through ingestion of T. gondii protozoal cyst containing numerous bradyzoites in warm blooded prey.

A number of investigators have pointed out that oocysts and bradyzoites of T. gondii are concentrated by oysters, clams and mussels during filter-feeding activity. It is noteworthy that the role of vertical transmission of toxoplasmosis in marine animals is unknown. However, experimentally oocyst sporulation occurs in seawater, remaining infective for animals for 6–24 months, depending on the temperature. Filter feeding sea animals may contribute to T. gondii infection. Also, the increasing amounts of anthropogenic toxicants discharged into the marine environment, as well as morbillivirus infection, can suppress the immunity of marine mammals and give rise to clinical toxoplasmosis susceptibility.

Each cat, as final host for T. gondii, shed over 3–810 million oocysts. The sporulation of the oocysts takes 1–5 days, and they can remain infective in the soil for up to 18 months. Furthermore, experiments showed that oocysts of T. gondii can sporulate in sea water and survive at 4 °C for

24 months and then infect mice. One important factor in infected hosts is the strain of the parasite, which plays a major role in the toxoplasmosis prognosis. As noted in cited article above, one interesting study has demonstrated strains of T. gondii in canids, coastal-dwelling felids, nearshore-dwelling sea otters, and marine bivalve shellfish. It is assumed that contaminated runoff to feline fecal material rapidly reaches sea from lands, and otters could be infected with T. gondii via the consumption of filter-feeding marine invertebrates.

Current studies indicate that the global prevalence rate of T. gondii infection is high in marine animals. It is well demonstrated that T. gondii parasite has a very successful adaptation in aquatic environments. Despite the worldwide range and broad marine animals host record of T. gondii infection, there was no evidence regarding toxoplasmosis in these animals in most parts of the world.[4]

The basic lifecycle of the parasite Toxoplasma gondii in warm blooded animals goes is: Toxoplasma reproduces inside the intestine of a cat, which sheds the parasite (oocysts) in its feces. The parasite is consumed from contaminated food or water with cat feces. The parasite takes up residence in the brain (as bradyzoite cysts) and, if that animal gets eaten by a cat, it starts the cycle all over again (by shedding oocysts in the stool).

Researchers have known for several years that a rat infected with Toxoplasma loses its natural response to cat urine and no longer fears the smell. And they know that the parasite settles in the rat's amygdala, the part of the brain that processes fear and emotions. Recent studies add another bizarre piece to the tale: When male rats infected with Toxoplasma smell cat urine, they have altered activity in the fear part of the brain as well as increased activity in the part of the brain that is responsible for sexual behavior and normally activates after exposure to a female rat. The double messages of "you smell a cat but he's not dangerous" and "that cat is a potential mate" lure the rat into the kitty's deadly territory, just what the parasite needs to reproduce. Scientists still don't know how the parasite works to alter the brain, though there apparently is a link to production of dopamine, an important neurotransmitter in the systems for decision-making and reward.[5]

When considering the risk of foodborne illness per unit weight of food consumed, seafood leads all other food groups as the most risk. Foodborne illness caused by pathogenic organisms in bivalve shellfish constitutes a significant health risk to consumers, and therefore carries economic risk and uncertainty to shellfish growers and the seafood industry as a whole. While attention to shellfish-borne disease to date has largely focused on bacterial and viral pathogens as well as algal toxins (e.g. paralytic shellfish toxins) - protozoan pathogens, including Cryptosporidium spp., Giardia duodenalis, and Toxoplasma gondii, have been identified as underrecognized foodborne pathogens from shellfish.

Importantly, concrete epidemiological or clinical data demonstrating a link between shellfish consumption and infections in people due to those protozoan pathogens have not been published to date. However, protozoan pathogens in shellfish have been likely underreported due to lack of standardized methods for their detection, delay between human infection and the development of illness, and/or nonspecific diarrheal illness. Evidence for their widespread contamination in shellfish, low infectious dose, potential severity of infection, and robust environmental parasite stages, demonstrates that protozoan parasites should be considered important foodborne pathogens in shellfish.[6]

According to the CDC: Toxoplasmosis is an infection caused by a single-celled parasite called Toxoplasma gondii. Cats play a key role in is spread. It is the leading cause of death from foodborne illness in the United States. The parasite occurs worldwide and can last for up to a lifetime in humans and other animals. People who are pregnant or immunocompromised with a weakened immune system can take steps to reduce their risk of infection due to Toxoplasma.

It is common for people to be infected with the parasite in the United States. Most with healthy immune systems who get toxoplasmosis do not have symptoms. Those with symptoms may experience flu-like symptoms, swollen lymph nodes, muscle aches, and pains. Severe toxoplasmosis causes damage to the brain, eyes, or other organs. Infants infected while still in the womb often have no symptoms at birth but can develop symptoms later in life.

Although anyone can become infected with toxoplasmosis, some people need to be more cautious given their health condition; including pregnancy and those who are immunocompromised. People who are at risk for developing severe toxoplasmosis include infants born to mothers who are newly infected with Toxoplasma gondii during or just before pregnancy, and people who are severely immunodeficient – those with HIV, taking certain types of chemotherapy, or those who recently received an organ transplant.

Humans can become infected with Toxoplasma through the following: Eating contaminated undercooked meat or shellfish or unwashed contaminated fresh produce, accidentally consuming the parasite through contact with cat feces (poop) or contaminated soil that contains Toxoplasma. Mother-to-child (congenital) transmission when a newly infected mother passes the infection to their unborn child, and receiving an infected organ transplant or infected blood via transfusion (though this is rare).

Recommended precautions to reduce the risk of becoming infected with Toxoplasma gondii: Use a food thermometer to cook food to a safe internal temperature high enough to kill Toxoplasma (160 degrees F), freeze meat for several days at sub-zero (0° F) temperatures before cooking, rinse fruit and vegetables under running water or cook them, do not drink unpasteurized goat's milk, do not eat raw oysters, mussels, or clams, clean areas where you handle food with hot, soapy water after preparing each food item, wear gloves when gardening or touching soil or sand that may be contaminated with cat feces, wash hands with soap and water any time you touch something that may be contaminated with cat feces, and change the cat litter box daily.

Proteins are biomolecules made up of amino acids. They are needed for the body to function properly and are the basis of body structures, such as skin and hair, and of other substances such as enzymes, cytokines, and antibodies. Proteins are used as medicines in a variety of ways, including as therapeutic drugs and to help identify the effect of other drugs.

Proteins are used to treat a wide range of diseases, including cancer, HIV, autoimmunity, inflammation, genetic disorders, and exposure to infectious agents. As medicines, proteins can act as catalysts, signaling molecules, transporters, scaffolds, and receptors. They have several advantages over small molecule drugs, including:

- Specificity: Proteins often perform complex functions that can't be mimicked by chemical compounds.

  They are less likely to cause side effects because they have evolved to play specific roles and are less likely to interfere with normal biological processes.

- Protein engineering: Advances in protein engineering technologies allow drug developers to fine-tune proteins to maintain or improve safety and efficacy. For example, recombinant protein drugs, also known as "biobetters", are improved versions of existing biopharmaceuticals that can produce effects for longer periods of time.

- Identifying drug effects: Proteins can also be used to help identify the unknown effects of existing drugs.

The blood-brain barrier (BBB) is a semi-permeable membrane that regulates the movement of molecules and ions between the blood and the brain's interstitium. The BBB's permeability is limited, which protects the brain from rapid changes in metabolic or ionic conditions, and from exposure to molecules that are toxic to neurons but harmless to other organs. The BBB also allows the brain to receive nutrients and filters harmful compounds into the bloodstream.

The BBB prevents macromolecules used for medicine and research that requires delivery into the central nervous system.

In a recent breakthrough study researchers engineered the 'cat parasite' Toxoplasma gondii to deliver drugs to the human brain. The parasite's ability to penetrate the brain and survive there in a dormant state, without reproducing, makes it a perfect candidate for the researchers' novel approach: genetically engineering Toxoplasma gondii to secrete therapeutic proteins.

One of the biggest challenges in treating neurological diseases is getting through the blood-brain barrier (BBB). It is very difficult to deliver drugs to the brain via the blood stream, and this is especially true for large molecules such as proteins, the critical 'machines' that carry out many important functions inside the cell.

Toxoplasma gondii, can infect a vast variety of organisms, but reproduces only in the guts of cats. The parasite is very effective in infecting humans, with an estimated third of the global population infected at some point in their lives. Most people don't even feel the infection or only experience mild flu-like symptoms. The parasite is, however, dangerous for people with immune failure due to conditions like AIDS, and for fetuses whose immune system has not yet developed. This is why pregnant women are advised not to eat raw meat which might contain the parasite, and to stay away from cats, that might deliver it through their feces. While ridding the body of the parasite, a healthy immune system has only limited access to the brain, and the parasite remains in the brain throughout the carrier's lifetime.

The parasite's ability to penetrate the human brain and survive there in a dormant state, without reproducing, makes it a perfect candidate for researchers' novel approach: genetically engineering Toxoplasma gondii to secrete therapeutic proteins. During infection, T gondii 'shoots' a 'harpoon' into neurons, to enable penetration. Once inside, the parasite forms a kind of cyst (bradyzoite) in which it continues to secrete proteins permanently. Scientists engineered the parasite's DNA to make it produce and secrete the proteins they wanted, which have therapeutic potential.

The parasite's ability to pass through the BBB and communicate with the neurons, combined with the ability to engineer the parasite, generates a golden opportunity for solving the great therapeutic challenge of delivering medications to the brain. This breakthrough can have far-reaching implications for a series of severe diseases. In the present study the researchers specifically demonstrated the delivery of a protein called MeCP2, whose deficiency is associated with Rett syndrome.[7]

Perhaps you're a cat lover. Perhaps you abhor the lazy critters. Either way, when you see a cat lounging on an armchair, napping all day but for the occasional stretch or window gaze, "useless" is by no means the last word that comes to mind. Cats, beloved or otherwise, don't radiate the message that they're indispensable, hard-working members of the household, or the world. But, in fact, they're just playing it cool (as usual). Experts say that if all the world's cats suddenly died, things would quickly go to hell in a handbasket.

Cats, both pets and strays, may fool us into thinking that they depend on our food and trash for survival, but they're expert predators with adaptable hunting behaviors. They are a significant predator of small animals, and can survive as almost solitary animals when the prey is scarce, while thriving in high density when the prey is abundant.

And that's just why we'd miss them. By killing mice and rats in barns and grain storage areas, cats are vital for keeping those pests in check. In India, cats are believed to play a significant role in lessening the amount of grain loss caused by consumption or contamination by rodents. In other words, it may be true that humans feed cats, but without cats, humans would have less food in the first place. So, how dramatically would the rodent population increase if cats suddenly vanished? It just so happens that several scientific studies have been conducted that paint a vivid picture. A 1997 study in Great Britain found that the average house cat brought home more than 11 dead animals (including mice, birds, frogs and more) in the course of six months. That meant the 9 million cats of Britain were collectively killing close to 200 million wild specimens per year — not including all those they did not offer up to their owners. A study in New Zealand in 1979 found that, when cats were nearly eradicated from a small island, the local rat population quickly quadrupled.

If the rodent population shot up, this would of course trigger a cascade of other ecological effects. On that same island in New Zealand, for instance, ecologists observed that, as rat numbers increased in the absence of cats, the population of seabirds whose eggs rats preyed upon declined. And let's not forget the emotional toll that a mass cat death would take on humans: In most countries, cats are much loved. While there are more dog-owning households (38 percent) than cat-owning households (34 percent), there are actually more domestic cats. Cats as pets have always been appreciated for the contact, relatively low maintenance, and pedomorphic (child-like) face and general morphology.[9]

Cats are nocturnal and roam the night, which led to the belief that they were supernatural servants to witches. In the 14th century the black cat was linked to the devil, it led to many of them being killed during the Black Death pandemic. The contagious bacterial disease was characterized by fever and delirium, typically with the formation of enlarged lymph nodes under the arm pits and in the groin called buboes (bubonic plague) and sometimes infection of the lungs (pneumonic plague). The pandemic, caused by the bacterium Yersinia pestis, swept through Europe, Asia, and North Africa from 1346 to 1353. The plague was spread by fleas carried by rodents and cats as hunters of rodents. The cats could become infected, but rarely transmitted the disease to humans. It appears unlikely that cats were responsible for the Black Death. The cats were actually helping to kill the rats that spread the plague, killing them was likely a mistake that cost many lives. However, both cats and rats harbored fleas that also bit the family and spread the plague. In the 16th century cats became associated with sorcery, magic, and witches, and were feared as signs of evil.

Luckily, even after 250 years of professionals documenting thousands of new plants and animals every year, the rate at which new species are discovered remains relatively stable. Somewhere between 15,000 and 18,000 new species are identified each year, with about half of those being insects. However, that number is somewhat misleading: it also includes the correction of taxonomic mistakes, movements from one family to another, and decisions that will end up being overruled in years to come. The new species are scattered all over the globe, with animals from the top ten list hailing from Morocco, Australia, eastern China, and central Mexico.

There are many scenarios that can lead to a new species being discovered: The archetypical researchers clad in multi-pocketed khaki clothing heading into the jungle certainly do locate new creatures. There are also cases of new species being found in museum collections, where they were collected 50 or 100 years ago and at the time nobody looked at the specimens closely enough. Technology has led to even more animals being identified - new species today are regularly detected through DNA. Often, two species live relatively near to each other and look exactly alike, which means they were formerly categorized as only one genus.

The political situation can unnerve researchers far more than a long and uncomfortable boat ride, and national and regional instability can lead to waves of scientists alternately heading to (or avoiding) large swaths of land.

Zoologists at the National Zoo in Washington, D.C. actually spent years being frustrated about their resident olinguitos' inability to mate. But the olinguito is a small carnivore in the raccoon family, commonly confused with its identical-looking cousin the olingo. They were trying to mate the olinguito with an olingo, not realizing that it was an entirely different species. Analyzing their DNA showed enough dissimilarities in their genes to now classify them as separate species.

According to panda.org, experts calculate that between and 0.1% of all species will become extinct each year. If the low estimate of the number of species out there is true – i.e. that there are around 2 million different species on our planet – then that means between 200 and 2,000 extinctions occur every year.

Cats have earned a reputation for being hard-to-read animals as they communicate differently than humans. With their posture, tails, eyes, ears, whiskers, and vocalizations, they can explain to you whether they are comfortable and secure or not. Changes in behavior can be unpredictable and its source difficult to resolve. Addition of another cat, a new family member, changes of seasons or other environmental stresses, or sickness can be an inciting cause.

Why is my cat suddenly not use its litter box, meowing, not eating, hiding from the family…the list can go on and on. Even with Google searches and vet visits, cats are known for not letting you know what is bugging them.

My cat Boo, owns a home that happens to be shared by me. He had been dropped off several times in a carrier by the side door of Camden Pet Hospital where I worked. Finally, the staff made Boo a part of the hospital in hopes that a new owner could be found. I eventually neutered him and took him home to supplement a couple of other outdoor cats for vermin control on our property. Watching him inside the house, it soon became apparent that letting him outside would not work. He didn't show caution or fear and I was afraid the behavior would lead to a quick meal for a coyote that occasionally made its way through the neighborhood. So, he became an indoor cat, set up his own routine and even walks us down the hall around 5 PM to the laundry room where he is given some food and the door closed until the next morning.

As near as I can tell; he sleeps about 20 hours a day, spends time looking out the window, plays with our dog BeBe and at times tentatively alertly watches the floor area near the refrigerator and dishwasher, where he has caught at least five mice. He playfully exhausted, spread their blood on the kitchen floor and placed the remains of each tortured victim in an obvious location as an offering for his family. When I dress in the morning, he insists on a soft rubber brushing while he rubs, rolls and meows. The behavior continues until I start vacuuming up his fur and he vacates the area. His 20-pound body routinely finds its way on my lap when I'm trying to read or take my daily blood pressure readings.

During these interruptions, I started vocally asking Boo his thoughts about my research findings on Felis catus and his ancestor's relationship to man. My interpretations of his responses are as follows:

— Don't you wish you had a perfect body structure like us cats. We may have brought a few diseases your way, but look at how we've kept vermin away from you and your food for at least 9,000 years. We even paired up with the protozoan parasite Toxoplasma gondii making it easier to catch rats and mice by making them less afraid of us and attracting them to the smell of our urine.

– You've really jumped all over us because we eat endangered species. You even resent us taking over your lands. What's the big deal? There are estimated to be 200 to 2000 animals that become extinct each year on this wonderful planet. We cats are blamed for only a few. Oh, by the way there are between 15,000 and 18,000 new species of animals discovered yearly. So, what's the big deal? You should appreciate a little more what we do for you.

– If us cats became suddenly extinct, you would have rats and mice eating a good portion of your food, filth and disease would be brought into your homes and there would be a huge loss of important birds from their eggs being eaten.

– You jump our bones because we are the only "known" source of T gondii infection. There are several types of T gondii known, so us cats question if there aren't other animals that produce T gondii infective oocysts that disseminate on land and in water, infecting warm blooded animals. Give us a break until you find out more about this important parasite and what it is doing for man.

– As an example, just imagine what recent research has found about T gondii's ability to transfer protein biomolecules of amino acids across the blood brain barrier into warm blooded animal's central nervous system. This discovery might advance science research towards treating diseases that need substances to penetrate the blood brain barrier.

– Because of your cat studies - you learned about bivalves filtering out Toxoplasma. You wisely decided to no longer order raw oyster shooters at your annual Survivor's Dinner. It wouldn't look good if one of the immune comprised or weakened attendees got a case of toxoplasmosis. Considering your profession and eating habits you shouldn't be very concerned getting the disease. However, you should think about bivalves being bottom feeders of all the decomposing plant and animal life, and the offal they produce. You will find us cats loving the stuff! However, I'd recommend you switched to cooked only if any.

Yes, us cats have got us covered in many ways…Even Leonardo da Vinci in the 1400s recognized our value: "In its flawless grace and superior self-sufficiency I have seen a symbol of the perfect beauty and bland impersonality of the universe itself, objectively considered, and in its air of silent mystery there resides for me all the wonder and fascination of the unknown."

1– *Skull morphology and functionality of extant Felidae (Mammalia: Carnivora): A phylogenetic and evolutionary perspective, Zoological Journal of Linnean Society, October 2010.*

2– *A global synthesis and assessment of free-ranging domestic cat diet, National Communications Volume 14, 2023.*

3– *Invasive Species and Toxoplasmosis: A Case for Hawaii's Native Wildlife.*

4– *Acta Parasitology, 2022; 67(2): 592–605.*

5– *The Parasite That Makes a Rat Love a Cat, Smithsonian, Sarah Zielinski, 09/22/2011.*

6– *Current Opinion in Food Science, Volume 55, February 2024.*

7– *Genetically Engineered Parasite Delivers Drugs to the Brain, GeneticsNeurologyNeuroscience, 08/05/2024.*

CHAPTER 23

LIVING WITH RABIES...

In 1970, attending a virology class in veterinary school, the professor told us a story: When he was a young man, on a full moon clear night he was walking on a deserted country dirt road with a log fence between him and a large meadow. He noticed an object off- in the distance erratically moving towards him in the meadow and he soon realized it was a skunk. In his part of the country when a warm-blooded animal showed this behavior the fear of rabies was upmost on one's mind. The skunk was rapidly closing in on him and he ran as far and fast as he could until he reached the safety of his home.

At the end of the class, he showed a silent movie made by Walter Reed Medical Center that was about a group of men that had been attacked and bitten by a rabid wolf. As I recall, the professor told that us that half of the men were given wound treatment only and the other half were given rabies post-exposure prophylaxis (PEP) and medical wound care. I will never forget the movie showing a group or Iranian men standing in a row with bandages on various parts of their bodies. I don't know for sure if the men not getting PEP received placebo injections or if anyone was given injections. Being a Walter Reed film, I can't imagine it not being a research study. If they did, it was not shown on the silent movie. The professor may have just been trying to get our attention.

The scientists waited and in time some of the men developed rabies. The movie showed one of them dying from rabies. He was first shown attempting to drink a glass of water and eat pieces of bread. This was to show the involuntary gag reflex that protects our throat and pharynx from foreign objects "going down the wrong pipe" and the characteristic hydrophobia symptoms of rabies. Later in the movie the man was shown with his arms and legs tied to the bed, open lid staring of the eyes and convulsion like movements of his mouth.

At the end of the movie, I and my classmates left the lecture hall in silence and the likes of a deer looking into a car's headlights. We had been given a look into how cruel life can be and the insensitivity man may show in the "interest of science." It wasn't long after that the class was given rabies shots with the duck embryo strain. I will always remember this because at the time I was taking allergy desensitization shots (I had severe allergies in my youth and two anaphylactic reactions); and a couple of weeks after the vaccine, I was walking down one of the clinic halls and overheard my classmates laughing "Hoge flunked." The test paper pinned on the wall was rabies titers from the vaccine we had received. I had no titer and was given the opportunity to have another rabies vaccine with the fear that I may have become allergic from the first one.

When writing this chapter, I looked on YouTube to see if I could find this film. It is still there and came up when I typed in "man with rabies." A few pictures I took are shown below.

Rabies is an ancient and much-feared disease. Over the centuries, many different authors—clinicians, veterinarians, surgeons, pharmacists but also writers, philosophers, and poets—have mentioned rabies in their writings. Rabies is one of the oldest known diseases, with cases dating back to 4000 years. For most of human history, a bite from a rabid animal was uniformly fatal. In the past, people were so scared of rabies that after being bitten by a potentially rabid animal, many would commit suicide.

Even in the 20th century, the fatal course of rabies is still predictable and there are consequences when one is negligent caring for their pet. Records from the BCE: This dialogue between Marduk, the God of Healing, and his father Enki was recited by priests over (thus blessed) water which was then administered orally. These incantations are striking, marked as they are by the caveat of likely—however divine—failure, and certain death should rabies develop:

"Oh! My Father! Concerning a man whom a [...] rabid dog attacks, and to whom it passes (lit. "gives") its venom [...], I do not know what shall I do for that man."

"Oh! My son! For what you do not know, What can I add for him?" *Nippur site (3rd dynasty of Ur III, 21st-20th-century BCE).* And, "If a dog becomes rabid and the ward authority makes that known to its owner, but he does not watch over his dog so that it bites a man and causes his death, the owner of the dog shall pay forty shekels of silver; if it bites a slave and causes his death, he shall pay fifteen shekels of silver." *Excerpts from the Sumerian Laws of Eshnunna, Northern Babylonia ca. 1930 BCE.*

Humans have lived alongside domesticated dogs for 14,000 years at least, with estimates reaching back to 32,000 years. They have also long been familiar with their diseases, which became more prevalent as populations and their animals congregated in the cities. Sumerian rules and regulations attesting to the fact that a causal link between the bite of a rabid animal and a human death from rabies was well recognized almost 4000 years ago.

Although circulation of rabies had reportedly increased, especially in Europe, great progress was being made in the prevention of dog bites in European cities. Regulations for keeping dogs or for the containment of domestic dogs and elimination of stray dogs were passed in as early as 1446. A similar approach led to the successful elimination of dog-mediated rabies from Denmark, Norway and Sweden by 1826.

Other long-known approaches including muzzling were implemented in other cities or territories. In a 1793 communication it was proposed to quarantine local and imported dogs to "eradicate rabies from the British Isles." The decision to implement an international plan to control canine rabies was made at the 2nd International Veterinary Conference in Vienna in 1865. Cities and states legislated, integrating and applying early forms of what are now termed One Health principles.

The understanding of the physiopathology of rabies also evolved: 1-1546, it hypothesized that rabies was transmitted by semina ("seeds") present in the saliva; 2-1555, writings mention that rabies transmission occurs after the bite of a rabid dog; 3-1698, the risk of transmission varies according to the anatomical site of the bite; 4-1766, biting dogs should remain in 15-day observation to ascertain the risk of rabies transmission to a bite victim; 5-1775, saliva is declared to be the source of rabies transmission and provided a clinical description in humans that remains relevant to date. Also, many animals being, like humans, susceptible to rabies without being capable of transmitting the virus, and of that susceptibility being variable among species; 6-1776 and 1793, proposed (dog bite) inoculation experiments to better understand the physiopathology of rabies, including in prisoners awaiting capital punishment, which was never put into effect.

The understanding of post-bite rabies prevention in animals or in humans, however, still made no progress. Published in 1684, the first edition of Medicina Curiosa, the first English-language journal wholly dedicated to medicine, describes post-exposure prevention failure in a suspected human case of rabies acquired from a cat. "Treatment" after a bite remained faith-based or otherwise fanciful, based for example on applying hair of the biting dog ("hair of the dog") to the wound or omelets flavored with "dog-rose root" (Rosa canina or cynorrhodon, as already suggested by Pliny the Elder in the 1stC CE). The same was true outside Europe. Suggested therapies—some even based on homeopathic approaches—were rightly criticized as ineffective. The fact that rabies is not transmitted in all cases even after the bite of an evidently rabid dog or wolf contributed to the illusion that each of the many preventive "treatments" had been effective.

These are all too easily disparaged as ludicrous recommendations made by self-assured and pompous clinicians, steeped from old-wives' remedies. They are, however, sure signs of desperate and all-out efforts by health providers of the time to save their patients from what to this day remains an intractable disease. Vigorous approaches continued to be used well into the mid-19thC: In the 1830s London, children bitten by potentially rabid dogs still underwent surgery or cauterization of the wound (still discussed by Babes in 1912). Patients with clinically declared rabies were plunged into cold water or hot oil as recommended by Celsus, or were later euthanized by being stifled between mattresses or made to bleed to death.

Around the turn of the 19thC, the scientific approach improved the understanding of the physiopathology and clinical epidemiology of rabies. Much experimental work was done on the transmission of rabies—and its prevention through the amputation or immunization of animals. In 1804 rabies was transmitted experimentally (without a bite) by applying the saliva of rabid dogs to animals' tissues. The same was demonstrated in 1813 by using saliva from a human rabies patient. In 1805 experimental transmission of rabies to dogs was shown by inserting sciatic nerve segments of rabid cats into a fresh wound. Clinicians progressively identified the seat of rabies infection in the midbrain and nerve ending density was positively correlated with risks of infection and migration.

In the struggle pitting the microbial theory against spontaneous generation, subsequent experiments provided solid scientific evidence to support the long-suspected transmission of rabies by "filterable" infectious agents present in the saliva. In 1842, the agent was causing rabies was suspected not to be a poison, but a "virus" capable of multiplying and developing in the host. In 1872, virulence was found to increase by serial passage (but these were with septicemia and anthrax bacteria, not with viruses). In 1880, saliva could be broken into two components; one non-infective and the other infective. These agents were now considered to progressively ascend from the infected wound to the brain not through the blood but through the nerves—as initially hypothesized in 1879 but not established—before diffusing centrifugally.

Resorting to nerve section as a means of prevention was contemplated in 1807 and this thought communicated with Louis Pasteur in 1881—who also postulated that the rabies "virus" could be destroyed in situ or by preventing it from reaching the medulla oblongata. This paved the way for the advent of post-exposure prophylaxis, based on the notion of taking advantage of the latency period and rapidly building the patient's immunity through timely and adequate vaccination.

An Italian physician claimed to have carried out experimental infections and successfully immunized dogs by injecting the saliva of infected dogs after submitting it to gastric juices of frogs in 1799. He claimed to have inoculated this mixture to at least two people that were bitten by a suspected rabid dog and who did not contract rabies. If confirmed, this would be the first attenuated vaccine and rabies vaccine, although the small numbers discussed and the absence of laboratory confirmation would not prove preventive effectiveness.

In 1879, at the Veterinary school in Lyons, rabies was inoculated into a rabbit through a cutaneous injection and administered rabid dog saliva intravenously to a sheep which did not contract rabies but became immunized. It was theorized that post-exposure prophylaxis could occur and they began experimenting on vaccination of dogs. It was also shown in 1883–1884 that the rabies virus lost virulence after desiccation and that this approach could be used in humans. It was in this already advanced research context that Louis Pasteur and his colleagues began to apply their systematic data-driven scientific methods to the study of rabies in1880.

The rabbit cord used in the Pasteur vaccination protocol was known to preserve its virulence despite preservation in carbolic acid. It was, however, not stabilized and therefore it needed to be "transported" by/in inoculated rabbits. Patients therefore had to travel to access post-exposure prophylaxis (PEP), in some cases across continents or oceans. After PEP spared the lives of 16 of 19 Russian patients who came to Paris from Smolensk after being attacked by a rabid wolf, rabies vaccine began to be produced in 1886.

In1889, the first description of immunity as a correlate of vaccine response and protection, discussed inactivated rabies vaccines and experimentally demonstrated protection of animals by antiserum in 1891. Solutions of attenuated virus mixed with serum immunoglobulin were experimented at the Pasteur Institute as early as 1902. Rabies antiserum was administered in humans to interrupt replication of the virus in bite wounds by 1911 and the use of rabies-specific immunoglobulin was generalized in the 1950s. Monoclonal antibodies (produced either in animals or by yeasts or plants) are now being developed to replace unaffordable equine—let alone human—rabies immunoglobulin (RIG), so far with mixed but promising results.

Semple's killed-virus vaccine using sheep brain tissue, remained the most used worldwide into the 2000s. Although the vaccine had limited immunogenicity and required a tedious protocol (and was painful when given) it was affordable and for decades saved countless human lives, especially in the developing world.

Advances have led to the validation of rabies vaccine effectiveness, of shorter and dose-sparing regimens and of the equivalence of the intradermal vaccination route. It also enabled the identification of nonfatal cases of RABV infection in animals and in humans. Human survivors of clinical rabies were first documented, mostly in the New World following bat exposure.

Whether or not these survived thanks to attempted treatment remains hotly debated. Despite our dramatic advancements in the knowledge and prevention of rabies, and with a handful of exceptions to date, all documented patients with clinically-declared rabies have died within a few hours or days. So far, efforts to test some traditional medicines and antivirals currently being explored as a therapeutic resource, have shown little success.

Current understanding of the mechanisms and primary and secondary prevention of rabies in animals and in humans has profoundly changed since the attempts made during the earliest known civilizations. Yet despite this, and great progress in symptomatic management of encephalitic patients, clinicians caring for animals or patients with symptomatic rabies remain as powerless today as they were

4000 years ago. Rabies remains today the most lethal disease known to man and the author is not aware of any other disease for which—once the disease is declared—modern medicine has offered no tangible improvement. We wait in hope for researchers to identify antiviral agents capable of controlling progression of clinically-declared rabies.

Rabies became a neglected disease when it was eliminated from Europe and North America. It is emerging in some island territories and remains uncontrolled in most of the developing world, where surveillance of dog bites, rabies exposures (syndromic or laboratory-confirmed) or rabies deaths, is poor. The prevention of human rabies deaths in the 21stC still rests on tools and strategies developed in the 19thC: Effective primary prevention of animal bites, responsible dog and cat ownership including rabies vaccines, and effective rabies post-exposure prophylaxis (developed by Pasteur and his team and first administered in 1885.

Duck embryo rabies vaccines include the purified duck embryo vaccine (PDEV) and the duck embryo vaccine (DEV). PDEV was developed in 1957, and DEV was developed in the late 1950s. Modern rabies vaccines include the human diploid cell vaccine (HDCV) -1980, the purified chick embryo cell vaccine (PCECV) - 1997, and the purified Vero cell rabies vaccine (PVRV) - 1985. An oral vaccine was developed for wildlife in 1971.[1]

As of 2022, researchers estimate that 30,000 to 70,000 deaths are attributable to rabies each year, with less developed countries affected more. In the United States, few human cases are reported, though that may be due to the widespread use of post-exposure prophylaxis and the prevention programs in place. In developed countries, domesticated animals have only been responsible for about 10% of cases of rabies transmission. In contrast, wild animals such as skunks, raccoons, foxes, and bats are responsible for the rest of the cases. Any mammal may carry rabies, and so while small rodents and the rabbit family are usually considered safe as they are not expected to survive an inoculating wound from a rabid animal, there have been anecdotal reports of rabies caused by transmission from rats. As animal carriers vary by region, it is important to know your region's carriers to help determine who may need prophylaxis.

Following viral transmission, the rhabdovirus travels through the peripheral nervous system, targeting the central nerves and leading to encephalomyelitis. In humans, the first symptoms seem like any other nonspecific viral syndrome (fever, malaise, headache). These benign symptoms may then progress to anxiety, then to agitation, and then to frank delirium. One very consistent symptom after a rabid bite is tingling at the bite site within the first few days. Interestingly, after the virus has spread from peripheral nerves to the central nervous system (CNS), it travels back to the peripheral nervous system, particularly affecting highly innervated areas (eg, salivary glands). The "frothing," as portrayed in the movies Cujo and Old Yeller, is due to hypersalivation, and victims can suffer from intense pharyngeal muscle spasms at the mere sight, taste, or sound of water. This is called "hydrophobia." Eventually, the virus progresses to complete failure of the entire nervous system, which causes a quick death. While animals tend to die within 10 days, the incubation period following inoculation can last 2 weeks to 6 years, averaging a few months. Determining factors for the onset time include the viral load, location of exposure, and wound severity. The virus ultimately affects the central nervous system, usually severely affecting the brainstem. The toxic effects occur through an inflammatory response, with functional changes not completely understood. Ultimately, the virus is suspected to affect neurotransmission, and apoptosis may occur through virus-dependent and cell-dependent routes. In biology, apoptosis refers to a process of programmed cell death, where a cell actively self-destructs through a series of controlled steps, essentially "committing suicide" to eliminate unnecessary or damaged cells in the body; it is often described as a "falling off" of cells, similar to how leaves fall from a tree, hence the name derived from Greek meaning "to fall off". Once clinical features are seen, rabies is universally fatal.

The history of a rabies-infected patient may be straightforward, with a known bite from a rabid animal. Unfortunately, it may be challenging to obtain a history pointing towards rabies due to the potential for a long incubation period and multiple potential transmission methods. There are 5 stages of rabies following inoculation: incubation, prodrome, acute neurologic illness, coma, and death.

1-Incubation is the period defined as an inoculation to the first onset of symptoms and can range from days to years. 2-The prodrome phase includes nonspecific symptoms similar to flu-like illnesses, with gastrointestinal symptoms, myalgias, and fevers being some of the possible symptoms. 3-The third stage of rabies is when neurologic symptoms occur. These are classified into 1 of 3 categories: encephalitic (also considered "furious"), paralytic (also considered "dumb"), and a rare non-classic form. The encephalitic form is most common and presents in approximately 85% of cases. These patients may exhibit hydrophobia or aerophobia when spasms develop due to stimuli such as swallowing liquids (hydrophobia). Agitation and changes in mentation can occur during the encephalitic form, with the potential for autonomic dysfunction, increased deep tendon reflexes, nuchal rigidity, and finding positive Babinski sign. The Babinski reflex is a reflex that occurs when the sole of the foot is stroked, causing the big toe to move upward and the other toes to fan out. It's normal in infants and children up to two years old, but it disappears as the child matures. In adults, the Babinski reflex is abnormal and can indicate a problem with the brain or spinal cord. Other examination findings outside the nervous system include tachycardia, tachypnea, and fever. This progresses rapidly to hyperactivity. 4-The paralytic form of rabies is less common and noted to occur less than 20% of the time. These patients may be confused with Guillain-Barre syndrome as the classically associated hydrophobia and irritability are not seen. Weakness is a hallmark, though patients may also have altered mentation, ongoing fevers, and bladder dysfunction.

Guillain-Barré syndrome (GBS) is a rare neurological disorder that occurs when the body's immune system attacks the peripheral nervous system. This damage makes it difficult for the nerves to send signals to the muscles, causing weakness, numbness, and sometimes paralysis. 5-The final form of rabies is considered non-classic and is rare, generally associated with seizures and more profound motor and sensory symptoms.

Stage 4 of rabies is the coma stage and usually begins within 10 days of stage 3. Patients may have ongoing hydrophobia, develop prolonged apnea periods, and have flaccid paralysis. Following the onset of stage 4, without supportive care due to cardiopulmonary failure, most patients experience death within 2 to 3 days. Even with supportive therapy, virtually zero patients survive rabies.

There is no effective treatment for rabies. Prevention is the mainstay of treatment, including domestic animal vaccination programs, education, and monitoring. Wound care is the first step in treating any individual with a feared rabies exposure. Appropriate wound care alone is almost 100% effective if initiated within 3 hours of inoculation. Recommendations include scrubbing the wound and surrounding area with soap and water (solutions include a 20% soap solution, povidone, and alcohol solutions) and swabbing deeply for puncture wounds with irrigation. After cleaning the wound thoroughly, a virucidal agent such as benzalkonium chloride or povidone-iodine is recommended.

In the United States, when a bite is known to be from a bat, skunk, raccoon, or fox, it is treated immediately with rabies vaccine and rabies immune globulin. Outside the United States, a dog bite should be treated immediately with a vaccine and rabies immune globulin.

Unimmunized patients are treated with human rabies immune globulin as well at a dose with a preference to infiltrate as much of that dose around the wound as possible. Any remaining dose of human rabies immune globulin not infiltrated into the wound is then given intramuscularly proximal to the wound. Recommendations have recently been updated in the United States. Since bats are the major source of rabies here, anyone who awakens from sleep and finds a bat in the room should be urgently immunized.[2]

The primary components of a rabies control program for companion animals are: immunization and licensing; stray animal control; reporting, investigation, and isolation of animals involved in bite incidents; and public education. Wild animal rabies virus control is maintained in populations of wild animals and occasionally spills over into domestic animals and humans. In most states, skunks and bats comprise most of the animal rabies cases reported each year. Prevention and control of rabies in bats and terrestrial mammals pose considerable challenges. It is generally not possible or desirable to control rabies by reducing the size of wild carnivore or bat populations. Selective population reduction may be attempted in terrestrial rabies outbreaks of limited geographic scope, but these efforts can be labor and resource intensive and provide effective control only until immigration or reintroduction of the incriminated species.

Immunization of wildlife by widespread distribution of vaccine-impregnated oral baits has shown variable success toward arresting the propagation of rabies in raccoons and coyotes. The effectiveness of oral rabies vaccination programs has not been demonstrated for skunks and such programs would be infeasible for bats. Principles of rabies prevention should focus on excluding wild animals from areas of human and domestic animal habitation and activity, and avoidance of contact with possibly rabid wild animals.

Public education on the risks of rabies transmission from wild animals is paramount to effective disease prevention.

Livestock All livestock species—horses, cattle, sheep, goats, llamas/alpacas, swine--are susceptible to rabies infection. Cattle and horses are the livestock species most frequently diagnosed with rabies. Unvaccinated livestock bitten or exposed to a rabid or suspect rabid animal should be euthanized.

For those who develop symptoms of rabies, survival is rare. Only a handful of survivors exist in the USA after acquiring rabies. For those without symptoms but with rabies vaccine prophylaxis, survival is assured. Individuals who have rabid animal bites need the rabies vaccine and immunoglobulin ASAP for survival- once the symptoms appear, death is inevitable. Interestingly, after the virus has spread from peripheral nerves to the central nervous system (CNS), it travels back to the peripheral nervous system, particularly affecting highly innervated areas (eg, salivary glands).

The World Organization for Animal Health and the Food and Agriculture Organization of the United Nations are currently spearheading an effort to eliminate dog-transmitted rabies worldwide by 2030. While one strives for all dogs to be vaccinated, a major effort is urgently needed to make the time-proven and well-tolerated vaccine (and immunoglobulin) geographically and financially accessible in a timely way to those people who remain the most vulnerable to rabies: the rural populations of developing countries.[3]

For most of human history, a bite from a rabid animal was uniformly fatal. In the past, people were so scared of rabies that after being bitten by a potentially rabid animal, many would commit suicide. Inoculation to the first onset of rabies symptoms can range from days to years and soap and water wound care alone is almost 100% effective if initiated within 3 hours of inoculation. However, once clinical features are seen, rabies is universally fatal.

The history of a rabies-infected patient may be straightforward, with a known bite from a rabid animal. Unfortunately, it may be challenging to obtain a history pointing towards rabies because it shares other disease symptoms. Also, rabies is often difficult to diagnose because of the potential for a long incubation period and multiple potential transmission methods.

Looks like God has given man an opportunity window to an almost 100% chance of dodging the rabies bullet if he but gives the wound a good cleaning and seeks medical care for a vaccine and immunoglobulin. However, if the wound is neglected, one may find themselves at death's door where there is no hope. Then one places themselves in God's hands. As John Rutter wrote in his song, "Look to the Day:"

Look to the light that will drive out darkness;
Look to the hope that will conquer fear.
God's strength upholds us till the fight is won.
Look to the Day; till we see our task
is done when the day is here.
Look for that day when there shall be no more pain.

1– *Four Thousand Years of Concepts Relating to Rabies in Animals and Humans, Its Prevention and Its Cure, Trop Med Infect Dis, 03/24/2017.*
2– *Rabies, NIH, 10/31/2022.*

3– *California Department of Public Health Veterinary Public Health Section, Rabies Control, 2012.*

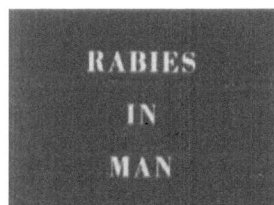

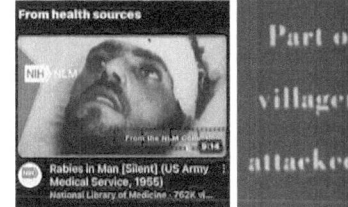

CHAPTER 24

DONKEYS...

The donkey is a domesticated equine. It derives from the African wild ass, was domesticated in Africa some 5000–7000 years ago, and has been used mainly as a working animal since that time.

There are more than 40 million donkeys in the world, mostly in underdeveloped countries, where they are used principally as draught or pack animals. While working donkeys are often associated with those living at or below subsistence, small numbers of donkeys or asses are kept for breeding or as pets in developed countries.

An adult male donkey is a jack or jackass, an adult female is a jenny or jennet, and an immature donkey of either sex is a foal. Jacks are often mated with female horses (mares) to produce mules; the less common hybrid of a male horse (stallion) and jenny is a hinny.

The first donkeys came to the Americas on ships of the Second Voyage of Christopher Columbus, and were landed at Hispaniola in 1495. The first to reach North America may have been two animals taken to Mexico by the first bishop of Mexico, who arrived there on 6 December 1528, while the first donkeys to reach what is now the United States may have crossed the Rio Grande with Juan de Oñate in April 1598.

From that time on they spread northward, finding use in missions and mines. Donkeys were documented as present in what today is Arizona in 1679. By the Gold Rush years of the 19th century, the burro was the beast of burden of choice of early prospectors in the western United States. By the end of the placer mining boom, many of them escaped or were abandoned, and a feral population established itself.

About 41 million donkeys were reported worldwide in 2006 with China having the most with 11 million. As of 2017, however, the Chinese population was reported to have dropped to 3 million, with African populations under pressure as well, due to increasing trade and demand for donkey products in China.

Donkeys vary considerably in size, depending on both breed and environmental conditions, and heights at the withers range from less than 35 in to approximately 59 in:Working donkeys in the poorest countries have a life expectancy of 12 to 15 years; in more prosperous countries, they may have a lifespan of 30 to 50 years. A donkey's weight can vary depending on its age, breed, and environmental conditions. For example, miniature donkeys can weigh between 200–450 lbs., while standard donkeys can weigh between 400–500 lbs. Wild donkeys can weigh up to 551 lbs., and the Mammoth Jack Stock donkey can weigh between 900–1200 lbs.

Donkeys are adapted to marginal desert lands. Unlike wild and feral horses, wild donkeys in dry areas are solitary and do not form harems. Each adult donkey establishes a home range; breeding over a large area may be dominated by one jack. The loud call or bray of the donkey, which typically lasts for twenty seconds and can be heard for over three kilometers, may help keep in contact with other donkeys over the wide spaces of the desert. Donkeys have large ears, which help pick up more distant sounds, and may help cool the donkey's blood. Donkeys can defend themselves by biting, striking with the front hooves or kicking with the hind legs. Their vocalization, called a bray, is often represented in English as "hee haw".

A jenny is normally pregnant for about 12 months, though the gestation period varies from 11 to 14 months, and usually gives birth to a single foal. Births of twins are rare, though less so than in horses. About 1.7 percent of donkey pregnancies result in twins; both foals survive in about 14 percent of those. In general jennies have a conception rate that is lower than that of horses (i.e., less than the 60–65% rate for mares).

Although jennies come into heat within 9 or 10 days of giving birth, their fertility remains low, and it is likely the reproductive tract has not returned to normal. Thus, it is usual to wait one or two further estrous cycles before rebreeding, unlike the practice with mares. Jennies are usually very protective of their foals, and some will not come into estrus while they have a foal at side. The time lapse involved in rebreeding, and the length of a jenny's gestation, means that a jenny will have fewer than one foal per year. Because of this and the longer gestation period, donkey breeders do not expect to obtain a foal every year, as horse breeders often do, but may plan for three foals in four years.

Donkeys can interbreed with other members of the family Equidae, and are commonly interbred with horses. The hybrid between a jack and a mare is a mule, valued as a working and riding animal in many countries.

Donkeys have a notorious reputation for stubbornness, but this has been attributed to a much stronger sense of self-preservation than exhibited by horses. Likely based on a stronger prey instinct and a weaker connection with humans, it is considerably more difficult to force or frighten a donkey into doing something it perceives to be dangerous for whatever reason. Once a person has earned their confidence, they can be willing and companionable partners and very dependable in work.

Although formal studies of their behavior and cognition are rather limited, donkeys appear to be quite intelligent, cautious, friendly, playful, and eager to learn. *Wikipedia Donkey*

Since 2013, Chinese traders have been buying the hides of millions of butchered donkeys obtained from various countries and shipping them to China. They're used to manufacture a gelatin product derived from collagen in the donkey's hide, called E-jiao - a traditional Chinese medicine. The trade has led to an animal welfare nightmare, along with a threat to donkey populations, the severity of which is only now emerging. Without drastic measures, the number of donkeys worldwide are expected to drop by half within 5 years. The crisis threatens many of the world's rarer donkey breeds and a vital means of transport for the poor. But it is also spurring new studies of donkey biology—including how to speed their reproduction.

E-jiao, in use for thousands of years, purportedly treats or prevents many problems, including miscarriage, circulatory issues, and premature aging, although no rigorous clinical trials support those claims. The preparation combines mineral rich water from China's Shandong province and collagen extracted from donkey hides, traditionally produced by boiling the skins in a 99-step process done at specific times of the year. Once reserved for China's elites, E-jiao is now marketed to the country's booming middle class, causing demand to surge. One producer, touts it as "a creation of heaven and earth" that's now passing "from the royal tribute to the home of ordinary people."[1]

With similar nutritional profiles, the main difference between gelatin vs. collagen is that gelatin only dissolves in hot liquids, whereas collagen dissolves in both hot and cold liquids. This means that the one incorporated into a diet often comes down to personal preference. Gelatin is further used as a thickener for foods, alongside being a nutritional supplement, whereas collagen is not.

Collagen is the most abundant protein in an animal's body. Its fiber-like structure is used to make connective tissue. Collagen protein supplements have become one of the more popular supplements on the market today. However, the majority of collagen products on the market are not a "complete protein". They do not contain all the essential amino acids present in protein (they lack tryptophan - unless it is added to the product). A protein must have 9 essential amino acids that a human body cannot produce on its own to be considered a complete protein. Some of these foods include beef, poultry, fish, eggs, dairy, soy, quinoa and buckwheat.

Collagen can be either fully hydrolyzed or partially hydrolyzed. If partially hydrolyzed, it's considered gelatin. Typically, gelatin is derived from collagen by heating it. However, they share a very similar nutritional profile and are both abundant in the amino acid glycine. Collagen is the most abundant protein in animals and essential for the healthy bones, joints, skin, hair, nails, digestion, & more.

Both collagen and gelatin contain almost 100% protein. There's very little difference between the two, with gelatin containing slightly fewer calories.

At the same time, it's important to note that their nutritional profiles may differ slightly depending on their animal source. With gelatin, nutritional variances may also happen depending on how it's extracted from collagen. In processing, sugar, artificial flavors, and artificial colors may also be added, again, altering each supplement's nutritional profile.

Collagen and gelatin are frequently discussed in relation to healthy aging. This is because as we age, our skin loses collagen, leading to increased wrinkles, thinness, and dryness. Research consistently shows that collagen supplementation improves skin moisture and slows down the loss of collagen in the skin. This, in turn, can reduce fine lines and wrinkles. One study even showed that collagen improved skin thickness by 18%.

Collagen and gelatin may help improve joint pain and reduce symptoms associated with osteoarthritis.

One study had individuals take gelatin across a 70-day duration. Researchers observed significant improvements in their pain and other symptoms when compared to the control group. Additional research revealed that collagen supplementation improved joint pain, mobility, and inflammation in 24 weeks.

As we age, the risk of osteoporosis increases—especially for women who are postmenopausal. But taking collagen might support bone health by improving bone density. Research suggests that bioactive collagen supplements may even help increase the production of new bone, leading to stronger and more resilient bones.

About 60-70 million Americans suffer from some form of gastrointestinal disease. While collagen is no replacement for other treatments or remedies, it can play a role in repairing damaged gut lining.

Since most collagen is fully hydrolyzed (as opposed to partially hydrolyzed), it's considered easier to digest when compared to gelatin. Look for the terms "hydrolyzed" or "peptides" on the label. Both of these terms mean that the collagen has undergone hydrolysis and has been broken down into easy-to-digest amino acids.[2]

Despite government incentives for new donkey farmers, farms in China can't keep up with the exploding demand, which the Donkey Sanctuary currently estimates at 4.8 million hides per year. Donkeys' gestation period is one full year, and they only reach their adult size after 2 years. So, the industry has embarked on a frenzied hunt for donkeys elsewhere. (Importing hides is not illegal in China, and the import tax was lowered from 5% to 2% last year.) This has triggered steep population declines.

In Brazil, the population dropped by 28% between 2007 and 2017. An equine veterinarian/researcher in Zaria,

Nigeria, reported that African populations are crashing. After buying donkeys at markets, traders often drive large herds to slaughter, sometimes covering hundreds of kilometers with no rest, food, or water. Those transported by truck fare worse: Handlers tie their legs together and sling them onto piles or strap them to the top of the truck. Animals that survive the journey—many with broken or severed limbs, as well as other injuries—are unloaded by the ears and tails and tossed in front of a slaughterhouse.[1]

The donkeys are slaughtered by placing a captive bolt gun on the forehead between the eyes that hits or pierces the skull and damaging the brain. In many slaughterhouses, this system is not used, and the animal is hit with a sledge hammer on the forehead. The animal is then hung by its hind legs and has its throat cut to bleed it out. Following this, the animal's skin is removed. One concern is that donkeys can spread zoonotic diseases - maladies that can pass from animals to humans - such as brucellosis and leptospirosis during the slaughter process or along shipment routes.

After slaughtering, the donkey skins are salted, placed on the ground in the open air and sun, dried for approximately 45 days and shipped to China. The cured donkey hides are prepared by soaking them in water, boiling, removing the hair and cutting into small strips. Gelatine is separated from the skin by adding the strips into boiling water. The separated hot gelatine paste is cooled.

China's demand for the traditional medicine, known as E-jiao, is fueling the slaughter of millions of donkeys every year, say animal welfare groups and veterinary experts. E-jiao, which is made using collagen extracted from donkey hides, is the vital ingredient in food and beauty products believed by many Chinese consumers to enrich the blood, improve the immune system, and prevent diseases.

Reuters spoke to more than a dozen experts, including veterinarians and academics, to examine how demand for E-jiao is rippling across communities in Africa, which rely heavily on the donkey, and how the trade in hide continues to boom despite efforts by some African nations to restrict it.

Once famed as a delicacy for the very wealthy, E-jiao is widely seen as a contemporary Chinese superfood and associated with gift giving, comparable to ginseng or expensive tea. Many E-jiao products are readily available on common online platforms such as Amazon and Taobao, which sell items including Shandong walnut E-jiao cake and E-jiao black sesame balls.

Traditionally, E-jiao was a luxury product. It gained favor among elites during the Qing dynasty that ruled China from 1644 until 1912. Its popularity has surged in recent years due partly to its use in the Chinese television series 'Empress in the Palace', which started airing in 2011. The rise in demand has also been fueled by China's growing middle class and rising elderly population.

As Africa has the world's largest donkey population, it has emerged as the key source of donkey skins.

The donkey is used extensively as a workhorse across the continent, particularly for transport, helping to alleviate poverty. It frees many women and girls from some hard physical labor and domestic chores. Its essential role in many African villages clashes with the sky-rocketing demand for donkey hides in China.

The donkey remains one of the most affordable means of transporting goods and people in many rural African communities. Even in harsh conditions, the animals can travel long distances with heavy loads.

China's E-jiao demand disrupts this role, decades before Africa's poor are able to replace donkeys with mechanized vehicles, this not only fails to foster prosperity but may also see a return to poverty, especially among women.

For donkey owners, selling their animal means quick cash—now more than $200 in parts of Africa—but it's often a shortsighted deal: The report estimates that working donkeys support the livelihood of half a billion people by carrying people and goods to markets, schools, and health clinics. Losing donkeys means the people become the donkey again. Women most often shoulder that burden.

Ironically, the booming E-jiao trade, along with a developing donkey dairy industry in Eastern Europe, has stirred scientific interest in donkeys. The number of PubMed-indexed papers with "donkeys" in the title shot up from six in 2000 to 46 so far in 2019, including this year, for example, including many from China.

A reproductive biologist at the China Agricultural University in Beijing, says Chinese efforts are focused on increasing yields, for instance through artificial insemination and harmonization of the estrus in female donkeys, which allows farmers to inseminate them more efficiently. They are improving techniques so jennies don't end up not pregnant. Those improvements include better techniques to freeze and thaw sperm; for reasons that are unclear, breeding with cryopreserved semen is much less successful in donkeys than in horses. The biologist said he takes E-jiao himself occasionally for "better color" and "more energy," although he says scientists "still don't know the bioactivity of the product."[1]

E-jiao products:

— The most common E-jiao product. Used in cooking or can be dissolved with warm liquids.

— Walnut e-jiao cake: A mixture of black sesame, walnut kernel, protein powder, rice wine, red dates, wolfberry, and rock sugar.

— Powder: Dissolved in drinks such as milk or black tea with honey.

— Bottled: Also sold as individual doses to drink.

— Pills: Can be manufactured as gel capsules.

— Paste: Can be dissolved in beverages and used in food.

Traditionally, E-jiao was a luxury product. It gained favor among elites during the Qing dynasty that ruled China from 1644 until 1912. Its popularity has surged in recent years due partly to its use in the Chinese television series 'Empress in the Palace', which started airing in 2011. The rise in demand has also been fueled by China's growing middle class and rising elderly population. Its price has leapt 30-fold in the past decade from 100 yuan per 500 grams to 2,986 yuan ($420), according to Chinese state media.

The E-jiao industry requires an estimated 5.9 million donkey skins annually, which has put unprecedented pressure on global populations, according to a report released recently by The Donkey Sanctuary, a British charity devoted to the animal's welfare, that China's donkey population has fallen more than 80% to just under

2 million from 11 million in 1992, prompting its E-jiao industry to source donkey skins from overseas.[3]

According to a 1723 account by the French Jesuit Dominique Parrenin, there was a well in Dong'e which was normally kept closed and sealed, and which was only opened when water was taken to be used in preparation of E-jiao for the emperor's court. The product was traditionally prepared during the late fall and winter (from after the harvest and until the beginning of March). It was supposed to be made from the skin of a recently killed well-nourished black donkey. Since the supply of this material was rather limited, it was said that a large amount of "fake" E-jiao was also manufactured, using skins from mules, horses, camels, pigs, and sometimes, it was said, even from old shoes; a bit of "real stuff" was added to it, to deceive consumers.

E-jiao is either prepared as dry gelatin or mixed with powdered oyster shell or pollen to form glue balls. It tastes sweet and slightly bitter. Jesuits noted that while the "real" E-jiao has no disagreeable taste or smell, the fake product could be distinguished by its unpleasant smell and taste, even when it was made from pig skins (which, supposedly, provided the best approximation of the real thing). *Donkey-hide gelatin, Wikipedia*

The supply of material to make donkey-hide gelatin, also called E-jiao (colla corii asini), is becoming more limited. There is also a large amount of "fake" E-jiao on the market and I could not find listed on the internet any Jesuit smell and taste specialists to authenticate the "real" versus "fake" health supplement used for "valuable Chinese medicine".

Its ever-growing demand and short supply make it a target for fraud, and many other animal gelatins can be found as adulterants. Authentication remains a quality concern. Therefore, scientists are investigating peptide markers by searching the protein database of animals used to produce fraudulent E-jiao. However, donkeys and horses share the same database, and there is no specific marker for donkeys. Here, solutions are sought following a database-independent strategy... The specificity and applicability of the tested markers were confirmed by testing multiple authentic samples and 110 batches of commercial E-jiao products, 57 of which were found to be unqualified. These results suggest that these markers are specific and accurate for authentication purposes. *Qualitative and Quantitative Analysis of Ejiao-Related Animal Gelatins through Peptide Markers..., Molecules, 07/27/2022; 27(14):4643.*

A Man and his son were once going with their Donkey to market. As they were walking along by its side a countryman passed them and said: "You fools, what is a Donkey for but to ride upon?"

So, the Man put the Boy on the Donkey and they went on their way. But soon they passed a group of men, one of whom said: "See that lazy youngster, he lets his father walk while he rides."

So, the Man ordered his Boy to get off, and got on himself. But they hadn't gone far when they passed two women, one of whom said to the other: "Shame on that lazy lout to let his poor little son trudge along."

Well, the Man didn't know what to do, but at last he took his Boy up before him on the Donkey. By this time they had come to the town, and the passers-by began to jeer and point at them. The Man stopped and asked what they were scoffing at. The men said: "Aren't you ashamed of yourself for overloading that poor donkey of yours and your hulking son?"

The Man and Boy got off and tried to think what to do. They thought and they thought, till at last they cut down a pole, tied the donkey's feet to it, and raised the pole and the donkey to their shoulders. They went along amid the laughter of all who met them till they came to Market Bridge, when the Donkey, getting one of his feet loose, kicked out and caused the Boy to drop his end of the pole. In the struggle the Donkey fell over the bridge, and his fore-feet being tied together he was drowned:

Upon this, the old man, vexed and ashamed, made
the best of his way home again, convinced that by
endeavoring to please everybody he had pleased nobody,
and lost his Ass in the bargain. *Aesop's*
Fable, The Boy and the Donkey

Looks to me like this Aesop's Fable, recorded probably somewhere between 600 BC and 230 AD, kind of hits the nail on the head. The 1723 account by the Jesuit Dominique Parrenin included very specific details as to how E-jiao was to be made that are not followed today. Fake products were being produced during his time as it is now. The horses DNA is so close to the donkey that it is stretching scientist's ability to identify peptides in proteins to tell a donkey from the horse in "fake" products.

For the life of me, I can't imagine gelatin (donkey skin from almost anywhere in the world is salted, placed on the ground in the open air and sun, dried for approximately 45 days and shipped to China) closely resembles – a special covered well which was only opened when water was taken to be used in preparation of E-jiao for the emperor's court. A well-nourished recently killed black donkey being traditionally prepared during the late fall and winter.

I would like to see clinical studies comparing donkey gelatin vs horse gelatin. If the proteins are so difficult to tell the difference – there clinically may not be any. I suspect Aesop's involving the miller, his son, and their ass wisdom may have it correct. *"Upon this, the old man, vexed and ashamed, made the best of his way home again, convinced that by endeavoring to please everybody he had pleased nobody, and lost his* (our) *Ass* (earth's donkeys) *in the bargain."*

1– *Surging Chinese trade in hides has led to global donkey massacre, Science | AAAS, Christa Leste'-Lasserre, 12/12/2019.*

2– *Is Collagen a Complete Protein? Amy Myers, MD.*

3– *How China's demand for donkey hide is devastating African communities, Donkey Sanctuary, Arranz et al. 04/15/2024.*

The Donkey's Dialogue. Fables Aesop 4

CHAPTER 25

DON'T GET SPOILED BEFORE YOUR TIME...

Even though our receptionist and business manager, Nanci Itri, at Camden Pet Hospital for nearing twenty years now lives in Florida and I retired in February of 2024, we each just before Christmas received our annual box of pears from the wonderful Kusumoto family. The event always brings back memories of my helping care for their pets (Sasha, Kerri and Tonka), beautiful daughter, her husband's traveling to Japan to watch Sumo wrestling and remembering that my family needed to start eating the green looking pears upon arrival because that's when they taste good and they aren't good when they turn yellow - what Mrs. Kusumoto calls BTW (Better To Wait syndrome).

Some of the general thoughts on keeping fresh fruits and vegetables edible for longer have been offered: Here are some suggested tips for making fruits and vegetables last longer: 1-Use sealed containers or bags to keep produce fresh longer. This helps prevent produce from drying out and helps protect it from ethylene gas. It is a natural plant hormone that occurs in all types of vegetation, and is produced by ripening fruit and some microorganisms. Ethylene is used in many industrial applications, including ripening and coloring fruit, and inducing flowering in pineapples. 2-Store in the right place: Some fruits and vegetables should be stored in the fridge, while others should be left at room temperature: Apples, grapes, and other produce that should stay crisp should be kept in the fridge. Leave at room temperature: Avocados and tomatoes should be left at room temperature to develop their best flavor and texture. 3-Separate fruits and vegetables: Some fruits, like bananas, apples, citrus, and tomatoes, produce ethylene gas which can speed up the ripening of other fruits and vegetables. To prevent this, store these fruits alone.

This is not the complete story – man has intervened through science to help them taste better sooner, hold back ripening until they can reach the market place and keep them for long years without losing all their flavor:

The story of extending freshness of fruits and vegetables is rooted in the history of modified atmosphere storage. It was found that low O_2 and high CO_2 atmospheres inhibited the respiration climacteric and were beneficial for long-term storage of apples. However, it was not until 1962 that it was found that the physiological and biochemical basis of these effects was not simply a reduction in respiration, but also an inhibition of the production and action of ethylene. Intrigued by the apparently competitive kinetics of the inhibition of ethylene action by CO_2, scientists proceeded to use a chemical approach to understanding the nature of the ethylene-binding site. They compared the properties of a range of olefins and other compounds with ethylene-like activity and noted a striking correlation between their activity in inducing ethylene responses.

Although they were on the track of the ethylene-binding site, they turned their attention to hypobaric storage, a technique that inhibited the effects of ethylene by reducing its partial pressure in plant tissues. The story therefore changed little until the mid-1970s it was found that low concentrations of silver (Ag) could inhibit the action of ethylene. Although the discovery of the role of Ag in preventing the action of ethylene were very exciting, its commercial application was limited because silver, a heavy metal, cannot be applied to edible crops. In addition, Ag in the form of silver nitrate is not very mobile in plant vascular systems and Ag solutions can cause black spotting of petals and leaves.

The commercial application of silver as an antiethylene treatment was made possible by the discovery that the silver thiosulfate (STS) complex was stable and highly mobile in the vascular system but was still very effective in preventing ethylene action. This finding was quickly exploited in commercial horticulture and led to the development of the famous "super carnations" that helped catapult the Colombian flower industry into prominence worldwide. STS also proved very effective in preventing the effects of ethylene in potted plants and other nursery materials. STS remains commercially useful today as an Environmental Protection Agency (EPA) -registered material in the United States for preventing the effects of ethylene in cut flowers and is a required pretreatment for certain ethylene-sensitive species marketed through the Dutch flower auctions.

Although horticulturists were fascinated with silver, others were pursuing a different approach in studies that were initiated because of the interest in using ethylene to accelerate coloring of tobacco leaves in curing sheds. Following this lead, they synthesized numerous olefins and other organic compounds with ethylene-like properties. To understand the relative effectiveness of these different compounds, they developed a radioactive assay for estimating ethylene binding. Among the compounds synthesized was 2,5-norbornadiene, which proved to be an effective inhibitor of ethylene action. This compound has been a very useful material for physiologists despite its obvious drawbacks; to inhibit ethylene action, plants needed to be continuously exposed to relatively high concentrations of 2,5-norbornadiene, and the gas itself had a foul odor, 1985.

1-methylcyclopropene (1-MCP) was then developed to be used commercially to maintain the freshness of ornamental plants and flowers and preventing the ripening of fruits. It can be used in enclosed sites, such as coolers, truck trailers, greenhouses, storage facilities, and shipping containers. It was approved in 1999 by the U.S. Environmental Protection Agency for use on ornamental crops. For cut flowers, potted flowers, and bedding, nursery and foliage plants, to prevent or delay wilting, leaf yellowing, opening, and death.

It is also used in the agriculture industry by growers, packers, and shippers to prevent or delay the natural ripening process. It is used in agricultural products including apples, kiwifruit, tomatoes, pears, bananas, plums, persimmons, avocados, and melons. Although benefiting from fresher produce and lower cost, the consumer however may be purchasing fruit that is older than expected. 1-MCP is also being developed as a crop protection technique. By spraying it on growing field crops during times of stress, the crops may be protected from moderate heat and drought conditions. *Several Sources*

Nicolas Appert was born the ninth of eleven children. His family ran an inn in the town and he worked in the family business until the age of twenty, he and his one of his brothers opened a brewery, he then served as head chef thirteen years for royalty, was a confectioner and chef in Paris eleven years, was married and had four children. Poor production years and the need to have edible food supplies for the traveling armies of the era created an environment where food could be preserved for long periods of time. So, who appeared to save the day – the man who was destined to become known as the "Father of Canning".

Appert was active during the French Revolution and politicly took part in the guillotine execution of King Louis XVI in 1793. Carrying out the deed was described as messy, since the King's neck was too fat to fit properly in the guillotine's groove. The guillotine was a method of execution that became popular during the French Revolution. The first execution by guillotine was in 1792 on a highwayman. The guillotine was a symbol of the Reign of Terror, when as many as 40,000 people were executed. It remained the only legal form of capital punishment in France until 1981. The last execution by guillotine in France was in 1977.

The execution was a turning point in French and European history, inspiring a range of reactions. Some saw it as the end of a thousand-year monarchy and the beginning of democracy, while others condemned it as senseless bloodshed. The execution of Louis XVI caused a shift in public opinion, with his name, image, and insignias removed from public view. His wife, Marie-Antoinette, was executed nine months later.

Appert fell under suspicion during the subsequent Reign of Terror and was arrested in April 1794, but he was able to avoid being executed himself. In 1795, he began experimenting with ways to preserve foodstuffs, succeeding with soups, vegetables, juices, dairy products, jellies, jams, and syrups. He placed the food in glass jars, sealed them with cork and sealing wax and placed them in boiling water (in later years, he switched to using an autoclave). It is believed that this technique was already being used by homemakers, but Appert was the first to do this on an industrial scale.

Appert then established a business to preserve a variety of food in sealed bottles. At first, he used champagne bottles, imperfectly sealed by a mixture of cheese and mineral lime. Appert's method transitioned to filling thick, large-mouthed glass bottles with produce of every description, ranging from beef, fowl, eggs, milk, and prepared dishes. Appert avoided using tinplate in his early manufacture because the quality of French tinplate was poor. He left air space at the top of the bottle, and the cork would then be sealed firmly in the jar by using a vise. The bottle was then wrapped in canvas to protect it, dunked into boiling water, and boiled for as much time as Appert deemed appropriate for cooking the contents thoroughly. In honor of Appert, canning is sometimes called "appertization", which is distinct from pasteurization.

Despite his technical successes, Appert had financial troubles due to the high cost of his equipment and the fact that he was not a very good businessman. He declared bankruptcy in 1806, but was able to continue his business. In 1795, the French army had offered a prize of 12,000 francs for a new method to preserve food. In 1806 Appert presented a selection of bottled fruits and vegetables from his manufacture but did not win any reward. In 1810 the Bureau of Arts and Manufactures of the Ministry of the Interior gave Appert an ex-gratia payment of 12,000 francs on condition that he make his process public. Appert accepted and published a book describing his process that year. Appert's treatise was entitled (The Art of Preserving Animal and Vegetable Substances), 6,000 copies of which were printed in 1810. This was the first book of its kind on modern food preservation methods.

Appert never truly understood why his method worked, as the science of bacteriology had not yet been developed, but it was so simple that it quickly became widespread. In 1810, British inventor and merchant Peter Durand patented his own method, but this time in a tin can, thus creating the modern-day process of canning foods. In 1812 Englishmen Bryan Donkin and John Hall purchased both patents and began producing preserves.

Despite the government grant, Appert's financial situation did not improve and was exacerbated by the destruction of his factory by Prussian and Austrian forces at the end of the War of the Sixth Coalition in 1814. With the support of the French government in the form of free rent, he opened a new factory in Paris to preserve food in tin cans, which lasted for ten years until the same government evicted him in December 1827.

Appert's canned goods were widely appreciated, especially by naval services as the products were far superior to the dried and salted provisions they had previously relied on. Cans were exported to Bavaria and Saint Petersburg, and received praise from newspapers across France. However, this did not translate into financial success. Despite being rewarded with silver and gold medals in 1816 and 1820 respectively, it was not until 1824 that he received the 2,000 francs associated with them.

In 1828, he opened yet another factory in the city. He petitioned Louis Philippe I for entry into the Legion of Honor but was denied, possibly due to his activities during the Revolution. Taking this as an insult, he retired in 1836 at the age of 86. Despite a pension of 1,200 francs a year from the government beginning that year, he died in poverty in 1841 and was buried in a pauper's grave. *Various Sources*

Thomas Jefferson once pointed out that while life is trying to educate us, it is also sorting us. Jusus expressed this idea in parables: the goats being separated from the sheep and the tares from the wheat so that the tares could be tied to the bundles and burned. Elder Sterling W. Sill related this principle to his experience in sorting apples. Apples were graded according to size, color, and freedom from defects. Sorters would put the Grade-A apples into one box. Grade-B would go into a second box. And smaller than a certain size or if it lacked color, it was considered to be Grade-B. Wormy apples and those with other defects that made them unfit for commercial use were carried away and fed to the pigs. Of course, the Grade-As fetched the highest price and were the most pleasant to work with. It was pretty hard to get buyers interested in less-developed apples, and no one wanted the culls at any price.

The similarities between growing apples and life are striking. To get the best results, a certain amount of cultivating, fertilizing, irrigating, and spraying must be done. And through the growing operations, one must always keep his mind on the harvest and the substantial premium paid for every Grade-A product. There is never a great demand for cull apples, scrubby potatoes, runt pigs, diseased beef, knotty lumber, or inferior human beings. No intelligent farmer would put his cull onions, rotten apples, wormy gooseberries, and knotty potatoes in the same package with those that are Grade-A. At a state fair, all of the choicest fruits are beautifully displayed. Culls are conspicuous by their absence. We know what happens when even one rotten apple gets into a Grade-A barrel.

Just as one integrated carrier of a contagious disease can cause an epidemic, so can the integration of evil destroy us individually and collectively. Sometimes, a tree is shaken in order to improve its health. Wormy apples have the weakest hold upon the tree. They are the most likely to fall when the tree is shaken to conserve the tree's strength in order to mature the Grade-A apples. This also prevents contamination of the barrel of Grade-A apples from a rotten apple.

Like the postal clerk who sorts mail according to its destination, we sort ourselves. Reaching out to others to cultivate their faith and strengthen them facilitates the sorting process. When a storm comes, the first structures to get blown away are those that aren't firm. Similarly, those with weak faith are the first to get blown away in a crisis. That's why we sometimes shake each other to rid ourselves of rotten attitudes and a wormy commitment. The Lord described this process through the Apostle Paul: "Yet once more I shake not the earth only, but also heaven... that those things which cannot be shaken may remain" *Hebrews 12:26-27*

After sorting ourselves in mortality, we are sorted in the spirit world, and the judgment, we are sorted further, not as apples (according to our size, color, or freedom from defects) but according to our *desire, perseverance, and meekness.* When we rid ourselves of resentment, we have taken the first step toward turning our stumbling blocks into stepping stones.[1]

We are a lot like fruits and vegetables when placed on this earth. There are some of us that need immediate attention if we are to succeed (crops ready to be eaten fresh), others of us need to have time to bloom and mature (crops that are kept under ideal conditions to remain nutritious), others need a boost from others input (compounds that slow down crop ripening until time to be used), and others will need constant love and care (preserved and canned).

1– *And Then There Were None Some – A Murder Survival Mystery, Jay D. Clark, MD, Pgs 150-152, 2024.*

THE ART

OF

PRESERVING

ALL KINDS OF

Animal and Vegetable Substances

FOR

SEVERAL YEARS.

———

A WORK PUBLISHED BY ORDER OF THE
FRENCH MINISTER OF THE INTERIOR,
On the Report of the Board of Arts and Manufactures,

BY

M. APPERT.

———

TRANSLATED FROM THE FRENCH.

———

LONDON:
PRINTED FOR BLACK, PARRY, AND KINGSBURY,
BOOKSELLERS TO THE HON. EAST-INDIA COM-
PANY, LEADENHALL STREET.

———

1811.

CHAPTER 26

NEAR SIGHTED – MYOPIA...

Bold hues of red, orange, yellow, blue and purple help plants and animals communicate with their own species and others in their efforts to survive. Vivid orange dart frogs warn predators of their toxicity. Different birds use a rainbow of plumage to attract mates. Flowers in a rainbow of colors lure birds and bees to disperse pollen and seeds.

The coloration of living things has evolved slowly: colorful fruitlike seeds started dotting an otherwise bland landscape around 300 million years ago, vibrant flowering plants appeared 100 million years later, and animals—namely cockroaches and butterflies—started sporting bolder pigmentation 70 million years after that. But now, in a puzzling twist, new research shows that animals' ability to perceive many colors came long before the colors themselves existed for them to see.

A recent study in Biological Reviews found that color vision dawned about 500 million years ago—against a drab backdrop of browns and grays and muted shades of some other colors. And it wasn't until around 400 million years later that bright colors expanded across vertebrates and arthropods (a group of invertebrates with an exoskeleton, such as insects and spiders). "There was this long lag time between the explosion of color and the origins of color vision," says John J. Wiens, a co-author of the study and a professor of ecology and evolutionary biology at the University of Arizona.

Researchers previously pinpointed the origination of various coloration using a diagram called a phylogenetic tree, which maps organisms' genetic relationships to one another. This, coupled with fossils that happened to include preserved pigments, allowed evolutionary biologists to trace bright coloration back to the first types of organisms to carry this feature. Wiens and his co-author Zachary Emberts, an integrative biologist at Oklahoma State University, took that work further, analyzing genes that encode protein receptors in animals' visual system to determine when a species could perceive color. By analyzing the timeline of color vision and that of conspicuous coloration, the study showed that hundreds of millions of years elapsed between the development of the former and the latter.

An evolutionary trait almost always occurs for a reason; this raises the question of why animals would gain the ability to see distinctions in bright color long before they would need to. According to the new study, color vision likely played an important role in early species' ability to see whether a plant had living green leaves or dead brown ones or to pick a predator out of the background. Color vision also probably proved especially important underwater, where vertebrate species first evolved, for differentiating hues that resulted when light was filtered through the liquid. "In a marine environment, there's a lot of motion where light is moving, so color vision would have been especially helpful in navigating underwater," Wiens says.

The study's scope is impressive but doesn't tell the whole story of color vision, says Innes C. Cuthill, a professor of *behavioral* ecology at the University of Bristol in England, who was not involved in the research but provided comments for the manuscript. This research focused on trichromatic color vision—the type of visual color perception that humans possess; it didn't look at ultraviolet (UV) vision, which most insects have. Bees, for example, use UV light to distinguish different flowers. "The colors that we see aren't what matters to most animals," Cuthill says. Wiens acknowledges that many aspects of color vision are still a mystery. "There's a very long fuse before this explosion of color occurred," he says, "and we don't really know why."[1]

Veterinarians are frequently confronted by questions such as "Why do cats see better at night?" "Is it true that dogs are color blind?" or "How sharp is my dog's eyesight?" Vision is a very complex sense that is affected by numerous factors, varies greatly between species and can be evaluated in numerous ways, so there is no simple answer to these questions. This talk was presented to not provide a comprehensive and detailed discussion of the subject, but instead focus (pun intended) on some of the significant differences in vision between humans, dogs, cats and horses. Why does my pet seem to be uninterested in watching TV? Responses to rapidly flickering lights are generated by cones. In between flickers cones undergo a brief process of recovery that enables them to generate the response to the next flicker. When the flickers become too rapid, the cones are unable to recover sufficiently between flashes.

At this point, the responses of the cones "fuse," and they generate just one response to a series of rapid flashes. In humans, cone responses fuse at 45 Hz. Therefore, pictures generated by computer or TV screens, which flicker at 50 or 60 Hz, are perceived as one continuous image. However, in animals cone responses fuse at 70–80 Hz. Therefore, when watching television, pets can perceive individual flickering images, which probably have a dramatic effect on their interest in the program! Similarly, pets can detect the flickering of fluorescent lights, a fact that may be taken into account when designing the lighting in a veterinary clinic. Yellow, incandescent bulbs that do not flicker provide for a friendlier environment, at least as far as the patient's vision is concerned.

Does my pet have color vision? Color vision is the domain of the cone photoreceptors. Based on wavelength sensitivity of the photopigment contained in their outer segments, four types of cones have been identified, with animals having anywhere from one to all 4 populations. The number of cone populations, and the degree of overlap in the absorbance spectrum of their photopigment, determine an animal's color vision capabilities. Humans have 3 cone populations, with peak absorbance in the blue, green and red wavelengths (and this is why these are our 3 primary colors), thus making us a trichromatic species.

Some species are monochromatic, having just one cone population, making them red, green or blue monochromats. Such a retina can be found in many nocturnal species, and their color vision is limited to shades of that single photopigment. At the other end of the spectrum, some species have 4 cones populations, with a 4th photopigment absorbing light in the ultraviolet part of the spectrum. These Tetrachromatic species, usually fish and birds, consequently have a much richer color vision than we do.

Contrary to prevalent public opinion, dogs and cats do not "see in black and white." Dogs have two populations of cones. One population absorbs light in the blue-violet spectrum, while the second population absorbs light in the red spectrum. Therefore, dogs can see colors, but are unable to distinguish between green shades. Similarly, cattle & horses have cones absorbing in blue and in green wavelengths, but are unable to see red shades of color (which means that bulls do not perceive the color of the red cloth used by bullfighters). Color vision in all of these species is analogous to that of "color blind" humans. Color blind people are rarely truly color blind. In most cases, they are missing either the red or the green cone population, making them, and the respective species, dichromats. Whales and other aquatic mammals are unique dichromats, who are missing the blue cone population. This means that these species cannot appreciate the blue shade of their aquatic environment. Cats, on the other hand, have 3 cone populations. However, numerous behavioral studies failed to reveal rich trichromatic color vision in felines.

Night vision? Domestic animals have very sensitive night (scotopic) vision. Studies show that the threshold light intensity needed to elicit vision in humans is x 6 the threshold intensity in the cat. Several physiological and anatomical mechanisms account for this improved visual performance in the dark. The first is the amount of light entering the eye. Animals (especially cats, cattle and horses) have very large corneas and pupils. Therefore, more light can pass through their cornea and pupil and reach the retina. It has been calculated that the amount of light that falls on a feline retina is x 6 the amount of light that reaches a human retina.

Furthermore, domestic animals are more capable of exploiting this light, thanks to the tapetum lucidum. This structure, located in the choroid, acts as a mirror. Photons that are not absorbed by photoreceptors are reflected back to the retina, thus doubling the probability that they will be absorbed. However, it should be remembered that the presence of a tapetum results in lower visual acuity, as the photons that are reflected by the tapetum are scattered in the eye and not absorbed by the photoreceptors that are in their original trajectory. In other words, the tapetum provides cats with higher sensitivity at night (when cones are inactive, and therefore reduced visual resolution is of less consequence) at a price of lower daytime visual resolution. However, the most important factor in determining sensitivity to low light levels is the proportion of rods and cones. Rods are very sensitive to low light levels, and can function in intensities that are 10-5 those required by cones. Cats have a much higher concentration of rods than humans throughout the retina, thus contributing significantly to their night vision, while detracting from their visual acuity. How sharp is my pet's eyesight? Visual acuity, or visual resolution, is determined primarily by two factors, the optics of the eye and the anatomy of the retina. Optically, an emmetropic eye is one in which light is properly focused on the retinal photoreceptors. In a myopic (or short-sighted) eye, the image is focused in front of the retina, while in a hyperopic (or far-sighted) eye the image is focused behind the retina. Myopia and hyperopia are collectively known as ammetropia, and the image in such eyes is blurred. A recent large study in which 1500 dogs were refracted showed that a majority of dogs are emmetropic. In other words, it could be said that in these dogs the combined optical power of the eye (mainly the cornea and lens) result in a focused image on the retina, and these dogs do not require corrective spectacles. However, the same study showed that about 25% of all dogs are myopic, with a refractive error ranging from -0.5 to -6.0 D.

Furthermore, some dog breeds have a mean myopic refractive state the average refractive error of some breeds is myopic. For example, in poodles, 77% of dogs were myopic, with a mean refractive error of -1.8 D. On the other hand, significant numbers of dogs were hyperopic, with some dog breeds (e.g., Alaskan Malamute) having a mean hyperopic refractive state.

However, visual acuity is also determined by retinal anatomy. As mentioned previously, the presence of a tapetum lucidum in the eye of domesticated animals causes scattering of light which reduces visual acuity in all these species. Furthermore, differences in the concentration of cones, and their associated ganglion cells, will also have an effect on visual acuity. Because in all domestic species the concentration of cones and their associated ganglion cells is lower than in humans, their visual acuity is lower than that of primates. This means that even if a dog or a cat are emmetropic, and have a well-focused image on their retina, their visual acuity will be low, because the resolving power of the eye is reduced by the low cone and ganglion cell concentration in these species.

Visual acuity is typically expressed as a Snellen fraction. The acuity of normal humans is 20/20. It is estimated that the visual acuity of the horse is 20/33, meaning that a horse needs to be 20 feet from an object to see it as well as a person standing 33 feet away. Visual acuity is 20/75 in the dog and 20/150 in the cat. In other words, a cat has half the acuity of a dog, and a fifth the acuity of a horse. Consequently, a cat has to be more than 7 times closer to an object to see it as sharply as we do! Again, these figures are based on the assumption that the animal is emmetropic. If an animal is ammetropic, then its visual acuity will be even poorer.[2]

According to recent research, people are becoming more short-sighted (nearsighted or myopic) globally, with studies indicating a significant rise in the prevalence of myopia, particularly among children, and projections suggesting that nearly half the world's population could be nearsighted by 2050. Myopia, is an eye disease where light from distant objects focuses in front of, instead of on, the retina. As a result, distant objects appear blurry while close objects appear normal. Other symptoms may include headaches and eye strain. Severe myopia is associated with an increased risk of macular degeneration, retinal detachment, cataracts, and glaucoma.

Myopia results from the length of the eyeball growing too long or less commonly the lens being too strong. It is a type of refractive error. Diagnosis is by the use of cycloplegics during eye examination.

Tentative evidence indicates that the risk of myopia can be decreased by having young children spend more time outside. This decrease in risk may be related to natural light exposure. Myopia can be corrected with eyeglasses, contact lenses, or by refractive surgery. Eyeglasses are the simplest and safest method of correction. Contact lenses can provide a relatively wider corrected field of vision, but are associated with an increased risk of infection. Refractive surgeries like LASIK and PRK permanently change the shape of the cornea. Other procedures include implantable collamer lens (ICL) inside the anterior chamber in front of the natural eye lens. ICL doesn't affect the cornea.

Presbyopia, also known as age-related long-sightedness or far-sightedness, is a normal part of ageing. It can happen even if you already have myopia because presbyopia is typically caused by loss of flexibility of the crystalline lens in the eye, while myopia is caused by the shape of your eye. The eye's natural lens is responsible for evenly refracting light and focusing it on to the right part of the retina, the part of the eye responsible for seeing light and images. The eye's lens can change its shape to bring objects at different distances into focus, a bit like adjusting the focus of a camera lens. As one gets older, they might experience a decline in the lens' ability to do this. This is known as presbyopia. The lens loses its flexibility, and the muscle around the eye becomes weaker. This means your lens isn't able to focus as easily, and you will notice your close-up objects appear a little blurry.

However, if you have myopia and begin to develop presbyopia, you might not notice it straight away. Myopia means the image of an object forms in front of the retina, the part of the eye responsible for seeing light and objects, but in presbyopia, the image is formed behind the retina.

Both issues can compensate, and you might temporarily feel as though your vision is actually improving, but this is just part of the process and you will still need glasses to retain sharp, comfortable vision at near and far distances.

Color blindness, also known as color vision deficiency, is a chronic condition that makes it difficult to see colors or distinguish between them. People with color blindness often have trouble telling the difference between shades of red and green. Other types include difficulty distinguishing between blue and yellow, or purple and red. Color blindness is usually inherited, but it can also be caused by certain eye diseases, medications, aging, diabetes, or multiple sclerosis. Men are more likely to be born with color blindness. *Various sources*

I recall my vision was 20/400 as a child. That means that I needed to be 20 feet away from what an emmetropic person could see at 400 feet away. Visual acuity less than 20/200 is considered legally blind, but to actually fit the definition, the person must not be able to attain 20/200 vision even with prescription eyewear. My myopic vision was not discovered by my parents until school eye exams alerted them to the problem.

I would identify classmates walking down the hall by the way they walked or hearing their voices. When I did start to wear corrective lenses, the view startled me and I can only describe it as a "mystical out of body experience". It took me some time to adjust to wearing glasses.

In my early 30s I was given progressive lenses and the first thing I noticed was that I lost sight of my feet and during the adjustment period tended to trip more often. In my late 40s presbyopia began to set in and I could see very close up objectives better with my glasses off even with adjustments made by the ophthalmologist. This vision changed until in my 70s the glasses come off automatically when I was doing computer work or reading. For five years before my retirement at 78, if my glasses became fogged from my surgical mask or if needing to see close up, I would ask the assistant to remove my glasses.

Being near sighted (myopia) is a true blessing for the aged. As the world begins to close in around us, it is wonderful to be able to see the printing on a page. However, one curse of my aging is finding where my glasses are when needed. "Honey, do you know where I left my glass?" Answer often is – "Can't you see them? They are perched on the top of your head!"

1– *Animals Evolved Color Vision before Bright Colors Emerged, Sara Novak Science Writer, 12/12/2024.*

2– *Vision in the Animal Kingdom, World Small Animal Veterinary Association World Congress Proceedings, Ron Ofri DVM, PhD, DECVO, 2014.*

CHAPTER 27

ANTHRAX ANYONE...

In September 11, 2001 terrorist attacks were a series of coordinated suicide attacks on the United States by the Islamist extremist group al-Qaeda. The attacks killed 2,977 people, making it the deadliest terrorist attack in U.S. history. Nineteen terrorists hijacked American Airlines flight 11 and United Airlines flight 175, crashing both planes into the World Trade Center's North and South Towers. The towers collapsed due to the impact and resulting fires. A third plane, American Airlines flight 77, was hijacked but passengers fought back and crashed he plane into a field in Pennsylvania. The plane was believed to be headed to the White House or the U.S. Capitol. The attacks led to the Global War on Terrorism. The GWOT included military operations, diplomatic actions, and financial measures to stop terrorist groups. The World Trade Center complex was rebuilt and the damaged Pentagon was restored. The National Commission on Terrorist Attacks upon the United States released a report on the attacks in 2004.

Seven days after the terrorist attacks of 09/11/2001, anonymous letters laced with deadly anthrax spores began arriving at media companies and congressional offices. Over the ensuing months, five people died from inhaling anthrax and 17 others were infected after exposure. In 2011, a panel concluded that scientific evidence was consistent with the idea that a government scientist alone sent the anthrax letters.

Because of the increased threat of terrorism, the risk posed by various microorganisms as biological weapons needs to be evaluated and the historical development and use of biological agents better understood. Biological warfare agents may be more potent than conventional and chemical weapons. During the past century, the progress made in biotechnology and biochemistry has simplified the development and production of such weapons. In addition, genetic engineering holds perhaps the most dangerous potential. Ease of production and the broad availability of biological agents and technical knowhow have led to a further spread of biological weapons and an increased desire among developing countries to have them.

Anthrax is a serious disease that came into public prominence in 2001 during the bioterrorism attack in the United States. Anthrax is caused by a bacterium called Bacillus anthracis (B. anthracis). The name anthrax comes from the Greek word for coal and refers to the black skin lesions it produces. Descriptions of a disease affecting both animals and humans that appear to be anthrax have been found as early as Biblical times, and in fact anthrax has been suggested to have been the fifth plague described in the book of Exodus.

The anthrax bacterium was first described in 1823 and was the first bacterium ever shown to be the cause of a disease - in 1876, Robert Koch obtained a pure culture of B. anthracis and demonstrated that it caused disease by injecting it into animals. B. anthracis was also the first bacterium to be used, by Louis Pasteur in 1881, for making an attenuated vaccine.

B. anthracis is a large, rod-shaped bacterium that forms spores. These spores can survive in a dormant state in the environment, usually in soil, for many years, even decades. Once ingested, the spores are activated, and the bacteria begin to reproduce. Reproducing bacteria make three different proteins (protective antigen (PA), lethal factor (LF), and edema factor (EF)) that combine to form two toxins known as lethal toxin (composed of PA and LF) and edema toxin (composed of PA and EF). The toxins cause a fatal buildup of fluid around the lungs that can kill infected cells and produce disease and death in infected animals or humans.

Anthrax is primarily a disease of livestock that become infected by ingesting spores found in soil. Humans usually become infected with anthrax by handling products of infected animals such as leather or wool or by inhaling anthrax spores from infected animal products. They can also become infected by eating undercooked meat from infected animals. Anthrax is not known to be spread person-to-person. Cases of transmission of anthrax from infected animals to humans are relatively rare in the United States, with an average of about five cases per year. However, in 2001, there were 22 cases of anthrax infection that were caused by deliberate spread through the United States Postal system. Letters containing anthrax killed five people and sickened 17 others. The attack caused a temporary disruption of mail service and forced the evacuation of several buildings including Senate offices and the Supreme Court. After a massive and difficult seven-year investigation, the Federal Bureau of Investigation concluded this case after its leading and sole suspect, an Army microbiologist, committed suicide.

Three Main Forms of Human Anthrax:

1– Cutaneous anthrax occurs when bacteria from infected animal products enter a break in the skin; black lesions occur at the site of infection. Other symptoms include fever and fatigue. This is the most common form of anthrax (greater than 95% of all cases). It can be controlled with antibiotics if it is treated before the infection spreads through the body; left untreated, it can be fatal in up to 20% of cases.

2– Gastrointestinal anthrax can result from the ingestion of contaminated meat that is eaten raw or undercooked. Symptoms include fever, nausea, vomiting, and abdominal pain. It can be fatal if not treated immediately.

3– Inhalation anthrax occurs when anthrax spores are inhaled. The spores travel to the lymph nodes near the lungs and produce toxins that cause severe breathing problems and shock. This form is the most dangerous because it is very difficult to treat and it is often fatal. Naturally occurring inhalation anthrax is very rare but, rather, occurs when anthrax spores are aerosolized.

The bacterium that causes anthrax is considered a highly dangerous potential agent for use in bioterrorism. It is classified as a Category A agent – the highest risk type - by the Centers for Disease Control and Prevention (CDC). This means that if a bioterrorist attack were to happen, B. anthracis is considered to be one of the most likely agents to be used. The anthrax bacterium has been a central component to biological weapons research for over 60 years, in multiple countries including Japan, the former Soviet Union, and Great Britain.

The reasons that anthrax is so dangerous is because of its highly toxicity – the mortality rate is nearly 100% for the inhalation form, in the absence of treatment. Its spores are easily disseminated through the air, extremely durable, antibiotics must be administered shortly after exposure and early symptoms are often confused with respiratory or gastrointestinal diseases. There is also concern that the anthrax bacterium could become resistant to currently used antibiotics. In fact, some strains are already resistant to certain classes of antibiotics (some strains are already resistant to certain classes on antibiotics).

There is an effective vaccine against the bacterium that causes anthrax, but its use is recommended only for adults aged 18 through 65 who have an occupational risk for anthrax exposure such as laboratory workers who handle B. anthracis, individuals who have direct contact with potentially infected livestock, and some military personnel. It is not recommended for the general public, and evaluation of its safety or effectiveness in children, pregnant women, the elderly, and people with weakened immune systems is incomplete. Therefore, most people would not be protected in the event of a bioterrorism attack.[1]

Biological weapons are unique in their invisibility and their delayed effects. These factors allow those who use them to inculcate fear and cause confusion among their victims and to escape undetected. A biowarfare attack would not only cause sickness and death in a large number of victims but would also aim to create fear, panic, and paralyzing uncertainty. Its goal is disruption of social and economic activity, the breakdown authority, and the impairment of military responses. As demonstrated by the "anthrax letters" in the aftermath of the World Trade Center attack in September 2001, the occurrence of only a small number of infections can create an enormous psychological impact-everyone feels threatened and nobody knows what will happen next.

The choice of the biowarfare agent depends on the economic, technical, and financial capabilities of the state or organization. smallpox, Ebola, and Marburg virus might be chosen because they have a reputation for causing a more horrifying illness. Images on the nightly news or doctors, nurses, and law enforcement personnel in full protective gear could cause widespread public distraction and anxiety. Biowarfare attacks are now a possibility. The medical community as well as the public should become familiar with epidemiology and control measures to increase the likelihood of a calm and reasoned response if an outbreak should occur. In fact, the principles that help clinicians develop strategies against diseases are relevant as the medical community considers the problem of biological weapons proliferation. For the medical community, further education focusing on recognition of this threat is both timely and necessary.

Primary prevention rests on creating a strong global norm that rejects development of such weapons. Secondary prevention implies early detection and prompt treatment of disease. The medical community plays an important role in secondary prevention by participating in disease surveillance and reporting and thus providing the first indication of biological weapons use. In addition, continued research to improve surveillance and the search for improved diagnostic capabilities, therapeutic agents, and effective response plans will further strengthen secondary prevention measures.[2]

Old-fashioned shaving tools are getting trendy with younger men these days, but one such tool has an interesting history: Men's shaving brushes made from animal hair were linked with cases of anthrax around the time of World War I. A recent report describes several hundred cases of anthrax, which occurred from 1915 to 1924, that were tied to shaving brushes, mainly among men in the U.S. military. Shaving brushes are small facial brushes that are used to apply shaving cream or soap. They were invented in the 18th century and a razor used on the skin can cause small cuts that allow the bacteria entrance into the body.

In 1921, researchers in New York City tested shaving brushes purchased from street vendors, and they found Bacillus anthracis, the bacteria that causes anthrax, in 78 percent of the brushes, a new report said.

Although the risk of contracting anthrax today from an animal-hair shaving brush is extremely low, the report "serves to remind those interested in a return to 'natural grooming' that use of untreated hair from horses, pigs, badgers, or other animals" poses a potential risk of getting anthrax spores into openings on the skin.

Traditionally, the brushes were made with hair from badgers, horses or boars, although badger hairbrushes were the most popular. In recent years, shaving brushes have made something of a comeback as part of a growing niche market of vintage shaving tools, according to the Los Angeles Times.

Given the renewed interested in shaving brushes, researchers from the Centers for Disease Control and Prevention, thought it was relevant to review information on cases of anthrax linked to these brushes. In the new report, the CDC researchers reviewed summaries of disease outbreaks and medical case reports. The outbreak summaries from 1915 to 1924 came from Europe and the United States, and the researchers found 149 cases of anthrax linked to shaving brushes among members of the U.S. military; 17 cases among American civilians; 28 cases among members of the British military; and 50 cases among British civilians.

The cause of the "mini epidemic" of anthrax cases appears to have been related to the disruption of commerce during World War I. Prior to the war, badger hair for the brushes was sourced from Russia, but this hair became difficult to acquire during the war. As a consequence, horsehair was used to make imitation badger brushes.

However, before the war, the animal hair had been disinfected in France or Germany before it was sent to the U.S. While the war was underway, the hair was shipped directly to the U.S. from Russia, China or Japan. Public health officials who investigated the anthrax outbreaks at the time speculated that some manufacturers used the horsehair as received, because they assumed it was already disinfected.

In addition, some manufacturers may have avoided disinfecting lighter-colored hairbrushes because the high-temperature treatment might have discolored the brushes and reduced their resemblance to badger hair. Lighter-colored brushes were more likely to be linked to cases of anthrax compared to dark-colored brushes.[3]

During WWI, Japan, allied with the British, took advantage of the situation to seize German territories in China, particularly the port of Tsingtao (Qingdao), and used this opportunity to further its own influence by issuing the controversial "Twenty-One Demands" to the Chinese government, effectively attempting to establish a sphere of dominance over China; while China officially declared war on Germany alongside the Allies, it did not actively participate in combat due to its internal instability and was largely forced to accept Japanese demands.

During WWI, Russia fought on the side of the Allies against the Central Powers, entering the war in August 1914 due to its alliance with Serbia; however, despite having a large army, Russia suffered major military defeats, severe economic hardship, and ultimately contributed to the downfall of the Tsarist regime through the Russian Revolution, which led to their withdrawal from the war in 1917.

The Allies, particularly Western powers Britain and France, viewed Russia with deep distrust and hostility due to withdrawing from the war early, signing a separate peace greatly, leaving the Allies feeling betrayed and concern about the spread of communist ideology across Europe. This sentiment further fueled interventions by Allied forces into the Russian Civil War, ultimately strengthening the Bolshevik regime in power.

The connection to horsehair causing Anthrax is not surprising. According to the Veterinary Merck Manual: "Anthrax is an often-fatal infectious disease that can infect all warm-blooded animals, including horses and humans. Under-diagnosis and unreliable reporting make it difficult to estimate the true frequency of anthrax worldwide; however, anthrax has been reported from nearly every continent. Under normal circumstances, anthrax outbreaks in the United States are extremely rare.

The Bacillus anthracis bacteria form spores, which are extremely resistant to environmental conditions such as heating, freezing, chemical disinfection, or dehydration that typically destroy other types of bacteria. Thus, the spores can persist for a long time within or on a contaminated environment or object. Horses may consume the spored while grazing in areas where anthrax has been a problem. Optimal growth conditions for the bacteria often occur in neutral or alkaline, calcium or lime-rich soils. Flies and other insects may also spread the disease from infected animals to other animals."

Studies have found that horses are more susceptible to anthrax than badgers and pigs. So, it's even possible that the hair used in these brushes was taken from horses that died from anthrax. Today, animal-hair shaving brushes are unlikely to be a source of anthrax because of modern decontamination processes and regulations on imports. Even the risk from used, vintage brushes would be extremely low. However, the anthrax cases linked to shaving brushes usually involved new brushes, and so shavers buying unused vintage brushes from the early 20th century might want to consider this small risk before using them for shaving.

"This historical information is relevant to current public health practice because renewed interest in vintage and animal-hair shaving brushes has been seen in popular culture," the researchers wrote in an issue of the journal Emerging Infectious Diseases. "This information should help healthcare providers and public health officials answer questions on this topic." The researchers do not recommend trying to disinfect vintage brushes at home because the risks of this process — which involves using steam, pressure and formaldehyde — are likely to outweigh the benefits. *Original article on Live Science*

No, anthrax found in hair and shaving bushes was not considered bioterrorism; it was typically a result of accidental contamination from animal hair used in the brushes, often stemming from animals that had died from anthrax, and not a deliberate act of terrorism; however, the potential for using such contaminated brushes as a bioweapon has been discussed historically, especially during WWI when cases of anthrax linked to shaving brushes were documented.[3]

But, can we be sure anthrax tainted brushes weren't influenced by bioterrorism? Russia withdrew from WWI early, signed a separate peace treaty, left the Allies feeling betrayed and they had to intervene in the Russian Civil War. Russia left the war in 1917 and anthrax cases appeared between 1915-1924 in the military and civilians of Europe (primarily Britian) and the US...Acts of terrorism?

Reading Rueben Ananthan Santhana Dass', Research Analyst at the International Centre for Political Violence and Terrorism Research (ICPVTR), studies makes me wonder whether anthrax, Covid-19 and many other biological tragedies may have been considered at the time as being benign neglect, mistakes, accidents, ignorance or acts of Nature- just might have been influenced by bioterrorism: COVID-19 has cast a spotlight on another potential global threat - that of bioterrorism. Several extremist and terrorist groups, including the Islamic State, Al Qaeda, and some far-right groups around the world, have sought to exploit the ongoing pandemic to promote their worldviews and recruit into their networks. The devastating impact of the virus, which has been acknowledged by these terrorist groups, has also reignited their interest in acquiring, developing and using biological weapons. Recent technological advancements have made the development of biological weapons easier, cheaper and more accessible. This has raised fears of threat groups being more capable of developing and deploying a virus of similar ilk in the near future. The COVID-19 pandemic, the bio-agents that could be exploited by various threat groups, as well as potential lessons that can be gleaned from the pandemic, which may be useful in dealing with a future bioterror threat. The COVID-19 pandemic has claimed more than 2.5 million lives, with more than 100 million cases of infection recorded worldwide since its outbreak in China in December 2019. The pandemic's impact has gone far beyond the disease itself, with far-reaching consequences for societies and economies around the world.

The devastating social, economic and physical impact of the pandemic has also raised questions about the consequences of a virus of similar ilk potentially being used deliberately as a weapon by a violent actor. Terrorist groups can see the havoc that the virus causes, and might potentially draw inspiration for future attacks. In this regard, advancements in the field of biotechnology, have given rise to the threat and possibility of future genetically engineered biological agents that could have a similar or worse strategic impact on the world.

What is a biological weapon?

The World Health Organization (WHO) defines a biological weapon (BW) as "microorganisms such as virus, bacteria, fungi, or other toxins that are produced and released deliberately to cause disease and death in humans, animals or plants." Any number of biological agents can be utilized as BWs, and are typically divided into three categories; 1-bacteria such as anthrax; viruses such as ebola and smallpox; 2-toxins such as botulinum and ricin.

Bacteria and viruses can be categorized as disease causing pathogens that have a self-replicating property, which enables them to keep spreading after an attack/ release under low initial concentrations. In contrast, toxins are poisonous substances produced by living organisms which, while not having a self-replicating property, have high toxicity and lethality.

A BW consists of three major components – a payload (biological agent); munition that keeps the agent stable and virulent; and a delivery system. BWs may be disseminated by air (aerosols), injection, food or water or through a zoonotic vector, where the agents are transmitted from animal to humans.

In recent decades, terrorist groups have repeatedly attempted to acquire, develop and carry out bio-attacks. This comprises groups across the ideological spectrum, including right-wing, jihadist, ethno-nationalist, and various fringe movements. However, to date, there has not been a successful large-scale attack using a biological agent by a terrorist group. This may be due to the technical complexities and expertise required to weaponize biological agents.

A three stage process is typically involved in the development of a biological weapon: acquisition; synthesis (growing and multiplying of the bio-agent to sufficient quantities and genetic modification); and delivery. Whilst the first stage of acquisition is relatively attainable, particularly in the case of plant-based agents such as ricin and abrin, the latter two stages are harder to achieve as the synthesis and delivery of bio-agents require controlled environmental conditions, proper equipment and advanced technical capabilities. Thus far terror groups have failed to go beyond the second stage of BW development due to the technological barriers and difficulties in obtaining the necessary equipment and conditions needed to synthesize and deliver the agent.

Ricin is produced from a plant-based source such as castor oil beans, which are readily available, while the toxin itself can be isolated in a simple laboratory setup like a household kitchen with makeshift extraction equipment. The most recent case involving an attempted ricin attack was that of a Canadian woman who attempted to send ricin-laced letters to the White House and a number of government offices in Texas, September 2020.

In 1999, AQ initiated an anthrax development program under the direct purview of an AQ deputy leader. The first phase of AQ's anthrax program involved the attempted acquisition of pathogenic strains of anthrax from a Pakistani microbiology researcher. He had used his professional capacity as a researcher to attend international conferences on biological weapons, and visit laboratories known to be developing anthrax. Through these activities, he reportedly sought to obtain information, resources and possibly acquire a pathogenic strain of anthrax for AQ. However, he was largely unsuccessful, going only as far as providing AQ with a crude mock-up of a biological lab. Following his failure, AQ initiated a second phase of the program in 2000, engaging a former Malaysian Army captain to develop anthrax. The microbiology researcher, then a member of the AQ-affiliated Jemaah Islamiyah (JI), had been recommended to the AQ leadership by then JI leader in Southeast Asia. He being a biochemistry major from the US, would spend several months setting up a biological laboratory in Kandahar, Afghanistan, and conducted research into the cultivation of anthrax. Following the US' military invasion of Afghanistan in 2001 the program would be disbanded. He then moved to Bogor, Indonesia, where he tried to revamp the anthrax program, but ultimately failed. The microbiologist has subsequently served a string of prison sentences on terrorism charges in Malaysia before being released in 2019. He remains under surveillance by the Malaysian authorities.

IS has likewise held a keen interest in carrying out BW attacks. However, it is unclear if IS had a centralized BW program like AQ. IS' BW plots have mostly involved lone actors and autonomous cells. In 2014, a laptop belonging was recovered in Syria, revealing a 19-page document containing various methods of developing BWs, weaponizing the bubonic plague from infected animals, and instructions on releasing virus laden grenades into densely-populated areas. He was a chemistry and physics university student in Tunisia. In 2016, authorities in Kenya apprehended an IS cell consisting of four medical interns at a local hospital, who had planned on carrying out "large-scale attacks" using anthrax. The cell was also involved in active recruitment and radicalization efforts but it is unclear if they had procured anthrax. Two years later, German police foiled a terrorist plot involving a Tunisian IS member. He had planned to carry out a biological attack using ricin in Cologne, Germany. Sief had received instructions from an IS member in Syria. While a failed plot, this was the first instance in which an individual had successfully produced the biological toxin (stage 2 of weaponization), with police later recovering 84.3 milligrams of already produced ricin from his house.

In October 2019, Indonesian police thwarted a suicide attack plot involving a cell linked to pro-IS group in Cirebon, West Java. They had planned to use the biological agent abrin, which is found in rosary pea seeds. Indonesian counter-terrorism unit found explosives together with the abrin poison during raids, which they believed was meant to be incorporated into suicide bombs targeting the Cirebon Police Headquarters.

Among far-right extremists, the researchers observed that far-right linked bioterrorism is predominantly a lone-actor phenomenon, in comparison to other plots that involve a larger organizational structure. In October 2001, soon after the 9/11 attacks, the US faced an anthrax attack, in which five people died and twenty-two others were infected with anthrax. This followed a series of anthrax laced letters being sent to five media offices and two US senators. The attacks were perpetrated by microbiologist and biodefence researcher Dr Bruce Ivins, who had no real political motivations but Nevertheless, was referred to by the 2011 Norway attacker, Anders Breivik as a "right-wing, Christian, cultural conservative." Subsequently, there has been a number of other bio-incidents involving white supremacists primarily involving ricin.

In recent years, advances in science and technology have made it easier and cheaper to produce biological agents, which could be developed into BWs. In turn, this has prompted fears that post pandemic, bad actors could view biological weapons as a cost-effective means to launch attacks. One such field is synthetic biology (SynBio), which encompasses biological systems engineering which have potentially reduced the cost and technical skills required to engineer highly lethal biological agents. One of these advancements is a gene editing technique known as Clustered Regularly Interspaced Short Palindromic Repeats or CRISPR. This technique is akin to using a pair of scissors or a pencil to alter and modify – in theory - the DNA sequences of biological systems. Prior to CRISPR, gene alteration would require sophisticated equipment and hence was prohibitively expensive. Today, simple DIY CRISPR kits are available commercially for less than $150.36 In 2018, the United Nations (UN) highlighted the potential threat posed by CRISPR techniques in developing more effective biological weapons and the proliferation of these so-called "DIY biological labs." The inherent characteristic that allows for the purposeful engineering of the biological system is modularity, or the ability to separate and recombine separate components of a system. The genetic material (DNA or

RNA) of a system, which contains all the information for the system's proper functioning, can be removed from one pathogen and inserted into another as a means of altering its function. Modularity enables a measure of predictability in altered systems, while allowing for the various functions of the system to be tweaked and manipulated.

SynBio techniques have been used to successfully create viruses. In 2002 & 2017, researchers at the State University in New York succeeded in chemically synthesizing the complete poliovirus genome, the recipe of which is available freely online. In 2005, another group of American researchers succeeded in reconstructing the 1918 influenza pandemic virus. The entire process was carried out in a regular laboratory setting using standard equipment available in university biology laboratories. Additionally, the methods employed were not beyond the capabilities of an amateur biologist. In 2016, a group of Canadian researchers constructed the horsepox virus using genetic information solely obtained from a public database.

In a broader sense, Wickiser et. al. observed that the "techniques used to propagate bacteria and viruses and to cut and paste genetic sequences from one organism to another are approaching the level of skill required to use a cookbook or a home computer." SynBio has also enabled the development of binary bio-weapons including, for example, weapons consisting of two agents which are harmless on their own but become lethal when combined. In future, the prospect cannot be discounted that malicious actors might be able to develop the components, store them separately and bring them together in a biological munition prior to delivery.

Largely, however, there has been no known evidence of terror groups exploiting these technologies to plot attacks as yet, and the challenges to develop bio-weapons remain formidable. Yet these advancements arguably reduce the technological barrier, and could be taken advantage by terrorists in future to perpetrate attacks, particularly in instances when lone actors/autonomous cells possess some technical knowledge. The three potential capabilities of SynBio that warrant the highest level of concern are in the re-creation of known viruses; the manufacture of harmful biochemicals; and the genetic modification of existing bacteria into more lethal forms. This is in contrast to the creation of novel bio-agents, which remains technically a very difficult task.

Several experts, have warned that the current pandemic "may lead to a resurgence in interest among terrorists for using such weapons. This is partly due to the devastating impact of COVID-19, which highlights the lethality and potentially far-reaching consequences of a bioterror attack involving a novel biological agent. Terrorist groups such as AQ and IS continue to retain an interest in using biological weapons. In a recent pro-AQ magazine published in November 2020 titled 'Wolves of Manhattan', AQ had called on its "wolves of Islam" to hand out "poisoned masks" to unsuspecting individuals in streets or stations. IS too recently released a poster titled 'The Biological Terror', via an online blog, which called on supporters to carry out attacks by spreading poison in food and at gatherings. Terrorist cells in Indonesia have planned poison attacks previously.

In 2011, a militant cell in Jakarta planned to kill policemen by poisoning their food in a canteen using ricin. Five years later, another attempt was made by a terrorist cell in Indonesia to deliver cyanide-laced food to police officers. At the other end of the ideological spectrum, far-right groups have actively called on their members to exploit the novel coronavirus as a bio-weapon, urging infected members to spread the virus amongst Jews and minorities by hugging, coughing and contaminating currency notes.

However, there have been little indications thus far that these calls have been adhered to by far-right elements. At present, it is unlikely that transnational terror groups such as AQ and IS have the physical and technical capability to mount large-scale, centrally-directed bio-attacks. Apart from leadership at the strategic level, the use of bio-weapons on a large scale is dependent on, among other factors, the existence of safe havens, the ability to acquire bio-agents at the operational level, and having the necessary technical capabilities to develop these agents into weapons at the tactical level. Such prospects have been significantly diminished, following the loss of territory, leadership and technical capabilities that both groups have experienced, as a result of several major counter-terrorism operations in their previous strongholds in Iraq, Afghanistan and Syria.

Nonetheless, as evidenced by the terrorist attacks in Europe in late 2020, there has been a clear shift in general attack trends from large-scale centrally directed attacks like 9/11, to smaller scale "pin prick" attacks involving 'isolated' lone wolves who are self-radicalized and do not have links to wider extremist networks. As such, authorities need to be wary of lone-wolf perpetrated, low casualty attacks involving crude bio-agents such as ricin, that have high psychological but low physical impact, and are inspired rather than centrally directed.

The three main threat categories include: lone actors/ autonomous cells who are remotely directed by terrorists with technical know-how; lone actors/autonomous cells who have the technical knowledge and capability and 'isolated' lone wolves. The latter two categories may involve insider threats, including individuals affiliated with research institutions who have access to materials and technical knowledge.

Overall, conventional attack methods such as knife and vehicular attacks, and the use of IEDs, will continue to pose the larger terrorist threat compared to bio-attacks, mainly due to the difficulties surrounding the weaponization of bio-agents. Yet the need for governments around the world to increase their bio-preparedness and fortify their bio-defense capabilities has taken on added urgency since the onset of COVID-19. The pandemic has highlighted preparedness gaps in several areas, including in data sharing, communication, medical equipment availability and distribution, travel management and pandemic testing. Governments have also had to ensure their healthcare systems are well-resourced, in addition to developing adequate surveillance and rapid response capabilities. In these efforts, swift inter-agency cooperation between law enforcement, defense, medical and public service agencies is required.

Further, governments must also channel resources into research and development as well as ensure the availability of an updated stockpile of vaccines against emerging diseases and antidotes against bio-agents such as ricin.

In the realm of disrupting attacks, the main threat still stems from lone actor/autonomous cells who draw inspiration from terror groups such as AQ and IS. As such, security services should implement measures to keep lone actors isolated, including by closer monitoring of social media spaces and networks of key individuals, arresting cell leaders and cutting off chains of command.60 Closer scrutiny of e-commerce platforms known to be used by extremists for the procurement of precursor agents for possible BWs is also required.

In part, this will require law enforcement collaborating with online platforms to develop better monitoring systems to detect, flag and report purchases of precursor materials, as part of disruption measures to thwart attack plots. Such electronic surveillance proved vital in the 2018 Cologne ricin plot, where British intelligence had detected, flagged and relayed information to Germany's Federal Intelligence Service, or a bioterrorism agency, were alert enough to monitor the online purchases of at least 1,000 castor oil beans and a coffee grinder on Amazon for the purposes of producing ricin. Governments should also collaborate with academic institutions to regulate the Global Preparedness Monitoring Board.[4]

In sum, the threat of bioterrorism must be taken seriously, and the development of robust bio-defense mechanisms are necessary, in order to mitigate against future bio-threats. While I was in veterinary school (1969-1973) the contamination of animal hair in shaving and hair brushes with Anthrax story was told to my classmates during microbiology class. This story imprinted on my mind enough to buy a plastic bristled hair brush. I've used it on a regular basis over many years and try to remember to shake the water off and dry it after each use. When neglected a sour smell, indicating the growth of microbiome, can be controlled by washing the brush with soap, warm water and drying it with a hair dryer. Since the bristles are plastic, I'm sure that Anthrax has never been a part of the microbiome growing on my brush.

Bioterrorism or not, nostalgic good old days memories from purchasing a shaving or hair brush produced from animal hair in the 1900s could result in a nostalgic experience one is sure to never forget.

1– *Anthrax, Department of Molecular Virology and Micro biology, Baylor College of Medicine.*

2– *Biological warfare and bioterrorism: a historical review, Baylor Univ Med Cent, 2004.*

3– *Strange History of Anthrax Cases Tied to Men's Shaving Brushes, News, Rachael Rettner, 04-12-2017.*

4– *Counter Terrorist Trends and Analyses, Vol. 13, Reuben Ananthan Santhana Dass, 2021.*

CHAPTER 28

TERRORISTS...

Two bombs exploded (04/15/2013) near the finish line of the Boston Marathon. A video of the scene from the bombing showed people running toward the wounded, trying to help. A flood of support and sympathy poured out all across the Internet. And Bostonians rushed to donate blood and offer spare bedrooms to those displaced by the blast. Even though humans caused the carnage at the finish line, such acts of kindness, as well as a sense of empathy, are actually hard to overcome — even for the terrorists, psychologists say.

A whole industry of propaganda is aimed at convincing potential terrorists that their intended victims are worthy of death. Part of the ideological persuasion to get them to do these things is to reduce the humanity of the victims so the victims are perceived not as other human beings, but rather as vermin, as subhuman creatures. Terrorists do not fit into a simple mold. There's no profile, there's no personality, there's no checklist and there is no silver-bullet solution that helps explain why and how people become involved in terrorism.

However, there may be some common psychology necessary to carry out such an act. The underlying motivation is what is call a "quest for personal significance." They try to do something important, either because they feel insignificant on their own … they were humiliated in some way, or their group was denigrated. While some people respond to feelings of powerlessness and insignificance by turning to humanitarian aims — becoming a peace activist, for example — would-be terrorists draw on violent ideologies. Violence is a quick shortcut to feelings of significance. Violence enjoys this very clear advantage, that by striking, by shooting, by exploding a device, a very simple action immediately makes you out to be a significant, heroic kind of person.

In this worldview, the innocent victims of a bomb are subhuman, at worst, and incidental, at best. Timothy McVeigh, whose 1995 bombing of a government building in Oklahoma City killed 168, famously described the 19 children who died in the blast as "collateral damage." For a person who engages in this kind of activity, the immediate victims are meaningless. They're simply a means to an end. It's hard work maintaining that belief. Some terrorists eventually come to feel remorse for the innocent lives they took. But especially in the moment, many work very hard to convince themselves that what they've done is righteous. Though stories of violence may dominate the news, there's good scientific evidence to suggest that humans are wired to care for others. By toddlerhood, children take it upon themselves to be helpful, for example. Even 6-month- and 10-month-olds prefer helpful characters over mean ones, studies suggest. As adults, we quite literally feel others pain.

A study found that when doctors see their patients in pain, the pain-processing regions in their own brains activate. It's easiest for terrorists to reduce their guilt when they choose a method like a bombing, so they don't have to be nearby to see the damage they've done.

Although it is a major goal, terrorism is hard to pre-empt, because terrorists don't fit into one demographic profile. Radicals tend to speak their minds, making them easy enough to identify in the community though not all of those radicals would ever turn to terrorism in any case. Detention centers and prisons also run de-radicalization programs for suspected and convicted terrorists. Typically, these programs run along two lines: direct and indirect. A direct approach would be to confront the terrorist's belief system. In the case of an Islamic terrorist, for example, clerics might come in to explain how fundamentalist interpretations of the Koran are flawed. This "dialogue" approach can work, but not for terrorists, who are very firm in their beliefs, or for leaders who don't appreciate criticism of their interpretations. In these cases, an indirect approach can sometimes help. The goal of these programs is to give a radicalized individual something else to live for, whether a vocation, art or even spiritual practices, such as yoga. It directs their attention from these collectivistic goals and on to their individualistic.

Measuring whether you've prevented someone from participating in terrorism in the future is a difficult task, but it's important to remember that even among radicals, most people won't resort to violence — though terrorists rely on the randomness of their acts to make civilians feel like they or their loved ones could be next.[1]

A study that examined the connection between education and terrorism implementing several models, found a positive association between education and terrorism which suggests that more educated people are more likely to engage in terrorism. They also found that terrorists are generally active in the labor market. These results are associated with socio-economic and demographic characteristics of the individual and institutional framework, especially attendance to religious school, gender, age, and the presence of law enforcement in the attack place.

Furthermore, they found evidence that unlike "the old paradigm," terrorists come more from urban than rural areas and are sensitive to spatial heterogeneity which contributes to reduce their motivation. The negative binomial results confirm that the higher the level of education of the terrorist, the greater the number of victims. Educated terrorists cause the most damage and are the most dangerous.[2]

In 1995, Landau et al. documented the prevailing threats to animal research in "Neuroreality I," which emphasized the importance of incorporating an understanding of biomedical research within the educational system. Two decades later, the threat against research involving animals has not receded but rather has escalated. This has occurred against the backdrop of exponential growth in neuroscience research and understanding of neurologic disease pathogenesis leading to innovative treatment strategies. These advances have occurred as a direct outgrowth of the seminal contributions of animal investigations. Therefore, the alarming trend of these direct attacks requires an appropriate response.

Most practicing neurologists and biomedical investigators involved in neuroscience research are cognizant of the pipeline of research initiatives required to demonstrate the efficacy of new therapies.

This involves a long series of experimental paradigms and repeated testing to ensure that patients are not the first living beings exposed to a putatively helpful but potentially harmful new therapy. Most professional neuroscientists agree about the importance of animal research. However, not everyone in the general public understands the issues involved. Unfortunately, a minority of individuals who oppose the use of animals in research have used threats and even terrorism to further their views. This threatens the very system upon which new treatment options depend. Messages designed to enlist support against animal research have been delivered for many years without overt challenge by the scientific community. A presumed fear of reprisals has been thought to enable the unchecked spread of misinformation. Outreach initiatives through presentations to schoolchildren have been used to gain support from the earliest stages of conceptual thought. These outreach initiatives have incorporated misleading information and contrived photographs through activists gaining employment in research labs and intentionally staging fake photographs in the laboratory setting for use in presentations and Web site postings. Misleading information typically remains on the Web sites and in brochures even after errors have been pointed out to anti–animal research groups. Activist organizations also attempt to identify themselves with the pro-environmental movement for recruitment and fundraising purposes.

Anti–animal research organizations deny that there are beneficial outcomes from animal research. As most clinicians and researchers are aware, a wide range of breakthroughs derived from animal studies have saved countless lives. Animal research continues to be critical for protecting patients from premature approval of potentially deleterious drugs. The tragedy of birth defects caused by thalidomide might have been prevented had more animal research been mandated. Most of the birth defects occurred in Europe, where thalidomide was prescribed to control morning sickness in pregnancy. The United States was largely spared thalidomide-related birth defects due to the vigilance of the US Food and Drug Administration in deferring approval of this drug's use pending investigation of its effects in pregnant animals.

Vaccines, which have been the most successful and cost-effective public health intervention ever introduced, have depended on animal research for their development. For example, the polio vaccination program that began 60 years ago could not have been achieved rapidly or safely without animal research. Effective control of more recent infectious disease threats, including Legionnaires' disease, HIV/ AIDS, severe acute respiratory syndrome, and avian flu, have also depended on animal research. Timely response to newly emerging infectious agents (influenza pandemics, hemorrhagic fevers) will also depend on animal research.

The most threatening acts of terror target researchers studying primates, cats, or dogs. However, investigators studying rodents increasingly require protection from harassment.

University scientists are not the only ones affected. The Chief Executive Officer of Novartis had his mother's ashes stolen, the graves of his family desecrated, and his vacation home burned by animal activists. Activists' efforts to impede transport of research animals affect a range of stakeholders, including the pharmaceutical industry. "Animal rights" groups have attacked other industries. They were responsible for disrupting the Westminster Dog Show at Madison Square Garden in New York, and activists have adversely interacted with various stakeholders in the food industry.

The centralized activities of the major public organizations are relatively easy to track, but the organizational structure of individuals involved with terrorist acts is considerably more difficult to trace. Activities such as posting personal information or false information about researchers are also difficult to trace and typically are not prosecuted. However, the Federal Bureau of Investigation (FBI)'s characterization of these activities as terrorism has assisted efforts toward prosecution. All extremist activities are destructive to scientific dialogue and disruptive to the pipeline of research yielding new therapies for both human and veterinary patients.

Financial support for the more extreme activities used by animal rights activists is complex. Funding for the more "mainstream" organizations opposing the use of animals in research can generally be traced. Activists involved in more violent activities are typically from smaller fringe groups not requiring large amounts of funding, and their sources of funding are more difficult to track.

The larger, more public groups dedicated to disrupting animal research use a variety of methods to raise funds. Their chosen titles are sometimes purposely misleading in order to accrue donations from individuals who may not fully understand the group's intentions.

One leading animal rights member was barred from entering the United Kingdom for being quoted as saying that millions of animal lives could be saved if a handful of researchers were killed. Donors intending to contribute to animal shelters may not be aware that <1% of its annual budget goes to grants for local animal shelters.

Another contemporary strategy favored by activists is to legally challenge in promotion of animal guardianship rather than ownership. Their goal is to grant animals "personhood," a title that would raise animal rights to a new category in which research is no longer possible. The activists' argument is that any lesser legal status of animals is "speciesism," analogous to racism and other forms of civil discrimination. Activists continue to lobby for larger cages for rabbits and rodents, ignoring the fact that rabbits and rodents in nature are fearful of open spaces. Furthermore, bans are moving forward for all research involving great apes. The strength of existing support for the welfare of research animals is evidenced by strict federal and local regulations with specific requirements that must be in place before research can proceed.

The customary silence of researchers has been a potent weapon for the animal rights activist. By avoiding discussion of animal research for fear of reprisals, many who would otherwise be highly supportive of animal research enable extremists' activities to proceed unchecked.

The threat to biomedical research has not receded. New threats are still emerging, including the potential for cyber-attacks, which must be taken into account for future research security planning. In order to preserve the research pipeline to better health, creative efforts must be invested to educate the public about how advances in neurology and neuroscience occur and to justify the use of animals to advance biomedical research.[3]

During my research years at Purdue University (1968-1972), animal extremist terrorizing of animal research was just coming into view. We were advised that we should keep copies of all our research at our homes in case antivivisectionists compromised our research animals or destroyed our lab data.

When confronted with this issue, I silently scoffed at the idea of considering rats as being harassed and even questioned some of the regulations that we needed to follow during our care and research protocols. I had slept with, bred and raised enough white rats as a youth to have my mother take the whole lot of them to Idaho State University for "educational purposes." I suspected their lack of laboratory quality led them to be fed to their lab reptiles (which I felt would be harassment).

Later in life, I felt the taste of harassment/terrorism by donating to a ballot initiative while living in California. The ballot initiative process is meant to give California citizens a way to propose laws and constitutional amendments without the support of the Governor or the Legislature. I felt it unfair that a monopoly electric utility, that our community was forced to use their services, was donating several hundred thousand dollars to support one side of an initiative. The mistake I made was sending a couple of hundred dollar checks in my company's name to support the other side. The donation wasn't as much that I supported the opposite point of view than that I didn't think it was fair for a supposed nonpolitical business to help drown out the opposite point of view through their huge donation.

Several days later my son, Jeremy, asked me why I had chosen to jump into a hornet's nest. Apparently social media (which I do not subscribe to) was all over our company, my good name and Jeremy's. He asked if I was trying to destroy the business? The unhappy lot had gone so far as to go to a nearby pet store and distribute fliers to store patrons and place them on car windows in the parking lot. I read some of the media and could not believe that the donation could have caused such an uproar.

I eventually wrote my first and so far, my last letter to social media. I explained the "what and why" I had made the donation. For me, it turned out to be an interesting experience. A short time after my comments were written, thoughts began coming in from many expressing kind comments about me and their feelings that I had every right to make the donation. Things returned to business as usual and several involved in the protest still visit our hospital.

When I say that terrorism is war against civilization, I may be met by the objection that terrorists are often idealists pursuing worthy ultimate aims - national or regional independence, and so forth. I do not accept this argument. I cannot agree that a terrorist can ever be an idealist, or that the objects sought can ever justify terrorism. The impact of terrorism, not merely on individual nations, but on humanity as a whole, is intrinsically evil, necessarily evil and wholly evil. *Benjamin Netanyahu*

World War II (09/01/1939-09/01/1945) was coming to a close when this radio program was aired October 1, 1944: For quite some time now, the war has been, and still is, our greatest immediate worry. The world is waiting prayerfully, solemnly, hopefully, for any news which will indicate the end in sight. Indeed, so absorbed have we become with this one great emergency, that it has overshadowed all else—to the point where we have more or less forgotten what were our worries before the war began. War takes so much of our attention and effort that there is seemingly little time to prepare for peace, but to prepare for peace is a grave and urgent obligation, because war is merely a symptom of a disease, the germs of which are already at work in times of peace.

Long before the actual outbreak of war, men are at war in their hearts. Our courts of law are filled with the evidence of private wars—of quarrels, hatreds, misunderstandings, lying, deception, covetousness, and infidelity—and war among nations is merely the organized evidence of what has been in the hearts and minds of men long before its actual outbreak—and the order to cease firing does not heal the souls of men, nor rid the world of its sorrows, nor quiet the hatreds and vows for vengeance, nor destroy the greed for power. And if perchance we have been guilty, any of us, of oversimplifying the problem, we should ask ourselves, in all frankness, what was the nature of our difficulties before war began? And then comes the next logical question: What have we done or what are we doing to justify the conclusion that those same conditions, or others equally aggravating, will not rise to plague us when war ceases?

Suppose we ask ourselves honestly what have we done to remove the basic causes of those troubles? What have we done, honestly, to clean our own house? And so, much as we yearn for peace, much as we shall rejoice when it comes, if peace should come without some changes in us and in others, it will inevitably fall short of our hopes and expectations. War is electrifying and absorbing. Despite its sordidness and sacrifice, its terror and its sorrow, in the preparation for war and in the waging of it, there is always an element of the dramatic and the spectacular which seems to fire the imaginations of men and stir them to heroic activity. But if men would have the peace they cherish, they must prepare for peace and pursue it as earnestly and heroically as they now wage war.[4]

1– *Inside Twisted Terrorist Minds — Where Is the Empathy?, Live Science Newsletter, Stephanie Pappas, 04/16/2013.*

2– *Are more educated people more likely to engage in terrorism, Taylor & Francis, Applied Economics, 10/11/2022.*

3– *Animal extremists' threats to neurologic research continue, Neurology; 85(8): 730-734, 08/25/2015.*

4– *Private Preface to Public Conflict, Music & The Spoken Word #789, 10/01/1944.*

CHAPTER 29

CANNIBALISM...

The strict definition of cannibalism is the eating of human flesh by humans. It is also often stretched to include other species of animals eating their own species or humans being eaten by animals of any species they consider as being human – cats, dogs, snakes, allegators etc.

While the existence of cannibalism, anthrophagy, has been disputed, particularly in tribal societies, there appears no doubt from multiple historical records that there have been many reliably reported cases. Cannibalism occurs for a wide variety of reasons and may be separated into two broad categories of exo- and endocannibalism. With exocannibalism, the victim is selected from outside the social group or community that is engaging in anthrophagy. The reasons for this may simply be nutritional in that outsiders are being hunted as a source of food, or tribal in that cannibalistic rituals form part of victory celebrations in warfare. The purpose of the latter is often to demonstrate complete dominance over a fallen foe and also to subjugate or incorporate their spirit into self. Endocannibalism refers to cases where victims derive from the same social group and may be subclassified as 'aggressive' when the victim is an enemy or 'affectionate' when family or friends are involved. Again, the motive may be simply nutritional or ritual with domination and/or incorporation of the victim into the perpetrators.

A more functional classification is based on motivations for consuming human tissues and has the following subgroups: (1) nutritional or gastronomic, (2) ritual and (3) pathological. Nutritional cannibalism has a long history and it has been hypothesized that early hominids engaged in cannibalism as fellow group members were readily available for consumption and also that it served to dispose of corpses thus decreasing the attention of animal predators around camps. The basis of nutritional cannibalism is simply the use of human tissues or organs for their calorific value. It most often occurs in situations of acute starvation when groups are deprived of food or become isolated from their usual food resources.

Consumption of their victims by killers is a recognized, although rare, occurrence with one of the most widely publicized being Jeffery Dahmer a serial killer in the USA who committed 17 murders between 1978 and 1991. He was found to have engaged in necrophilia, consuming parts of his victims and keeping skulls and body parts as souvenirs. A slightly different case was that of Armin Meiwes in Germany who advertised on the internet for a victim to kill and consume. (Necrophilia is a rare paraphilia characterized by a persistent and intense sexual attraction to dead bodies. It is a form of paraphilia, which is a sexual interest or behavior that deviates from typical societal norms).

Individuals who engage in such practices are usually either severely mentally ill or suffering from a significant paraphilia. The same applies to those who suffer from clinical vampirism where they drink human blood, usually from a deceased or dying victim. A review of cannibalistic homicides showed that the offenders were older and the victims younger than in other homicides, that deaths were inflicted manually (beating, strangling and stabbing) rather than by gunshots and that kin-avoidance occurred with more victims being strangers. When family members were victims, the perpetrators were usually suffering from more serious psychiatric illnesses.

It has been suggested based on animal studies that the transmission of pathogens from victims to consumers may account for the rarity of cannibalism in human populations; however, ethnographic and sociological factors are probably of more importance. The presence of certain genetic polymorphisms in human populations has been proposed as evidence of an evolutionary protective mechanism against kuru-type diseases (rare, fatal neurodegenerative diseases that was once prevalent among the fore people of Papua New Guinea. It is caused by an infectious protein called a "prion"), associated with cannibalism possibly indicating that cannibalism may have been more common during earlier stages of human evolution.

On occasion, the consumption of human tissues and blood has been promoted for medical purposes. In Europe, particularly in the sixteenth and seventeenth centuries, remedies were dispensed that contained blood, fat and bones derived from recent graves or from Egyptian mummies. Human skull bones in alcohol, and moss growing over a buried skull was used to treat epilepsy and nosebleeds. Some have considered that drinking blood as being therapeutic.[1] The word BSE is short but it stands for a disease with a long name, bovine spongiform encephalopathy. Bovine means that the disease affects cows, spongiform refers to the way the brain from a sick cow looks spongy under a microscope, and encephalopathy indicates that it is a disease of the brain. BSE is commonly called mad cow disease. BSE is a progressive neurologic disease of cows. Progressive means that it gets worse over time. Neurologic means that it damages a cow's central nervous system (brain and spinal cord).

Most scientists think that BSE is caused by a protein called a "prion". For reasons that are not completely understood, the normal prion protein changes into an abnormal prion protein that is harmful. The body of a sick cow's immune system does not recognize that abnormal prion is present.

Prions are simply proteins, not living organisms, and they can survive almost anything, even hundreds of degrees of heat. Placing infected tissue in a landfill simply removes it, but scientists worry that the prions can leach through soil and groundwater, and spread. Incineration is possible, but it isn't as easy as burning the carcass in a fire. Unlike most bacteria, regular cooking won't destroy it. Even many of the sterilization techniques used in hospitals, such as autoclaving, are not necessarily effective — though some may be when infected material is dipped in sodium hydroxide, or lye and heated well above the boiling point of water.

A common sign of BSE in cows is incoordination. A sick cow has trouble walking and getting up. The cow may also act very nervous or violent, which is why BSE is often called "mad cow disease." It usually takes four to six years from the time a cow is infected with the abnormal prion to when it first shows symptoms of BSE. This is called the incubation period. During the incubation period, there is no way to tell that a cow has BSE by looking at it. Once a cow starts to show symptoms, it gets sicker and sicker until it dies, usually within two weeks to six months. There is no treatment for BSE and no vaccine to prevent it.

The parts of a cow that are not eaten by people are cooked, dried, and ground into a powder. The powder is then used for a variety of purposes, including as an ingredient in animal feed. A cow gets BSE by eating feed contaminated with parts that came from another cow that was sick with BSE. The contaminated feed contains the abnormal prion, and a cow becomes infected with the abnormal prion when it eats the feed. If a cow gets BSE, it most likely ate the contaminated feed during its first year of life. Remember, if a cow becomes infected with the abnormal prion when it is one-year-old, it usually will not show signs of BSE until it is five-years-old or older.

People can get a version of BSE or kuru-type diseases, called variant Creutzfeldt-Jakob disease (vCJD). As of 2019, 232 people worldwide are known to have become sick with vCJD, and unfortunately, they all have died. It is thought that they got the disease from eating food made from cows sick with BSE. Most of the people who have become sick with vCJD lived in the United Kingdom at some point in their lives.

Neither vCJD nor BSE is contagious. This means that it is not like catching a cold. A person (or a cow) cannot catch it from being near a sick person or cow. Also, research studies have shown that people cannot get BSE from drinking milk or eating dairy products, even if the milk came from a sick cow.[2]

While cows, mink, sheep, cats, elk, mule deer, hamsters, and some zoo animals including a lion, tigers, pumas, a bison, and eland (a spiral-horned African antelope that lives in open woodland and grassland. It is the largest of the antelopes), have died from species-specific versions of the spongiform diseases, other animals seem immune. For example, to date, no pigs, chickens, horses, or dogs appear to contract the disease (updated).

The practice of prescribing human remains or their byproducts for healing goes back hundreds of years. Galen, a Roman physician and philosopher who lived in the second century, advocated the curative effect on epilepsy and arthritis of an elixir of burned human bones, and Paracelsus, a Swiss alchemist and physician who lived from 1493–1541, observed that the noblest medicine for man is man's body and promoted the medicinal power of mummy, human blood, fat, marrow, dung, and cranium in the treatment of many ailments.

Between at least the 12th and 17th centuries and well into the 18th century, according to Noble — mumia or "mummy" was widely used as a drug in European countries. According to an 18th-century pharmaceutical treatise, the term could refer to various substances extracted from embalmed and mummified human remains. Ailments listed to be cured by mumia remains were: Blood thinner, painkillers, cough suppressants, anti-inflammatory, menstrual aid, and promoting wound healing. Other parts of human remains could be used such as: cadaver's skin for difficult labors and hysteric affection; fat to ease pain and "mollify the hardness of cicatrices," and bones to treat "catarrh, flux of menses, dysentery, and diarrhea."

Some 16th- and 17th-century physicians were particularly concerned that many of the "mummy" drugs were not extracted from real Ancient Egyptian mummies, but counterfeits procured from the cadavers of more recently executed criminals.

For a long time, charges of cannibalism were used as an effective slur against tribal peoples in the Americas and Australasia. Yet for centuries, Europeans had no qualms about consuming human remains for health — particularly if those remains came from ancient tombs in the Middle East. While this practice began to die out in the 18th century, Egyptian mummies remained at the center of an intense European trade for another hundred years or so — as mummy brown, a pigment obtained from mummified remains, continued to be popular with painters in the west. Finally, however, medicinal cannibalism fell out of fashion completely, partly thanks to shifting attitudes toward human remains, which by the 20th century, had become decidedly less palatable to the public at large.[3]

My uncle, Walter Bithell, had a home and acreage just north of Blackfoot Idaho called Wapello. There was a grain shed, garden and some corals that separated a few cows and pigs. Visiting my cousin, I noticed that occasionally a dead farm animal, including pigs, had been placed in with the pigs. Over time the carcasses turned into scattered bones and hair in the pig coral. I eventually concluded in my mind that my uncle was saving the cost of pickup and rendering of his dead animals because pigs will eat pretty much anything.

Pursuing a career and practicing as a veterinary into my 50th year, I have come to the conclusion that my uncle may have been more knowledgeable in animal husbandry, using a disposal method called "feedback", or just was following animal disposal customs in the area during this time. Either way, it was a poor choice. However, a better choice than disposing the carcasses into the Wapello canal contaminating the irrigation water as it floated to who knows where.

"Feedback" was a common practice used in the pork industry where infected deceased pigs and their manure are fed to breeding pigs. It is also called controlled oral exposure or sometimes oral controlled exposure. It is done in an attempt to make the breeding pigs garner some degree of immunity to circulating diseases. There was no standard protocol, resulting in some swine researchers calling the procedure potentially risky and noting that it is often done in an unsafe manner. The practice has also been criticized by animal welfare and animal rights groups calling it disturbing and/or unethical. The practice extended to many countries and regions.

Feedback appears to have been originally researched in the 1950s. In the decades since, its usage in the pork industry has become widespread due to increases in the pork industry's size and increases in overcrowding. The change in the industry's size has led to a growing spread in diseases such as E. Coli and PEDv. (Porcine Epidemic Diarrhea

[PEDv] is a TGE-like virus [Transmissible Gastroenteritis virus] and causes diarrhea in a large proportion of all ages of swine when epidemic). Additionally, PEDv presents with various other clinical signs; including vomiting, anorexia, dehydration, and weight loss. A lack of effective vaccines for these diseases in the past led to feedback being used in their place. Feedback practices extended beyond diseases where vaccines did not yet exist.

Some veterinarians recommended against its use due to the risk of exposing pigs to more diseases than intended. The Humane Society of the United States has called the practice "beyond disturbing" and that its use is indicative of the rise of intensive pig farming. The Animal Legal Defense Fund has called it "disgusting, unethical and unlawful". *Wikipedia*

A Ripley's Believe It or Not (2020) reported: It was autumn, 2012, in coastal Coos County, Oregon, and a 69-year-old farmer named Terry Vance Garner had gone out to feed his hogs and never returned. Concerned, his family went looking for him, and what they found was a gruesome sight. There, in the pig enclosure, were his dentures and pieces of his body. Either because of attack or by medical emergency, it seemed Garner had fallen and been overwhelmed by the 700-pound hogs, which then consumed his remains—almost all of him. It was a terrifying revelation.

Reports from the newspaper reported that the animals were his life and for all they knew - it was a horrific accident. However, it was so weird that that they began looking into all possibilities. They found that it is not at all uncommon that pigs have eaten people: 1-In 2019, a Russian woman fell during an epileptic seizure while feeding her hogs. She was eaten alive, and her remains were found in the pen. 2-In 2015, a Romanian farmer died of blood loss after being attacked by his hogs. And a year prior, a 2-year-old toddler from China was eaten when he wandered into a hog enclosure. 3-In 2013, a mob boss was still alive when he was fed to hogs by a rival family. In fact, it's been whispered for years that the Mafia uses hogs to help them dispose of bodies.

All awfulness aside—we know a hog will eat a human. But, can they really make a body disappear? There's one problem with answering this question: If a person disappears, there's no way to prove one way or the other where they've gone—or how.

The thing is, it seems pigs will eat a lot—but there's always a little bit left behind. In 2003, two brothers were convicted of murdering two hunters even though their bodies were never found. Many think the two killers fed the bodies to their hogs. In the book Darker than Night: The True Story of a Brutal Double Homicide and an 18-Year Long Quest for Justice, outlines the theory, which admittedly was divulged by a controversial witness who said the men told her they'd used the pigs. Still, it seems most of these situations end up with people being arrested when some remains are found.

Like Terry Garner's dentures, there are always some leftovers. Susan Monica (born July 8, 1948) is an American former sailor and convicted murderer. She garnered public attention after being convicted of murdering two men at her residence in rural Wimer, Oregon. Both of the victims had worked as handymen on her farm, and each had gone missing under mysterious circumstances in 2012 and 2013, respectively. In both cases, Monica dismembered the victims before feeding portions of their remains to her farm pigs. Partial remains of the two men were discovered at her 20-acre residence after authorities interrogated her for identity theft of one of the men. In April 2015, after a trial that lasted six days, Monica was sentenced to two consecutive 25-year sentences, for a total of 50 years to serve in prison for her crimes *Wikipedia*).

So, hogs won't eat everything? The TV Tropes website seems to verify this, explaining that a pig will "eat meat, even pork, if they are able to come by it. Fact of the matter is, pigs can eat almost anything they can chew." The site goes on to say, however, that pigs cannot chew the larger bones of the human body, but that they will break them into smaller bits to make them more manageable. Human hair and teeth, on the other hand (or hoof), are not digestible to hogs and will get left behind.

But, the site concludes, "it should be a simple matter to shave your victims' heads and pull out their teeth before chow time, right?" Good advice. Just remember all of this the next time you eat bacon.

The first scientists to research cannibalism studied patterns among cannibalistic creatures. In 1981, a project examined data from hundreds of studies regarding cannibalism, or "intraspecific predation," as the author called it. The author identified five main patterns among cannibalistic behavior. To start, the young were more apt to be eaten than mature adults. Eggs, in particular, were most vulnerable because they were both defenseless and nutrient-rich. Researchers observed cannibalism in almost every egg-laying creature from spiders to lizards, to birds. The study also found that many animals didn't recognize their own kind. To them, an egg was just an egg.

The study also found females were more cannibalistic than males. When researchers observed both the sex of the predator and prey, they found females munched on males 88 percent of the time, and 76 percent of these were related to courtship and mating rituals. Killing a mate could benefit a female's offspring. If a female devours the male after mating, she would eliminate any possibility for the male to mate with another female and create competition for her young. And although cannibalism increased with hunger, scarcity wasn't a requirement for the behavior. But cannibalism was directly related to overcrowding. The more an animal felt the pressure of overcrowding, the more likely they were to seek a same-species meal. Since this ground-breaking study was published in the early 1980s, researchers have worked within the framework and found more nuanced behavior. Some species, for example, would rather not eat family members.

For some animals, cannibalism begins soon after hatching or birth, and their siblings are one of their early snacks. Researchers were curious if the dyeing poison dart frog (Dendrobates tinctorius) had cannibalistic behavior. They are confined to small pools, which is an environment that can breed cannibalism. Dyeing poison dart frog fathers take their tadpoles one by one and drop them in small pools of water. The tadpoles remain there until they undergo metamorphosis and hop away. These pools aren't exclusive, and some older tadpoles might still be there. Any given pool can have tadpoles of varying ages and relatedness.

In a 2022 study, researchers wondered if the dyeing poison dart tadpoles were as likely to eat a sibling as they would a stranger. In their laboratory, they created small pools and then made pairings of tadpoles that were either siblings, half-siblings, or unrelated. Researchers put plexiglass to keep the tadpoles apart and then put them together for observation. If one of the tadpoles became too aggressive, as in biting for two seconds or more, researchers broke up the fight. The researchers found larger tadpoles were more apt to attack smaller ones, but full siblings were less likely to fight to the death. The concept of half-sibling didn't have much meaning to the tadpoles, and didn't stop aggressive behaviors.

In the wild, tadpoles with parental support, meaning parents who bring food to the pool, are less likely to turn to cannibalism to survive. If parents are slacking, the nutrition from eating a pool mate can support metamorphosis and help the tadpole leave the problematic pool sooner. The study concluded that family bonds have their limits, and although tadpoles are less likely to eat their own, they will if needed.

For animals like the dyeing poison dart frog, cannibalism in the early years can supply necessary nutrients. But research shows that cannibalism can also bring undesirable side effects. Scientists are not in agreement about the impact that parasites and deadly diseases have on cannibals. Some argue that cannibals have a greater chance of exposure to deadly parasites or diseases when they eat one of their own. As parasites evolve to successfully survive in certain species, they develop defenses against the animal's immunity.

Others suggest that cannibalism kills the infected host, thus limiting the parasite or disease and its spread. Another downside to cannibalism is that it decreases inclusive fitness. Parents, siblings and offspring share their genetic makeup, and eating them means deleting more of the cannibal's own DNA from the gene pool. For species that recognize siblings, it also means taking out others who might have recognized the cannibal as kin and spared them from a similar fate.[4]

There are documented cases of cats eating their dead owners. Once the owners have died, they're another carcass, so domestic cats will eat them to avoid starvation. How long the cat waits will depend on its age, size, metabolism, and health. Cats prefer eating the body while it's in the earlier stages of decomposition as it's easier to chew. Cats can differentiate between what is living and dead, are not scavengers by choice, and house cats are accustomed to eating cat food, not raw meat.

Cats are obligate carnivores. As such, they eat the meat of newly dead animals in the wild constantly. This is natural behavior and plays into their instincts for hunting, surviving, and staying healthy. While a person may seem like a non-option from a sentimental perspective, a deceased human will still become a food option for a cat if there is no other food to be found. However, domestic cats are far less likely to eat a dead human than a feral cat. That's because they are accustomed to eating cat food. When all of a cat's needs are provided for, it will be less likely to eat anything that isn't cleanly provided in its food bowl.

More importantly, cats are rarely scavengers. Since the cat did not hunt and kill the human, it will not be naturally driven to eat any part of it. Nonetheless, a cat will resort to scavenging for food if the situation calls for it. If the feline is in dire need of a meal, and a human corpse is the first thing readily available, it will eat it to survive. Feral cats are less fussy. Meal options can be scarce, leaving the cat hungrier and more willing to scavenge. Therefore, a human corpse left in reach of a feral cat is more likely to be eaten. Even though domestic cats have more access, feral cats have more reason to.

It is very rare but a documented case of cats eating their dead owners was published in 1994. According to The American Journal of Forensic Medicine and Pathology, it found postmortem injuries inflicted on a deceased owner by its own cat. Most of the injuries were localized around softer areas of the body, such as the face. The researchers proposed that this is more likely to occur if the: Cat is free to roam the house, owner is socially isolated (and thus, less likely to be found by others before consumption), or the owner had a sudden death (i.e., due to a pre-existing illness). One study published in 2001 documented house cats eating a human corpse. Although this human did not own any felines, domestic cats that frequented the area were found consuming parts of it at the time of discovery. Another study purposefully offered feral cats this opportunity. The human corpses were donated to Forensic Investigation Research Station in Whitewater, Colorado, specifically for research purposes. The study found that a colony of feral cats did eat human corpses. In the controlled environment, they regarded them as scavenged meat, no different than animal corpses. The study proved that feral cats would regularly eat human corpses if given the chance. Although this doesn't concern house cats, it still provides insight into the fact that cats do eat human corpses.

Cats will usually eat a human corpse right away if they eat it at all. We know this from studies regarding feral cats. Researchers found that feral cats are more likely to consume human corpses that were in the earlier stages of decomposition. These stages are also known as the moist decomposition stage(s) since the body has not quite stiffened. Furthermore, it was discovered that these cats would gravitate more towards softer tissue areas of the body. These included the shoulders, arms, and surface of the body (the skin, rather than the head). That's likely due to the strength of a cat's jaw. A feral and domestic cat's jaw is not powerful enough to tear through tough fibers as well as its ancestors. That's especially true for large carcasses, like a human's. As a result, felines consume the softer areas of the corpse before the corpse becomes too stiff to eat.[5]

Other studies have also shown that, while not common, there are documented cases of dogs eating their deceased owners, especially if left alone for an extended period without food, where they may resort to scavenging the body as a source of sustenance; this behavior is often attributed to their natural instinct to forage for food when hungry, even if it means consuming their owner's remains.

James S. Jameson was the great-great-grandson of John Jameson, the founder of the famed Irish Whiskey company, and as such was heir to the family fortune. Like many rich heirs of the era, Jameson considered himself something of an adventurer, and would tag along on the expeditions of more accomplished explorers. In 1888, he joined the Emin Pasha Relief Expedition, led by renowned explorer Henry Morton

Stanley, across central Africa. The journey was ostensibly to bring supplies to Emin Pasha, the leader of an Ottoman province in Sudan that was cut off by a revolt. In June 1888, Jameson was in command of the rear column of the expedition at Ribakiba, a trading post deep in the Congo known for its cannibal population. At the time, Jameson's group were dealing directly with Tippu Tip, a slave trader and local fixer. A Sudanese translator on the trip testified that Jameson expressed interest in seeing cannibalism first hand.

Farran would later tell Stanley, when he returned to check up on the rear column, his account of the events, and would later recount them in an affidavit that was published by the New York Times.

He said that Tippu then talked to the chiefs of the village and produced a 10-year-old slave girl, who Jameson paid six handkerchiefs for. According to a translator, the chiefs then said to their villagers, "This is a present from a white man, who wishes to see her eaten."

"The girl was tied to a tree," said Farran, "the natives sharpened their knives the while. One of them then stabbed her twice in the belly." In James Jameson's own diary he then wrote, "Three men then ran forward, and began to cut up the body of the girl; finally her head was cut off, and not a particle remained, each man taking his piece away down the river to wash it."

"The most extraordinary thing was that the girl never uttered a sound, nor struggled, until she fell," wrote Jameson. "Jameson, in the meantime, made rough sketches of the horrible scenes," recounted Farrad in his later testimony. Jameson oddly doesn't even fully deny making these drawings, writing, "When I went back to my tent I tried to make some small sketches of the scene while still fresh in my memory."

In his account in his diary and his wife's later account of the incident, the two attempt to play it off as though Jameson went along with the proceedings because he believed it be a joke, and could not imagine that the villagers would actually kill and eat a child.[6]

Jameson seems to not be severely mentally ill or have, at least outwardly, persistent and intensive sexual attraction to dead bodies, or be a sexual deviate from societal norms. However, for Jameson to pay for such an event, let such a horrible experience occur to that young child, make some small sketches at the scene and then while still fresh in his memory going to his tent where he finished his sketches in watercolors – he must have had serious mental issues.

In his own diary, Jameson oddly doesn't even fully deny making these drawings. I suspect he was a sadist who enjoyed seeing other people hurt, inflicting pain on others, and sometimes getting off sexually. Fortunately for the richly famous Irish Whiskey Jameson family, the account never faced justice. James S. Jameson died from a fever he contracted during his tag along expedition in central Africa. The Jameson's family, with the help of the Belgian government, were able to hush up many of the atrocities. However, this mission became the last of its kind. Non-scientific civilian expeditions into Africa were suspended after this time, though military and governmental ones would continue.[6]

1– *Cannibalism, Forensic Sci Med Pathol, Roger W Byard, 04/14/2023.*

2– *All About BSE (Mad Cow Disease) FDA.*

3– *A liquament of carcases' Medical News Today.*

4– *Why Cannibalism Is A Common Behavior For Some Animals, Emilie Le Lucchesi, 03/05/2022.*

5– *Will Cats Eat You If You Die in Your Home? Richard Parker, 09/30/2022.*

6– *When James Jameson Bought A Girl Just To Watch Her Be Eaten By Cannibals, Gabe Paoletti, 07/08/2018.*

CHAPTER 30

SHOCKING WHAT MAN WILL DO...

It is said that modern, industrialized, civilized human beings are uniquely nervous and jumpy, unprecedentedly disturbed by the future, despaired by the present, sleepless at memories of the recent past, all because of the technological complexity and noisiness of the machinery by which we are surrounded, and the rigidified apparatus of cold steel and plastic which we have constructed between ourselves and the earth. Incessant worry, according to this view, is a modern invention. To turn it off, all we need do is turn off the engines and climb down into the countryside. Primitive man, rose-garlanded, slept well.

I doubt this. Man has always been a specifically anxious creature with an almost untapped capacity for worry; it is a gift that distinguishes him from other forms of life. there is undoubtedly a neural center deep in the human brain for mediating this function, like the centers for hunger or sleep.[1]

Recently watching the Turner Classic Movie channel, I viewed the *The High Cost of Loving*. It is a 1958 comedy film that according to MGM made a loss to the studio of $350,000. A summary of the plot reads: Around the same time that Jim Fry learns that his place of work is merging with another company, his wife of nine years Ginny reveals she might be pregnant with their first child. Jim celebrates with friend but when invitations are extended to a company luncheon to meet the new executives, Jim is excluded.

The word goes around quickly that the new president is planning a few changes. Jim feels upset and betrayed after 15 years of loyalty to the firm.

Ginny is pleased about the baby, but after her friend speaks happily of the upcoming luncheon and improved prospects for their husbands, Jim confesses to Ginny that he's actually about to be fired. His nervous and jumpy, unprecedentedly disturbed by the future, despaired by the present, sleepless at memories of the recent past, leads to anger. The angrier he gets, Jim decides to write a letter of protest, then confronts the new president face-to-face, particularly after seeing his name being removed from his office door.

Jim is unaware that the new president is planning a promotion for him and has been informed of the invitation slight, an oversight. He is eager to invite Jim to the luncheon personally, which results in Jim's needing to humbly request his angry letter be returned. When all is resolved, he and Ginny toast his new success and their future parenthood.

Watching this movie, I recalled when I was struggling with a biochemistry class at the U of Idaho. The genetic alpha helix had recently been discovered and I was having trouble understanding the concept. It is a secondary structure in proteins where amino acids are twisted into a right-handed coil, the most common structural arrangement in proteins and the most easily predicted local structure from an amino acid sequence.

What made the situation worse was that the instructor gave oral final exams. I knew that if I didn't pass biochemistry; thoughts of medical, veterinary or graduate studies in animal science may be doomed. My capacity for worry constantly flooded my mind with visions of failure and the fearful event of facing the professor or dropping the class. I began to feel ill, tossed and turned till I fell asleep and awakened feeling like a rat being played with by a cat - soon to be a meal.

Nancy Colier, LCW, Rev, asks the question: "Do you have repetitive negative thoughts? If so, the diagnosis is confirmed: You're human. The Laboratory of Neuro-Imaging reports that the average person experiences 70,000 thoughts per day. As a psychotherapist, I can say with certainty that a large percentage of the 70,000 are about what can go wrong, what did go wrong, what will go wrong, what you've done wrong, and what everyone else is doing wrong.

What makes negative repetitive thoughts so challenging is that they often stem from core self-beliefs, like I'm not good enough, I won't get what I want, or the world is not trustworthy. Because they're built out of these deeply held beliefs, repetitive thought loops are powerful and sticky; we believe our repetitive thoughts, as if their persistence is somehow evidence of their truth. As a result, we are compulsively compelled to attach and engage with their content.

Further, we learn early in life that we need to do something with and about our negative thoughts: Either prove them wrong, convince them (and ourselves) that they're false, or actively replace them with positive thoughts that feel less threatening. Either way, we're taught, we need to put up a fight.[2]

Seemingly everyone is concerned about concentration these days. Medical facilities are being "inundated" with clients who don't actually have ADHD – they're just worried they do. It's hard to blame them for worrying. ADHD diagnostic rates are on the rise in the U.S. and social media platforms have convinced even more people that they have attention issues. There's a shortage of medications to treat ADHD, largely driven by rising demand. And even among people who haven't sought medical care, there seems to be a sense—probably enhanced by regular studies about shrinking attention spans—that focusing is getting harder. A recent U.K. survey found that about half of adults think their attention spans are getting shorter, and plenty of teachers say the same thing is happening with kids.

Distractibility is nothing new. Focus naturally waxes and wanes depending on a range of factors, from how much sleep the night before to how interested they are in the task at hand. But the "cocktail" of anxieties inherent to modern life can make for a particularly potent drain on attention.

Most people without chronic attention issues could likely focus fairly well if given a task in a quiet, empty room—but they'd probably perform worse if they did the same task in a room where people are talking and music is playing. In modern life we're essentially living in a room filled with distractions all the time, thanks to the competing demands of work and home life, societal stressors like the pandemic, and the constant temptation of phones, social media, and the internet.

Screens present a unique minefield of distractibility, with their constant flow of notifications and information. At its core, the internet was designed to capitalize on how humans think. It's little surprise that people are drawn to it. It's not just the fact that there's algorithms catching our attention. We have this sense that we have to respond, we have to check.

Human brains want novelty, excitement, and social connection, and devices play into those desires. Checking a notification flashing across your screen can provide a small hit of dopamine, creating a sense of reward that keeps you coming back for more. When you give in to temptation by pausing a task to check your phone, your brain also has to shift gears to stop what it was previously doing and move to a new task. This process negatively affects the overall speed and quality of your work in the short term and in the long term. The more you engage in task switching, the more your brain wants to wander and look for that new thing. In other words, your brain gets used to constant diversions and engages in them out of habit—hence why you might find yourself mindlessly checking your phone even as you watch your favorite television show.

Research suggests we're giving into digital temptation more and more. In the early 2000s, a team tracked people while they used an electronic device and noted each time their focus shifted to something new—roughly every 2.5

minutes, on average. In recent repeats of that experiment, she says, the average has gone down to about 47 seconds.[3]

At some point today you will disengage from the rest of the world and just think. It could happen any number of ways: if your mind wanders from work, while you're sitting in traffic, or if you just take a quiet moment to reflect. But as frequently as we drift into our own thoughts, a new study suggests that many of us don't like it. In fact, some people even prefer an electric shock to being left alone with their minds.

To conduct the study, social psychologists recruited hundreds of undergraduate student volunteers and community members to take part in "thinking periods." Individuals were placed in sparsely furnished rooms and asked to put away their belongings, such as cellphones and pens. They then were given one of two tests that lasted between 6 and 15 minutes. While some were told to think about whatever they wanted, others chose from several prompts, such as going out to eat or playing a sport, and planned out how they would think about it during the period.

Afterward, the team asked the volunteers to rate their experience on a nine-point scale, where the higher the number, the more enjoyable their time was. In both the free-thinking and planned-prompt scenarios, about 50% of people did not like the experience, reporting an enjoyment level at or below the midpoint of the scale. Also, participants generally gave high ratings of boredom.

To see if a change of scenery would help, the team let participants do the studies in their own homes, but still found similar results. Overall, the subjects said they enjoyed activities like reading and listening to music about twice as much as just thinking.

The researchers then decided to take the experiment a step further. For 15 minutes, the team left participants alone in a lab room in which they could push a button and shock themselves if they wanted to. The results were startling: Even though all participants had previously stated that they would pay money to avoid being shocked with electricity, 67% of men and 25% of women chose to inflict it on themselves rather than just sit there quietly and think. The research report commented: "We went into this thinking it wouldn't be that hard for people to entertain themselves. We have this huge brain and it's stuffed full of pleasant memories, and we have the ability to construct fantasies and stories. We really thought this [thinking time] was something people would like. The results may be mixed signs of boredom and the trouble that we have controlling our thoughts. Our mind is built to engage in the world. So, when we don't give it anything to focus on, it's kind of hard to know what to do.

Although daydreaming is spontaneous and can be enjoyable, the pressure to think on command—whether it's being demanded by researchers, or while you're waiting in line with nothing else to do—may be what's difficult and unpleasant for so many.

It was surprising and a bit disheartening that people seem to be so uncomfortable when left to their own devices; that they can be so bored that even being shocked seemed more entertaining. One researcher commented: "But I can't help but feel that there has to be more to the story. I'm confident that there are conditions in which at least a subsample of the population enjoys this quiet opportunity for self-reflection." Some people seem to enjoy thinking more than others. For instance, the study found that people who are more agreeable or cooperative were more likely to enjoy themselves when they were told to think about anything. Individuals who admitted that their daydreams normally leave them happy fared better, too.

Because people so often find themselves intentionally or unintentionally wrapped up in their thoughts, the research team suggests that meditation or other techniques to relax and learn how to gain control of the mind could be helpful. If we knew how to steer our thoughts in a pleasant direction and enjoy the experience, maybe we wouldn't hate to be alone with ourselves.[4]

In a Facetious Little Essay entitled "On Transcendental Metaworry," the science writer Lewis Thomas observes that "Worrying is the most natural and spontaneous of all human functions Man is the Worrying Animal."

This rare capacity to worry, Thomas continues, "is a trait needing further development, awaiting perfection. Most of us tend to neglect the activity, living precariously out on the thin edge of anxiety but never plunging in." To remedy this, Thomas recommends the practice of Transcendental Worry (or TW), preferably "before work and late in the evening just before insomnia."

To practice TW, Thomas recommends the following: make yourself as uncomfortable as possible; tense all your muscles; close your eyes tight "until the effort causes a slight tremor of the eyelids"; focus on the muscular effort required to breathe (preferably attempting to breathe through one nostril at a time); then repeat to yourself a suitable mantra like "worry." After a few minutes, you will experience the vertiginous pleasures of angst. Worries will circle in and out of your consciousness and you will begin to hear the *sing* pounding in your head – originating from rushing blood from your heart that is most likely rushing through vessels of artery plaque buildup, a bent artery or rising blood pressure.

Nothing remains but to allow the intensification of TW to proceed spontaneously to the next stage, termed Primal Wince. En route, you pass through an almost confluent series of pictures, random and transient, jerking and running at overspeed like an old movie, many of them seemingly trivial but each associated with a wince of dropping abruptly through space…a shrieking plumed bird, a current electric light bulb, or the vision of numbers whirring too fast to read on a gasoline pump, or the last surviving humpback whale, singing a final song into empty under seas…The ascending slopes of chalked curves on academic blackboards, interchangeably predicting the future population of pet dogs in America, rats in Harlem, nuclear explosions overhead and down in the salt mines, suicides in Norway, crop failures in India, number of people at large…These images become confluent and then amorphous, melting together into a solid, gelatinous thought of skewness. When this happens, you will be entering the last stage, which is pure worry about pure worry. This is the essence of the Wisdom of the West, and I shall call it "Transcendental Metaworry (TMW)."

Now, as to the usefulness of TMW. It tends to fill the mind completely at times when it would otherwise be empty. Instead of worrying at random, continually and subliminally, wondering always what it is that you've forgotten and ought to be worrying about, you get the full experience, all in a rush, on a schedule which you arrange for yourself. Practicing TMW will help make the times of the day when there is nothing to worry about more intensely pleasurable.[1]

During the movie, *The High Cost of Loving,* I thought about Apostle Paul's advice: "When I was a child, I spake as a child, I understood as a child, I thought as a child: but when I became a man, I put away childish things" (1 Corinthians 13:11). My childish thought patterns of insomnia became my adultish insomnia. My mind has created millions of mountains out of mole hills in the crevices my mind. The fears, anxieties, tossing and turning until sleep often came near the crack of dawn, mostly churning my what if's of the moment that usually became so what's. The TMW's differed when "I spake like and did childish things" and as I have gone through changes of life during my manhood.

Since I have this huge brain that has also been stuffed full of pleasant memories, fantasies, stories and visions of who I am becoming – why can't my TMW's be forgotten and the pleasant thoughts and dreams become as they were at times as a child?

One pleasant memory I still remember as an adult after suffering from a severe TMW: I finally approached the biochemistry professor at the U or Idaho about my grade. He visited for a few minutes and took out his grade book. He told me that he did not recommend that I drop the class. It just so happened that my 50+% grade average was within the top 10% of the class. I received a B and was able to continue my animal science studies, eventually becoming a veterinarian.

1– *The Medusa and Snail: More Notes of a Biology Watcher, Lewis Thomas MD, Pages 82-87, 1979.*

2– *How to Live Peacefully With Repetitive Negative Thoughts, Psychology Today, Nancy Colier, LCSW, Rev., 03/08/2017*

3– *Why Everyone's Worried About Their Attention Span—and How to Improve Yours, Time, Jamie Ducharme, 08/10/2023.*

4– *People would rather be electrically shocked than left alone with their thoughts, Science, Nadia Whitehead, 07/03/2014.*

CHAPTER 31

A CARING MOMENT...

On April 27, 2020, Sam brought into Camden Pet Hospital a shoe box containing a cold limp hummingbird wrapped in a wash cloth that appeared to be in a comma. He had found the bird lying stiff on the ground on a cool morning in San Jose, California. A physical exam noted that the bird's only signs of life was a very slow heart rate (the average heart rate during flight is 1200 beats per minute. When resting, heart rate reaches 250 beats per minute). Exercising the "Uniform Good Samaritan Law", we cleaned debris off the bird, mixed some sugar in warm water and placed several drops at the base of the beak in hopes that some would seep onto the tongue. We then placed the bird in a portable incubator, waited and watched.

In 1994, the American Animal Hospital Association recommended the adoption of a Uniform Good Samaritan Law by all states and provinces, such as the following: "Any veterinarian or veterinary technician who, in good faith, renders emergency care, without remuneration or expectation of remuneration, to a sick or injured animal shall not be liable for any civil damages resulting from his or her acts or omission, except for such damages as may result from acts of gross negligence or wanton acts or omissions." This law serves to encourage veterinarians and veterinary technicians to assist with emergency veterinary care.

For example: Using the Uniform Good Samaritan Law, Camden Pet Hospital over the years has cared for abandoned and lost pets; as well of lots of kittens without homes and compassionate euthanasia. About five years ago Laila was looking through Petfinder and saw a cat, named Rico, that looked like a cat CPH was no longer caring for, Fivill.

Laila and Megan went and meet Rico at the foster home and soon they brought him back to the clinic. How he got to the foster home? He had been injured with a broken back and front right legs. Somehow or another he got to the shelter and a rescue group picked him up and had him operated on. He has two legs plated and it cost the rescue group about $7000 to plate them both. When he was all healed, they adopted him to a couple. He lived with them for a while before the woman became pregnant and they gave him up saying they were going to have a child. They couldn't have a cat and they returned him to the rescue. From records, it appeared that he had two homes before he came to Camden. He was only about 4 years old when Camden adopted him.

During this time no money changed hands except for the cost of surgery (which I'm sure was discounted a bunch) and there was probably an adoption fee when first adopted. Care was an act of love for one of god's creatures that was suffering. (See Rico's photo below)

National Good Samaritan Day on March 13th recognizes the unselfish actions of those who provide help when needed. The term "good Samaritan" comes from the Bible parable where a Samaritan helped a stranger who had been robbed and beaten and left to die by the side of the road. The Samaritan not only cleaned the man's wounds and clothed him but took him to an inn where he paid for the man's care.

This day honors the death of Catherine "Kitty" Genovese, who was murdered near her home on March 13, 1964, in New York City. That night, if one Good Samaritan had stepped forward, Miss Genovese would have lived. Something interrupted her killer twice that night, each interruption witnessed by neighbors or passersby. Still, no one called the police. One person called after his third and successful attempt, but too late for Miss Genovese.

A good Samaritan law protects someone who provides aid in an emergency from being sued for injuries or damages. The laws vary from state to state but generally have the expectation that the good Samaritan, if possible, asks permission from the ill, injured, or in danger and that they do not act in a reckless or negligent manner. Federal laws protect good Samaritans, too.

Hummingbirds have less feathers when compared to other birds (less than 1000), but are known as "the flying jewels" because they are able to change the color of their feathers when they fly. This unique characteristic is the result of the iridescence coloring of the feathers and the influence of light, moisture and other factors. They are called humming birds because of the humming sound which is produced by their wings during flight.

They are very intelligent animals and have larger brain size (compared to the rest of the body) than other birds. Their brain weighs 4.2% of the hummingbird's total body weight. Hummingbirds can remember which flower they have already visited and they know how much time each flower requires for nectar refilling.

Hummingbirds have excellent hearing and their can even detect ultraviolet light. They prefer red flowers with a tubular shape that support their long beaks which helps them reach the bottom of the flowers with a forked (W shaped) tongue that is used for licking of the nectar inside. They do not have a sense of smell.

They are well known for their ability to move their wings fast. Unlike other birds, they move their wings making a full circle. The number of times a hummingbird's wings beat is different from one species to another, and ranges from 720 to 5400 times per minute when hovering. Hummingbirds are the only birds that can fly backwards and some hummingbirds fly at speeds greater than 33 miles per hour.

This type of flying requires a lot of energy and that is the reason why hummingbirds eat a lot of food each day. Hummingbirds digest carbohydrates (both fructose and glucose, a unique trait other vertebrates cannot achieve) as the main source of energy for flight. Nectar from flowers is the best source of sugar and humming birds drink it 5 to 8 time each hour. It spends 30-60 seconds during each feeding. They usually visit 1000 flowers per day. Hummingbirds also eat insects, which provides proteins.

Hummingbirds do note mate for life and vocalize during the mating season. After mating which lasts less than 4 seconds, females leave the male and start preparing a nest to her eggs. Females usually lay 2 eggs, which are very small (just ½ inches long). Eggs represent 10% of the mother's body weight (less than a nickel on average). Chicks cannot fly and they spend the first three weeks of life in the nest. Most hummingbirds die during the first year of their life. Those that survive, have an average lifespan of 5 years in the wild. They can live up to 10 years during captivity.

During flight they have a heart rate of 1200 beats per minute. When resting, the heart rate reaches 250 beats per minute. Each night they enter a hibernation-state called torpor which helps them preserve the energy. Heart rate slows down, temperature drops and their metabolic rate decreases to 1/15 of the normal rate. They usually hang upside-down in the tree during this phase. *Several sources*

Birds and mammals spend a large proportion of their energy expenditure on maintaining high euthermic body temperatures (Tb). This optimizes many physiological functions, such as mobility, digestion, and brain function, but becomes costly during periods of cold exposure, which require substantial heat production that is impossible to sustain during food shortages. The only 'logical solution' for animals that cannot escape harsh environmental conditions by migration is to suspend the maintenance of high body temperatures and employ a mode of living that saves energy. This is the strategy used by many birds and mammals that employ hypometabolism, i.e., periods of profoundly reduced metabolic rate (MR) and Tb, which typically occurs on a seasonal basis. States of profound but controlled reductions of MR and Tb in endotherms are called torpor (cold-lethargy). Birds and mammals that use torpor are traditionally classified as either hibernators or species using daily torpor (i.e., daily heterotherms). The main distinguishing trait that is often invoked, is that species regarded as hibernators are capable of consecutive multiday torpor bouts, lasting on average for more than a week, whereas torpor in animals traditionally viewed as daily heterotherms usually lasts only between ~3 and 12 hours.

Other traits that point to functional differences are the minimum metabolic rate (MR) during torpor (TMRmin), which in animals categorized as hibernators appears to be much lower, as well as the minimum body temperature (Tb min) that is defended during torpor, which seems higher in species regarded as daily heterotherms, although the variation among species in Tb min is large. It appears that body mass also differs between the two categories with species conventionally viewed as hibernators being significantly bigger than species classified as daily heterotherms. *Biol Rev Camb Philos Soc, 2014.*

The migration of hummingbirds is an amazing thing since hummingbirds have many different fly zones or paths in which they travel from one habitat to another. These little birds can fly far and fast. There are a few types or species of hummingbirds that make this journey every spring and fall. It is believed that hummingbirds are very keen on the changes in daylight and the declining insect and flower population every year before migration. It is also believed that a chemical change occurs pushing the hummingbirds to migrate. Some report that hummingbirds will follow the flower population; still others state that they follow the insect population. No one really knows for sure why hummingbirds migrate.

Each time before a hummingbird starts migration, they need to eat a lot of insects and nectar to fatten up. A hummingbird will gain 25-40% of their body weight before they start migration. When migration occurs on the same common fly zones, they do so alone for several reasons. First of all, hummingbirds are so small that most predators have difficulty seeing them. If they flocked together, they would be a larger, more readily seen, target. Also, a hummingbird must stop frequently to feed at a flower or feeder, even during migration. To have a flock of hummingbirds waiting in line for a flower to refill doesn't work. Plus, during hummingbird flight, there is just not enough body mass to make a wake in the air currents for others.

When hummingbirds are migrating, they usually do not stay very high off the ground. They have been reported to fly just above treetop level over land or pretty much skimming the top of the water ways. It is believed they do this to keep an eye out for a food or nectar opportunity on their long journey.

While migrating, hummingbirds generally will fly during the day and sleep at night. When the Ruby-Throated Hummingbirds are flying over the Gulf of Mexico during migration, there is no place to land to sleep, so they must keep on going. Many years ago, fisherman and oil rig workers would report seeking hummingbirds zip by them out in the gulf 200 miles away from land. The hummingbirds could be seen flying low over the water toward shore. The workers started to notice this happening every year, recording the common migration routes taken by the Ruby-Throated

Hummingbirds. It's amazing to think that these little tiny fluffs of feathers would travel over 450 miles of water with a 20 mile an hour headwind (with more than 20 hours of travel time) to make it to their favorite breeding grounds.

Many hummingbirds will also have to cross other obstacles during migration, like the Mojave Desert. There have been reports of an occasional Rufous Hummingbird falling out of the sky on the migration route to and from Alaska. *John James, Audubon*

We continued to watch over the hummingbird laying in the incubator and the heart rate began to increase and we noticed that it began taking obvious breaths. In about 10-15 minutes its small feet attached themselves to the wash cloth, it righted itself, the ruffled feathers smoothed into place and it looked at us. We took the incubator to the outdoor dog run and opened the door. In a couple of minutes it flapped its wings, flew out of the incubator and perched itself on a fence nearby for a for several seconds before it flew up above us as if to say thank you before it flew off.

Yes, you probably guessed it. The hummingbird reduced its body temperature and employed a mode of living to save energy – torpor. I suspect that it was in a suspended state of sleep during the cold night and hanging upside down in a state of torpor when it slipped off the branch and fell to the ground. It needed to be warmed up, given some energy and time to fully awaken. It was now having a better day and our day was a little more brightly lit from being "Good Samaritans" and knowing that we had the opportunity to do at least one good deed and it was still early in the day. (below is the photo of our hummingbird rescue just before it flew from out incubator)

William Hoggan recorded a similar experience while at a Young Women camp in the mountains of California, as girls and leaders waited for dinner in an A-frame lodge. Waiting, some girls noticed something under a table. A hummingbird had somehow flown into the lodge, couldn't find its way out, and finally collapsed on the floor. They asked him to help. They treated the bird basically the same way we did at Camden Pet Hospital and the bird opened its eyes, its ruffled feathers fell instantly into place and after drinking a couple more drops of sugar water, it started its wings, warmed them for a second, and flew straight up. It hesitated a moment above them, and then shot away.

He later wrote: "We stood there, stunned. And then, as suddenly as the bird had flown away, the spiritual lessons came. Often, as we reach out to the less active, our efforts don't seem to make a difference. But the love we offer does slip into the cracks—like the nectar into the unmoving beak of the hummingbird—providing spiritual nutrition that one day may produce results. At times we can't go further on our own; we need a kind, caring hand up. Sometimes people get tangled in the cobwebs of sin or addiction and need the help of a friend or priesthood leader and the Savior's assistance to get free. We need regular spiritual nutrition in order to endure, else we run out of spiritual strength and fall victim to evil influences.

The hummingbird kept hanging on. Literally. Hanging on made all the difference. At times, we must simply endure in faith as we deal with the painful and sometimes horrible challenges of life. The New Testament says that the Master is aware of even the sparrow's fall (see Matthew 10:29–31).

I now know He is also aware of a hummingbird's fall. And He is aware of you." *William Hoggan, June 2015.*

"To be a Good Samaritan is to wonder how your words and actions will impact others rather than to wonder how you will be impacted. This is not to say that we should abandon personal safety or exhaust ourselves in unhealthy ways. Instead, we should build the faith to understand that when we are unselfish, our needs will also be taken care of." *Megan Sanborn Jones, BYU Speech, 2022.*

CHAPTER 32

FINALLY GOT IT RIGHT...

There is much confusion of the true symbol of medicine. The single staff with one snake-entwined is the current American Medical Association logo. The history of this ancient symbol with a heritage stretching over two millennia is shrouded in the fog of history. Many physicians as well as the public are unaware there are two distinct symbols commonly used which have two different origins.

Aesculapius was the god of medicine and was the son of Apollo, the god of healing. The Staff of Aesculapius is a rough-hewn branch representing plants and growth entwined by a single snake. Aesculapius was known as the god of medicine. He was killed by his grandfather, Zeus, with a thunderbolt because not enough people were passing onto the underworld due to his healing skills.

Aesculapius, God of Medicine, was the son of Apollo, the God of Healing.

Hermes (Mercury) was the messenger of the gods and known for carrying a staff known as the Caduceus. The caduceus included two snakes topped off with a set of wings. The Caduceus is from the Greek root meaning "herald's wand" and was a badge of diplomatic ambassadors associated with commerce, eloquence, alchemy, thievery, and lying. This is why the same symbol has been used on businesses of commerce such as banks.

The popularity of the caduceus with two snakes is probably attributed to being more aesthetically appealing than the single snake on the Staff of Aesculapius. The symmetry is more balanced than the single snake. The caduceus if often used in medically related industries such as pharmaceuticals and hospital supplies.

Two wings and two snakes are the difference in the Caduceus and the Staff of Aesculapius. The snake is a powerful symbol. The ancients looked on the snake as a symbol of health and healing because it could shed and regenerate its's skin. The snake also produced venoms which killed many parasites in the body. Many patients suffering from sickness such as depression were put into a temple healing rooms containing snakes to shock them out of their stupor.

Hippocrates of Kos was a physician the father of Western Medicine, ca. 450-380 BCE. It was believed that Hippocrates was a direct descendant of Aesculapius. The Hippocratic Oath begins with the words "I swear by Apollo, the physician, and by Aesculapius…."

The question to ask is how did the caduceus become popular so quickly in the United States? The role of the United States Army Medical Corps (USAMC) is crucial. In 1902, at the suggestion of an assistant surgeon, Captain Frederick Reynolds, a new uniform code was established, and the caduceus became a collar insignia for all personnel in the USAMC. From Captain Reynold's correspondence with the Surgeon General's office, it is apparent that he was unaware of the distinction between the caduceus and Aesculapius. He recommended the combined use of the "cock of Aesculapius" and the caduceus. His statement to the Surgeon General that the Medical Corps of "several foreign powers, notably the English" all displayed the caduceus was also erroneous. In fact, no other western medical military ser vice of that time displayed the caduceus; they all used the Aesculapius symbol. Medical Associations in Asia, India, Canada, Great Britain, France, Germany, Africa, and Scandinavia all share the Staff of Aesculapius.

Thus, the adoption of the caduceus by the USAMC seems to have been simply a misunderstanding of classical mythologic iconography. Ironically, this mistake was nearly avoided. In March 1902, when Captain Reynolds initially suggested the switch to the caduceus symbol, the Surgeon General, G.W. Sternberg, dismissed his request outright. However, Captain Reynolds was persistent and, later that year, he sent a second letter to the new Surgeon General, W.H. Forwood; this time, his proposal was approved. Thus, on 17 July 1902, the "caduceus of gold" was adopted as the branch insignia of the USAMC. This mistake did not go entirely unnoticed. In 1917, Lieutenant Colonel McCulloch, the librarian to the Surgeon General, discovered original documents showing that the coat of arms adopted by the USAMEDD a century earlier had displayed the Aesculapius and not the caduceus. McCulloch lamented the error, but did nothing to correct the error. The U.S. Army Medical Corps and the U.S. Navy Medical Corps still use the caduceus with the two snakes. The U.S Air Force Medical Service uses the Staff of Aesculapius with one snake.

In conclusion: The Staff of Aesculapius has represented medicine since 800 BCE, and most knowledgeable medical authorities support its use as the symbol of medicine. The New England Journal of Medicine, The American College of Physicians, and the World Health Organization use the Staff of Aesculapius. The Staff of Aesculapius has represented medicine since 800 BCE and most authorities support its use as the symbol of medicine. The Staff of Aesculapius is the only true symbol of medicine.[1]

In 2013, the AVMA replaced the insignia the Association has used on its publications, awards, and office buildings since 1971. The new AVMA logo likely will still include the Aesculapian staff with the superimposed "V" that is central to the current logo. The current logo is only the third since the Association's founding as the United States Veterinary Medical Association 150 years ago.

"As much as we value and take pride in our past, we need to be forward-thinking and focused; the new logo will help us to do that—and to convey this to our members," Dr. Ron DeHaven, AVMA CEO, told JAVMA News. Dr. DeHaven notes that the AVMA wants to show it is changing to maintain relevance and value to its members, and that includes developing a new look and feel that conveys that the Association is evolving. Aesculapius, known as the Greek god of healing, was the son of Apollo and the pupil of the centaur Chiron. The image of Chiron was central to the first logo adopted by the United States Veterinary Medical Association in 1863.

The AVMA logo showed Chiron holding a scroll and standing above the Latin phrase "non nobis soblum," meaning "not for us alone." (Chiron was held to be the superlative centaur amongst his brethren since he was called the "wisest and justest of all the centaurs"). He was replaced in the early 1920s with a caduceus, a staff topped with wings and wrapped with two snakes facing one another. The caduceus is the symbol of the Greek god Hermes, and is used to represent commerce. The AVMA House of Delegates voted in June 1970 to replace the symbol, and the current logo was first displayed on the cover and in the pages of the Jan. 1, 1971, issue of Journal of the American Veterinary Medical Association.

JAVMA news coverage stated at the time that Dr. Joseph Arburua of San Francisco, who initially supported adoption of the caduceus, had fought for 38 years to replace it as the AVMA's insignia.

"Since 1932, when he realized that the winged wand of the caduceus was a symbol of the Greek god Hermes, who was associated with such unsavory callings as highwaymen, thieves, intrigues, and the fat purse, Dr. Arburua has been trying valiantly to get the AVMA to change its insigne to the staff of Aesculapius," JAVMA archives state.

1– *The Caduceus vs. Staff of Aesculapius - One Snake or Two?, Mo Med, George Bohigian, MD, Nov-Dec, 2019.*

www.ingramcontent.com/pod-product-compliance
Lightning Source LLC
Chambersburg PA
CBHW020914140626
46545CB00015B/35